MÁZANDARÁN
AND
ASTARÁBÁD

By

H. L. RABINO

DI BORGOMALE

WITH A NEW PREFACE BY

Charles Melville

Gibb Memorial Trust

Published by
The E. J. W. Gibb Memorial Trust

First printed London, 1925
This edition printed 2018

ISBN 978-1-90972-492-1

A CIP record of this book is available from the British Library

Printed in Turkey by Mega Print, Istanbul

Further details of the E. J. W. Gibb Memorial Trust and its publications are available at the Trust's website

www.gibbtrust.org

MÁZANDARÁN
AND
ASTARÁBÁD

THE E. J. W. GIBB MEMORIAL TRUST

The Gibb Memorial Trust was founded in 1902 in memory of Elias John Wilkinson Gibb, a scholar who devoted his life to researching the history, literature, philosophy and religion of the Turks, Persians and Arabs. His particular interest was the poetry of Ottoman Turkey, the fruits of which were published, mostly posthumously, in the six-volume *History of Ottoman Poetry*.

The objectives of the Gibb Memorial Trust are to promote the study and advancement of the areas of Elias Gibb's interest. This is done through the preparation of scholarly publications, and through the awarding of scholarships to researchers working in the field.

Further details of the E. J. W. Gibb Memorial Trust and all its current publications are available at the Trust's website, www.gibbtrust.org

PREFACE

Hyacinth Louis Rabino di Borgomale (1877–1950) was a professional diplomat who spent many years in Persia in a variety of consular posts, first in Kirmanshah and particularly at Rasht, where he served as vice consul from 1906 to 1912. He was then posted to the Arab world (first Morocco and ultimately to Cairo, via Smyrna and Salonika), but retained his interest in the Caspian provinces, as is evident not only from his continuing publications in both English and French, but also, of course, from the work reprinted here, *Mázandarán and Astarábád*, first published as volume VII of the new series of the E.J.W. Gibb Memorial Series (London, 1928, printed in Cairo). Among his other significant contributions in this area are his edition of the *Tārīkh-i Gīlān va Dailamistān* by Ẓahīr al-Dīn Mar'ashī (Rasht, 1912) and "Les provinces Caspiennes de la Perse: Le Guilan" (Paris, 1917). A fuller picture of his numerous and valuable researches, not least in the field of numismatics, is provided on pp. 167–69 of the current book.[1]

Rabino's *Mázandarán and Astarábád* is a remarkable work, the product of many years of the careful accumulation of information about a region cut off from the Iranian Plateau by the formidable barrier of the Alburz Mountains and enjoying a complex history commensurate with its peculiar physical geography and inaccessible valleys. As the author notes in his brief Preface, in addition to his documentary researches, much of the data was retrieved in the course of two expeditions, one in spring of 1908 and the other between November 1909 and January 1910, the latter providing the chronological framework

[1] See also the brief but appreciative obituary by Vladimir Minorsky in the *Journal of the Royal Asiatic Society* 84, iii–iv (1952), pp. 180–81, who notes that his work on the Caspian provinces will long remain sources of information.

for Rabino's observations along his itinerary. His Persian introduction is rather more expressive of his fondness for the region, which he calls one of the best parts of Iran for its natural beauty and climate, quoting verses from the *Shāhnāma* story of the reign of Kay Kavus to support this view.[2] He notes the province's somewhat separate history and the preservation of much of its pre-Islamic culture, as in the use of Pahlavi script on the coinage, until Shāh 'Abbās brought it back into connection with the other regions of Iran. He mentions too the unfortunate fact that it was prey to the destructive raids of the Central Asian nomads who periodically invaded the area – that is, in the Safavid period, the Uzbeks, though many covetous eyes had previously fallen on this rich territories and attempted to subdue them.

The book is a remarkable mixture of gazetteer and travelogue, informed by detailed research not only in the historical sources available (one of which he had edited himself, as noted above),[3] but also in the works of previous European and local writers. In the Persian preface he excuses himself for any inaccuracies, due to the impossibility of verifying in person the names of every single village. It is clear, nevertheless, that he had a very intimate knowledge of the territory and a genuine attachment to it. Although he was a British consular official, and wrote reports along with his colleagues as required on the state of the country, its products, inhabitants and communications, the result is a poke in the eye for Edward Said's critique of the orientalist agenda of acquiring knowledge to achieve domination and

2 Firdausī, *Shāhnāma*, ed. Dj. Khaleghi-Motlagh, vol. II (Costa Mesa & New York, 1990), pp. 4–5, verses 26–31.

3 For a lengthy analysis of the mediaeval chronicles of the region, see Charles Melville, "The Caspian provinces: a world apart. Three local histories of Mazandaran", *Iranian Studies* 33, i–ii (Winter-Spring 2000 [2001]), pp. 45–49.

emphasise western superiority; he does mention (p. 8) that the roads do not lend themselves to "military purposes", but it is hard to imagine that this was his main concern. Here we have a scholarly and sensitive account of two Iranian provinces full of character and variety.

Among the valuable qualities of *Mázandarán and Astarábád* is the selection of inscriptions provided in the Persian section of the text. These are not directly integrated into the main text, and it is a pity they are not listed separately or cross-referred to, but generally they follow the order of Rabino's itinerary, the inscriptions in Astarabad, for instance, on pp. 25–52 of the Persian text being described on pp. 73–76 of the English text. The inscriptions themselves are of varying nature and a range of dates, including *waqf* (endowment) deeds, tombstones, foundation and restoration inscriptions and several interesting *farmāns* (decrees), notably from the Safavid era, although 15th century is also well represented as well as the Qajar period, as one would expect, Astarabad being the homeland of the dynasty.

Overall, this is a classic work that has long been out of print,[4] and an essential resource for subsequent work on the Caspian provinces, which is indeed copious. The late Manouchehr Sotoudeh was a leading figure in this respect, especially in his massive multi-volume work, *Az Astārā tā Istārbād*;[5] we may also note the numerous contributions of Wilferd Madelung, among many others, to the study of the region, its dynasties and religious sectarian history. All these works continue to draw on

4 The WorldCat website states that 25 editions were published between 1928 and 1987 in four languages. The Gibb Memorial Trust archives contain have no details about reprints under its auspices.

5 Published by the Anjoman-i Asar-i Melli, 7 vols, Tehran, 1349/1970ff., repr. 1380/2001.

the pioneering efforts of H.L. Rabino, and it is the hope of the Trustees that this reprinted edition and a full-size scan of the excellent accompanying map will allow it to remain accessible to a new generation of scholars.

Cambridge
June 2016

Charles Melville

PREFACE

THE present book is the outcome of persistent research carried on from 1906 to 1922, and of data collected during two journeys in Mázandarán, one in the spring of 1908, the other in the late autumn of 1909[1].

Owing to the official position I held I was debarred from touching upon any subject that savoured of politics, and, because of the cost of printing, I had to suppress all anecdotes, descriptions and quotations, thus reducing the volume to a third of its original size. In its present form the work will, I am afraid, only appeal to the student.

With the papers referred to in pages 167 to 169 of this volume I have now exhausted all the materials I had accumulated, except various papers on agriculture and kindred subjects written in collaboration with the late Monsieur D. F. Lafont, which were irretrievably lost in the sack of Anzalí[2], and my notes on the dialects of the Caspian provinces and on wood-carving in Gílán and Mázandarán (15th to 18th centuries), which were too sparse for publication.

I am fully sensible of the shortcomings of my work, but am confident, nevertheless, that its perusal will facilitate the work of all such as are desirous of extending their knowledge of the Caspian provinces. There is yet much information to be gleaned either locally, or from the lost chronicles alluded to by Persian historians[3], should these ever come to light again.

[1] My itinerary in 1908 was Bandargaz, Astarábád, Ashraf, Sárí, Bárfurúsh and Mashhadisar, and in 1909, Rasht, Láhiján, Ámul, Bárfurúsh, Mashhadisar, Faraḥábád, Sárí, Dhaghmarz, Ashraf, Bandargaz, Astarábád, Aq-Qal'a, Gunbad-Qábús, Qumish-tappa, Khwája-Nifis, Astarábád, the Jahánnumá Pass, Rádkán and Bandargaz.

[2] These papers, which were ready for the press, comprised: La Culture de l'Olivier en Guilan; La Filature de la Soie en Perse; Essais de Cultures nouvelles en Perse par le Prince Kâchef-es-Saltané; Culture des Plantes textiles (Coton, Chanvre, etc.) en Guilan et en Mazandéran; Contribution à l'étude de la Faune du Nord de la Perse; and Contribution à l'étude de la Flore du Nord de la Perse (comprenant les plantes cultivées, légumes, céréales, etc.). The last-mentioned was the most important as it dealt with over one thousand specimens, giving their names in Latin, Persian and local dialect, as well as the industrial or medicinal purposes they serve.

[3] The chronicles of Mázandarán which are known to us are:

The *Báwand-Náma*; the *Ta'ríkh-i-Gáwbara* of Abu'l-Ḥasan Muḥammad al-Yazdádí; the *Kitáb-i-Futúkh-i-Jibál-i-Ṭabaristán* of Abu'l-Ḥasan 'Alí ibn Muḥammad al-Madá'iní; the *Ta'ríkh-i-Ṭabaristán* of Mawláná Auliyá'ulláh Ámulí; and the *Ta'ríkh-i-Ṭabaristán* of 'Alí ibn Jamálu'd-Dín ibn 'Alí ibn Maḥmúd an-Najíbí ar-Rúyání. The chronicles of Astarábád and Gurgán are mentioned in page 161, note 99.

I am deeply grateful to Professor E. G. Browne not only for most valuable advice, but also for his generous assistance in the correction of all but the last proofs for the Press. Dr Nicholson kindly undertook to supervise what remained of the publication of the work when Professor Browne was prevented from proceeding with it through ill-health. Mr G. H. Selous, H.B.M. Consul at Casablanca, revised the original text before its final emendation. To M. F. von Stahl and his publishers I am indebted for permission to make full use of his surveys, the results of which were given in Petermann's *Geogr. Mitteilungen.*

The texts of inscriptions given in the appendix relate also to Gílán. I deemed it useful to reproduce them, as many of the original inscriptions have been destroyed in recent years. The misprints which mar the Persian text were due to my inability to superintend personally its printing owing to my transfer from Cairo.

H. L. RABINO.

BRITISH CONSULATE GENERAL, SMYRNA.
26 *November*, 1925.

CONTENTS

PREFACE . . . . p. xi

BIBLIOGRAPHY . . . . p. xvii

NOTE ON MÍR ẒAHÍRU'D-DÍN'S *HISTORY OF GILAN AND DAYLAMISTÁN* . . . . p. xxiii

GLOSSARY . . . . p. xxiv

CHAPTER I . . . . p. 1

Ṭabaristán. Limits. Name superseded by that of Mázandarán. Mountains of Ṭabaristán. Former limits of Mázandarán. Situation. Districts. General description. Mountains. Rivers. Harbours. Communications. Sháh 'Abbás's causeway. Other roads. Climate. Towns. Resources. Population. Sayyids. Tribes. Qájárs. Armenians and Georgians. Jews. Language. Religion. Administration. Military works.

CHAPTER II . . . . p. 16

Rasht to Khurramábád. Bazaar of Kúchisfahán. Safíd-Rúd. Láhiján. Langarúd. Kilídbar. Rúdisar. Nawdih. Miyándih. District of Sakhtsar, products, language, inhabitants. The hot springs of Áb-i-Garm. District of Gulayján, inhabitants. The Amír-i-As'ad.

CHAPTER III . . . . p. 21

District of Tunakábun. Products. Industries. Clans. Hereditary chiefs. Origin of the name Khal'at-barí. Khwájawands. Khurramábád. Oil wells at Átishkada. Castle of Ḥabashabur. Khurramábád to Ámul. Subdistrict of Nishtá. 'Abbásábád. Subdistrict of Langá. The Namakábrúd. Subdistrict of Kalár-rustáq. Road from Chálús to Ṭihrán. River-mouths. Chalandar. Ruins of Ḥawdkútí. Ṣarínkalá. District of Kujúr, its subdistricts, inhabitants, and roads. Ṣuladih. District of Núr, its subdistricts and mines. Maḥmúdábád. Arrival at Ámul.

CHAPTER IV . . . . p. 33

Ámul. Foundation of Ámul. Islám. History of Ámul. The great mosque. Ibn Ḥawqal's description. Sack of Ámul by Tímúr. Present town. Bridge over the Harhaz. Town quarters. Principal buildings. Shrine of Mír Qiwámu'd-Dín. Masjid-i-Jámi'. Imámzáda Ibráhím. The *Gunbads* or tower-tombs of Ámul. Districts of Ámul. Roads. District of Láriján: subdistricts. History of Láriján. Basin of the Lár river. The Harhaz. District of Sawádkúh: subdistricts. Road from Fírúzkúh to Sárí. Ámul to Bárfurúsh. Bridge of Muḥammad Ḥasan Khán. Arrival at Bárfurúsh.

CHAPTER V . . . . p. 45

Bárfurúsh: situation. Foundation. Mámṭír. Population. Mosque of Káẓim Baygí. Masjid-i-Jámi'. Mashhadisar: district. Shrine of Abú Jawáb. Maḥmúdábád to Faraḥábád. Districts of Bárfurúsh. Bárfurúsh to Faraḥábád. District of Faraḥábád. Stenka Razin. Faraḥábád to Sárí. Road from Sárí to Bárfurúsh.

CHAPTER VI . . . . p. 51

Sárí. Foundation. History. Muqaddasí's description. Sack of Sárí by Tímúr. Situation. Gates and town quarters. Public buildings. Chief mosque. Gunbad-i-Salm-wa-Túr. Shrines. Imámzáda Zaynu'l-'Ábidín. Shrine of Mullá Majdu'd-Dín. Districts of Sárí. Subdistricts. Districts of Hazárjaríb: Dúdánga, Chahárdánga, Yánisar, Surkhgiriya, Yakhkash.

CHAPTER VII . . . . p. 58

Sárí to Nárinjbágh; bridge over the Tijin. Imámzáda 'Abbás. Shrine of Niká. Niká bridge and river. Road to Chahárdih. Nárinjbágh to Dhághmarz. Excursion to Miyánkala; fort of Palangán. The Miyánkala peninsula. Dhághmarz to Ashraf. Direct road from Niká to Ashraf. Ashraf: foundation, history, town quarters, public buildings, streams. Road to Sháhrúd. Districts. Ashraf to Nawkanda: Buland Imám. District of Kulbád. Galúgá. Road from Galúgá to Sháhrúd. The Jar-i-Kulbád. Nawkanda. Arrival at Bandargaz.

CHAPTER VIII . . . . p. 67

Bay of Astarábád: Count Voinovitch. Streams. Áshúráda. Gaz. District of Anazán: description. Gaz to Kafshgírí: Kharába-Shahr. Tamísha. Kurd Maḥalla. District of Sadan-Rustáq. Streams. Shrine of Rawshanábád. Kafshgírí to Astarábád. Astarábád: origin. Chronicles. Muqaddasí's description. Situation. Walls. Gates. Town-quarters. Public buildings. Masjid-i-Jámi'. Inscriptions. Governor's palace. Inhabitants.

CHAPTER IX . . . . p. 78

Province of Astarábád: limits. Description. Districts. Population. Roads. Attacks of tribes. Qizil Álán. Castle of Mubárakábád. Áqá Muḥammad Khán and the Turcomans. District of Sháhkúh and Sáwar. District of Anazán-Rustáq. *Bulúk* of Fakhr 'Imádu'd-Dín. District of Katúl. District of Findarisk. District of Kúhsár. Ḥájjílar. Kabúdjáma. Castles.

CHAPTER X . . . . p. 85

Astarábád to Gunbad-i-Qábús: Sulṭán-Duwín. Sháhmarz. The Qaráṣú. Áq-Qal'a. Founding of Mubárakábád. Qizil Álán wall. The Gunbad, or dome, of Qábús. Climate of Gurgán. City of Gurgán: its origin. History. Ibn Ḥawqal's description. Mustawfí's description. Ábasgún. Ním-Mardán. Former villages of Gurgán. The river Gurgán. Ruins of Gurgán. Shrine of Qarangí Imám. Dahistán: laid waste by successive invasions, desolate and uninhabited at the present day.

CHAPTER XI . . . . p. 93

Gunbad-i-Qábús to Unchalí. Unchalí. The Band-i-Amír. Khwája-Nifis. Persian Turcomans: intertribal feuds. Authority of Persian Government. *Sarkardas*. Iḥtishámu'l-Wizára's account of the Turcomans. Marriage. The Yamút. Country. *Chumúr* and *Chárwá*. Cultivation and industries. Business honesty. Sharaf and Chúní. Permanent settlements. Relations with the Atak villagers. Raids. Possible pacification. The Gúklán. Country. Relations with the Yamút and other neighbours. Tradition as to origin of name. Astarábád to Rádkán. Kútal of Jahánnumá. Caravanserai of Rádkán. Tower of Rádkán. Inscriptions. Descent to the Caspian.

APPENDIX I. VILLAGES AND LOCALITIES OF MÁZANDARÁN AND ASTARÁBÁD . . . . p. 105

A. Tunakábun. B. Kalár-Rustáq. C. Kujúr. D. Núr. E. Ámul. F. Láriján. G. Sawádkúh. H. Mashhadisar. I. Bárfurúsh. J. Faraḥábád. K. Sárí. L. Hazárjaríb. M. Ashraf. N. Anazán. O. Sadan-Rustáq. P. Sháhkúh and Sáwar. Q. Astarábád-Rustáq. R. Katúl. S. Findarisk. T. Kúhsár. U. Localities unidentified or not otherwise mentioned.

APPENDIX II. RULERS OF MÁZANDARÁN . . . . . p. 133

I. House of Gushnasp. II. Kayús. III. House of Zarmihr. IV. The Súkhrániyán or Qárinwand. V. House of Dábúya (Dábuwán). VI. House of Báwand. VII. Governors of Mázandarán: Caliphate, Ṭáhirid, Caliphate, Ṣaffárid, Caliphate, Sámánid, Buwayhid, Saljúq, Khwárazmsháhs, Mongols, Tímúrid, Ṣafawid. VIII. 'Alíd Rulers. IX. Asfár b. Shírúya. X. House of Kákí. XI. House of Ziyár. XII. Kiyás of Chuláw. XIII. Kiyá-i-Jalál. XIV. Mar'ashí Sayyids. XV. House of Rúzáfzún. XVI. Díw. XVII. Murtaḍá'í Sayyids of Hazárjaríb. XVIII. House of Pádúsbán. XIX. Vassals: Tamísha, Amír-Ká, Miyándúrúd, Láriján, Mámṭír, Landak, Lafúr, Kabúdjáma, Gulpáygán or Gúshwára, Lesser Báwands and others. Governors of Tunakábun. Governors of Karjiyán and Gulayján.

NOTES . . . . p. 150

OTHER WORKS BY THE AUTHOR . . . . . p. 167

INDEX OF NAMES OF AUTHORS AND OTHER PERSONS . . . . p. 170

INDEX OF NAMES WHICH DO NOT APPEAR IN THE PERSIAN INDEX . . . . p. 171

PREFACE IN PERSIAN . . . . p. 3

INSCRIPTIONS. PERSIAN TEXT:

Tijin Gúka: Shrine of Sayyid 'Alí . . . . p. 7
Láhiján: Masjid-i-Jámi' . . . . p. 7
Shaykhánbar: Shrine . . . . p. 11
Ámul: Imámzáda Ibráhím; Imámzáda Sih Tan . . . . . . p. 12
Bárfurúsh: Masjid-i-Káẓim Baygí; Masjid-i-Jámi'; two doors; a caravanserai . . . . p. 14
Imámzáda Sulṭán Muḥammad Ṭáhir . . . . p. 18
Abú'l-Ḥasankalá . . . . p. 19
Mashhadisar: Imámzáda Ibráhím Abú'l-Jawáb; a shrine . . . . p. 19
Sárí: Imámzáda Zaynu'l-'Abidín; Imámzáda Yaḥyá; letter of Imám Ja'far in the shrine of Majdu'd-Dín Makkí . . . . . . p. 21
Áẓádgala: Imámzáda 'Abbás . . . . p. 23
Niká: Imámzáda . . . . p. 24
Galúgáh: Buland Imám . . . . p. 25
Astarábád: Masjid-i-Jámi'; Madrasa-i-Muḥammad Taqí Khán; shrine of Sháhzáda Muḥsin; Takiya in the Na'lbandán quarter; Minaret in the Sabz-Mashhad quarter; Imámzáda Murád Bakhsh; Cistern near the Imámzáda Murád Bakhsh; Takiya-i-Dabbághán; Imámzáda 'Abdu'lláh; Gate of Government House; Madrasa-i-Áqá Muḥsin; Masjid-i-Qájárhá . . . . p. 25
Waqf-Náma relating to the water-supply of the town of Astarábád . p. 46
Kharába-Shahr; Imámzáda Qásim . . . . p. 53
Imámzáda of Raushanábád . . . . p. 54
Lamisk: Imámzáda-i-Panj Tan . . . . p. 55
Láhiján: Shrine of Chahár Pádsháh . . . . p. 56
Sumám: Sar Turbat . . . . p. 60

INSCRIPTIONS (*cont.*):

Rasht: Masjid-i-Jámi‘; Khákhar-i-Imám; Masjid-i-Ḥájjí Muḥammad Khán; Former gate of Government House; Minaret of Ságharísázán; Sulaymán Dáráb . . . . p. 65
Fíldih: Shrine . . . . p. 71
Láhiján: Masjid-i-Akbariya . . . . p. 73

ERRATA . . . . p. 76

INDEX IN PERSIAN

Names of persons . . . . p. 79
Names of places, tribes, rivers, etc. . . . . p. 124

MAPS

Sketch Map of Mázandarán and Astarábád . . . . . . *in pocket*
Fírúzkúh to Bárfurúsh . . . . *to face* p. 40

ADDENDA AND CORRIGENDA

p. 2, note 2. Add: M. R. Vasmer has just pointed out to me that my account of the mountains of Ṭabaristán is erroneous although based on the descriptions of some of the Persian geographers and historians. According to Ṭabarí there were three mountains of Ṭabaristán: that of Wandá Hurmuzd, which was in the centre of Ṭabaristán; that of his brother Wandásfahán, son of Alandá b. Qárin; and that of Sharwín b. Shahryár b. Báw. Ibn Rustah states that the mountain of Wandá Hurmuzd was Damáwand, while al-Faqíh informs us that the Banú Sharwín resided in the mountains of Ṭabaristán which bordered on Qúmis. It is evident therefore that Kúh-i Sharwín was to the east, Kúh-i Wandá Hurmuzd in the centre, and Kúh-i Wandásfahán to the west.

p. 12, l. 11. *Read* Ṣadr-i A‘ẓam.
p. 14, l. 1. ,, Abu'l-Khaṣíb (cf. Ṭabarí, III, 136).
p. 14, l. 19. ,, Kayúmarth.
p. 21, l. 5. ,, ‘Abbásábád.
p. 22, l. 16. ,, Maḥáll-i Thalátha.
p. 25, l. 15. ,, al-Mu'ayyad.
p. 34, l. 13. ,, ‘Abdu'lláh b. Kházim.
p. 34, l. 15. ,, Kházima-Kúy.
p. 40, l. 15. ,, Áḥ.
p. 40, l. 20. ,, Áḥ.
p. 42, l. 16. ,, Talár.
p. 42, l. 12 from foot. *Read* Talár.
p. 44, l. 6. *Read* ‘Álamdár.
p. 48, l. 9 from foot. Read *maḥall.*
p. 52, l. 16. *Read* Abu'l-Khaṣíb.
p. 53, l. 9. ,, Mu'ayyad bi'lláh.
p. 59, l. 9. ,, ‘Abdu'l-Muḥíṭ.
p. 65, l. 3. ,, Wala-múzí.
p. 65, l. 23. ,, ‘Imránlú.
p. 66, l. 12. ,, Shiháb.
p. 74, l. 5. ,, Abú ‘Abdu'lláh.
p. 89, l. 3. ,, ‘Ámir.
p. 93, l. 16 from foot. *Read* Aqíra-jár.

BIBLIOGRAPHY

ANET, CLAUDE. *Feuilles Persanes.* (Paris, 1924.)

BAKER, V. *Clouds in the East.* (London, 1876.)

BARBIER DE MEYNARD, C. *Dictionnaire géographique, historique et littéraire de la Perse, extrait du Modjem el-Bouldan de Yaqout.* (Paris, 1861.)

BAUER. *Dattelpalmen an den Ufern des Kasp. Meeres.* (*Bull. de l'Ac. des Sciences de St Pétersbourg.* February 1859.)

BELL, Dr C. M. *Geological notes on part of Mázandarán.* (*Geological Transactions*, Series 2, Vol. V, p. 577. London.)

BODE, VON. *Yamút und Gúklán.* (*Abhandl. der russisch. geograph. Gesellschaft*, 1847, Vol. II, p. 209.)

BROWNE, EDWARD G. Abridged translation of Ibn Isfandiyár's *History of Ṭabaristán.* ("E. J. W. Gibb Memorial" Series, Vol. II, 1905.)

—— *Ta'ríkh-i-Guzída* by Ḥamdu'lláh Mustawfí-i-Qazwíní. ("E. J. W. Gibb Memorial" Series, Vol. XIV, 1, 1911 (Persian Text), Vol. XIV, 2 (Abridged translation), 1913.)

—— *Ta'ríkh-i-Jahán-gushá of Juwayní.* Vols. I and II (Vol. III not yet published). ("E. J. W. Gibb Memorial" Series, Vols. XVI, 1, 1913, and XVI, 2, 1917.)

—— Dawlatsháh's *Tadhkiratu'sh-Shu'ará*, or *Memoirs of the Poets.* (*Persian Historical Texts*, Vol. I, 1901.)

—— *A Year among the Persians.* (London, 1893.)

—— *A Literary History of Persia.* (2 vols. London, 1902, 1906.)

—— *Account of a Rare MS. History of the Seljúqs.* (*J.R.A.S.*, July, 1902.)

BRYDGES, Sir HARFORD JONES. *Dynasty of the Kádjárs.* (London, 1833.)

BUHSE, Dr F. A. *Bergreise von Gílán nach Asterábád.* (*Beitrage zur Kenntniss des russischen Reichs*, 1849, Vol. XIII, p. 125.)

CHARDIN, Sir JOHN. *Travels of Sir John Chardin into Persia, and The Coronation of Soleiman III.* (London, 1686.)

CHODZKO, A. *Specimens of the Popular Poetry of Persia.* (London, 1842.)

CURZON, Hon. GEORGE N. *Persia and the Persian Question.* (2 vols. London, 1892.)

DARMESTETER, J. *Lettre de Tansar au Roi de Ṭabaristán.* (*Journal Asiatique*, 1849, pp. 185–250 and 502–555.)

DEMORGNY, G. *Organisation du Ministère de l'Intérieur.* (Téhéran, 1313/1895–6.)

DIEZ, ERNST. *Churasanische Baudenkmäler mit einem Beitrage von Max van Berchem.* (Bd. I. Berlin, 1918.)

DORN, B. *Die Geschichte Tabaristán's und der Serbedare nach Khondemir.* (Persischer Text. Petr. 1850.)

DORN, B. *Muhammedanische Quellen zur Geschichte der Südlichen Küstenländer des Kaspischen Meeres.* 4 vols.:

I. Sehir-eddin's *Geschichte von Tabaristan, Rujan, und Masanderan.* (Persischer Text. Petr. 1850.)

II. Aly ben Schems-eddin's Chanisches Geschichtswerk, oder *Geschichte von Gilan* (880 bis 920 A.H.). (Persischer Text. Petr. 1857.)

III. Abdu'l Fattah Fumeny's *Geschichte von Gilan* (923 bis 1038 A.H.). (Persischer Text. Petr. 1858.)

IV. *Auszüge aus Muhammedanischen Schriftstellern, betreffend die Geschichte und Geographie der Südlichen Küstenländer des Kaspischen Meeres.* (Arabische, Persische and Türkische Texte. Petr. 1858.)

—— *Reise nach Masanderan im Jahre* 1860, I. Abschnitt: St Petersburg —Aschref. Bemerkungen auf Anlass einer wissenschaftlichen Reise in dem Kaukasus und den Südlichen Küstenländern des Kaspischen Meeres in den Jahren 1860–1861, herausgegeben von der Kaiserlich-Russischen Archaeologischen Gesellschaft. (Petr. 1895.)

—— *Atlas zu Bemerkungen etc.* (Petr. 1895.)

—— *Caspia.* (*Mémoires de l'Ac. des Sciences de St Pétersbourg*, 1875, Vol. XXIII, No. 1[1].)

DORN, B. and Mírzá MUḤAMMED SHAFí'. *Beiträge zur Kenntniss der Iranischen Sprachen.* Theil I. Masanderanische Sprache. Theil II. 1 u. 3 Lieferung, Die Gedichtsammlung des Emir-i-Pazewary. (Petr. 1860–1866.)

DROUIN, ED. *Observations sur les Monnaies à légendes en Pehlevi et Pehlevi Arabe.* (*Revue Archéologique.* Paris, 1884.)

EASTWICK, E. B. *Journal of a Diplomate's Three Years' Residence in Persia.* (2 vols. London, 1864.)

EICHWALD, ED. *Reise auf dem Caspischen Meere und in den Caucasus.* (Stuttgart und Tübingen, 1834.)

FERTÉ, H. *Vie de Sultan Hossein Baikara.* (Paris, 1898.)

FORSTER, G. *A Journey from Bengal to England.* (2 vols. London, 1808.)

FORTESCUE, L. S. *The Caspian Provinces.* (Lecture given on Feb. 14th, 1924, to the Central Asian Society at the Royal United Services Institution.)

FRASER, J. B. *Travels and Adventures in the Persian Provinces of the Southern Banks of the Caspian Sea.* (London, 1826.)

—— *A Winter's Journey from Constantinople to Tehran.* (2 vols. London, 1837.)

—— *Narrative of a Journey into Khorasan in the years* 1821 *and* 1822. (London, 1825.)

GASTEIGER-RAVENSTEIN-KOBACH. *Rundreise durch die nördlichen Provinzen Persiens.* (*Z. f. allgem. Erdkunde*, XII n. F. 1862.)

GMELIN, SAM. G. *Reise durch Russland zur Untersuchung der drei Naturreiche.* (4 vols. 1770–1784.)

[1] See also H. L. Rabino, *Le Guilan*, p. 9.

GREWINGK, Dr C. *Die Geognostischen und Orographischen Verhältnisse der Nördlichen Persia.* (Petr. 1853.)

ḤABLU'L-MATÍN. *Ṭabaristán bihtarín nuqṭa-i dunyá.* (Jumádá I, 1345/ November, 1926.)

HAENTSCHE, Dr J. C. *Topographie und Statistik der persischen Turkmanen.* (*Zeitschrift für Allgemeine Erdkunde*, Berlin, 1862. No. 10.)

HANWAY, JONAS. *An Historical Account of the British Trade over the Caspian Sea, with a Journal of Travels and the Revolutions of Persia.* (4 vols. London, 1753; 2 vols. London, 1762.)

HOLMES, W. R. *Sketches on the Caspian Shores.* (London, 1845.)

HOMMAIRE DE HELL, X. *Voyages en Turquie et en Perse.* (Paris, 1854–1860.)

HUART, CLÉMENT. *Les Ziyârides.* (Extrait des *Mémoires de l'Académie des Inscriptions et Belles-Lettres*, Tome XLII.) (Paris, Imprimerie Nationale, 1922.)

I'TIMÁDU'S-SALṬANA, MUḤAMMAD ḤAṢAN KHÁN. *Kitábu't-Tadwín fí Aḥwál-i-Jibál-i-Sharwín.* (Ṭihrán.)

KHANIKOFF, N. *Mémoire sur la partie méridionale de l'Asie Centrale.* (Paris, 1861–1862.)

—— *Voyage Scientifique de M. Dorn dans le Mâzandérân, le Caucase et le Dâghestan.* (*Journal Asiatique*, fév. 1862, pp. 214–225.)

KHWÁNDAMÍR. *Ḥabíbu's-Siyar.*

LE STRANGE, GUY. *The Lands of the Eastern Caliphate, Mesopotamia, Persia, and Central Asia.* (Cambridge, 1905.)

—— *Nuzhatu'l-Qulúb* by Ḥamdu'lláh Mustawfí Qazwíní, edited and translated by G. Le Strange. ("E. J. W. Gibb Memorial" Series, Vol. XXIII, 1, 1915, and XXIII, 2, 1918.)

LOVETT, Col. C. BERESFORD. *Report on Astarábád.* (March 1882. *Consular Reports.*)

—— *Itinerary Notes of Route Surveys in Northern Persia in* 1881 *and* 1882. (*Proceedings R.G.S.*, Vol. V, 1883, with Map. February number.)

MALCOLM, Sir JOHN. *History of Persia.* (2 vols. London, 1829.)

MARQUART, J. *Ērānšahr nach der Geographie des Ps. Moses Xorenac'i.* (*Abhandlung der Königl. Gesellschaft der Wissenschaften zu Göttingen.* Neue Folge, Bd. III, 1899–1901.)

MELGUNOF, G. *Das Südliche Ufer des Kaspischen Meeres.* (Leipzig, 1868.)

—— *Essai sur les Dialectes der Mazendéran et du Ghilan, d'après la prononciation locale.* (*Z.D.M.G.*, Vol. XVII, pp. 195–224.)

MORDTMANN, A. D. *Münzen der Sassaniden.* (1880. *Z.D.M.G.*, Vol. XXXIV, pp. 1–162.)

MORGAN, J. DE. *Mission Scientifique en Perse.* 5 vols. Paris, 1889–1891. (*Mission Scientifique en Perse.* Carte des Rives Méridionales de la Mer Caspienne. Paris, 1895.)

MURAVIEW. *Voyages en Turcomanie et à Khiva.* (St Petersburg, 1823.)

NAPIER, Hon. G. C. *Collection of Journals and Reports from Capt. the Hon. G. C. Napier, on special duty in Persia.* (1874. London, 1876.)

NÁṢIRU'D-DÍN SHÁH. *Journey to Mázandarán.* (In Persian.) (Persia, 1877.)

NOEL, Capt. J. B. *A Reconnaissance in the Caspian Provinces of Persia* (*J.R.G.S.*, June 1921, Vol. LVII, No. 6, p. 401.)

NÚRU'LLÁH TUSTARÍ, SAYYID. *Majálisu'l-Mu'minín.* (Lith. Ṭihrán, 1268/1851-2.)

O'DONOVAN, E. *The Merv Oasis.* (Vol. I. New York, 1883.)

OLSHAUSEN, D. JUSTUS. *Mazdoran und Mazanderan.* (*Gesammtsitzung der Akademie,* 23 Nov. 1876. Vienna, pp. 777-783.)

—— *Die Pehlewi-Legenden auf den Münzen der letzten Sasaniden.* (Copenhagen, 1843.)

OUSELEY, Sir WILLIAM. *Travels in Various Countries of the East, more particularly Persia.* (3 vols. London, 1819-1823.)

POSLAWSKI, Général. *D'un voyage sur les rivières Atrek et Gurgan,* 1900. (Extrait des *Comptes rendus des Séances du Cercle Turkestanais des Amateurs d'Archéologie,* Protocole 4.)

PUSCHIN, Capt. *The Caspian Sea.* (In Russian.)

QUERRY, A. *Le Qabous-namé.* (Paris, 1886.)

RABINO, H. L. Mír Ẓahíru'd-Dín's *History of Gílán and Daylamistán.* (Persian Text. Rasht, 1330/1912.)

—— *A Journey in Mázandarán* (*from Rasht to Sárí*). (*J.R.G.S.* Nov. 1913. pp. 435-454.)

—— *Report from March* 20, 1903, *to March* 20, 1907, *on the Trade of the Consular district of Resht and Astarábád.* (*Dipl. and Cons. Reports,* Ann. Series, No. 3864.)

—— *Report from March* 21, 1907, *to March* 20, 1909, *on the Trade of the Persian Caspian Provinces.* (Consular district of Resht and Astarábád. *Dipl. and Cons. Reports,* Ann. Series, No. 4398.)

—— *Report from March* 21, 1909, *to March* 20, 1911, *on the Trade of the Persian Caspian Provinces.* (Consular district of Resht and Astarábád. *Dipl. and Cons. Reports,* Ann. Series, No. 4828.)

—— *Report on the Trade and General Condition of the City and Province of Astarábád.* (*Dipl. and Cons. Reports,* Ann. Series, No. 4381.)

—— *Report for the Year* 1910-11 *on the Trade and General Condition of the City of Bárfurúsh and the Province of Mázandarán.* (*Dipl. and Cons. Reports,* Ann. Series, No. 4812.)

—— *Les dynasties Alaouides du Mazandéran.* (*Journal Asiatique,* Avril—Juin, 1927, pp. 253-277.)

RABINO, H. L. and LAFONT, D. F. *L'Industrie Séricicole en Perse.* (Montpellier, 1910.)

—— *La Culture du Riz en Guilan et dans les autres Provinces du Sud de la Caspienne.* (Montpellier, 1911.)

—— *Culture de la Gourde à Ghalian en Guilan et en Mazandéran.* (*Revue du Monde Musulman,* 1914. T. XXVIII.)

RABINO, H. L. and LAFONT, D. F. *Culture de la Canne à Sucre en Mazandéran.* (*Revue du Monde Musulman*, loc. cit.)

RAWLINSON, GEORGE. *The History of Herodotus.* (4 vols. London, 1858–1860.)

REHATSEK, E. *The Báw and Gáobarah Sepahbuds along the Caspian Shores.* (*Journal Bombay Br. R. Asiat. S.*, 1876, Vol. XII, pp. 412–445.)

RIḌÁ QULÍ KHÁN. *Rawḍatu's-Ṣafá.*

RIES, P. *Voyages dans le Guilan et le Mazandéran.* (*Zapisk. Kavkask. Geogr.*, Vol. VI, 1864. In Russian.)

RITTER, K. *Erdkunde von Asien.* (Leipzig, 1863.)

ROLLIN, CHARLES. *The Ancient History of the Egyptians, Carthaginians, Assyrians, Babylonians, Medes and Persians, Grecians and Macedonians. With notes by James Bell.* (2 vols. Glasgow, 1842.)

SCHINDLER, A. H. *Notes on Damavand.* (*Proceedings R.G.S.*, Feb. 1888.)

—— *Eastern Persian Irak.* (*R.G.S.*, 1897.)

SEIDLITZ. *Handel und Wandel an der Kaspischen Südküste.* (*Pet. Geog. Mitt.*, 1869, pp. 98 and 225.)

SHARAF KHÁN ibn SHAMSU'D-DÍN BIDLÍSÍ. *The Sharafnáma.*

SHEIL, Lady. *Glimpses and Manners in Persia.* (London, 1856.)

STAHL, A. F. *Teheran und Umgegend.* With map. (*Pet. Geog. Mitt.*, 1900, Tafel 6.)

—— *Reisen in Nord und Zentral Persien.* With maps. (*Pet. Geog. Mitt.*, Ergänzungsheft, No. 118, Blatt I, 1895.)

—— *Reisen in Nord- und Westpersien.* With map. (*Pet. Geog. Mitt.*, 1907, Heft VI, pp. 121–132. Tafel 10.)

—— *Notes on the March of Alexander the Great from Ecbatana to Hyrcania.* (*J.R.G.S.*, October 1924, Vol. LXIV, pp. 312–319.)

—— *Die orographischen und hydrographischen Verhältnisse des Elbursgebirges in Persien.* (*Pet. Geog. Mitt.*, 1927, Heft 7/8 (mit karte, s. Tafel 13).)

STICKEL, J. G. *Aelteste Muhammedanische Münzen bis zur Münzreform 'Abdul Melik's.* (Leipzig, 1870.)

STRABO. *The Geography of Strabo, translated with notes, the first six volumes by H. S. Hamilton, the remainder by W. Falconer.* (3 vols. Bohn's Classical Library. London, 1912.)

STUART, Gen. CHARLES. *Journal of a Residence in Northern Persia, and the adjacent Provinces of Persia.* (London, 1854.)

SYKES, Major P. M. *A sixth Journey in Persia.* (*J.R.G.S.* London, January, 1911.)

TODD, E. D'ARCY. *Memoranda to accompany a Sketch of part of Mazanderan etc.* (In April, 1836. *J.R.G.S.*, Vol. VIII, No. 5, pp. 101–108.)

TREZEL, Colonel. *Notice sur le Ghilan et le Mazandéran. Dans le Voyage en Arménie et en Perse de P. Amédée Jaubert.* (Paris, 1821.)

VASMER, R. *Die Eroberung Tabaristans durch die Araber zur Zeit des Chalifen al-Manṣur.* (Verlag der Asia Major, Leipzig. Separatdruck aus *Islamica*, Vol. III, fasc. I, pp. 86—150.)

—— *Die orographischen und hydrographischen Verhältnisse des Elbursgebirges in Persien.* With map. (*Pet. Geog. Mitt.*, 1927, Heft 7/8, pp. 211-215, Tafel 13.)

—— *Die Münzen der Ispehbede und Statthalter von Tabaristan* (in preparation).

WELLS, Lt.-Col. H. L. *Across the Elburz Mountains to the Caspian Sea.* (*The Scottish Geographical Magazine*, January, 1898.)

YATE, Col. C. E. *Khurásán and Sístán.* (London, 1900.)

NOTE ON MÍR ẒAHÍRU'D-DÍN'S *HISTORY OF GÍLÁN AND DAYLAMISTÁN*

The work opens as usual with a doxology, followed by a preface in which the author mentions the advantages to be derived from the study of history, states why he wrote the present chronicle, concludes with a panegyric of his benefactor Sulṭán Muḥammad of Láhiján, and explains the arrangement of his book, which is as follows:

(*a*) Preface (*muqaddama*). Etymology of Gíl and Daylam.

(*b*) Chapter I. Rulers of Gílán and Daylamistán prior to the Amír Kiyá'í dynasty. Description of those districts.

(*c*) Chapter II. Rebellion of Sayyid Amír Kiyá Maláṭí, to the death of Sayyid 'Alí Kiyá and his brothers at Rasht, in 29 sections (*faṣl*).

(*d*) Chapter III. Sayyid Hádí Kiyá of Tunakábun drives out of Biyapísh the rulers of the Náṣirwand clan and of Biyapas who had established themselves there after the death of Sayyid 'Alí Kiyá. (5 sections.)

(*e*) Chapter IV. Rule of Sayyid Raḍí Kiyá b. Sayyid 'Alí Kiyá and of Sayyid Muḥammad b. Mahdí Kiyá over Láhiján and Ránikúh. They expel their uncle Sayyid Hádí Kiyá. (18 sections.)

(*f*) Chapter V. Rule of Kárkiyá Náṣir Kiyá and of his brother Kárkiyá Amír Sayyid Aḥmad. (17 sections of which two are numbered 5.)

(*g*) Chapter VI. Rule of Kárkiyá Sulṭán Muḥammad. (26 sections.)

(*h*) Chapter VII. Events from 881–894/1476–1489. (19 sections.)

This chronicle was written by Mír Ẓahíru'd-Dín, so he informs us, under the dictation of Kárkiyá Sulṭán Muḥammad, in 880/1475–6. It was then carried down year by year to 894/1489 by the author himself.

The only known copy of this work was presented in 1602 to the Bodleian Library (Bodl. Or. 156) (see Ethé's *Bodl. Pers. Cat.*, No. 309, col. 162) by Sir Richard Lee, formerly Ambassador to Russia, who probably received it from one of the companions of Sir Anthony Jenkinson who had visited Gílán.

The manuscript comprises 203 pages and is dated Rabí' I, 993/March 1585. It was apparently copied by a scribe of Láhiján under the dictation of one of his friends. This would explain the numerous mistakes to be attributed to bad hearing, lack of grammatical knowledge, and influence of local dialect.

The handwriting is very clear throughout, and at first very carefully done.

Although intact, the manuscript is incomplete and was copied from an original, some leaves of which had disappeared. Thus there are missing:

(1) The concluding lines of the Preface.

(2) The Introduction.

(3) The first chapter. It has been impossible to fill up this lacuna although I have gathered from Arab and Persian historians notices on local dynasties such as the Wahsúdániyán, the Muẓaffarís and certain 'Alawí princes who reigned in Gílán and Daylamistán. A section, the loss of which is greatly to be regretted, is that relating to the history and doctrines of the Assassins of Alamút.

(4) The first, second and part of the third sections of the second chapter. These sections contained no doubt the genealogy and early history of the family of Sayyid Amír Kiyá. This information is given briefly in the *Majálisu'l-Mu'minín* of Sayyid Núru'lláh-i-Shustarí.

(5) The conclusion of section 8, sections 9 and 10, and the beginning of section 11 of the fourth chapter. These sections dealt with an expedition to Mázandarán of which an account is given in the author's *History of Ṭabaristán, Rúyán and Mázandarán*.

Notwithstanding all these lacunæ the manuscript gives us a complete history of the Amír Kiyá'í dynasty of Láhiján from 750 to 894/1349–1489.

Ẓahíru'd-Dín's *History of Gílán and Daylamistán* is the second book published at Rasht, Gílán, and, though misprints are numerous, the '*Urwatu'l-Wuthqá* Press can be congratulated on having successfully carried out the printing of this volume notwithstanding all sorts of difficulties with which it had to contend, such as want of skilled and literate staff, the closing of the press for four months by the Russian Consul, Mr A. Necrasof, the exile of Áqá Riḍá, owner and manager of the press, and the departure of Mr Rabino when the work was only half through the press.

For a biographical notice of Mír Ẓahíru'd-Dín, see Dorn, *Sehır-eddin's Geschichte von Tabaristan, Rujan und Masanderan*, pp. 13–22.

GLOSSARY

Áb-bandán.	Irrigation reservoir.
Áb-dang.	Tilt hammers for husking rice worked by water power.
Aghúz.	Walnut tree.
Asal *or* Isṭalkh.	Water reservoir.
Ázád.	The Zelkowa crenata or Planera crenata.
Bun.	Above.
Charwá.	Turcoman nomad.
Chumúr.	Turcoman cultivator.
Dár.	Tree.
Dunbál *or* Dunbála.	Overflow canal.
Duwín.	Mound, tumulus.
Gálish.	Herdsmen, cowherd.
Gálish-Nishín.	Camp of cowherds.
Gílak.	Inhabitant of Gílán.
Jú *or* Júb.	Ditch, canal.
Kalá *or* Kaláta.	A fortified village.
Kála.	Elevated land not liable to be swamped.
Kíla.	Canal, stream.
Laylakí.	Gleditschia caspica.
Mázú.	Oak.
Rú *or* Rúd.	River, stream.
Talú.	Thicket (Mázandaráni).
'Ubba.	Turcoman camp.

CHAPTER I

Ṭabaristán. Limits. Name superseded by that of Mázandarán. Mountains of Ṭabaristán. Former limits of Mázandarán. Situation. Districts. General description. Mountains. Rivers. Harbours. Communications. Sháh 'Abbás's causeway. Other roads. Climate. Towns. Resources. Population. Sayyids. Tribes. Qájárs. Armenians and Georgians. Jews. Language. Religion. Administration. Military works.

MÁZANDARÁN, formerly known as Ṭabaristán, is a district forming part of the old province of Farshwádgar[1], which comprised Ádharbayján, Áhár, Ṭabaristán, Gílán, Daylam, Ray, Qúmis, Dámghán, and Gurgán (1).

"Ṭabar" has the signification of "mountain" in the local dialect, whence Ṭabaristán would mean "the mountain land[2]."

The frontier of Ṭabaristán was fixed by Minúchihr as follows: east, Dínárjárí,—west, the village of Malát, which was to the south of Húsam,—south, the crest of all the mountains whose waters reach the Sea of Ábasgún (the Caspian), which borders the province to the north.

Ṭabaristán (2) thus comprised Gurgán, Astarábád, Mázandarán (3), and Rustamdár, to which were occasionally added Basṭám, Dámghán, Fírúzkúh, and Kharraqán.

"In the 7th (13th) century, about the time of the Mongol conquest, the name of Ṭabaristán appears to have fallen into disuse, being replaced by Mázandarán (4), which since that date has been the common appellation of this province....Practically the terms Ṭabaristán and Mázandarán were synonymous, but while the former name was applied primarily to the high mountains, and only included in a secondary use the narrow strip of lowland along the sea-shore running from the Delta of the Safíd Rúd to the south-eastern angle of the Caspian, Mázandarán appears in the first instance to have denoted these lowlands, and then included the mountain region as subsidiary thereto. The name Tabaristán is at the present day obsolete[3]," although revived for a short period (1250–1290/1834–1873) as a Mint name on coins struck at Sárí.

[1] For the derivation of the name Farshwádgar see Darmesteter, "Lettre de Tansar," *Journal Asiatique*, 1894, p. 507.

[2] Le Strange, *Lands of the Eastern Caliphate*, Cambridge, 1905, p. 369. For other derivations of the name Ṭabaristán see Dorn, *Reise nach Masanderan im Jahre* 1860, St Petersburg, 1895, pp. 51–52, and for the name Tapuri, *ibid.*, p. 160.

[3] Le Strange, p. 369. See also J. Marquart, "Ērānšahr nach der Geographie des Ps Moses Xorenac'i" in *Abhandlung der Königl. Ges. der Wissenschaften zu Göttingen*, Neue Folge, Bd III, 1899–1901, pp. 129–135.

Ibn Ḥawqal in the 4th (10th) century describes three mountain districts of Ṭabaristán. The first was Jabal-i-Fádúsbán, *i.e.* the mountain of Pádúsbán, this being the name of the ruling family, who, as semi-independent chiefs, held Rustamdár from about 45 to 1005/665–6—1595–6. "The whole of this mountain district was covered with villages, of which the largest was named Qaryat Manṣúr, 'Manṣúr's village,' and another was Uram Khwást with an upper and a lower village, these places all lying about a day's march from Sáriya, but throughout the mountain side there was no town of sufficient size to have a Friday Mosque[1]."

Adjoining Fádúsbán was the mountain district called Jabal-i-Qárin after the famous family of that name. This district comprised the present Láriján, Ṣawádkúh and Hazárjaríb. The third mountain range was the Jabal-i-Rúbanj lying north of Ray, and must have comprised, therefore, the present districts of Áranga and Ṭálaqán. It could not possibly have been Ránikúh which is a small district north of the Ishkawar mountains.

Kúh-i-Qárin (5) was the general appellation of the eastern mountain range, but the range of mountains extending from Ámul to Astarábád was itself subdivided into various mountain districts which usually bore the name of some prince of the ruling family. Thus we have Wandád-Ummíd-Kúh immediately south of Ámul; Ummídwár-Kúh which became later Amíra-Kúh; Hurmazd-Kúh, probably the same as the Wandád-Hurmazd-Kúh which was to the east of the Kúh-i-Sharwín on the road to Khurásán (Álárd was in Wandád-Hurmazd-Kúh). Kúh-i-Sharwín lies between Sawádkúh and Fírúzkúh and is known now-a-days as Kúh-i-Shalfín. Shahriyár-Kúh, which Ibn-Isfandiyár gives as in Farím, was south of Sárí and on the road from Dámghán to Ṭabaristán. From Wíma to Ṭabaristán one could pass by Wandáhaza-Kúh; there was also a path over the Shahriyár-Kúh. Wandáhaza-Kúh is mentioned as on the way from Níshápúr to Ṭabaristán; and Farrukhán-Fírúz-Kúh, to which the Ispahbad Khurshíd banished his cousins who had conspired to kill him, may possibly be the present Fírúz-Kúh[2] (6).

[1] Le Strange, p. 372.

[2] See Ibn Isfandiyár's *History of Ṭabaristán*, abridged translation by E. G. Browne, Vol. II. of *E. J. W. Gibb Memorial*, p. 29, lines 13–14, Cháh-i-Wíjan in Ummídwár-Kúh; but for "thence they carry logs and planks to Ámul" read "passed by people on their way from Farasp and Pulúr to Ámul"; pp. 40–41, Wandád-Hurmazd-Kúh; Ummídwár-Kúh and Pá'íza-Kúh; pp. 41–42, Shahriyár-Kúh.

Gurgán, which included Astarábád, extended from Dínárjarí, the western limit of Dahistán and the eastern limit of Ṭabaristán, to the forest of Anjadán, the eastern limit of Mázandarán. Anjadán was probably not far from Tamísha which was immediately west of the moat dug by the Ispahbad Farrukhán the Great as a protection against the people of Túrán. Astarábád was called Bírún Tamísha, and the extreme eastern districts of Mázandarán, Andarún Tamísha[1].

Mázandarán extended from Tamísha and the forest of Anjadán to Namakábrúd which separated it from Rustamdár. The latter district extended originally from Sí-Sangán, or the Mánhír stream, to Maláṭ, but, through the cession of certain territories to the Assassins and the acquisition of certain others which were brought to the Ustundárs by their wives as dowries, the boundaries were removed to Namakábrúd (Namakáwarúd) on the Gílán side and to the Alísharúd west of Ámul.

Eastern Mázandarán is often spoken of as Ispahbad or Ispahbadán from the title of its princes, just as Rustamdár was called Ustundáriyya.

Mázandarán "was originally called Múz-Andarún because Múz was the name of a mountain on the confines of Gílán extending as far as Lár-i-Qasrán and Jájarm (7); and since this territory was 'within (the mountain of) Múz,' it received this name[2]."

Mázandarán lies between the southern coast of the Caspian and the Alburz range, and extends from latitude 35° 45′ to 37° and from longitude 50° 40′ to 54° 30′. Its boundary on the western side lies to the west of the Surkhání stream; to the east the province is bounded by the *jar*, or ditch, of Kulbád and the Sháh-Kúh range. The greatest length of Mázandarán is 292 miles from east to west; in following the sinuosities of the coast, it is, of course, more. Its greatest breadth to the south of Faraḥábád is about 68 miles, of which about one third is flat, the remainder being mountainous.

Mázandarán is divided into 13 districts, viz. Tunakábun, Kalárrustáq, Kujúr, Núr, Ámul, Bárfurúsh, Mashhadisar, Sárí, Faraḥábád, Ashraf, Láriján, Sawádkúh, and Hazárjaríb (8).

Geographically the province may be divided into two distinct

[1] Ibn Isfandiyár gives the names of 28 cities in Andarún Tamísha, thus extending the application of the name to Western Mázandarán. See Ibn Isfandiyár, p. 28.

[2] *Ibid.*, p. 14. For the name Mázandarán see Dorn, *Reise*, pp. 58–61 and 157. See also Olshausen, *Mazdoran und Mazanderan* in Gesammtsitzung der Akademie of 23 November 1876, Vienna, pp. 777–785.

belts (9); the low, marshy, and impenetrable, jungle-clad plains, varying in breadth from 10 to 30 miles along the coast of the Caspian, and the elevated and forest-clad spurs thrown out from the northern face of Alburz. Both districts, owing to their natural impenetrability, are very difficult of access.

Fraser's description of Mázandarán[1] is so excellent that I have quoted freely from it in this chapter[2]:

"The surface, where not cultivated, consists of natural or artificial swamps, overgrown with forest trees and thorns, particularly bramble bushes of incredible luxuriance and absolutely impenetrable.

"Above the flat space tower the mountains, assuming the appearance of two ranges, the first being clothed with forests as dense as those below, which throw forward spurs and shoulders that sometimes reach the coast. Beyond this wooded and buttressed wall, which is traversed in all directions by the most wild and romantic glens, and which forms a sort of velvet lining to the principal range, the peaks and masses of this last are seen rising in naked, rocky grandeur, and snow-spotted even in September. It is in ascending these that you meet with the most desperate passes, and amongst their recesses, and even on their summits, as well as on those of the wooded hills below, are found the *yayláqs*, or summer quarters, to which the inhabitants resort in the heat of that season. The whole of these wooded mountains are pervaded by paths and passes so intricate that none but an experienced guide can find his way from one place to another; but the long winding tracks that lead through the skirts of the hills and the low plain are equally perplexing and more difficult, following, as they do generally, the windings of streams and rivers that keep to no particular bed, and involving the traveller in swamps, creeks, and quicksands, against which, as they shift with every flood, no experience can guard. It is these dense jungles and swamps which are the breeding-places of all the ill-health and disease, the hosts of flies, insects, and reptiles, and all the other abominations that infest Mázandarán.

"The beach which bounds this flat is a strip of sand and gravel, thrown up by the wash of the surf, which is driven against the southern shore with great violence by the prevailing wind from

[1] See Ibn Isfandiyár's description of Mázandarán, *History of Ṭabaristán*, p. 33, lines 2–29 and p. 34, lines 1–6.

[2] J. B. Fraser, *A Winter's Journey (Tâtar) from Constantinople to Tehran*, London, 1838, Vol. II, p. 468.

the north. In truth, the whole coast is lined by a chain of sand-hills, rising sometimes 25 to 30 feet in height, and 200 yards in breadth, behind which lies a morass of stagnant water from the numerous streams and rivers that, descending from the mountains, are prevented by these sand-hills from finding their way into the sea. Wherever a river does force its way through them, there is a continual battle between it and the surf, which latter throws up a bar that shuts up the channel entirely, so that its waters will accumulate and spread behind the sand-hills for miles, sluggish and dead, only finding their way to the sea by filtration, or very small streams beneath the sand, until a flood enables it to sweep bar and all before it. It is by these stagnant waters or *murdábs* (dead waters), as the natives call them, that the lakes and harbours of Sáliyán, Anzalí, Langarúd, Mashhadisar, Astarábád, and others, have been formed.

"The banks of these dead, or rather back waters, to speak more properly, are overgrown with alders of enormous size, with plane-trees, elms, ashes, poplars, and other trees which love a moist soil; and in the rainy season the country around is all flooded, so as to exhibit the singular spectacle of a boundless forest in a swamp. Yet scattered among these swamps, behind these *murdábs*, and sometimes between them and the sand-hills, the traveller may find numerous villages and clusters of houses inhabited by the cultivators of the rice-fields around. But a stranger would pass a dozen of these, and never suspect the existence of a human being, unless he chanced to see the smoke curling upwards from some of their fires, or to hear the bark of one of their dogs; and yet from each of these *maḥallas* there are always several pathways leading to the sea-beach, for the inhabitants have a considerable traffic which is carried on by sea, and at certain seasons the people live on fish, salmon, mullets, and other excellent kinds, which come to the coast, particularly in autumn and winter[1]."

The mountain system of Mázandarán consists entirely of the northern spurs thrown out from the Alburz range towards the Caspian. The length of these spurs varies from 30 to 50 miles. The distance of the mountains from the coast varies considerably; sometimes, as at Sakhtsar, they sweep down to the sea, forming headlands; at others, they form irregular curves, none of which are far from the Caspian.

[1] Fraser, *l.c.*, p. 470.

The main range is lofty and bare, but the lower hills are covered with every kind of forest tree and slope down by degrees to the belt of virgin forest. They are all of a very difficult and impracticable nature, being covered with dense forest for a great portion of their slopes.

The rivers of Mázandarán all rise in the northern slopes of the Alburz, and consequently none of them have any great length, and are really no more than mountain torrents, most of them being very low in dry weather, but subject to sudden and dangerous rises during and after the melting of snow.

Their names in succession from west to east are as follows: Surkhání, Turkrúd, Áb-i-Ṣakhtsar, also called Ṣafárúd or 'Isárúd, Náranjbun, Palangrúd called lower down Salmrúd (10), Áb-i-Ramak or Ramakábrúd, Shúrábsar, Áb-i-Sayyid-Maḥalla or Rúda'a, Baríshrúd, Mísha-Kaláya, Pahdarrúd, Niyása-Rúd, Zamínjúb, Júb-i-Pádangrúd, Chalkrúd, Chawarrúd, Shírrúd or Áb-i-Tahram, Áwsiyá, Wáchak, Fíkárúd, Zamínjúb probably the same as Mackenzie's Naṣírkalá, Áb-i-Karímábád, Gúsarí, Mazar, Chashmakíla, Sangsará, Tílpurdsar, Halíkalá, Palatkalá-dunbála (11), Izarúd, Sulṭánkalá, Nishtárúd, Káẓimrúd, Pasandarúd, Galabúsí, Kúchabúsí, 'Abbásábád, Muḥammad-Ḥusaynábád, Ganjarúd, Múmadamarda, Aspchín, Kharrakrúd, Chika-i-Aṣgharábád, Chika-i-Gulúr, Tílrúdsar, Zardkíla, Isparúd, Chika-i-Khájakasar, Palangrúd (12), Namakábrúd, Nawrúdsar, Ḥacharúd, Dújamán, Sardábrúd, Áwrang or Ábrang, Chálús, Gandábrúd, Kurkrúd, Girdú, Mashánkíla, Sháhmurádkíla, Mashalak, Dirázabál-kíla, 'Alíábádkíla, Sham'járán-Dunbál, Latangán-Dunbál, Amír-Rúd, Marúrdí, Khayr-rúd, Mázígáh, Duzdakarúd, Mulkár stream, Anárwar stream, 'Alíábád stream (13), Núrrúdbár, Khushklát, Ṣarínkalá (Ṣaláḥu'd-Dín Kalá), Namakábrúd, Kulírúd or Kalírú, Kunusarúd (14), Shaykhrúd, Kacharúd, Nahr-i-Ḥasanábád, Bunjákul, Falímarz, Siyáhrúd, Alamrúd, Suladih, Rustamrúd, Háshimrúd, 'Izdih, Alíshaṛúd or Ahlamrúd, Harhaz, Siyáhrúdbár, Ahlama, Shilít, Mullákíla, Surkhrúd, Shírarúd, Faríkinár, Bábul, Mírrúd, Chapukrúd or Tálár, Lárím or Siyáhrúd, Tijin, Niká (falling into the Caspian in four branches: Qal'a-i-'Alí Naqí Bayg, Qal'a Zardí, Gawharbarán and 'Abdu'l-Malikí-Kíla).

Holmes remarked that all the rivers on the Mázandarán coast have a long sandbank at their mouth projecting from the western bank towards the east, at which point they take a turn, flowing almost parallel to the shore before entering the sea; this occurs even when the rivers approach the coast from a south or south-west direction. From this fact it is evident that the prevailing winds are from the west and north-west, and that the waves running one way and the streams another have gradually raised banks between them.

Most of the rivers of Mázandarán are well stocked with fish.

The principal harbour, if we may call it by this name, is Mashhadisar. The next port in importance is Faríkinár, after which comes Faraḥábád.

There are two made roads leading from Mázandarán to the interior across the Alburz, that from Ámul to Ṭihrán, striking the eastern base of Damáwand, and constructed by Gasteiger Khán, an Austrian engineer in the service of Náṣiru'd-Dín Sháh, and that from Bárfurúsh to Ṭihrán via Sawádkúh, which follows the old causeway. Both are tolerably good.

In 1031/1621[1] was terminated the famous causeway which Sháh 'Abbás the Great had instructed the Wazír of Mázandarán, Mírzá Muhammad Taqí, to construct from Faraḥábád on the Caspian to Khwár, via Sárí, 'Alíábád, Sawádkúh, Halírúd, and Fírúzkúh, a total distance of about 45 *farsakhs*, divided into nine stages. Another causeway was constructed about the same time from Jájarm to the plain of Múghán traversing the whole of the Persian provinces along the southern shore of the Caspian.

The road consisted of a causeway, generally 20 feet wide, and was, apparently, laid down with great care and labour, being paved throughout with large water-worn stones taken from the numerous mountain streams which cross the forest-covered plain, drained by deep ditches, and fenced with a stout hedge of white thorn and wild pomegranate, which is equally thorny and impenetrable; it was not, however, sufficiently raised and no gaps for cross drainage were made. This, with the inevitable Persian indifference to repairs, has rendered it what it is at the present day, a monument to the wisdom of a single sovereign, and a reproachful witness to the neglect of a long line of his successors (15).

To the east of Astarábád, the causeway, in the shape of a wide road clearing the Gurgán pass or gorge 50 miles lower down the valley, is now said to be covered with impenetrable forest, and two

[1] The date of the completion of the causeway is given in the chronogram *kár-i-khayr* = 1031, and not *amr-i-khayr* = 1051, as mentioned by some authors.

ruined hostels known as Rubáṭ-i-'Ishq and Rubáṭ-i-Qarábil (16) alone remain to afford a comparison between the past and the present. The road from Astarábád to Ashraf is so completely ruined through neglect that the traffic of the country generally passes on either side of it, through deep sloughs which are, however, preferable to the broken pavement of the road with its dangerous pitfalls. From Ashraf to Sárí the present road for the greater part follows the causeway which is full of deep holes and ruts; in many places the mud is a yard deep, but a good road might easily be constructed on the foundation of the old one. From Sárí to 'Alíábád and thence to Ámul traces of the causeway are still to be seen. From Ámul to Tamíján in Ránikúh the causeway ran through the jungle, and I have heard of a section still in existence between Dániyál and Píshambur in Kalár-rustáq, a distance of about 20 miles. From Tamíján the road skirted the foot of the hills, passing Maláṭ and continuing thence to Láhiján, Rasht and the Múghán plain. The only traces of it in Gílán are seen at Maláṭ, near the former Gúráb-i-Gaskar, and perhaps on the way from Rík in Kargánrúd to Áqavlar, where Fraser thought he saw traces of the famous causeway leading over the mountains to Ardabíl.

The other roads in the interior are a trifle better than those of Gílán, but still are bad enough to occasion great fatigue, if not death, to horses. The only tolerable road from Rúdisar in Gílán to Bárfurúsh, which is always chosen by muleteers, when possible, lies along the sands of the sea-shore; but experienced guides are necessary to point out the fords of the numerous rivers, which are full of quicksands; and the fatigue of crossing these streams may be conceived when the number of them is taken into account.

The following is Fraser's description of the internal communications of Mázandarán: Certainly I never saw, nor can I imagine, a stronger or more impracticable country, from a military point of view, than these provinces. Roads—that is, made roads—there are none, except the great causeway, made of old by Sháh 'Abbás, and this has now so nearly disappeared, that it requires a guide to find it; and, even when found, it would be useless for military purposes, from the numerous breaks and gaps in its course, and from the impenetrable jungle which surrounds it on all sides, and affords cover for all sorts of ambuscades and surprises.

As for their paths, who, except themselves, could discover

them? A dense hedge, a perfect wall of bramble, blackthorn, and thick boxwood, cemented with wild vines, and other creeping plants that run up and overtop the trees, of great thickness, often approaches within 30 yards of the water's edge, and usually terminates in one of those swamps and jungles I have described. No one in his senses would be mad enough to attempt to penetrate it, but a guide will show you a "hole in the wall," a crevice, a thing like a rabbit-run, through which he introduces you to a pathway at first scarcely perceptible, winding like a snake through the bushes, but which increases in size as you get on, not, however, in facility, for it is intersected by at least a dozen deep natural creeks, through the mire and water of which your horse must flounder; or you may have the choice of a precarious bridge of boughs; or, for variety, after a little space you may have to tread through artificial cuts, made for irrigation, no less deep and difficult than the natural creeks, as your poor load-horses soon find out, and which flood the whole vicinity, so that you travel girth-deep in the soil; and thus, if you survive after a circuitous and perilous pilgrimage, you reach the *mahalla* or village.

The climate of Mázandarán is universally condemned. It is extremely capricious, and not naturally divided into wet and dry, or cold and hot, seasons: one year it pours for a month without cessation, and the same month in the next year may be quite dry. Though not nearly so damp as Gílán, it must be termed a humid climate, for there is no day throughout the year in which the people can rely on dry weather. The rainfall is five times as great as it is to the south. From December to April are the wettest, as also the coldest, months. The summers are very hot, and the weather then is subject to very great changes of temperature, which occasion much sickness. It is the same in winter; the inhabitants are then sometimes forced to throw off their warm clothes, and in summer they are obliged to have recourse to their *púst*í*ns*, or sheepskin cloaks, and furs. Snow often falls heavily, and though it does not remain so long as in the higher country to the south, it is a mistake to think that it does not lie at all. The cold of summer is damp and unwholesome, causing many diseases. Rheumatisms and dropsies are common, and complaints of the eye still more so.....Many of the inhabitants certainly have a sallow look, but others are remarkably sturdy and athletic[1].

[1] Fraser, *l.c.*, p. 48.

Along the sea-shore fevers are less prevalent than on the skirts of the hills.

The principal towns in Mázandarán are Sárí, the capital, Bárfurúsh, the centre of trade, Mashhadisar, and Ashraf.

The chief products of Mázandarán are rice, cotton, a little sugar[1], and a variety of fruits.

"The whole extent of the country, between the foot of the hills and the sea, is said to present a succession of large and populous villages, embosomed indeed in wood, quite surrounded also with cultivation; the greater part of this is rice, for which the country is best adapted.

"The land in Mázandarán yields only one full crop in the year, but barley is sown occasionally in spring, for horses and cattle, as a green crop; after it is cut they plough up the ground and plant it with rice[2]."

Silk cocoons are exported to Milan and Marseilles via Russia; some silk is reeled locally and used in native manufactures, mixed with cotton. Beans, wheat, and barley are grown in the mountainous districts, and some flax in the lowlands. During the winter a great many labourers come from the upper country and are employed here.

The principal fruits are a great variety of the orange, lemon and citron species. These are evergreens, and in winter give a lively and cheerful appearance to the gardens, which are filled with them. There are also to be found apples, pomegranates, quinces, pears, peaches, walnuts, grapes, and melons. The vines are seen climbing the trunks of the forest trees, and their stems are sometimes 8 and 10 inches in diameter.

Mázandarán produces mineral pitch, which is found in abundance in different states, from petroleum to the choicest kind of naphtha, and is applied to many useful purposes. Iron also is produced.

The cattle of Mázandarán are very small and have humps like the Indian cattle: the sheep are likewise small, and have not fat tails, like those of 'Iráq.

The mountains of Mázandarán abound with wild beasts; among others the tiger, panther, bear, wolf, goat, deer of different kinds, and wild boars are found in great quantities. Pheasants,

[1] See D. F. Lafont et H. L. Rabino, "Culture de la canne à sucre en Mâzandérân," *Revue du Monde Musulman*, Paris, Vol. XXVIII, Sept. 1914, pp. 237–243.

[2] Fraser, *l.c.*, p. 86.

woodcocks, and wild ducks are abundant all over the province. All the rivers are exceedingly well stocked with fish, which is the staple food of the peasantry[1].

The Mázandaránís (17) are a somewhat more manly race than the Gílaks, although there is not much difference between the two. This is perhaps owing to the fact that a great portion of them reside in the mountains in summer, as also to the smaller weight of taxation they have to endure. As far as honesty goes they are no better than they should be, and they are far inferior in point of intelligence to the Gílak: *en revanche* they are of sturdier build (18).

"The intellect of the Mázandaránís has been decried by the rest of their countrymen, as was that of the Boeotians by the Greeks, for stupidity and brutality, but, I suspect, on no sufficient grounds[2]." The poor classes are extremely ignorant, and according to our ideas can be considered but slightly civilized. The bigotry of the people in religious matters is great but concerns chiefly matters of ritual (19), and many indulge in liquor and opium, whilst the women of Sárí have the reputation of being of easy virtue.

Sayyids in Mázandarán are countless. At the death of Imám Riḍá, his relatives sought refuge in Daylam and Ṭabaristán, where some of them suffered martyrdom, their tombs (20) becoming celebrated. Their descendants, however, remained there. When Yaḥyá b. 'Umar b. Yaḥyá b. Ḥusayn rebelled at Kúfa and claimed to be an *imám* amongst the sect of Zayd, such of the *sayyids* as escaped from the battle in which he was captured fled to Ṭabaristán and Daylam. Under Sayyid Ḥasan b. Zayd, *sayyids* of the House of 'Alí and the Banú-Háshim began to flock to Ṭabaristán from Hijáz, Syria and 'Iráq, "like unto the number of the leaves on the trees," and this continued under the other 'Alid rulers.

In addition to the aborigines of the province and *íls* (21), there are many tribes disseminated over the country: 'Abdu'l-Malikís, Khwájawands, Laks, Giraylís, Úṣánlús, Balúchís, Afgháns, and Kurds, who have been brought into Mázandarán at different periods by various Persian Monarchs, and who hold their land

[1] For further information on the resources and trade of Mázandarán see Diplomatic and Consular Reports, No. 4812, Annual Series, *Report for the year* 1910–11 *on the trade and general condition of the city of Barfrush and the Province of Mazanderan*, by H. L. Rabino.

[2] Fraser, *l.c.*, p. 478.

by virtue of military service. They have become so mingled with the country folk that they cannot be distinguished from them; apart from the Kurds and a few Turks, they have altogether forgotten their original languages and are now Mázandaránís to all intents and purposes.

The 'Abdu'l-Malikís were at first settled at Darragaz; they were subsequently removed to Shíráz, and thence to Shahriyár, where they spent three years. Áqá Muḥammad Khán later transplanted them to Núr, where they remained for 40 years. They then left their country for their country's good, being moved on by Mírzá Áqá Khán Núrí Sadr-i-'Aẓam, about the year 1855, to Dhághmarz in the neighbourhood of Sárí. The territory they now occupy extends from Nawdharábád in Miyándúrúd on the west, to Qarátappa on the east, and from Atrap and Láktaráshán in Qaráṭughán on the south, to the Caspian. The Khwájawands are originally from Luristán. They were brought from Ardalán and Garrús to Western Mázandarán by Áqá Muḥammad Khán Qájár, together with the 'Abdu'l-Malikís from Shahriyár, to protect the capital, Ṭihrán, against any rising of the inhabitants of these parts, then noted for their turbulence.

The Laks inhabit Kalárdasht.

The Giraylís were brought to Mázandarán from Kálpúsh by Áqá Muḥammad Khán and are to be found in Andarúd, Miyándúrúd and Qaráṭughán. Like the Úṣánlús they are a Turkish race. The Úṣánlús were also imported by Áqá Muḥammad Khán. They numbered 150 families in the town of Sárí and many others in the villages, but are now dispersed.

We find a few Ṭálish in Kulít and others dispersed in the neighbourhood of the former Royal Residences of Mázandarán, and in the district of Tunakábun. A few Qawí Ḥiṣárlús reside in the latter district. Sheil estimated the number of Qájárs in Mázandarán at 2000 families[1]. Their number is now greatly reduced.

The few Balúchís, who came from the province which bears their name, numbered about 30 or 40 families settled in Sárí, but none are now to be found. Some 30 families of Afgháns had settled at Sárí but were massacred during some disturbances many years ago. There are still 60 families of Ghilzá'í Afgháns at Qarátappa, who were first brought to Mázandarán by Nádir.

[1] Lady Sheil, *Glimpses of Life and Manners in Persia*, London, 1856, notes by Sir Justin Sheil.

At his death they retired to the neighbourhood of the Gúklán country, but were brought back here by Áqá Muḥammad Khán.

The Kurdish tribes of Jahánbayglú and Mudánlú inhabited the villages of Shírkhwást, Miyánrúd, and Faraḥábád. The Mudánlús were, in Sir Justin Sheil's time, the most important tribe of Mázandarán. Jahánbayglús are reported as residing in Andarúd, Chapukrúd, and at Mashhadganjrúz; Mudánlús at Mishkábád, Júbár, Panbachúlí, Kurdkalá, and Lárím; Zayds at Isfandín.

Another important Turkish tribe is that of Imránlú which is settled in the village of Galúgá.

A few Arabs were brought to Eastern Mázandarán by Áqá Muḥammad Khán, and they introduced buffaloes into Mázandarán.

Some Gúdar families, Bankashís, Barbars and Karáchís or gypsies are also to be found in Mázandarán[1].

Of the 30,000 families of Armenians and Georgians brought to Mázandarán by Sháh 'Abbás (1585–1628 A.D.) few if any remain. They have either succumbed to the climate or been absorbed by the native population.

There are over 700 Jews in Bárfurúsh. In 1859 the *kadkhudá* told Mackenzie[2] that the colony to which he belonged had been formed from the remnants of those Jewish colonies planted in Mázandarán by Sháh 'Abbás, who, in accordance with his usual policy, established many Armenians and Jews on the Caspian.

The total population of Mázandarán is estimated by Demorgny[3] at between 250,000 and 300,000 souls.

The inhabitants generally speak Mázandarání (22), an old Persian dialect. In Tunakábun Gílakí is spoken, whilst Kurdish is the language of the Kurdish tribes, and Turkish, but to a lesser degree, that of the tribes of Turkish origin. In the towns Persian is the usual language.

Ẓahíru'd-Dín informs us that the first follower of Islám to come to Ṭabaristán was Ḥasan b. 'Alí, who was accompanied by 'Abdu'lláh b. 'Umar, Málik b. al Ḥárith al-Ashtar, and Qutham b. al 'Abbás, and that this occurred during the caliphate of 'Umar.

At the time of the conquest of Mázandarán by the Arabs, the people of Sárí, who, like their brethren of Tabaristán, were fire-

[1] For further information regarding these tribes see H. L. Rabino, Diplomatic and Consular Report, Annual Series, No. 4812, pp. 21–24.

[2] Capt. F. Mackenzie, *Report on the Persian Caspian Provinces*, Resht, 1859–1860. Unpublished.

[3] Demorgny, *Organisation du Ministère de l'Intérieur*, Téhéran, 1331, p. 48.

worshippers (23), embraced Islám under Abu'l-Khuḍayb and became Shí'ites. When Ámul was occupied by 'Umar b. 'Alá, the people, being disgusted with the Ispahbad's arrogance, came in in crowds and embraced Islám. They were apparently at first of the Málikí sect and the old Masjid-i-Jámi' of Ámul, called in Ẓahíru'd-Dín's time (880/1475–6) Ṭashtazanán, was built by people of that sect.

When Mázyár (d. 224/839) cast off his allegiance to the Caliph, he resumed the Zoroastrian girdle and treated the Muslims with contempt. He conferred various offices and distinctions on Bábak, Mazdak, and other Magians who ordered the Muhammadan mosques to be destroyed and all traces of Islám to be removed.

Ḥasan b. Zayd (250–270/864–884), when his authority was firmly established, issued a proclamation to all the regions of Ṭabaristán, bidding them add the Shí'ite clause *ḥayya ila khayri'l-'amal* to the call to prayer, and to say the *bismi'lláh* aloud in their prayers, and the like[1].

The people of Rustamdár were Sunnís, but Malik Kayumarth b. Bísitún (807–857/1404–1453) compelled the people of Rúyán and Rustamdár to embrace the tenets of the Shí'ites, with the exception, however, of the inhabitants of the village of Kadír who presented him with 700 geldings in order to be allowed to remain Sunnís. Two centuries later people of that sect were still to be found in the village.

Amongst the Shí'ites the Imámí doctrines prevailed, although there were many followers of Zayd, especially in Tunakábun. It was only under the Ṣafawís that the Imámí doctrines became universally accepted amongst the Shí'ites of Mázandarán.

At present the majority of the inhabitants of Mázandarán are Shí'ites, but amongst the Kurdish tribes there are still many 'Alí-alláhís and a few Sunnís.

The Bábís secured many adherents in Mázandarán towards the middle of last century, and the stand which they made at Shaykh Ṭabarsí against the Sháh's troops is one of the great episodes of their history[2].

The administration of Mázandarán is entirely in the hands of the governor general, and all the governors of the different

[1] This proclamation is given in Ibn Isfandiyár, p 175.

[2] See E. G. Browne, *Materials for the study of the Bábí religion*, Cambridge, 1918, p. 241.

districts in the plain are appointed by him. The governorships of Tunakábun, Kalárrustáq, and Kujúr, and those of the mountain districts of Láriján, Sawádkúh, and Hazárjaríb, were until quite recently hereditary.

The revenue of the province was said to be about 150,000 *túmáns*, but it is not known what proportion of this amount reached the Imperial Treasury.

There are no modern military works in the province, but at various times in olden days strong works were erected to protect Mázandarán from invasion. These works are: (1) The famous Sadd-i-Anúsharwán, or Qizil-Álán wall, which was erected by Anúsharwán (531–578 A.D.) to protect the Gurgán valley against invasions by the wild Túránian tribes, Úzbaks, Turkomans, etc. (24). (2) The Fírúzkanda, a ditch or moat made by Fírúz Sháh, husband of Ámula the founder of Ámul, from Gurgán to Múghán on the sea-shore. (3) The dyke of Farrukhán the Great[1], traces of which may yet be seen at Kharába Shahr, the former limit of Mázandarán, the country east of it being termed Bírún-Tamísha, and that west of it Andarún-Tamísha. (4) The wall built by Mázyár from Jájarm to Gílán, where there were gates. Every gate had a keeper, and no one was allowed to leave or enter the place which was called Máz, and inside it Mázandarán. (5) The Jar-i-Kulbád, or Kulbád moat, dug during the reign of Karím Khán by Muḥammad Khán of Sawádkúh, then governor of Mázandarán, to protect Ashraf and eastern Mázandarán from the depredations of the Turkomans. (6) The Sháh-Marz, east of Astarábád and between that city and the Qarású, probably dug under Náṣiru'd-Dín Sháh by order of the Atábak, Muḥammad Taqí Khán, as part of his defensive scheme against the Turkomans.

[1] See Ibn Isfandiyár, pp. 30–31.

CHAPTER II

Rasht to Khurramábád. Bazaar of Kúchisfahán. Safíd-Rúd. Láhiján. Langarúd. Kilídbar. Rúdisar. Nawdih. Miyándih. District of Sakhtsar, products, language, inhabitants. The hot springs of Áb-i-Garm. District of Gulayján, inhabitants. The Amír-i-As'ad.

NOV. 14th, 25 miles. From Rasht we followed the road constructed a few years ago by the Sipahdár-i-A'ẓam, passed the bazaar of Ájíbísha, the village of Khúnácháh, the canal of Khumámrúd, Gúrábjúr, the canal of Ḥájjí Bikanda and that of Gílámúsh, and the village of Balasabuna, and reached the Gaysha-damarda canal. This name means in *gílak* "dead bride," and the legend is that a young bride, whilst being taken to the bridegroom's house, was drowned at this spot. We crossed the Nawrúd, also called Lálarúd, by the Murghánapurd, "chicken-egg bridge." We were told that an old woman spent the best part of her life selling eggs at this crossing, and that with her hard-earned savings she built this bridge, which ascends at a steep slope from both sides, thus forming an angle or point in the centre. The bazaar of Kúchisfahán consists of two rows of shops with a gateway at the western end, but open to the east. These bazaars, called *gúráb*, are places where markets are held periodically, and they are usually destitute of inhabitants on other days. Such bazaars are only found in Gílán and western Mázandarán, and, as a rule, they should be at least 4 miles distant from one another. An hour's ride from Kúchisfahán brought us to Rashtábád on the left bank of the Safíd-Rúd, from which Láhiján is 8 miles distant.

After crossing the Gíwdarra or Siyáhrúd by a brick bridge near Gúka, we saw near the village of Tijin-Gúka the shrine of 'Alí Ghaznawí, a descendant of Imám Ja'far. The strong stream of Shímrúd, which rises in the mountains of Daylamán, and flows into the Safíd-Rúd, is crossed by a pointed bridge of brick (the angle to the summit of which is certainly not less than 30°) consisting of two large centre arches and a smaller one on each side. Fording the Surkhwáy, a very small stream, though boasting the traces of a former bridge, we soon afterwards crossed the Láhiján river and entered the town.

The women in Láhiján, as in Langarúd, turn their faces to the wall whenever they meet anyone of consequence in the street, this being a sign of respect as well as of modesty on their part.

Nov. 17th, 24 miles. On leaving Láhiján we passed the *Sabz-Maydán* with its lake, and held on in an easterly direction. Two miles further on we came upon the picturesque shrine of Shaykhánbar with its blue tiled dome. The road winds along the slope of the low hills as far as Lílakúh, and is bordered with trees and boxwood. For nearly 7 miles from Láhiján the road has the same low wooded hills with stony blocks on their sides to the right, and jungle, rice fields, and mulberry plantations, intermixed with occasional *tilimbars* or silk granaries and houses, sloping down to the left; it follows generally the line of the old route constructed by Sháh 'Abbás, but at Lílakúh, one mile from Langarúd, it leaves the old causeway, which turns to the right towards Malát near the mountains. The villages passed on the way from Láhiján to Langarúd were: Chahárkhánasar, Nakhjír-kaláya, Qaṣṣáb-Maḥalla, Shaykhánbar, Sayyid Maḥalla, Nalqa-shar, Liyáristán, Dizbun, Díwshal, and Lílakúh. Outside Langarúd there is an open plain, and the road which was nearly east is raised above the rice fields. The last village belonging to the Langarúd district is Kíkaláya; its houses were all thatched and evidently belonged to cultivators in easy circumstances. At Dariyásar, a small stream running down from an *isṭalkh* or reservoir, fed by the Shalmán, is crossed by a most picturesque bridge with a thatched roof. We then entered the Shalmán district of Ránikúh and crossed the Gilsafíd and Fatídih streams, both branches of the Shalmán, which latter we forded at a point where there is a large village on the right bank.

The Balísa stream, which joins the Shalmán, is crossed by a brick bridge. The road here is bordered by *túsa* and much *shund*, or *palam* (*Sambucus Ebulus*), which reaches to a height of five or six feet. We passed Chiníján and the Miyánpushta, another tributary of the Shalmán, beyond which lies the village of the same name. The Rúdisar river is crossed by a very lofty and very steep bridge. The bazaar of Rúdisar is built like a huge caravanserai with four entrances.

Outside Rúdisar is an old grave-yard called the cemetery of Mullá Amíra; it is an open space covered with grass and adorned with venerable *ázád* trees. Before coming to the Caspian, we passed the Shírarúd, a branch of the Pulúrúd, and crossed the Kaldarra, which is no doubt the Nawrúd mentioned by Holmes and Mackenzie. We then came to the Dústkúh stream about 2 miles from Shírarúd. After the Dústkúh stream we crossed five small *rúdkhánas*: (1) the Rúd-i-Bálálam or Rúd-i-Gaskarí-Mahalla, (2) the Nawdarra, called by Mackenzie Sálú-Mahalla, (3) another branch of the Nawdarra stream, (4) the Gílakján stream, and (5) another stream the name of which is given by Mackenzie as Shír Maḥalla.

About 2 miles from the Dústkúh we came to the Pulúrúd, a large river which rises in the Sumám-Kúh. Leaving Kíkaláya and Límújú to our right, we crossed the Gizáfrúd and reached Nawdih where we stayed the night.

Nov. 18th, 16 miles. Outside Nawdih we crossed the lazy stream of Lazarján and a little further on the Áb-i-Khushkalát (25), which is very broad and in springtime can only be forded higher up at the hamlet of Raḍí Mahalla; then followed two streams belonging to Siyáhkalarúd, and another one near the village of Cháyján. The country here is well wooded. From the mouth of the Khushkarúd to the river of Qásimábád is about 4 miles. We then came to the Úshiyán Rúd, beyond which are a few brooks (26), and then comes the muddy Acharúd, also called Khushkalát. The mountain here approaches to within 2 miles of the coast. A bit of jungle and the Chashma-i-Malikjúb had still to be traversed before reaching Chábuksar and its stream. The village of Miyándih, which lies concealed in the forest, is 2 miles from Safíd Tamísha. The Júrdih hills, to which many of the people of Tunakábun retreat in summer, rose above us to the right, whilst in front, the Sakhtsar hills, and to the S.S.E. the Mázandarán hills, were visible in the distance. After the Ismalí rivulet we came to the Surkhání, a stream which forms the boundary of Gílán and Tunakábun in Mázandarán, and on the further side of which are the pastures of Safíd-Tamísha. Rounding the Sakhtsar hills, which here reach very nearly to the water's edge, we continued through the jungle to Dariyápushta which numbers thirty houses, boasts a mosque and a shrine, and is rich in fields and mulberry plantations. We forded the Turkrúd and rode through Ákhúnd Maḥalla with its mosque and *madrasa* and numberless orange trees. The next features of our ride were the Ṣafárúd or Áb-i-Sakhtsar, the fine village and stream of Náranjbun and the hamlet of Siyáhlam, after which we reached Áb-i-Garm, our halting place for the day.

Sakhtsar is a small district of Tunakábun and extends from the Surkhání stream on the west to the Nasiya Rúd on the east; to the south it is bordered by the Ishkawar mountains of Gílán which separate it from Rúdbár-i-Alamút. Most of the inhabitants spend the summer months in the mountains, and only return to their villages towards the beginning of winter (27). The mountains immediately south of Sakhtsar are known under the general appellation of Bálában d or Júrband; beans, wheat, and barley are grown there in small quantities. The inhabitants are mostly *sayyids*, whilst the language spoken is *gílakí*. Melgunof[1] mentions 100 Úsánlús and Khwájawands as residing here, but this is no longer the case.

Sakhtsar is celebrated for its hot springs. These are in the village of Áb-i-Garm. There are six large and many minor ones. The temperature of the largest, called Áb-i-Garm-i-Buzurg, is 114° F.; of the second, called Bacha-Garmáb, 111° F.; of the third, that for the ladies, 109° F.; and of the fourth, named Anjírabun, 98° F. On the left bank of the small river, which flows through a nicely wooded glen a little further down, there are two others, Khalak, 98° F., and Sangabun, 101° F. The people of the country only use these springs externally and follow no diet rules; they go to them for skin diseases, rheumatism, and the after-effects of fever.

Nov. 19th, 16 miles. The hills from Sakhtsar to the neighbourhood of Bárfurúsh form a magnificent amphitheatre of considerable breadth; they rise one above the other, and there are several ranges which slope down from the snow-capped peaks of Júrdih, Dú-Hazár, etc. The intermediate space between the mountains and the sea was covered with fields producing the much esteemed rice of Tunakábun, the roads through which are as bad as the evil paths of Gílán.

We crossed the Palangrúd by a stone culvert; this river, which is deep and full of large boulders, is called the Salmrúd lower down. Further on is the village of Ramak, through which flows the Áb-i-Ramak. We next came to the villages of Chawarsar, Shúrábsar, and Sayyid Maḥalla, which latter has extensive mulberry plantations and kitchen gardens. Sayyid Mahalla gives its name to a stream which is also called the Áb-i-Rúda'a. The road from Safíd Tamísha to Zír-Márkúh, east of Sayyid Maḥalla, was made by the Sipahdár-i-A'ẓam. and was to be continued to Khurramábád. We crossed the Barashí stream, not far from the mouth of which is the village of the same name. The road then leads behind sand-hills to the village of Míshakaláya and the

[1] G. Melgunof, *Das sudliche Ufer des Kaspischen Meeres*, Leipzig, 1868, p. 216.

Pahdar Rúd, which runs down from the village of Kúdih. After that comes the Niyása, between which and the Mazar lies a bay 8 miles in length. The next streams to be crossed were the Zamínjúb, the Pádangrúd, and the Chalkrúd which abounds in salmon. Beyond the Chalkrúd is Chawarsar, a *maḥalla* of Shírrúd, then the hamlet of Tamíjána, where we crossed the Chawarsar stream; and after that the Shírrúd river (28), also called Tírum or Tahram, which cannot be forded when in flood. Further on we forded a branch of this river and soon after reached the *maḥalla* of Shírrúd. The next water to be crossed was the Áwsiyáh Rúd (29), a shallow stream flowing immediately east of the village of Lapasar, after which we rode alternately along the beach and through the thorny jungle as far as the small Wáchak stream.

From Wáchak there is a path to the village of Gulayján, the chief place of the district of that name, which is bounded by the Niyása Rúd on the west, the Mazar on the east, and on the south by the mountains of Límraz and Girdkúh, beyond which lie the *yayláqs* of Ishkawar. The inhabitants of the district of Gulayján are mostly from Ishkawar, whilst a few come from Gílán, Tálaqán, and Alamút.

Beyond Wáchak flow the Fíkárúd with Tárík-Maḥalla on its right bank, and, further on, the Zamínjúb (probably the same as Mackenzie's Nasiyakalá), on the right bank of which is Nasiya Maḥalla. Then we followed the Áb-i-Karímábád, the Gúsarí, and an arm of the Mazar, before we reached the Mazar or Sháhsuwár river which is shallow and has a pebbly bottom. At Sháhsuwár we turned to the S.E., coming into open country, and, crossing the bed of the Mazarlát, which we followed for a quarter of an hour, and the broad pebbly bottom of the Chashmakíla torrent which was almost dry, emerged at Kúkaláya on a built road. We passed Karát and Shírakraz soon after, and reached the *maydán* of Khurramábád, on the northern side of which is the house of Amír-i-As'ad, the eldest son of the Sipahdár-i-A'ẓam.

CHAPTER III

District of Tunakábun. Products. Industries. Clans. Hereditary chiefs. Origin of the name Khal'at-barí. Khwájawands. Khurramábád Oil wells at Atishkada. Castle of Habashabur. Khurramábád to Ámul. Subdistrict of Nishtá. 'Abbasábád. Subdistrict of Langá. The Namakábrúd. Subdistrict of Kalár-rustáq. Road from Chálús to Tihrán. River-mouths. Chalandar. Ruins of Hawdkútí. Sarínkalá. District of Kujúr, its subdistricts, inhabitants, and roads. Suladih. District of Núr, its subdistricts and mines. Maḥmúdábád. Arrival at Ámul.

TUNAKÁBUN (30), of which Khurramábád is now the chief place, is the most westerly district of Mázandarán, and is bounded on the north by the Caspian, on the west by the Surkhání stream, on the south by the Alburz range and the Qazwín districts of Rúdbár and Ṭálaqán, and on the east by the district of Kalár-rustáq. It is divided into the following eight subdistricts: (*a*) Balada, or the chief place, (*b*) Gulayján, (*c*) Langá, (*d*) Nishtá, including Zawár, (*e*) Sakhtsar, (*f*) Sarḥadd, (*g*) Siyáh-rustáq, and (*h*) Tawábi'[1].

The *yayláqs* of the inhabitants are the mountains of Dú-Hazár, Sih-Hazár, and Ishkawar (31). The inhabitants of western Tunakábun also frequent the following *yayláqs* in the Ishkawar subdistrict of Gílán: Gara, Lúshkán, Kasháya, Púrandán, Dargáh, Liyásí, Darísanak, Chákul, Tukamján, and Ziyádí.

The products of Tunakábun are rice, which is much esteemed for its whiteness and delicacy, silk, *ghee*, and wool. Flax and sugar are no longer cultivated, but tea has been introduced and a small quantity is now grown. There is a great abundance of walnuts as also of oranges and lemons. In the forests, amongst a great variety of other trees, are boxwood and numerous oak-trees of great size. The rivers are rich in fish, and cattle and sheep are plentiful. Beans, wheat, and barley are grown in the highlands.

The chief industry is the manufacture of textiles, such as silk cloths, woollen tissues, felt cloaks for the peasantry, and coarse linen. Rugs or *gilíms* are also made by the tribeswomen.

The inhabitants trade with Qazwín and Ṭihrán. Periodical markets are held at the following villages: Siyáhwaraz on Mondays, Khurramábád on Tuesdays and Saturdays, Zawár on Mondays, Sulaymánábád on Wednesdays, Sádát Maḥalla of Sakhtsar on Thursdays, and Dárkalá.

There are eleven great clans in Tunakábun, viz.: Khal'atbarí,

[1] Villages of Tunakábun; see Appendix I, A.

Qawí-Úsallú or more correctly Qawí-Ḥiṣárlú, Kalántariyya (32), Faqíh, Tálish, Gulayj, Daj, Asás, Shúrij, Ṭálaqání, and Rúdbárí.

The chieftainship of the district has been hereditary in the family of the present Sipahdár-i-A'ẓam since the end of the 18th century, when Mahdí Bayg Khal'atbarí went to Shíráz to complain of the oppression of the Qawí-Úsallú governor, and received from Karím Khán Zand the title of *khán* and the governorship of Tunakábun (33). This Mahdí Khán was later a staunch supporter of Áqá Muḥammad Khán and he joined the troops which the latter sent against Hidáyat Khán of Gílán. A blood feud between the inhabitants of Rasht and those of Tunakábun resulted from this expedition, and, at the request of Mahdí Khán, Tunakábun was separated from Gílán and added to Mázandarán, and was, together with Kalár-rustáq and Kujúr, entrusted to Mahdí Khán. These three districts have ever since been known as Maḥall-i-Thalátha or "the three districts."

Mahdí Khán[1] was succeeded by his eldest son, Hádí Khán. The latter's son, Walí Khán, was killed at the siege of Herát, and to his grandson, Habíbu'lláh Khán, a lad of 13, better known under the title of Sa'du d-Dawla, who had accompanied the expedition, were given the governorship and command held by his father. Sa'du'd-Dawla was succeeded by his son Muḥammad Walí Khán, the present Sipahdár-i-A'ẓam. The Khal'atbarí clan claims descent from a certain Aḥmad Shumayd of Aleppo, who, during the caliphate of 'Alí, was the bearer of a robe of honour to one of the provincial governors, whence his surname of *Khal'atbar*. His sons, Náṣir and Yáṣir, came to Rustamdár in Mázandarán, the former settling in Núr, the latter in Gulayján. I am of opinion, however, that this surname is a corruption of Khalábar, the name given to certain retainers or boarded servants of the kings of Gílán.

In 1855 the Sadr-i-A'ẓam Áqá Khán Núrí removed the 'Abdu'l-Malikís from Núr to Dhághmarz near Ashraf, but Ḥabíbu'lláh Khán was unable to pay the sum asked for the removal of the Khwájawands from Kujúr and Kalár-rustáq. The Khwájawands, although now inhabiting villages, still move about in tents during the hot season. They keep cattle, and breed a fairly good race of horses. They are also employed in cultivation, most of their fields being *daymí*, *i.e.* not requiring artificial irrigation. The Khwájawands and Laks, as a whole, are hated by the other

[1] Son of Ḥájjí Ṣádiq b. Hájjí Báqir.

inhabitants of these parts, not only on account of their religion, but also and principally because they occupy the best *yayláqs* of the district.

The Rúzakí Kurds brought here by Sháh Ṭahmásp I have entirely disappeared.

Khurramábád, lat. 36° 45′, long. 51° 0′, the chief place of Tunakábun, is situated amongst rice fields in a green and pleasant prairie, about 5 or 6 miles from the foot of the nearest hills. It numbers about 250 houses (there were only 30 in 1859) scattered through the thicket, and has a telegraph station which connects it with Rasht, and a good brick caravanserai. Three fine gardens belonging to the late Sa'du'd-Dawla, the Sipahdár-i-A'ẓam, and the Amír-i-As'ad surround the *Sabz-Maydán* on three sides, the fourth or southern side being open.

There are five stages from Khurramábád to Ṭihrán: Márán, Alamút, Ṭálaqán, Kurdán, and Ṭihrán.

The port of Khurramábád is Sháhsuwár, about 2 miles north of it, to the east of the mouth of the Mazar river. The Mazar, which is not navigable, is formed by three streams, the Walamrúd, Dú-Hazár, and Sih-Hazár. Mackenzie says that it rises in two places, Márán and Dú-Hazár, and that its two branches unite at a distance of one *farsakh* (4 miles) from the sea.

Nov. 20th. Having heard of the existence of oil wells in the district, I decided to visit them. We passed Ḥasankalá about one mile from Khurramábád, then Kárdgar Maḥalla and Isṭalkhsar, and crossed the Kúrjú or Karájú stream. Off the road to the left were Miyán Maḥalla and Naṣrábád, and, to the right, Zamínkín. The jungle became thicker as we proceeded, some of the oaks being of great girth. We finally reached a spot called Átishkada, or "the fire-temple," at the foot of the hills, about four miles from Ḥabashabur where we first entered the jungle. We were shown four wells, which were, however, of small depth. A greasy substance could be seen floating on the surface of the water in two of the wells, but it is quite certain that no oil had been obtained here for many a century. The name Átishkada clearly indicates, however, that a fire temple had stood at this spot, and this is still further confirmed by the existence of low mounds and broken bricks in the close vicinity of the wells. The district was formerly named Túshkún (*túsh* = *átish* or fire, and *kun* = make), and there is still a village of this name not very far from Átishkada.

Oil was reported from Mazarlát near Khurramábád, and from Ḥasanábád in Kujúr, but no indications of it could be found.

As Tunakábun is on the longitudinal axis of symmetry of the Caucasian oil fields, and as we also find indications of oil in Samnán and Hazárjaríb, we may safely infer that oil does exist in Tunakábun, but at what depth and whether in paying quantities or not it is difficult at present to tell.

On our way back from Átishkada we passed the hamlets of Karakúh, Shántásh or Shánatarásh, and Barashabur, all belonging to Ḥabashabur. A few hundred yards east of Habashabur there is an old fortified enclosure of great strength. It is in the form of a square, measures 83 paces in either direction, and is composed of a mud embankment 30 feet high surrounded by a moat. The gate faces east. I was told that similar *qal'as*, or castles, existed in other parts of Tunakábun; one of these is called Qal'a Gardan and is near Balada, another is to be seen near Lashkarak, and a third one, called Qal'a Paraz, at Siyáhwaraz. From Barashabur we took a short cut through the villages of Kinársar and Miyán Maḥalla to Khurramábád.

In the evening the Amír-i-As'ad accompanied us to Sháhsuwár. Sháhsuwár and Khurramábád are in the subdistrict of Tawábi', the largest in Tunakábun, although it only extends from Tílpurdsar to the Izarúd.

Nov. 21st, 16 miles. Riding out of Sháhsuwár, we forded the Chashmakíla, and crossed over a wooden bridge which spans the Sangsará, a stream coming from the village of the same name. We then forded the Ḥájjí Mahalla (34), passed the village of Walíábád, and reached the Tílpurdsar or Tílpurdáb, which is about 30 yards wide and is spanned by a rough bridge of planks. The Halíkalá, which joins the Tílpurdsar at its mouth, is also crossed by a wooden bridge. After the village of Halíkalá we reached Palatkalá, which possesses a bath and extensive groves of orange trees and a stream of the same name. Passing through the jungle, which here comes close to the beach and conceals the village of Faqíhábád, we came to the Izarúd and beyond it to a rivulet named Sulṭánkalá. At this point begins the subdistrict of Nishtá which numbers about 1000 houses.

The Nishtá Rúd is crossed by a wooden bridge. Medlars, boxtrees, wild pomegranates, brambles, etc., were plentiful in the jungle up to the Pasandarúd. These jungles near the sea in which pomegranates usually abound are termed *anárkala*. We then forded the Káẓimrúd, Pasandarúd, Galabúsí, and Kúchabúsí streams, and soon afterwards entered the pretty village of ʻAbbásábád, which is pleasantly situated on a gravelly bank partially covered with grass and bushes, at a pistol shot from the water's edge. It has 25 houses, a bath and a mosque.

Langá, to which subdistrict ʻAbbásábád belongs, is bordered on the west by the Káẓimrúd, on the south by Mashalábád, and on the east by Aspchín. The *alíja*, or silk fabrics, of Langá are celebrated. Langá is divided into Júrband (or Báláband), usually known as Langá, and Jírband (or Pá'ínband). The low wooded hills which separate the plain from the *yayláqs* are known as Miyánband. The inhabitants of Nishtá, Zawár, and Langá go to Dákúh (Písh-Dákúh and Pas-Dákúh) for the summer. In the mountains behind Nishtá are Siyáhmushtad and other localities.

Sayyid Abu'l-Ḥusayn al-Mú'ayyad bi'lláh, who carried on propaganda in Daylamán which he occupied and where he had established himself, died in 421/1030, and was buried in his house at Langá. His grave was still venerated in the 10th (16th) century.

Nov. 22nd, 24 miles. The first part of the road after ʻAbbásábád was very good, passing over a belt of turf situated between the sea and the rice-fields as far as the river of Muḥammad Ḥusaynábád, on the right bank of which stands the *maḥalla* whence it derives its name. After crossing the Ganjarúd we reached a spot called Pakíbágh where mulberry plantations had been recently laid out. This place was formerly a village, but its inhabitants had abandoned it and gone to Umíchkalá. The *maḥalla* of Umíchkalá extends along both sides of a stream; the road here turns aside and passes through jungle for about a mile: we noticed some fine forest trees on the right, where there was a path through the thicket leading to the remains of an old building which is used as a brick mine by the natives. There is nothing above ground to indicate the site of a fortress, and so many holes have been dug in the search for bricks, that the inquisitive traveller would have no chance of discovering or reconstituting the outworks of an old castle or fortalice. Its name all over the neighbourhood is Aspchín (35), and it is said that a great man called ʻUthmán Khán dwelt there in bygone days.

After crossing the Múmadamarda, a small brook, and continuing for about a mile, we came to the Aspchín, a fairly broad stream with a sandy bottom, on the left bank of which stands the village of the same name. The road now lay through a jungle of lofty box trees close to the sea-shore, and 2½ miles from 'Abbásábád we crossed the Kharakrúd, a very winding and sluggish stream. On its right bank is the village of Jamshídábád. We crossed a rivulet, the Chika-i-'Abbásábád, near the village of 'Abbásábád, and a hundred paces further on the Chika-i-Gulúr. Some 2 miles from Jamshídábád we arrived again on the beach, at a place where two streams, one of which is the Tílúrasar or Tílrúdsar, flow into the sea. Passing into the jungle again, we threaded our way through the brambles and acacias and rejoined the sandy beach at a point where the Isparúd (36) falls into the sea. Crossing the small Khájakasar brook, and another one soon after, we once more entered the jungle and, passing the Palangrúd, came to the Namakábrúd where Kalár-rustáq begins.

The Namakábrúd was formerly the western boundary of Rustamdár. The real limits of Rustamdár, according to Ẓahíru'd-Dín, were Sí-Sangán or the Mánhír river to the east and Malát to the west. When in 492/1098-9 Táju'l-Mulúk Mardáwíj rebelled against his brother, Sháh Ghází Rustam, the latter obtained the help of the Ustundár Shahrnúsh b. Hazárasf by promising him the hand of his sister, who received as dowry the district extending from Pá-yi-Dasht to the Siyáhrúd. In 558/1163 'Alá'u'd-Dawla Ḥasan, also called Sharafu'l-Mulúk, who, on the occasion of his incurring his father's wrath, had been befriended by the Ustundár, succeeded his father, Sháh Ghází Rustam, and granted the Ustundár Kay-Ká'ús all the territory from Kunus to the Alísharúd, this river thus becoming the eastern limit of Rustamdár. In 590/1194 the Ustundár Hazárasf b. Shahrnúsh, who had rebelled against Sháh Ardashír b. Ḥasan of Mázandarán and entered into an alliance with the Isma'ílís or Assassins, ceded to the latter the territory between Malát and Sakhtsar. In 640/1242-3 the Ustundár Shahrákím b. Namáwar was compelled by the rulers of Gílán to retire to the Namakáwarúd, which thus became the western limit of Rustamdár. To the south Rustamdár extended to the crest of the mountains whose rivers flowed into the Caspian, which bounded it to the north. Rustamdár was also called Ustundár or Ustundáriyya, a name derived either from *ustun*, a word meaning mountain, or from Ustun, the name of a former ruler of this district. The Namakábrúd rises not far from Khushámiyán.

Passing the Nawrúdsar, the Hacharúd, the village of Imámrúd, and the stream of Dújamán, we came to the Sardábrúd (37), which runs down from the *yayláqs* of Kalárdasht. After some very stony ground we crossed the Áwrangkíla and reached the broad stream of Chálús which, rising in the Dalír and Núr hills, falls into the sea some 19 miles from 'Alíábád and forms the boundary between Kalár-rustáq and Kujúr.

The district of Kalár-rustáq[1] extends along the coast from the Namakábrúd on the west, to the Chálús on the east, and is situated between the districts of Tunakábun and Kujúr. It comprises four subdistricts: (*a*) Bírún Bashm (Bažham); (*b*) Dasht; (*c*) Kalárdasht; (*d*) Kúhistán. Mackenzie in 1860 said that there were about 100 villages in the *yayláqs* of Kalár-rustáq, and some 600 houses of Khwájawands.

The chief product of the plain is rice, whilst wheat and barley grow in the hills, but cattle and sheep constitute the principal source of wealth of this district.

The ancient rulers of Fárs had a castle at Chálús where armed horsemen were kept in constant readiness to protect the inhabitants against the raids of the Ḍaylamites, while the city was surrounded by a strong wall built at the command of a daughter of the King of Fárs. The defences of Chálús were destroyed in 287/900 by Sayyid Ḥasan b. Qásim. This town, formerly also written as Sálúsh and Sálús, is described by Muqaddasí as a city having a castle built of stone with a Friday Mosque adjoining[2]. Near it lay two other towns, namely al-Kabíra (38) and Kajja (39). Here was buried with great pomp the mother of Ḥasan the Buwayhid. Of the Mar'ashí *sayyids* of Mázandarán, Ẓahíru'd-Dín b. 'Alí b. Qiwámu'd-Dín and his son, Faḍlu'lláh, were laid to rest at Chálús. The town also gave its name to a district called Chálúsa-rustáq. The Arab geographers give the following stages from Ámul to Daylam: Nátil, a stage; Chálús, a short stage; Kalár (40), a stage; and Daylam[3], a stage.

The summer road from Chálús to Ṭihrán has four stages: Bábúdih, Alámul, Shahristának or Imámzáda Dá'úd, and Ṭihrán. The winter road has six or seven stages: Tuwár, Walíábád, Gachasar, Shahristának, Áhár which is optional, Úshán, and Ṭihrán.

Beyond the Chálús river we passed the village of Majídábád

[1] Villages of Kalár-rustáq; see Appendix I, B.
[2] Le Strange, *loc. cit.*, p. 373.
[3] See Marquart, *loc. cit.*, pp. 126–127.

and, after crossing the Damarú, reached the village of Bahársará. Here on the beach were some of those elevated platforms where the inhabitants sleep in summer and store their rice-straw for the winter. Next came the Gandábrúd, and then a branch of the Kurkurúd (41). On the further side of some stagnant waters we saw the village of Kurkurúsar. Later we crossed a broad but shallow stream called Chashma-i-Áb, which joins the sea at this point. I may here mention that the traveller on the shores of the Caspian knows that he is near the mouth of a river long before he reaches it, owing to the fact that the stream of fresh water as it flows from the river-mouth into the sea shows up conspicuously to a considerable distance from the shore in the form of a long, silvery streak, which is visible when one is yet several hundreds of yards away; in rainy weather the silver streak becomes mud-coloured.

On the banks of the Chashma-i-Áb is the village of Ḥabíbábád, formerly known as Kháchak[1], where we alighted. Ḥabíbábád, which is in the subdistrict of Girán, numbers 65 houses, is pleasantly situated near the beach, and is watered by the Kháchak and Chashma-i-Áb streams.

Nov. 23rd, 18 miles. We crossed the Girdú stream and reached the village of Ḥasanábád, through which flow the Mashánkíla and the Sháh-Murádkíla, which latter is full of aquatic plants, and joins the Mashalak at its mouth. From here we rode for about 2 miles over a mass of limestone, and, continuing in an easterly direction, crossed a stream, the 'Alíábád-Dunbál, above which and to our right lay the large village of 'Alíábád-i-Buzurg, also called 'Alíábád-i-Mír. The next streams to be crossed were the Sham'járán and Latangán, then the Amír-Rúd and the Mar-Úrdí stream, with the village of the same name on its left bank. Continuing on our road, we crossed the river Khayr-Rúd, a broad and formidable one, the bed of which is calcareous and was nearly dry. It gives its name to the small subdistrict of Khayr-rúdkinár. We were now in the jungle of Bandpay, and crossed the Suṭulkiyá (Sulṭán 'Alí Kiyá) stream. The Mázígáh stream was the next water encountered, soon after which we forded the Chálak stream and, passing through the village of the same name[2], reached the Duzdakarúd and a little later 'Alíábád-i-Aṣghar-Khání and the Mulkár-Rúd. From Mulkár a path,

[1] Zahíru'd-Dín has Khwáj and Khwájak.
[2] See Ẓahíru'd-Dín, *History of Gílán and Daylamistán*, Rasht 1330, p. 146, l. 17

paved with logs and often submerged, leads to Chalandar which is surrounded by a marsh. If a horse strays at night and flounders into the mud there is but little hope of extricating him. Mackenzie, who visited the ruins about one mile from Ḥawdkútí, a village to the east of the Chalandar stream, found distinct evidences of the existence in former days of a large fortress surrounded by a double ditch and wall; the inner fosse was at least twenty feet deep and the outer was not more than ten; the central mound contained many bricks, and on it grew two of the most splendid forest trees he had ever seen. Thence to the hills is rather less than a mile, where there is a cavern formed in the calcareous rock at a height of about 30 feet from the ground; this cave is about 6 feet in height, 4 feet in breadth, and as many in length. It commands a fine view of the country in front and of the sea (42).

We read in Ibn Isfandiyár's *History of Ṭabaristán* that, when pursued by Afrásiyáb, Minúchihr came to Rustamdár and, after wandering about for some time in Kúrshíd Rustáq, took refuge at Chalandar, where the mountains are nearest the sea. Here, between the villages of Wanúshadih and Kunus, he dug a great moat behind which he remained with his army. He sent his family to the village of Múz (another manuscript says Múr), at that time Mánhír, where in one face of the mountain is a great cave. Here Minúchihr concealed his treasures and stores and at its entrance had a castle built, which in the author's time was known as Diz-i-Minúchihr. In the time of Kúchik-'Alawí (the little 'Alawí) this cave was entered and much treasure found there.

Isma'íl, the *kadkhudá* of Warzan (43), told Lt.-Col. H. L. Wells[1] legends of an impregnable castle that once existed near Núrrúdbár, the name of which was Qal'a-i-Múr.

Leaving Mulkár, we re-entered the jungle, and, passing the Anárwar stream, the village and stream of 'Alíábád, and two more streams, the Núrrúdbár (Mackenzie calls it the Nírúd), and the Khushkalát, both of which were dry, arrived at Ṣarínkalá.

The village of Ṣarínkalá (Ṣaláḥu'd-Dín-Kalá) numbers 100 houses, has a bath, and lies in the jungle some 200 yards south of the road which runs along the beach.

[1] "Across the Elburz Mountains to the Caspian Sea," by Lt.-Col. H. L. Wells, in *The Scottish Geographical Magazine*, January 1898.

Ẓahíru'd-Dín relates in his *History of Mázandarán* that Minúchihr, when compelled to retire before Afrásiyáb, took up his residence at Kúsh. The plain of Kujúr, above Kúsh, was then under water as the river of Kujúr had no outlet to the sea. Minúchihr had the rocks which dammed the river removed, and some of them were carried down by the water to the sea-shore, where they are still to be seen at a place called Sí-Sangán (between Khayrrúdkinár and Kalár-rustáq). The plain when drained was cultivated and Minúchihr built on it the town of Rúyán[1].

Abu'l-Fidá says that the city of Rúyán was also known as Shahristán, and that it crowned the summit of the pass 16 leagues from Qazwín. According to Yáqút, Rúyán was the capital of the mountain district of Ṭabaristán as Ámul was of the lowland plains; it had fine buildings, and its gardens were famous for their productiveness. Near Rúyán lay the little town of Sa'ídábád (44).

On the 21 Dhú'l-hijja, 740/1340 the Ustundár Jalálu'd-Dawla Iskandar began rebuilding the castle and town of Ḳujúr (*i.e.* Rúyán, also called Shahr-i-Kujúr) which had been completely destroyed during the invasion of the Mongols. He surrounded the town with walls and completed its citadel on the 21 Dhú'l-ḥijja, 746/1346. He also built at the same time in the district of Rúyán the castle of Sháhdiz where he resided.

The district of Kujúr[2] is bounded on the west by the Chálús which separates it from Kalár-rustáq, on the east by Suladih in Núr, on the south by the district of Núr, and on the north by the Caspian. It is subdivided into the following *bulúks*: (*a*) Balada and Kúrshíd-rustáq, (*b*) Angás, (*c*) Bandpay, (*d*) Fírúzkalá and 'Ulwíkalá, (*e*) Girán, (*f*) Kálíj, (*g*) Kacha-rustáq, (*h*) Kalúrúdpay, (*i*) Khayrrúdkinár, (*j*) Kúhpar, (*k*) Panj-rustáq or Panjak-rustáq, (*l*) Ránús-rustáq, (*m*) Chalandar, (*n*) Zand-rustáq.

The inhabitants of Kujúr are Ḳhwájawands and Gílaks, each having their own governor. The inhabitants of the districts of Tunakábun, Kalár-rustáq, and Kujúr, which were formerly part of Rustamdár, do not choose to be looked upon as Mázandaránís, whilst the Mázandaránís say they are Gílaks.

The shortest route from Ṭihrán to the Caspian is via the Afcha pass to the Lár valley, and thence by the Yálú or Áb-i-

[1] Rúyán, le Raoidhita du Zamyad Yasht, 2; le Royishn-mand de Bundahish, XII, 2, 7 (*Zend-Avesta*, II, 416, note 25). Darmesteter, *loc. cit.*, p. 508, note; see also Marquart, *loc. cit.*, p. 136.

[2] Villages of Kujúr; see Appendix I, c.

Safíd pass out of the Lár valley to that of the river Núr; thence by a third pass over the Kúh-i-Qurúq into the Kujúr valley, and along the course of the stream which drains the last-named down to the sea. By this route a traveller can reach the sea in three easy, or two long, days without changing horses. This route is said to be closed for five months in the year The stages, according to native information, are Ṭihrán to Afcha, 24 miles; Núr, 24 miles; Kujúr, 16 miles; Ṣarínkalá, 16 miles.

Nov. 24th, 18 miles. We crossed a succession of streams in the following order: the Ṣarínkalá, the Namakábrúd, a nameless brook from Wanúsh, the Kulírúd, the Kunusarúd (45), and the Shaykhrúd, a branch of the last-named, on the left bank of which was a large village named 'Alawí Mahalla (pronounced 'Ulwí Maḥalla) belonging to Fírúzkalá. Next followed another village, Bazawár, and then more rivers, the Kacharúd, the Nahr-i-Ḥasanábád, the Bunjákul, the Falímarz, near which was a village of the same name, and the Siyáhrúd.

The district of Núr begins at the Alamrúd, a river with very steep banks.

Suladih is a large village half a mile from the sea-shore. A brick bridge of three arches spans the Suladih river which rises in the hills of Lábíj. The hills visible from Suladih are the Sardár, which lie to the south-west and are covered with snow, the Láshkinár, the Pímat, and the Lábíj; the country between them and the sea is open, or sparsely covered with very thin and scattered jungle. We followed the shore for some 4 miles to the Rustamrúd (46), on the left bank of which and close to the sea lies the village of Rustamrúd. A little further on we crossed the Háshimrúd and, passing south of the sand-hills, reached 'Izdih.

The district of Núr, to which belongs the village of 'Izdih, extends along the coast from the Suladih on the west to the Ahlamrúd on the east, but away inland it is of far greater extent and reaches from near Kalár-rustáq on the west to the Harhaz river on the east. To the south it is bounded by the Lár and Láriján mountains.

The upper Núr valley is very arid, and it might be in the highlands near Iṣfahán or Shíráz so far as the lode of the hills enclosing it and the villages is concerned[1].

[1] Col. C. Beresford Lovett, "Itinerary notes of route surveys in Noithern Persia in 1881 and 1882," *Proc. R.G.S.*, vol. v, February 1883.

Núr is divided into the following districts: (*a*) Balada, (*b*) Kamarrúd, (*c*) Kúp, (*d*) Miyánband, (*e*) Nayjkúh, (*f*) Namár-rustáq, (*g*) Nátilkinár, (*h*) Nátil-rustáq, (*i*) Rúdbár-i-'Ulyá, (*j*) Rúdbár-i-Suflá, (*k*) Tata-rustáq, (*l*) Úzrúd, (*m*) Yálúrúd[1].

We crossed the 'Izdih river by a wooden bridge and continued to the village of Sút'akalá, and then to the Ahlamrúd (47), a branch of the Harhaz. The village of Ahlam (48) lies about 3 miles from the sea and 12 miles from Suladih. We then reached the Harhaz, whose three branches (which, we were told, unite before joining the Caspian) we crossed by bridges of planks, and came to Mahmúdábád[2]. Striking south from Maḥmúdábád, we passed Lakamúzí, a hamlet belonging to Talíkasar, then Talíkasar itself and Tarsú. We continued through thick forest and joined the old railway track, which formed the only means of communication between Maḥmúdábád and Ámul and was reduced to a very narrow, seldom used, path, where thorns assailed one from above and from either side. Leaving Gálishbar, the village of Karchak, and Ma'súmábád on our right, we came to comparatively open country again. Újíábád, with its large whitewashed villa and garden belonging to the governor of Láriján, lay conspicuous on our left, whilst to the right we saw the shrine of Áqá Sayyid Ma'ṣúm nestling in a grove of magnificent trees. From here the old tower-tombs of Ámul were visible, and we soon reached the *Sabz-Maydán* just outside the town.

[1] Villages of Núr; see Appendix I, D. For produce, etc., of the district see H. L. Rabino, Diplomatic and Consular Report, No. 4812, pp. 14–15.
[2] See H. L. Rabino, Diplomatic and Consular Report, No. 4812, pp. 15–16.

CHAPTER IV

Ámul. Foundation of Ámul. Islám. History of Ámul. The great mosque. Ibn Hawqal's description. Sack of Ámul by Tímúr. Present town. Bridge over the Harhaz. Town quarters. Principal buildings. Shrine of Mír Qiwámu'd-Dín. Masjid-i-Jámi'. Imámzáda Ibráhím. The *Gunbads* or tower-tombs of Ámul. Districts of Ámul. Roads. District of Láriján: subdistricts. History of Láriján. Basin of the Lár River. The Harhaz. District of Sawádkúh. subdistricts. Road from Fírúzkúh to Sárí. Ámul to Bárfurúsh. Bridge of Muhammad Ḥasan Khán. Arrival at Bárfurúsh.

ÁMUL[1] was founded by Ámula (49), the wife of Fírúz, whose capital was at Balkh. She first chose as the site of the city a place in Pá-yi-dasht which was later called Shahristána Marz, but, as it was impossible to bring the water of the river Harhaz to this spot, the projected city was founded on its present site, a spot then called Máta and, later, Astána-saráy. The city wall was built of baked bricks and was surrounded by a moat 33 cubits in depth and a bow-shot across; it was pierced by four gates, called respectively "of Gurgán," "of Gílán," "of the mountains" (50), and "of the sea." Ámula's palace stood near the street of the washermen, Kúcha-i-Gázarán, and behind the "cloth-sellers' market," and here her tomb also was built. When the King's son, Khusraw, succeeded to the throne, he greatly enlarged Ámul and made it his capital and residence, surrounding the original wall with another of clay[2].

The people of Ámul embraced Islám and renounced fire-worship under the Ispahbad Khurshíd when 'Umar b. 'Alá (51), who had been sent to Ṭabaristán at the head of the Moslem army by Mahdí, the son of the caliph Ma'mún, took the city in 137/754–5 according to Ẓahíru'd-Dín, or in 140/757–8 according to Ibn Isfandiyár. Ámul now became the capital of the caliph's governors in Ṭabaristán.

Khálid b. Barmak, who was appointed governor of Ṭabaristán in 766 A.D., took up his abode at a place called after him Khálida-saráy. He also built for himself a castle at Ámul.

It is said that the Masjid-i-Jámi' of Ámul, called the mosque of Ṭashtazanán, was built by Málik b. al-Ḥárith al-Ashtar an-Nakha'í who accompanied Ḥasan b. Álí to Ṭabaristán, but Ẓahíru'd-Dín contradicts this statement, since, according to him,

[1] See Marquart, *loc. cit.*, p. 136. [2] See Ibn Isfandiyár, pp. 20–27.

it was built by a man of the Málikí sect whose descendants, in Ẓahír's time, were still at Lár-i-Qasrán (52), and came every year to Ámul to repair the mosque. The shrine known as Lala-parchín contains the tombs of their *shaykhs* and *sayyids*. The people of Ámul who embraced Islám were at first of the Málikí sect, and most of them remained so until the time of Dá'í'l-Kabír, when they were converted to Shí'ism. The plain known as Málikadasht takes its name from 'Abdu'lláh b. Malik and not from Málik-i-Ashtar.

The great mosque of Ámul was built in the time of Hárúnu'r-Rashíd in 177/793–4 by Ibráhím b. 'Uthmán b. Nahík[1]. 'Abdu'l-Malik b. Qa'qa', who was appointed governor of Ṭabaristán in 179/795, repaired the walls of Ámul. After him came 'Abdu'lláh b. Ḥázim who built there a house and *saráy*, and gave his name to the Ḥázima-Kúy quarter of the town. Muḥammad b. Músá, Ma'mún's deputy, was besieged in Ámul for eight months by the Ispahbad Mázyár, who, when the town fell, ordered the walls to be destroyed[2]. Shortly afterwards Mázyár repaired the fortifications of Ámul and Sárí and attempted to render himself independent of the caliph.

Ibn Isfandiyár relates that there were many persons at Ámul of whose allegiance Ḥasan b. Zayd entertained doubts, and who in the time of the Ṭáhirids had been people of rank and opposed to the doctrine of Ḥasan b. Zayd, though outwardly conforming to it. Ḥasan b. Zayd, therefore, feigned illness and had news of his death proclaimed and preparations made for his funeral, whereupon these disaffected persons threw off the mask. Ḥasan b. Zayd then sallied forth and had them all killed in the great mosque of Ámul and thrown into a recess to the east of the mosque, which was still called "the tomb of the martyrs" in Ibn Isfandiyár's day. Then Ḥasan b. Zayd ordered to be built in the quarter of Rást-Kúy a tomb and large cupola for himself, which was still existing in Ẓahíru'd-Dín's time; and *Mawláná* Awliyá'u'lláh Ámulí has written that in his childhood this building was going to ruins, and that in it there was an old wooden sarcophagus and in the wall steps leading to the top of the dome, and that 70 villages in the neighbourhood of Ámul, apart from gardens, farms, baths, and shops, were made *waqf* for its upkeep.

In 307/919–20 Ḥasan b. Qásim, Dá'í'ṣ-Ṣaghír, had his palace at the Muṣallá, near Ámul. He built lofty houses for his officers

[1] See Ibn Isfandiyár, pp. 26, 27. [2] *Ibid.*, p. 26.

around his palace, so that they should not dwell in the town and molest the inhabitants.

The tomb of Abú 'Alí Muḥammad b. Aḥmad b. al-Ḥasan 312–313?/924–5? was in the Rást-Kúy quarter opposite the cupola of Dá'í.

According to Ibn Ḥawqal, Ámul was in his day a larger place than Qazwín and very populous. Muqaddasí describes the town as possessing a hospital and two Friday mosques, one, the old mosque (53), standing among trees on the market-place, the new mosque being near the city wall. Each mosque had a great portico. The merchants of Ámul did much trade[1]. The city was sacked by the troops of Mas'úd b. Maḥmúd the Ghaznawid, in Jumádá I, 426/1035. Ámul was also besieged by the Ustundár Kay-Ká'ús who set fire to the palace of the Ispahbad Sháh Ghází Rustam (533–558/1138–9—1163) at Qarákaláta.

When in 606/1210 the nobles of Ṭabaristán submitted to Sulṭán Jalálu'd-Dín Muḥammad of Khwárazm, it was at Ámul that the *khuṭba* was read in his name, and thence was sent the annual tribute to Khwárazm. This was discontinued at the death of 'Alá'u'd-Dín Muḥammad in 617/1220–1 when Mázandarán was traversed to and fro by armies of destroying Mongols.

Ḥusámu'd-Dawla Ardashír b. Kínkwár, who in 635/1237–8 rebelled against the Mongols, transferred the capital from Sárí, which the house of Báwand had always made its metropolis, to Ámul which was less exposed. Here he built, at Kharáṭakaláya on the banks of the Harhaz, the palace which in 880/1475–6 was still in the occupation of the governors of Ámul.

In the time of Malik Táju'd-Dawla Yazdijird b. Shahriyár b. Ardashír, Ámul was again a flourishing city and had 70 colleges. Outside the town was the plain of Búrán where stood at Qarákaláta the palace of the King of Mázandarán.

Not long after the year 743/1342–3 cholera broke out at Ámul, and many of the house of Báwand and the wife and children of Fakhru'd-Dawla Ḥasan died of the disease, so that he with two of his sons alone remained. In 750/1349–50 the disease broke out again and all those of the house of Báwand who were at Ámul were wiped out, whilst of the Chuláwís only Kiyá Afrásiyáb and his sons were left.

In 795/1392–3 Ámul and Sárí were plundered by Tímúr who ordered a general massacre of the inhabitants of Ámul. He appointed

[1] See Le Strange, p. 370.

as governor Iskandar Shaykhí who was very unpopular, so that whilst Sárí was soon flourishing again, Ámul remained in ruins. On their return from exile the Mar'ashí *sayyids* rebuilt the city but it has never since played any part in the history of Persia (54).

Ámul is an open town (55) with four entrances called *darwázas*, although there are no gates. They are the Ṭihrán or Láriján, Bárfurúsh, Talíkasar, and Núr *darwázas*.

The city numbers 2000 houses. It is situated on the western bank of the Harhaz river, but there are two small quarters on the eastern bank joined to the city by a bridge of twelve arches called Pul-i-Duwázdah-pilla (56).

The inhabitants are divided into ten clans: Askí, Írá'í, Rína'í, Háshimí, Niyákí (*sayyids*), Shúndashtí (*i.e.* Sháhándashtí), Daylárustáqí, Mashá'í, Ámulí and Núrí. There are also a few Barbars and Bankashís.

The town comprises nine quarters: (1) Cháhṣar, including Rúdgar Maḥalla; has a bath. (2) Pulbiyúr, inhabited by the Írá'í clan; has a mosque called Masjid-i-Írá'íhá, which replaces the former Masjid-i-Rúḥiyya, and another built by Áqá 'Abdu'l-Karím. Hárún Maḥalla, part of Pulbiyúr, has a bath and a small *madrasa*. (3) Gurjí Maḥalla, also called Ásiyábsar or Ábdangasar; contains the Imámzáda Ibráhím, the Masjid-i-Gurjí Maḥalla, now in ruins, an *ábanbár* built in 1898 by the Amír-i-Mukarram, the famous shrine of Mír-i-Buzurg, an old *ábanbár* or water-cistern built by Sháh 'Abbás, the Sabz-Maydán, and the ruins of the garden and palace of Sháh 'Abbás. (4) Maḥalla-i-Masjid-i-Jámi', with the Masjid-i-Jámi', its *madrasa*, and a very old mosque and bath known as Áqá 'Abbásí. (5) Maḥalla-i-Shúndashtí, or Maḥalla-i-Háshimí, with the Háshimí mosque and *ábanbár* and the bath of Yúsuf Khán, which is now in ruins. (6) Maḥalla-i-Ámulíhá, or Pá'ín Bázár, with a *takya*, an *ábanbár*, the Imámzáda Ma'ṣúm, and the bath of Ashraf Sulṭán (7) Maḥalla-i-Niyákí, with the *takya* and mosque of Mírzá Muḥammad 'Alí and a new bath. (8) Maḥalla-i-Ispíkalá, with the takya-i-Askíhá and the bath of Rafí' Khán Yáwar (9) Maḥalla-i-Mashá'íhá with a *takya* and a bath. To these we may add the two *maḥallas* of Barbarí-Maḥalla or Barbaríkhayl and that of Bankashíkhayl, which are both known by the name of Darwísh Maḥalla (57)[1].

[1] For trade, produce, industries, etc., of Ámul see H. L. Rabino, Diplomatic and Consular Reports, Annual Series, No. 4812, pp. 15–16.

Nov. 26th. We visited this morning the Mashhad-i-Mír-i-Buzurg or shrine of Mír Qiwámu'd-Dín al-Mar'ashí (781/1379), founder of a dynasty of *sayyids* who reigned in Mázandarán from 760 to about 989 (1359–1581). "The Mausoleum...is a square brick building....There is a lofty gateway in the southern face of the building, and three blind arches on each of the other sides, which are about 20 yards in length. An octagon picturesquely broken, and overgrown with verdure, is placed upon the square, and a circular tower, with a low dome, rises above all. The whole edifice seems to have been formerly cased with glazed tiles, red, green, blue, yellow and purple, arranged in various fantastical patterns: some beautiful specimens remain, particularly about the gateway. That part of the interior containing the shrine of the saint is handsome and imposing[1]." The monument lies to the north-west of the town near the Sabz-Maydán and is much decayed, having suffered from want of repair and from earthquakes (58). Inside, a border of beautiful blue tiles runs round the building beneath the dome. The grave of the saint occupies the centre of the building and was covered with a wooden sarcophagus, the framework of which is all that now remains. On this framework were carved some verses by Muḥtasham; the writing is exquisite and the letters have been gilded, the background being painted in dark blue.

The Masjid-i-Jámi', which is not far from the Sabz-Maydán, is a very ancient building, but its western part was destroyed by earthquake and rebuilt in 1225/1810 by Áqá 'Alí Ashraf Mashá'í. Attached to the mosque is a *madrasa* at the entrance of which are two slabs of marble with an edict of Sháh Sulṭán Ḥusayn (1694–1722), forbidding, amongst other things, the sale of intoxicating liquor and of that most deleterious drug, *bang*, which is made of hemp seed. According to the same edict, houses of ill repute were to be closed, and pigeon-flying, cock-fights, ram-fights, and bull-fights were to be discontinued.

In the afternoon we visited the towers with conical roofs, which Hanway[2] attributes to the Guebres, but which are merely the sepulchres of holy Muḥammadan personages.

[1] Gen. Charles Stuart, *Journal of a Residence in Northern Persia, and the adjacent Provinces of Persia*, London, 1854, p. 279.

[2] Jonas Hanway, *An historical account of the British Trade over the Caspian Sea, with a journal of travels and the revolutions of Persia*, 4 vols., London, 1753; 2 vols., London, 1762.

Imámzáda Ibráhím is a shrine held in great veneration, and in summer a market is held here on Thursdays and Fridays. It is situated inside a walled burial-ground and consists of a square tower with an octagonal, conical roof. To this has been added a large building for prayer meetings. A wooden sarcophagus bears an inscription informing us that here are buried Imámzáda Ibráhím, his brother Yaḥyá and his mother. The genealogy of the saint is Ibráhím, son of Músá Káẓim, son of Ábú Ja'far, son of Muḥammad Taqí, son of Imám Riḍá. The date of the sarcophagus is 925/1519. Outside the walls of the tower lies a stone which is said to cover the remains of seventy-two of the saint's companions. Near the principal entrance to the graveyard stands a square tower in which was buried a certain Hájjí Námdar of Khurásán, who came to Ámul with two of his friends to repair the shrine of Imámzáda Ibráhím.

The Gunbad-i-Kabúd is a tower with a ruined cupola formerly covered with blue tiles, whence its name.

The Gunbad-i-Náṣiru'l-Ḥaqq, which was erected by Sayyid 'Alí Mar'ashí, ruler of Mázandarán, is a tower where lies buried Ḥasan b. 'Alí an-Náṣiru'l-Kabír. Ibn Isfandiyár mentions that the tomb, college, and library founded, and the endowments bestowed, by him, were still flourishing in Ámul in the seventh century of the Hijra, while his grave was accounted holy and visited by many pilgrims.

The Gunbad-i-Shams-i-Ṭabarsí is a tower in which lies buried Sayyid Shamsu Áli-Rasúli'lláh, a dervish learned in the traditions, and of ascetic and devout life (59). His tomb stood outside the gate of the 'Awámma-Kúy quarter. This tower had a double cupola, inner and outer, which was destroyed by an earthquake. Close to this tomb was that of Qádí Hishám[1].

The Gunbad-i-Sih-Tan is so called, I believe, from a tombstone on which was the representation of three cupolas[2]. The inscription on this stone informs us that this was the grave of Abu'l-Qásim, son of Abu'l-Maḥásin ar-Rúyání, who died in Sha'bán 514/1120. Ibn Isfandiyár mentions 'Abdu'l-Wáḥid b. Isma'íl Abu'l-Maḥásin who is called the second Sháfi'í, and for whom the Niẓámu'l-Mulk built a college at Ámul. He was the author of many works on Jurisprudence and various

[1] See Ibn Isfandiyár, p. 81.

[2] See Dorn, *Atlas zu Bemerkungen auf Anlass einer Wissenschaftlichen Reise in dem Kaukasus und den Sudlichen Kustenlandern des Kaspischen Meeres in den Jahren 1860–1861*, St Petersburg, 1895, Part II, Pl. 1.

religious subjects, and fell under the dagger of the Assassins. The *Gunbad* is a hexagonal tower surmounted by a cupola, beneath which stands a plastered tomb. The doors were dilapidated, many of the panels having disappeared. On one of those still remaining we read the name Sayyid 'Azíz b. Sayyid Bahá' u'd-Dín Ámulí.

From here we were conducted to a magnificent *afrá* tree, near which was a small burial monument called Panj-Tan.

The graves in all these monuments have been desecrated by treasure-hunters.

Ibn Isfandiyár gives the names of the following holy personages buried at Ámul: Sayyid Abu'l-Qásim Ḥasan, son of Ḥamza al 'Alawí, whose tomb was opposite the college of Zaynu'sh-Sharaf and was renovated by King Ardashír b. Ḥasan of Mázandarán. Ibn Fúrak, the preacher of the Masjid-i-Sálár, for whom the Sálár built the Masjid-i-Sálár, and for whom was erected the pulpit which stood by the *miḥráb*, was buried in the quarter of 'Alí-Kaláwa near the Dome of the cross-roads (Gunbad-i-Chahár-Ráh). Shaykh Abu'l-'Abbás Qaṣṣáb, whose tomb was still frequented in the time of the writer. Shaykh Abú Ja'far al-Ḥanáṭí, in whose shrine was preserved a *Qur'án* said to have been written by 'Alí's son, Muḥammad, called Ibnu'l-Ḥanafiyya. Shaykh Záhid, whose tomb was in the quarter called 'Alí-ábád near the gate of Zindána-Kúy (60). And, finally, Shaykh Abú Turáb, whose tomb was hard by the gate of the mosque in the quarter of Darlabash.

We also passed an old mosque named Masjid-i-Imám Ḥasan, which was constructed, it is said, under Hárúnu'r-Rashíd, but as Imám Ḥasan was seen praying here the mosque was named after him.

Another tower, called Qadamgáh-i-Khiḍr, stands near the Sabz Maydán in a cemetery known as Muṣallá or the oratory. This is probably the site of the old Muṣallá of Ámul where Dá'í'ṣ-Ṣaghír had his palace and which is often mentioned in the history of Mázandarán.

Melgunof mentions the Gunbad-i-Muḥammad Ámulí, but already in 1860 it was a heap of ruins and the foundations alone remained. The same author states that there formerly stood in the centre of the town a lofty tower, the tomb of Firídún[1]. In 1860 many tons of bricks were removed from its foundations,

[1] See Dawlatsháh, *Memoirs of the Poets*, p. 298.

and during the excavations numerous burial chambers were discovered (61).

Ámul has suffered much from earthquakes and from the Harhaz when in flood. When they require bricks, the inhabitants simply dig anywhere to a depth of a few feet, and obtain as many as they require. Some of these bricks measure 16 inches by 16 by 3, and are known as Guebre bricks[1].

The district of Ámul is subdivided into the following eight *bulúks*: (*a*) Balada; (*b*) Ahlam-rustáq; (*c*) Chuláw; (*d*) Dábú; (*e*) Dashtsar; (*f*) Garmrúdpay; (*g*) Harhazpay; (*h*) Lítkúh[2].

The ordinary road from Ámul to Ṭihrán, which is the highway for trade between the capital and Mashhadisar, goes from Ámul to Parasp, 19 miles; Panjáb stream 3½ miles; Kahrúd 3¼ miles; Báyján 4¼ miles; Wana 6 miles; Rína 6 miles; Ask 13 miles; Imámzáda Háshim pass, elevation 8700 feet, 15 miles; Áh 6 miles; Jájrúd 11 miles; Ṭihrán 21 miles; total 110½ miles. This road practically follows the Harhaz from Ámul up to near Imámzáda Háshim (62).

Another road leads from Ámul to Galiyá, Nashil, Arjumand or Lazúr, Nawá, Áh, and Ṭihrán; total about 144 miles. It is seldom or never taken by caravans, and part of the country it traverses is little inhabited except during the summer months.

The district of Láriján is so completely enclosed by mountains and narrow gorges as to be almost inaccessible to an invader, and on this account its inhabitants are often unmanageable, being always ready to revolt and unprepared to pay taxes. It comprises the whole country watered by the Lár river and the upper reaches of the Harhaz. It is divided into four *bulúks*: (*a*) Amírí or Pá'ín Láriján; (*b*) Bálá-Láriján; (*c*) Bihrustáq; (*d*) Daylárustáq[3].

Three-fourths of the inhabitants desert their villages during the winter, which they spend in the lowlands of Mázandarán. The district is said to contain between four and five thousand families. The products are wheat and barley.

Láriján is the oldest settlement in Ṭabaristán. Here, in the village of Warka, Firídún was born and here he kept Ḍaḥḥák prisoner. Ibn Isfandiyár informs us that Sahl b. al-Marzubán possessed Láriján. He constructed a road through the country,

[1] *Loc. cit.* pp. 297–8. For the herb gunduya zúma see Ibn Isfandiyár, p. 40.
[2] Villages of Ámul; see Appendix I, E.
[3] Villages of Láriján; see Appendix I, F.

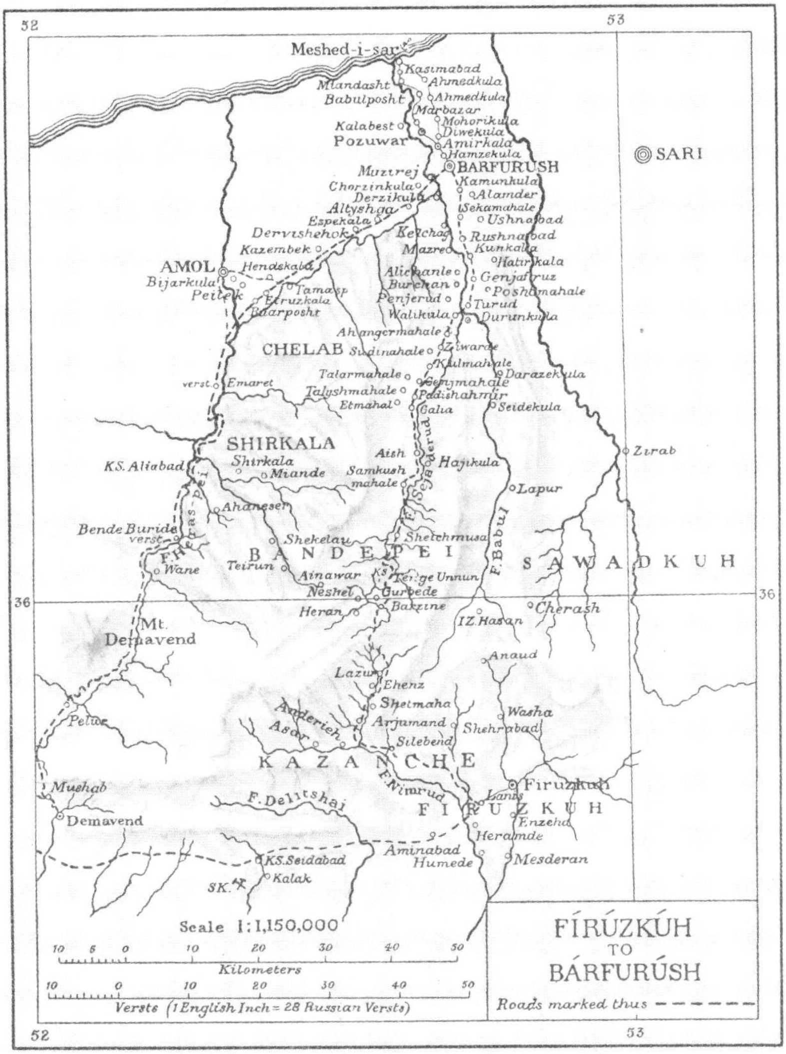

A. F. Stahl's Reiseroute zwischen Barferusch, Firuzkuh u. Djadjerud.
Petermann's Geogr. Mitteilungen, Jahrgang 1907, *Tafel* 10.

which, before his time, was impracticable both in summer and winter, by cutting and tunnelling the mountains, making bridges, and building rest-houses. Asfár b. Shírúya was a native of Láriján[1] and belonged to the Wardadáwand clan. Láriján is mentioned by Yáqút as a small town between Ray and Ámul, 18 *farsakhs* distant from either. It was protected by a castle often mentioned in the history of the Buwayhids.

The basin of the Lár river, which also lies in the district of Láriján, is bounded on the north by the mountains of Surḥak, Kahú, Surkhak, Piyázak, Díw-i-Siyáh, Alarú Walarú, and Damáwand[2], on the west by the Kutumbasta, and on the south by the Harasang, Ashtar, Khátúnbárgáh, Kazúnak, Lárkúh, Lawasán, Fílzamín, Bastán, and Siyáhchál (63). There are no trees or bushes but excellent grazing in Lár. The only inhabitants are nomads who spend the summer here with their sheep and cattle, and descend in winter to the shores of the Caspian (64).

The Lár river is formed by two streams running down from the Kutumbasta, Harasang, Ashtar, and Sútak mountains, at an elevation of about 10,000 feet. They unite at Dú-áb in the Yúrt-i-Sihdarra and flow south-east. The first valley is very narrow but widens below Yúrt-i-Gilurdak and becomes very broad below Bastak. It contracts again at Yúrt-i-Khánlar-Khán, and, after receiving the Dillícháy, it follows a narrow gorge as far as the Pulúr bridge. The river is then known as the Harhaz and flows at the foot of the Damáwand in a deep and narrow channel of rock past Ask. It then turns north-east, leaves the Damáwand to the left, and, after running in a deep channel of perpendicular rock, enters the plains at a spot about 4 or 5 miles south of Ámul. From this point it flows due north to Ámul where it is very broad and is crossed by a bridge of twelve arches. It finally joins the Caspian in two arms, the western at Maḥmúdábád and the eastern, known as the Surkhrúd, at the village of the same name.

The tributaries of the river Lár are: on the left: the united Safíd-Áb (65) and Gilagach, the Alarm, the united Ábbárán and Safíd-Áb, and the Dillícháy; on the right: the Yánisar, Khushkrúd, Chihilbarra, Gulkhána, Siyáhpalas, the united Umm-i-

[1] See Ẓahíru'd-Dín, *History of Mázandarán*, p. 313, ll. 9 and 10.

[2] The height of Damáwand is about 19,000 feet. For information about this mountain see A. H. Schindler, "Notes on Damavand," *Proc. R. G.S.* Feb. 1888, and "Eastern Persian Irak," *Proc. R. G. S.* 1897; Melgunof, *Das Sudliche Ufer des Kaspischen Meeres*, pp. 21–27; Le Strange, *The Lands of the Eastern Caliphate*, p. 371; Ibn Isfandiyár, pp. 35–37; and E. G. Browne, *A year amongst the Persians*, p. 559; see also Marquart, *loc. cit.*, pp. 127–129.

Muhának and Tang-Áw, and, below the Pulúr bridge, the Ziyár which comes from the south-east, and which has received on its right the Dhághrúd and Shírish. Below the Pulúr bridge the Lár changes its name to Harhaz. The principal tributaries of the Harhaz are: the Kahrúd on the left, the Annáwar on the right, the Hardarúd, which I take to be the same as the Núr river (66), on the left, and the Kamarrúd on the right.

The district of Sawádkúh (formerly known as Kúlá-pay), which takes its name from the mountain of Sawát, south-east of the village of Chirát, is bordered on the south by Fírúzkúh, from which it is separated by the mountain of Shalfín or Sharwín (called, near Qadamgáh, Piyázmarkar, and, in other parts, Munkíchál, Shárak, and Gadúk-i-Sháh). To the east lies Hazár-jaríb, and to the west are Láriján and Bandpay. Northwards Sawádkúh extends to Shírgáh where the Rástábpay and Walúpay streams unite at a place called Dú-áb to form the Tálár.

The houses in the *yayláqs* are of stone or wood with a roof of wooden tiles kept in place by stones. Half-way down the Gadúk pass towards the north begin the *qishláqs*, where the houses are double-storied with pointed roofs of thatch or tiles.

Sawádkúh[1] is formed by two valleys, called Rástpay or Rástábpay to the east, and Walúpay to the west, *i.e.* the district of the stream flowing to the right and that of the stream flowing to the left. Rástpay is subdivided into five *bulúks*: (*a*) Surkh-Rubáṭ; (*b*) Dú-áb-bálá; (*c*) Khánqáhpay; (*d*) Khánqáh; (*e*) Rás-tábpay-i-Kúchik. Walúpay is subdivided into seven *bulúks*: (*a*) Chirát; (*b*) Anand; (*c*) Alásht; (*d*) Karmarzd; (*e*) Kiláríján and Kamandayn; (*f*) Zíráb; (*g*) Kasliyán (67).

The Tálár, which rises immediately south of the Shahmírzád mountain on the Samnán border, is spanned in Sawádkúh by the Pul-i-Safíd, a bridge of two arches, 30 miles north of Fírúzkúh and 42 miles south of Sárí, and by another bridge on the road from Sárí to Bárfurúsh, 10 miles east of the latter town. It falls into the Caspian in three arms, the Mírrúd, the Chapukrúd, and the Siyáhrúd or Lárím river.

The road from Fírúzkúh (elevation 5580 feet) ascends to the caravanserai of Gadúk, 12 miles from Fírúzkúh and half a mile south of the top of the Gadúk pass (6620 feet). This inn stands at the dividing line of the provinces of 'Iráq and Mázandarán, and is a large, substantial, stone building, now sadly out of repair,

[1] Villages of Sawádkúh; see Appendix I, G.

built by Sháh 'Abbás on his causeway from Iṣfahán to Faraḥábád, which followed the Rástpay valley of Sawádkúh. Descending towards Mázandarán the path narrows and becomes very difficult. The ruins of the castle of Kalíp (68), a bandit chief of the reign of Sháh 'Abbás the Great, are romantically perched upon a rocky precipice, which seems to close the pass of Gadúk and divide it from another gorge opening to the south-east[1]. A wider and partially cultivated valley succeeds. Another castle, that of the Díw-i-Safíd, commands the junction of a lateral valley and its stream. A second gorge, as narrow but not so striking as the first, was in former times closed by a solid wall, five feet thick, whereof considerable remains are still visible. Surkh-Rubát (elevation 2340 feet) is 12½ miles from the Gadúk pass. Lower down, the road passes to the right of the Tálár river by a pretty bridge of two arches called Pul-i-Safíd and at 16½ miles from Surkh-Rubáṭ reaches Zíráb (elevation 2210 feet). From here the road still follows Sháh 'Abbás' causeway and is for the first 9 miles completely broken up. After crossing a tributary of the Tálár by a fine bridge of two arches, the road arrives at Shírgáh, 14 miles north of Zíráb. Seven miles from Zíráb is Haft-Tan (elevation 310 feet) and 3 miles further on 'Alí-ábád, whence to Bárfurúsh is another 12 miles. The Tálár is forded 2 miles north of 'Alí-ábád.

I'timádu's-Salṭana says that to the left of the road near the Gadúk one sees the ruins of a castle called Qal'a-i-Awlád-i-Díw-i-Safíd (this is the Qal'a-i-Awlád of the Persian historians), and that to the right are the remains of many ruined castles. Before reaching Surkhrubáṭ one passes through the defile of Tanga-i-Chihil-Dar. The Pul-i-Dukhtar, a bridge over the Áb-i-Kasliyán, marks the boundary between Sawádkúh and Shírgáh. Past Shírgáh one crossed the Utiján stream which joins the Tálár, and then another bridge built by Sháh 'Abbás and known as Pul-i-Bastal[2].

From Dú-áb, half a mile north of Surkhrubát, a track leads to Samnán via Kumrú, the distances according to native information being: Kumrú 16 miles; the pass 14 miles; Shahmírzád 1½ mile; and Samnán 16 miles; total 47½ miles.

Nov. 27th, 8 miles. Proceeding east from Ámul, we crossed

[1] See Stuart, *loc. cit.*, p. 255.
[2] Muhammad Hasan Khán I'timádu's-Saltana, *Kitábu't-Tadwín fí Ahwál-i-Jibál-i Shalfín* (or *Sharwín*). (Tihrán, 1311/1893–4.)

the Harhaz by the Duwázda-pillah bridge, the Hárún Maḥalla, the Shírrúd, the Ishkaraz, and another branch of the Ishkaraz formerly spanned by a small brick bridge now in ruins. Continuing east we crossed the Ispiyárbun stream, passed the village of the same name and that of Hindúkalá, crossed the Bá'ú stream and came to Álamdar Maḥalla. The Párúd and Kútalkash streams were crossed by small stone bridges, then came the Mullayt stream, and finally we reached a spot named Sihpul, or "the three bridges," where we joined the main Ámul-Bárfurúsh road which runs along the left bank of the Kárí river which is a branch of the Harhaz. Passing Káẓimbaygí we stopped for the night at Aḥmad-Chála-pay commonly called Amjalapay, a village of 40 houses with a mosque and a shrine (Darwísh 'Azízu 'lláh).

Nov. 28th, 12 miles. Turk Mahalla is half-way between Amjalapay and Bárfurúsh. Other villages we passed were: Ispúkalá, Darwíshakhák, Matíkalá, Kalágar-Maḥalla, and Múzúraj. We then came to a bridge which Muḥammad Ḥasan Khán Qájár built over the Bábul just below its junction with the Áb-i-Hárún which comes from the west. Two of the arches of this bridge were destroyed by an earthquake about the year 1820 and were rebuilt shortly afterwards. In 1907–8 two out of the nine arches of the bridge were carried away by the river in spate. A shopkeeper of Bárfurúsh who was childless spent most of his savings on repairs to this bridge, which is now in perfect condition again. The stream is deep, with a slow current and treacherous bottom. Bárfurúsh lies immediately on the other side of the bridge.

CHAPTER V

Bárfurúsh: situation. Foundation. Mámtír. Population. Mosque of Kázim Baygí. Masjid-i-Jámi'. Mashhadisar: district. Shrine of Abú Jawáb. Mahmúdábád to Farahábád. Districts of Bárfurúsh. Bárfurúsh to Farahábád. District of Farahábád. Stenka Razin. Farahábád to Sárí. Road from Sárí to Bárfurúsh.

BÁRFURÚSH is the chief commercial city of Mázandarán; it is situated to the east of the Bábul river, about 12 miles from Mashhadisar, and about as many from the foot of the mountains.

Bárfurúsh which was first known as Bárfurúshdih, or the village where loads were sold, was founded about the beginning of the 16th century on the site of the former city of Mámṭír[1]. When Muḥammad b. Khálid was governor of the province he constructed there a market and other buildings, to which, in 160?/776–7, Mázyár b. Qárin added a mosque.

Although the largest town in Mázandarán, Bárfurúsh[2] is not the residence of the governor general, who lives at Sárí.

Beyond the bazaars, which are dark and badly built, the houses are so much scattered that it is difficult to form an idea of the town, which covers a large extent of ground. There are said to be 9122 houses with a total population of 25,000 inhabitants, of whom 750 are Jews. There are 63 quarters, 26 mosques, 8 *madrasas*, 31 *takyas* used during the religious ceremonies of the month of Muḥarram, 10 shrines, 3 graves of venerated *darwíshes*, 31 caravanserais for merchants, 13 caravanserais for caravans, 36 baths, many elementary schools, and 1471 shops (69). The town has prospered and made great progress during the last 50 years. Outside Bárfurúsh to the south-west beyond a plain covered with dwarf alder lies the Bágh-i-Sháh (Bahru'l-Iram), a royal garden originally laid out by Sháh 'Abbás.

According to two inscriptions, one over the entrance and the other over the *miḥráb*, the mosque of Káẓim Baygí was built by

[1] See Ibn Isfandiyár, pp. 27–28. Ibn Isfandiyár visited the tomb of Ibn Mahdí Mámtírí at Mámtír; see Ibn Isfandiyár, p. 76.

[2] See H. L. Rabino, Diplomatic and Consular Report, Annual Series, No. 4812, pp. 3–4.

Muḥammad Khán (Qawánlú), a governor of Mázandarán under Muḥammad Ḥasan Khán, in 1169/1755-6. It was endowed with the totality or part of the revenues of the following villages: Káẓim Baygí and Dihak (in Lálábád); Sannú (in Jalál Azrak); Qal'akash and Áqá Malik (in Sásíkalám); and Ganjúrúz.

In the Masjid-i-Jámi' an inscription records that, by command of Muḥammad Sháh, Faḍl 'Alí Khán, governor of Mázandarán, abolished in 1251/1835-6 all taxes on bakers. Another inscription informs us that the mosque was destroyed by an earthquake during the reign of Fatḥ 'Alí Sháh and that it was rebuilt by Mír Muḥammad Ḥusayn in 1220/1805-6.

Ẓahíru'd-Dín relates that there was at Bárfurúsh a mound known as Pushta-i-Azrak-Dún which was the site of the house of Azrak, a cousin of Kiyá Fakhru'd-Dín and Kiyá Wishtásp, two chieftains of the Jalál clan who for a short time ruled eastern Mázandarán after the death of Fakhru'd-Dawla Ḥasan.

The port of Bárfurúsh is Mashhadisar which is situated at the mouth of the Bábul river[1]. The road from Bárfurúsh passes Ḥamzakalá, Na'lkalá, Amírkạlá, Pázawár (the birthplace of the poet Amír-i-Pázawárí), and Mír Bázár which is 7 miles from Mashhadisar and has a Tuesday market. There is here a ford across the Bábul to Kalbast which is on the opposite side. From Mír Bázár the road follows the precipitous banks of the Bábul to Mashhadisar, which lies about 12 miles north-north-west of Bárfurúsh.

Between Mashhadisar and the sea on the right bank of the Bábul stretches a line of sand-hills, on which a light-house has been erected. No traces are now to be seen of the large tower mentioned by Gmelin as having been built at the time of the descent on these shores of the Don Cossacks under Stenka Razin.

The district of Mashhadisar comprises the following *bulúks*: (*a*) Balada; (*b*) Bánṣarkalá; (*c*) Pázawár; (*d*) Rúdpusht; (*e*) Tálárpay[2].

Mashhadisar signifies "the burial place of the Martyr," and the Martyr is Imámzáda Ibráhím Abú Jawáb or "He of the answer."

The building of the *Imámzáda* lies to the east of the place and consists as usual of a round tower with a conical roof in an

[1] See H. L. Rabino, Diplomatic and Consular Report, Annual Series, No. 4812, pp. 4-6.

[2] Villages of Mashhadisar; see Appendix I, H.

enclosure filled with orange trees. There are four doors of carved wood, each bearing an inscription. Eastern door. Made by order of *Sayyid* 'Azíz, son of *Sayyid* Shamsu'd-Dín Bábulkání. Carpenter *Ustád* Muḥammad, son of *Ustád* 'Alí ar-Rází; date Muḥarram, 841/1437. Southern door. Door and building due to *Bíbí* Faḍḍa *Khátún*, daughter of *Amír* Sá'id. Carpenter Ḥasan, son of *Ustád* Báyazíd; date 905/1499–1500. Western door. Made by order of *Sayyid* Shamsu'd-Dín, son of *Sayyid* 'Abdu'l-'Azíz Bábulkání. Carpenter *Ustád* Muḥammad, son of *Ustád* 'Alí ar-Rází; date Jumádá I, 858/1454. Northern door. Made by order of *Sayyid* Shamsu'd-Dín, son of *Sayyid* 'Abdu'l-'Azíz Bábulkání. Carpenter *Ustád* Muḥammad, son of *Ustád* 'Alí ar-Rází; date Dhú'l-hijja, 857/1453. There is also an inscription written by Taqí al-Ámulí and carved by *Ustád* Isma'íl *Najjár* Ámulí ar-Rází, invoking God's blessing on the Prophet and the twelve *Imáms*.

In an adjoining building, now in ruins, was a door with an inscription, dated Muḥarram, 906/1500, to the effect that the building was due to *Sayyida Bíbí* Faḍḍa *Khátún*, daughter of *Amír* Sá'id and wife of *Sulṭán Amír* Shamsu'd-Dín deceased, and that the carving was the work of the carpenter *Ustád* 'Alí son of *Ustád* Fakhru'd-Dín, son of *Ustád* 'Alí, while the inscription was traced by Aḥmad b. Ḥusayn.

There is also in Mashhadisar the shrine of *Bíbí* Sakína, the door of which bears an inscription, dated 873/1468–9, informing us that this building was erected over the grave of *Bíbí* Sakína, daughter of Imám Músá Káẓim, and that the door was due to *Sayyid* Khujasta, son of Fakhru'd-Dín Bábulkání, and that the carpenter Shamsu'd-Dín, son of *Ustád* Aḥmad, was responsible for the carving. Another door bore an inscription which I could not decipher.

The road from Maḥmúdábád to Faraḥábád crosses the Siyáhrúdbár which has a village on either bank, the Tufangá, the Ahlama, the village of the same name being about 2 miles from the sea (70), the Shilít, and the Mullákalá with two *maḥallas* where is the boundary between Ámul and Bárfurúsh. Then it passes the *maḥallas* of Surkhrúd, which are divided by the stream of the same name (a branch of the Harhaz), and the village of Wazrá, crosses the Shírrúd and reaches Faríkinár where there is a ferry across the river and which is 7 miles from Mashhadisar. Three miles east of Mashhadisar is the river Mírrúd which is deep but not broad and has a ferry; before reaching it one passes the old mouth of the Bábul which was turned in its present direction by the people of the country in about the year 1850. On the right of the Mírrúd just above the ferry is the Maḥalla Báqirtanga. The road then crosses the Tálár called the Chapukrúd, the Lárím or Siyáhrúd (71), and reaches 8 miles further on the river of Faraḥábád.

Two lofty octagonal brick towers were built about 1857 to the west of the Faraḥábád river, at no great distance from each other, to prevent the Turcomans from landing on the coast. There are two others of similar build beyond on the road to Nawdharábád and Dhághmarz. The names of these towers between the Tijin and Miyánkala are given on De Morgan's map as Burj-i-'Alí Naqí, Burj-i-Zardí, Burj-i-Niká, and Burj-i-Gawharbárán.

The following are the *bulúks* of Bárfurúsh: (*a*) Balada; (*b*) Bálá-Bulúk; (*c*) Bálá-Tijin; (*d*) Bandpay (72); (*e*) Bísha; (*f*) Jalál-Azrak; (*g*) Lafúr (73); (*h*) Lálábád; (*i*) Mashhad-Ganjúrúz; (*j*) Sásíkalám[1].

Dec. 2nd, 16 miles. Leaving Bárfurúsh we crossed a small branch of the Bábul and passed the villages of Aghúzbun, Ḥájjíkalá, and Ḥaydarkalá; then a second Aghúzbun, after which we reached Bíshasar. The next village was 'Azízak, north of which is a large irrigation reservoir. The Tálár is spanned by a wooden bridge 33 paces in length. Passing through a jungle of pomegranate, we came to the village of Bahnamír. The next village was Rawshandún, and then we entered the jungle of Iznawá. Our road now lay through a marshy plain, and, after crossing by means of a small wooden bridge a branch of the Tálár called the Chapukrúd, we arrived at the village of Anármarz.

The small *maḥal* of Chapukrúd, which was formerly part of Bárfurúsh but has since been added to Sárí, is bordered on the east by Kurdkalá, on the west by Rawshandún, on the south by Misdán, and, I believe, Júbar, and on the north by Lárím and the Caspian. It comprises the villages of Anármarz, 30 houses; Dínachál, 50 houses; Pítrúd, 40 houses; and Imámzáda 'Abdu 'lláh, 30 houses. Under Sháh 'Abbás the inhabitants were settled near the sea-shore, but as they were constantly exposed to the attacks and depredations of Turcoman pirates, they retired inland to

[1] Villages of Bárfurúsh; see Appendix I, 1.

their present settlements. Near the beach is a spot called the grave of Sulṭán Ibráhím Adham, but no building exists. Oil is said to be found at a place called Gílaward which is near Chapukrúd, or part of it. We were told that the following rivers and streams had to be crossed on the way from Chapukrúd to Mashhadisar, namely the Zíkash, Halíkalá and Tálár.

Dec. 3rd, 16 miles. The plain between Anármarz and Lárím is flat, with but little cultivation. We passed through the *maḥalla* of Pítrúd, and saw to the right Kurdkalá and Kúhíkhayl. A large mound named Dímtappa marks the site of some former settlement. The village of Lárím numbers about 200 houses and is traversed by the Siyáhrúd. After crossing the Zarrínkalá stream and passing the village of the same name, we continued to 'Abbás 'Alí Kash (40 houses), to which belongs the hamlet of Sayyid Maḥalla, and crossed the Khúrdrú stream. The country between 'Abbás 'Alí Kash and Qájárkhayl is an open expanse of saltish ground which serves as grazing ground for cattle. We soon afterwards passed Faraḥábád, north of which flows an arm of the Tijin spanned by a wooden bridge of 60 paces, and reached the *bandar* or port of Faraḥábád at the mouth of the Tijin.

Faraḥábád, 17 miles north of Sárí, comprises Faraḥábád, Dazníkanda, and Súta, and consists of 70 houses all told of the meanest kind. A quarter of a mile east-south-east of the mouth of the Tijin (which flows in a deep bed in a north-north-west direction to the sea) lie the remains of the town of Faraḥábád, which was a favourite residence of Sháh 'Abbás (74). It was sacked in 1668 by a horde of Cossacks who were led by the famous Stenka Razin, chief of the Don Cossacks[1]. The Tijin was spanned here in former days by a substantial brick bridge, the piers of which are still visible.

The district of Faraḥábád comprises: (*a*) Balada; (*b*) Andarúd; (*c*) Shahrkhwást; (*d*) Gílkhwárán; (*e*) Miyándúrúd; (*f*) Rúdpay[2].

Dec. 4th, 17 miles. Passing Ḥamídábád and Dazníkanda we reached Ákand (70 houses) on Sháh 'Abbás's causeway (75). Traces of former reservoirs and irrigation works which we saw in the forest show that this part of Mázandarán must have enjoyed great prosperity under the Ṣafawí dynasty. At Máhfírúz Maḥalla,

[1] For a description of the sack of Farahábád see *Travels of Sir John Chardin into Persia*, London, 1686; *The Coronation of Soleiman III*, pp. 152–154.

[2] Villages of Faraḥábád; see Appendix I, J.

which lay to our left, near the Tijin, there is a ford called "Karbalá'í 'Alí kusht," *i.e.* "which drowned Karbalá'í 'Alí." We next came to Fírúzkanda to the left of the road 4 miles from Sárí, and further on to 'Alíwák which was on our right, and finally reached the Faraḥábád gate of Sárí.

The direct road from Sárí to Bárfurúsh passes the Imámzáda Isandij ('Ísá-Khandaq), 3½ miles; Tírkalá and Az, 3 miles; Siyáhrúd stream, ½ mile; Falláḥ, ½ mile; Fútam, 2¾ miles; Sayyid Maḥalla, 1¾ miles; Tálár river, 1½ miles; Mihrí, ½ mile; Kupúrchál, 1 mile; Imámzáda Sulṭán Muḥammad Ṭáhir (76), 1 mile; Bárfurúsh, 3 miles. This is a mere village path through dense forest and in places over very marshy ground, and a guide is absolutely necessary. There is an alternative route to Sárí via 'Alí-ábád along Sháh 'Abbás's causeway, which, however, is much out of repair. Between the Siyáhrúd and Sárí lie the villages of Afrákútí, Arata, and Surkhkalá (77).

CHAPTER VI

Sárí. Foundation. History. Muqaddasí's description. Sack of Sárí by Tímúr. Situation. Gates and town quarters. Public buildings. Chief mosque. Gunbad-i-Salm-wa-Túr. Shrines. Imámzáda Zaynu'l-'Ábidín. Shrine of Mullá Májdu'd-Dín Districts of Sárí. Subdistricts. Districts of Hazárjaríb: Dúdánga, Chahárdánga, Yánisar, Surkhgiriya, Yakhkash.

THE modern town of Sárí is built near the site of one of the oldest towns of Persia, variously identified as Phanáca, Zadrakarta, and Syrinx. When Minúchihr, to avenge his father Írij, slew Salm and Túr, he buried them at Sárí near Írij, and above each tomb he built a cupola which in the time of Ẓahíru'd-Dín was known as Sih-Gunbad, or the three cupolas, and was so strong that it was impossible to destroy it (78).

Rustam, after the fatal fight which took place between him and his son Suhráb, intended to carry the latter's coffin back to Zábulistán, but owing to the heat he deposited it at Sárí, at the place called Qaṣr-i-Túr, where, it is said, it was eventually buried.

Farrukhán the Great ordered one of his nobles, Báw by name, to build Sárí on the site of the village of Awhar (known later as Nárinja Ḳútí), which was chosen because of its high position, abundant streams, and pleasant surroundings. The inhabitants, however, bribed Báw to leave them in peace and choose another site, which Báw accordingly did. On becoming aware of Báw's disobedience, the King cast him into bondage, and had him hanged at the village of Ávíján (or Báw-ávíján), while with the money taken by Báw as a bribe he built a village called Dínár-Ḳafshín[1].

Yazíd b. Muhallab, who in the time of the Caliph Sulaymán b. 'Abdu'l-Malik (96–99/715–17) was sent to conquer Ṭabaristán, occupied Sárí, where he alighted at the *Ispahbad's* palace, but he was soon compelled by the Ispahbad Farrukhán-i-Buzurg to retire from Mázandarán.

Sárí takes its name from Sárúya, the son of Farrukhán, who was regent during the minority of his nephew the Ispahbad

[1] See Ibn Isfandiyár, p. 17.

Khurshíd. The palace of the *Ispahbad*, called Ispahbadán, was restored by Dázmihr, Sárúya, and Khurshíd. The latter also enclosed 400 *jaríb* (dialect *garí*) of land (called in Ibn Isfandiyár's time Kísa), which was used by King Ardashír as a breeding-ground for Arab horses, built a strong fortress called Sihdila, or Shihdila, and a market-place where he settled skilled artisans chosen from all parts of Ṭabaristán, and gave the city five gates which were called the Highland gate (darwáza-i-Kúhistán), the Sea gate, and the Gílán, Gurgán and Hunting gates (darwáza-i-Sayd). He also had a channel cut from the mountains to the sea to bring water to the town, and called it Gílána-Júy. Further he made fish-ponds, and outside the Hunting gate a great *maydán* and a deep ditch, of which traces still remained in Ibn Isfandiyár's time[1].

The first building erected by Muslims in Ṭabaristán was the great mosque of Sárí, which Abu'l-Khuḍayb, the first 'Abbásid governor of Ṭabaristán, caused to be built in the year 140/757–8.

This building was soon replaced by another Masjid-i-Jámi', as Ibn Isfandiyár mentions that "the mosque of Sárí was built in the reign of Hárúnu'r-Rashíd by Yaḥyá b. Yaḥyá and completed by Mázyár b. Qárin."

Sárí was the metropolis of the 'Alíd rulers, Ḥasan and Muḥammad b. Zayd, of the Ṭáhirid governors during the third century of the Hijra, and of the Báwand dynasty until 635/1237–8.

The walls of Sárí were repaired in 179/795–6 by 'Abdu'l-Malik b. Qa'qa' and destroyed afterwards by Mázyár who, however, soon repaired them again. Not long after he fell into the hands of 'Abdu'lláh b. Ṭáhir who brought him to the Caliph, by whose orders he was put to death at Sámarrá in 224/839.

The town was burnt by the Russians (in 298/910–3) who had come by sea and wasted the Mázandarán coast. In 325/936–7 Sárí suffered greatly from floods so that the people fled into the highlands.

Muqaddasí (375/985) describes Sárúya as "a populous place where much cloth was manufactured, and its markets were famous. There was a small castle with a ditch, and a Friday Mosque where a fine orange-tree grew, also an immense fig-tree on the town bridge. The bridges of boats here were renowned[2]."

[1] Ibn Isfandiyár, p. 115.

[2] Le Strange, p. 370

Ḥusámu'd-Dawla Shahriyár repaired the fortifications of Sárí in about 500/1106–7. This *Ispahbad* had a palace at Dawlatábád, near Sárí.

In 578/1182–3 Sulṭán Tukush marched against Sháh Ardashír of Mázandarán, by way of Gurgán and came to Sárí; he burned his palace and castles, plundered the city, and ravaged the countryside beyond all description. During the reign of Sulṭán Muḥammad of Khwárazm, Sárí was again plundered, and such was the havoc wrought by Mú'ayyid bi'lláh, one of the Sulṭán's generals, that nowhere in the town could one find shelter from the sun.

Sárí suffered much in the 7th (13th) century during the Mongol invasion, and, when Mustawfí wrote, it was almost a complete ruin, though its lands continued to produce an abundance of grapes and corn, and silk was still manufactured from the cocoons of silkworms reared here[1].

In 635/1237–8 Ḥusámu'd-Dawla Ardashír b. Kínkhwár removed the capital from Sárí, which was exposed to the attacks of the Mongols, to Ámul, where he took up his abode.

During the short time that the Jalál ruled in Mázandarán, they erected a few buildings at Sárí, but the greater part of the town remained in ruins and was soon overrun by the jungle and became the haunt of wild boars. Sayyid Kamálu'd-Dín b. Qiwámu'd-Dín Mar'ashí built a wall round the town and surrounded it with a deep moat; inside the wall he erected a castle and a palace and rebuilt the town. The work was begun in 769/1367–8 and ended in 777/1375–6.

In 795/1392–3 Tímúr's troops plundered the city, and the conqueror ordered a general massacre of its inhabitants. Under its new governor, Jamshíd b. Qárin Ghúrí, it soon recovered from this disaster, and remained the capital of Mázandarán until the province was conquered by the Zands, who transferred the capital to Bárfurúsh. As soon as Áqá Muḥammad Khán Qájár was firmly established in Mázandarán, he removed the seat of government back to Sárí.

Sárí suffered greatly during the disorders which followed the death of Nádir. It was plundered by the Turcomans when Muḥammad Ḥasan Khán Qájár was compelled to retire from Shíráz to Hazárjaríb before Shaykh 'Alí Khán Zand's troops. It was destroyed later by Muḥammad Khán of Sawádkúh who was

[1] Le Strange, p. 370.

appointed governor of Mázandarán after the departure of Naẓar Khán Zand. When Gmélin in 1771 passed through this part of Mázandarán, the town, which had very nearly been reduced to a heap of stones, was just being rebuilt, the capital having, as already mentioned, been transferred to Bárfurúsh. Forster was in Sárí in January, 1784. The city had grievously suffered from the effects of a recent fire. He describes it as a fortified town and the residence of Áqá Muḥammad Khán Qájár. Sárí has since remained the capital of Mázandarán. The earthquake of 1225/1810 caused much destruction, and in 1830 the plague carried away a large portion of the inhabitants.

Traces of the old walls still remain. There are four gates at the present time called the Bárfurúsh, Chihildar (Chihil-Dukhtarán), Faraḥábád or Mullá Majdu'd-Dín, and Astarábád gates.

The principal quarter of the town is Mír Maṣhhad; the others are Chahár-Takya, Shukrábád, Na'lbandán, Bayrámtar, Shipish-kushán, Sháhgházíbun, Bágh-i-Sháh-i-kuhna, Isfahání Maḥalla, Mír-Sih-Rúza, and Úsánlú. Melgunof also mentions the following quarters: Sabz-Maydán, Balúchíkhayl, Afghán, Chála-bágh, Qilíjlí Maḥalla, Mullá Majdu'd-Dín, Dar-Masjid, Pá-yi-Chinár, Shíshagar, Bahárábád, Sháhzáda Ḥusayn, Imámzáda 'Abdu'lláh, and Imámzáda Yaḥyá.

There are 7 mosques, 5 colleges, 7 *ábanbárs*, 5 shrines inside and two outside the town, 15 *takyas*, 17 caravanserais, and many baths[1] (79). The chief mosque, or Masjid-i-Jámi', was formerly a guebre temple near which stood, it is said, the tomb of Firídún, no traces of which, however, now remain. Another monument, the site of which is shown, but of which no traces remain, was the Gunbad-i-Salm-wa-Túr. It has been described as a tower of cylindrical shape with a cement top about 100 feet in height and 30 feet in diameter. Fraser says that according to the inhabitants it bore an inscription that the Daylamite King, Ḥusámu'd-Dawla[2], who died in the 5th century of the Hijra, was buried here. This would prove that the so-called Gunbad-i-Salm-wa-Túr was not the original building mentioned by Ibn Isfandiyár and Ẓahíru'd-Dín. It was, however, so solid that it resisted many earthquakes. Áqá Muḥammad Khán Qájár tried unsuccessfully to destroy it. It was finally shattered by the earthquake of

[1] See H. L. Rabino, Diplomatic and Consular Report, Ann. Series, No. 4812, p. 19.

[2] This should no doubt be the Báwand King of Mázandarán. See Fraser, *Travels and Adventures in the Persian Provinces of the Southern Banks of the Caspian Sea*, London, 1826, pp. 42–44.

1225/1810 and pulled down by order of the governor of Mázandarán, the Mulk-Árá, Muḥammad Qulí Mírzá, son of Fatḥ 'Alí Sháh. When Stuart visited Sárí he saw no trace of it, and only found at the place where it once stood a hole in the ground.

The name of the shrines of Sárí are: (*a*) Imámzáda Yaḥyá; (*b*) I. Z. 'Abdu'lláh, also called Mír-Sih-Rúza; (*c*) I. Z. Sháh-ghází; (*d*) I. Z. Mullá Majdu'd-Dín; (*e*) I. Z. Qásim, a son of Imám Músá Káẓim, near the above; (*f*) Sháhzáda Ḥusayn, outside the town; (*g*) I. Z. Sa'ídsar in Maḥalla Bayrámtar; (*h*) I. Z. Sháhzáda Sulṭán Muḥammad Riḍá; and (*i*) I. Z. Zaynu'l-'Ábidín.

Near the Bárfurúsh gate were formerly to be seen the ruins of the Imámzáda Ibráhím which was thrown down by an earthquake about 1810 A.D. Not far distant at the further extremity of a small open *maydán* is another tomb called the Imámzáda Zaynu'l-'Ábidín, which is still in a tolerably good state of preservation; it is probable that the Imámzáda Ibráhím was of similar construction to this one. It is of excellent brickwork; beginning as a square to a height of some 20 feet, it then takes the form of an octagon, and terminates in a conical spire, formerly covered with blue glazed tiles, of which, however, none is now to be seen. In the interior were two old chests of beautifully carved wood standing over the graves of Amír Zaynu'l-'Ábidín and Amír Shamsu'd-Dín, sons of Sayyid Kamálu'd-Dín, a former ruler of Mázandarán. The first chest had been partly destroyed by fire some 20 years previously; the second bore an inscription giving the date of Amír Shamsu'd-Dín's death as Sunday 25 Jumádá II, 905/1500. Over the entrance was an inscription recording that the building had been erected by 'Alá'u'd-Dín, son of Darwísh Muḥammad 'Abdu'l-Wafá. Higher up was a further inscription—a quotation from the *Qur'án*—in mosaic tile work and of great beauty. A small outer building had been added to the tower but was in ruins. A door leading from it to the tower bore the date 894/1489 (80).

In the same *maydán* at a few yards distance is the I. Z. Yaḥyá, consisting of a lofty tower finishing in a conical roof, with an outer building adjoining it. A chest of carved wood covers the graves of Yaḥyá and Ḥusayn, sons of Imám Músá Káẓim, and of their sister, Sakína.

The shrine of Mullá Majdu'd-Dín is outside the town on the road to Faraḥábád. It possessed an autograph letter of Imám Ja'far dated 10 Shawwál, 133/751, instructing Majdu'd-Dín

Makkí to proceed to Ámul and Sárí to convert the inhabitants of those cities to Islám (81).

The Governor's palace at Sárí was built by Áqá Muhammad Khán Qájár on the site of a former palace of Sháh 'Abbás. It was partially destroyed by fire and rebuilt by the Mulk-Ará. On the other side of the *maydán* facing the Governor's palace is the Bágh-i-Sháh, formerly known as the garden of the Mulk-Ará. To the north of Sárí is the old Bágh-i-Sháh laid out by Sháh 'Abbás (82).

The streets of Sárí are paved, but the pavement is usually out of repair and slopes down to a gutter which runs along the centre of the road[1].

The district of Sárí is one of the most productive tracts of Mázandarán, and much rice, cotton, and sugar-cane are grown. The district extends from the river Niká on the east to the Tálár on the west. Sárí stands nearly half-way between these two rivers and is watered by the river Tijin. On the south, the district of Sárí is bordered by Sawádkúh and Hazárjaríb, whilst the shores of the Caspian form its northern limits.

The *bulúks* of Sárí are: (*a*) Balada; (*b*) 'Alí-ábád; (*c*) Bíshasar; (*d*) Isfíward and Shúráb; (*e*) Gulayján Rustáq; (*f*) Kárkanda; (*g*) Kiyákalá; (*h*) Mishkábád; (*i*) Nawkandaká; (*j*) Sárí-Rúd-pay; (*k*) Sawádkúh; (*l*) Shírgáh[2] (83).

The *bulúk* of Hazárjaríb consists of two principal divisions, Chahárdánga and Dúdánga. It is related that Hazárjaríb belonged to Fakhr 'Imádu'd-Dín, son of Imám Zaynu'l-'Ábidín. Before his death he divided his property amongst his three sons, one of whom was of a different mother. The two full brothers received jointly, therefore, four-sixths or *chahár dáng*, and the half brother two-sixths or *dú dáng*.

Hazárjaríb is bounded on the east by Sáwar and Dámghán, on the south by Samnán and a portion of 'Iráq, on the west by Fírúzkúh and Sawádkúh, and on the north by different *bulúks* of Astarábád and the lowlands of Mázandarán[3].

Dúdánga lies south of Chahárdánga and is bordered on the south by the Kúh-i-Bashm, which separates Sangsar from Shah-mírzád, on the east by the Kúh-i-Díwtanga, which extends to the village of Túdarwár of Dámghán, on the north by the *bulúk* of Yánisar, whilst on the west it is separated from Sawádkúh by

[1] See H. L. Rabino, Diplomatic and Cons. Report, Ann. Series, No. 4812, pp 19–20.
[2] Villages of Sárí; see Appendix I, K.
[3] See H. L. Rabino, Diplomatic and Cons. Report, Ann. Series, No. 4812, pp. 17–18

the Sháhdarkúh mountain. Dúdánga has four *bulúks*; Pusht-i-Kúh, Nahramán, Banáft, and Farím. The river of Dúdánga rises in the Kúh-i-Bashm and neighbouring mountains; it flows through the village of Pá'ínkalá, and then enters Chahárdánga, subsequently joining the river Tijin east of Sárí.

Chahárdánga is divided into four parts: Yánisar, Surkhgiriya, Yakhkash, and Súrtij.

Yánisar extends from Anazánkúh on the north to Sháhdarkúh on the south, and from Sáwar on the east to Surkhgiriya on the west. It is subdivided into 9 *bulúks*: Bálárustáq, Anazánkúh, Anazán-pusht-i-Áb, Ghulámí, Kúhsár, Andarún-Tanga, Láy, Ramadán, and Bard. The chief place is Yánisar; in this district there are three mountains—Khúsh-angúr, where the Governor has a summer residence and on the summit of which stands an *Imámzáda*, Kúh-'Abdu'lláhí, and Kaywánkúh; in the last named 68 *imámzádas* are said to be buried.

The streams of Sháhkúh, Tásh, and Chahárbágh run down the Chaman-i-Sáwar to Yánisar and Surkhgiriya, and thence, joining, become the Zárimrúd, which in turn flows into the Niká between Sárí and Ashraf.

The *bulúk* of Surkhgiriya, containing that of Yakhkash, is bordered on the south by Kúh-i-Tírparú and Kaftarkulí, on the north by Kúh-i-Khúsh-angúr, on the east by Khaṭírkhayl, and on the west by the Astálam or Astáram stream. It is subdivided into four *bulúks*: Zárimrúd, Tírkár, Achrustáq, and Bálárustáq. The small *bulúk* of Yakhkash numbers about 11 villages.

I was unable to obtain precise information about Súrtij. Its chief place is Kuyúsar, a village numbering 200 houses, where the Governor spends the summer.

The above information on the district of Hazárjaríb was obtained from well-informed chiefs but does not tally with that culled from the official Revenue Register, according to which the divisions of Hazárjaríb are:

Dúdánga: (*a*) ....; (*b*) Niyáft (or Banáft?).

Chahárdánga: (*a*) Achrustáq; (*b*) Anazánkúh; (*c*) Bálárustáq; (*d*) Bard; (*e*) Barkár; (*f*) Chálú; (*g*) Darká; (*h*) Ghulámí; (*i*) Kúhsár; (*j*) Kuyúsar; (*k*) Láy; (*l*) Mawáḍi'; (*m*) Miyánsí; (*n*) Payraja; (*o*) Sa'ída; (*p*) Sartíka; (*q*) Tírkár including Kháṣa-i-Ramadání; (*r*) Wardíma; (*s*) Wilwíma and Warí; (*t*) Zárimrúd. Yakhkash is given as part of Ashraf[1].

[1] Villages of Hazárjaríb; see Appendix I, L.

CHAPTER VII

Sárí to Nárinjbágh; bridge over the Tijin. Imámzáda 'Abbás. Shrine of Niká. Niká bridge and river. Road to Chahárdih. Nárinjbágh to Dhághmarz. Excursion to Miyánkala; fort of Palangán. The Miyánkala peninsula. Dhághmarz to Ashraf. Direct road from Niká to Ashraf. Ashraf: foundation, history, town quarters, public buildings, streams. Road to Sháhrúd. Districts. Ashraf to Nawkanda: Buland Imám. District of Kulbád. Galúgá. Road from Galúgá to Sháhrúd. The Jar-i-Kulbád. Nawkanda. Arrival at Bandargaz.

DEC. 6TH, 18 miles. We forded the Tijin river, as the great bridge of 17 arches built by Áqá Muḥammad Khán Qájár 2 miles from Sárí had had two arches carried away by the floods of the preceding spring. The Tijin is a fine stream with a gravelly bed. It rises in the mountains between Pulwar and Fúlád Maḥalla and drains the Hazárjaríb plateau; it enters the plain of Sárí 4 or 5 miles above the town and flows into the Caspian at Faraḥábád, 17 miles north of Sárí, having travelled in all about 75 miles. Below the present bridge are the remains of the piers of a former bridge said to have been built by Sháh 'Abbás.

Beyond the river lay the village of Ázádgala where we saw the Imámzáda 'Abbás. The shrine had two pairs of beautifully carved doors, on the outer pair of which was an inscription giving the names of the donor, Áqá Ḥusayn, and of the carpenter, Bahrám-i-Sárawí, residing at Iskandábád; the date—Jumádá II, 897/1492—was given in a chronogram. On the wooden chest over the grave were some verses from the *Qur'án*, the names of the donor, Sayyid Murtaḍá b. 'Alí b. Shamsu'd-Dín b. 'Abdu'ṣ-Ṣamad b. Shamsu'd-Dín, and the carpenter, Bahrám.

Passing Buland Újá, the village of Zughálchál, and Haywalá, which is on our left and closed in with the hills which at this point are low and close to the road, we reached a place called Qabr-i-Khátún, or the Lady's Tomb. Simiskanda is about 6 miles north-east of Sárí. We continued along Sháh 'Abbás's causeway which here ran close to the hill-side over uneven ground through a forest of lofty trees. We passed a square brick building on the road side called Sháṭir-Gunbad, or the Courier's Tower. We crossed over a brick bridge spanning the Bádila, a stream issuing from the hills to the east-south-east where lies the *maḥalla* of Lálím. The village of Súrak lay to the left of the road. In the hills to our right was a village called Dárábkalá, from which flowed between steep banks a rivulet named Khúra (84) which we crossed by a brick bridge. In the hills, with rocks towering above it, lay the village of Asram, about a mile to the south of the road. Beyond the villages of Askam and Bádila stood the hill of Valíja and a little further on was Takht-i-Rustam, a hill to the left of the road, 2½ miles west of Niká. The *Imámzáda* of Niká, where lies buried Sayyid 'Abdu'l-Muḥammad b. Mír Tawání, is a small building covered with tiles and containing two rooms, in the inner one of which is the tomb. The door is exquisitely carved and was made to the order of Darwísh Sikandar b. 'Izzu'd-Dín, known as al-Khudá, by the carpenter *Ustád* Ḥusayn b. Aḥmad al-Azárí (ar-Rází?). The date of the inscription is 1 Muḥarram 870/1466.

Twenty minutes through wheat fields and mulberry plantations brought us to the left bank of the Niká river which is spanned by a large bridge of two arches known as Pul-i-Niká. The river higher up is called Shamshírbur and is formed by the junction of two streams, the northern one rising in the Sháwar, Balambarán, and Siyáhmarkúh mountains, about 3 *farsakhs* north-west of Basṭám, while the southern one runs down from Sháhkúh. The Áb-i-Shamshírbur then receives the Barkúh on its left, the Lúliyán (Lúdiyán?) on its right, and the Túrúdbár on its left; it is then known as the Asp-wa-Nayza river, and, after receiving many tributaries, notably one coming from the Tang-i-Shúráb to the south-west, enters the plain of Niká. Here it changes its direction from east-south-east to north-west and flows into the Caspian in four branches.

We stop for the night at Nárinjbágh, a hamlet of 20 houses, which is part of Niká.

From Niká a road leads to Rádkán, 40 miles, thence to Asp-wa-Nayza, 5 miles, Rusú, 3 miles, and, passing the Tamash-Tang and Shamshírbur passes, ascends across a wide open level plain to Ḳushtaladasht, 5½ miles, and 2 miles further on to Sar-i-Halála (elevation 6500 feet), whence to Chahárdih, 4 miles. Total about 59½ miles.

Dec. 7th, 15 miles. On our right we saw Ismilí, then 'Alíkanda on our left, as well as the shrine of Sházdán, nearly a mile distant. Next we came to the village of Siyáhwashkalá. An hour out from Nárinjbágh we saw Ṭúskalá on our right, nearly hidden in the jungle, and an hour later, Walínawá. The next village was Khurshíd, also on our right. The path now lay through a jungle of lofty trees and followed for some time the bank of an old irrigation reservoir known as Báqilí-Ábbandán. Our direction was north by north-north-east. A small stream without a name marks the boundary of the *maḥall* of Dhághmarz, which is inhabited by the 'Abdu'l-Malikí tribe. Later on we crossed the 'Abdu'l-Malikí-kíla, a small branch of the Niká river.

Leaving the jungle here, the road wound its way through fields overgrown with gigantic ferns. After passing the hamlet of Táza-ábád-i-Kalak, we reached Dhághmarz where we were hospitably entertained by Qásim Khán, Huzhabr-i-Kháqán, the chief of the 'Abdu'l-Malikí tribe.

Dec. 8th, 14 miles. We crossed a barren plain, the Ṣaḥrá-i-Sháh Ḥusayn, which extends from the mouth of the Túskárúd stream, about 1 mile from Dhághmarz and 8 from Palangán. East of Túskárúd are the pastures of Yaktút, Gusháda, Yakwar-lapú (*lapú* = *murdáb*), and Shírkhánlapú. Later we passed a tree at the foot of which flowed a small stream called Chashmasar or Mullá Ṣádiq.

The peninsula of Miyánkala runs out eastwards from the mainland near Dhághmarz to a distance of about 30 miles and terminates in the three islands of Áshúr-áda. It is a low sandy stretch of land never over 3 or 4 miles in breadth, bordered to the north by low sand-hills, behind which there is an abundance of sour pomegranate and thorny bushes forming in places impenetrable thickets known here and in Astarábád by the name of *talú*. To the south the soil is very marshy and covered with tall rushes. On the south-west the peninsula is much indented, numerous shallow arms of water running inland (85). The few trees to be seen on the peninsula serve as landmarks; thus a mulberry tree marks the beginning of Ya'qúblanga and an old fig tree that of Palangán. The fort of Palangán (86), which is at about $1\frac{3}{4}$ hours' distance from Dhághmarz, is built on the western extremity of the peninsula. It is of octagonal shape with a tile-roofed tower at each corner, the distance between the towers being 80 paces.

By order of Náṣiru'd-Dín Sháh, and until about 1901, 35 soldiers from Ashraf were stationed at this fort as a protection against Turcoman pirates and to guard the royal preserves, as at that time it was strictly forbidden either to shoot over the peninsula or to graze cattle on it. Under Muẓaffaru'd-Dín Sháh, Miyánkala was thrown open and it now affords during the winter rich pastures for the numerous buffalo herds from Anazán and Faraḥábád.

Beyond Qal'a Palangán is the reservoir of Palangán-Asal, used for watering cattle, and further on that of Turk-Asal. After these we passed a venerable fig-tree, Ispí-Anjíl, which stood in the Changúr pasture and had given its name to this spot, and reached Dághdághán-Asal a reservoir full of filthy black mud where we camped for the night. The peninsula was well stocked with game, deer, wild boar, pheasants, woodcock, duck, etc., being plentiful; in fact the noise made at night by the various kinds of water-fowl was so deafening that we were prevented from sleeping.

From Túskábun, which is about a mile from Dhághmarz, it is about 8 miles to Palangán; next come Gú-Asal (*Gáw-Isṭalkh*), 8 miles; Tanga-Muqímí—the narrowest point on the peninsula —3 miles; Gúklashawar (*Gáw-kalla-shawar* = cow-head-depression, so named, it is said, because it is so muddy here that it is impossible to pass, and the buffalo herdsmen have to collect the skulls of dead cattle for stepping-stones), 3 miles; Lalawanga and then Khurmá, 4 miles. Khurmá is said to be the site of a former city. From Khurmá to Sartúk it is about 4 miles, and 2 miles from Sartúk to the end of the peninsula (87). We were told that it was possible to cross over to Áshúr-áda as the water between Miyánkala and the island was nowhere very deep. At Sartúk there stood formerly a fort built by order of Náṣiru'd-Dín Sháh and garrisoned until about 1903 by soldiers from Ashraf.

Dec. 12th, 17 miles. On leaving Dhághmarz we passed Zaynawand and Amírábád, crossed the Kaftarkhán stream by a brick bridge, then another stream, and reached the Chahár-Imám stream (88). On the farther side, near the small bridge which spans this stream, stands the Imámzáda Chahár-Imám, a small, square, tile-roofed building with an inner and an outer room.

The road now crossed an extensive grassy plain, marshy in parts, but consisting chiefly of firm, rich, meadow land. Similar plains occur between Faraḥábád and Dhághmarz, and, according to de Morgan's map, bear the following names: Anármarz Chul, Lalamarz Chul, Sihpushta Chul, Zulánkútí Chul and Múẓak Chul. To the south we could see two mounds, Surkhdím and Imám Taqí (89).

Qarátappa numbers 160 houses and has a mixed population of Gílaks and Afgháns, and is built on a large mound. West of the village flows the Bahrám 'Alí-Kíla spanned by a two-arched bridge, whilst south of it is the Atrip-Kíla which is crossed over by a small bridge of 5 arches. To the north of Qarátappa is another mound called Sháltappa or Shigháltappa. Qarátappa has a small landing-stage on the bay of Astarábád, about 2 miles north of the village at a place called Kinára.

From Qarátappa to Ashraf is about 6 miles. Beyond Turújan, where we crossed the stream of the same name and joined Sháh 'Abbás's causeway, were some houses and the *Imámzáda* of Zírwán, and a place called Qádí-Kiyáb, above which on high ground stood the ruined palace of Ṣafí-ábád.

Mackenzie, who went from Niká to Ashraf by the ordinary route, relates that from Qizillí, at the foot of the hills, he rode over the bridge which spans the Niká river into the *bulúk* of Miyándúrúd. On his left were Nárinjbágh and 'Imáratsar. Several streams were forded, and at length he reached a rivulet near the village of Chálapul which lay to his right. Further on to the left was the village of Miyánkalá, and, a little distance from it, Shayṭán Maḥalla. Near the village of Shúrábsar is a salt spring which gives its name to the *maḥalla*. The road all day lay along the foot of the hills, and to its left beyond Shúrábsar was a village of 95 houses called Kulít. Here the *bulúk* of Panj-Hazár began. To the north of the road was the *maḥalla* of Rustamkalá and Gurjí Maḥalla, then the Kúsán stream (90) was crossed and the road led through mulberry plantations and pomegranate bushes to Turújan.

Ashraf, latitude 36° 41′ 55″ north, longitude 53° 32′ 30″ east, is about 5 miles from the Caspian. It lies at the foot of mountains and is backed by lofty wooded spurs; to the north extends a fine view over the bay of Astarábád. Several springs rising upon the hill-sides behind flow through it.

Ashraf owes its now fallen greatness to Sháh 'Abbás-i-Ṣafawí, and its decline dates from that of the Ṣafawí dynasty. It was formerly named Kharkúrán and belonged to an old woman, from whom Sháh 'Abbás bought it. He founded the new town in 1021/1612 (the date is recorded in the chronogram *Dawlat-i-Ashraf*), chose it for his residence in Mázandarán, and endowed it with numerous palaces and gardens. Suffering much from civil wars and the invasions of Turcomans, it was plundered and destroyed during the Afghán rule in Persia, and suffered again when the Zand armies came to Mázandarán.

Gmélin mentions that it was not the intention of Sháh 'Abbás to build a large city or a fortified palace. He wished nature alone to afford him the innocent and rural pleasures which he purposed tasting here. Ashraf, therefore, was at first simply a collection of large farm-houses constructed without any art and scattered in a plain interspersed with small woods. Some of these farms surrounded the royal castle, whilst others were spread along the avenue which led from Sárí. At the time of Gmélin's visit there only existed at Ashraf a few ruined huts, and the royal palaces had become the haunts of wild beasts. They had been devastated and were almost totally destroyed, whilst the wonderful gardens had degenerated into thickets into which it was wellnigh impossible to penetrate (91).

Nádir spent some time here during the famous campaign against the Lasghís. 'Ádil Sháh, who succeeded him, also visited Ashraf occasionally, but after his death this part of Persia seems to have become the refuge of insurgents who wreaked their vengeance on anything they could lay hands on. Nevertheless, Muḥammad Ḥasan Khán had a marked predilection for Ashraf, where he often resided, and undertook the principal repairs of the royal residence. When he succeeded Naẓar Khán Zand as Governor of Mázandarán, Muḥammad Khán of Sawádkúh, by whose treachery Muḥammad Ḥasan Khán Qájár was defeated and killed at Qaráduwín, thought it necessary for his own safety to reduce Ashraf to ruins. Faraḥábád, 'Alí-ábád, and Sárí suffered the same fate. His excuse for this wanton destruction was that he thus rendered it more difficult for the Turcomans to reach the other districts of the province. It was only after he had, by order of Karím Khán, built a rampart east of Kulbád, from the mountain to the sea, as a protection against the Turcomans, that he began rebuilding the three last-mentioned towns. He did nothing, however, for Ashraf, which was almost uninhabited until Áqá Muḥammad Khán Qájár escaped from Shíráz and came to Astarábád and induced the people to rebuild Ashraf. Since then Ashraf has recovered something of its old prosperity, although it can never attain the position it occupied when it was the residence of the Court of Persia.

The inhabitants are of mixed race; there are descendants of a Georgian colony, brought from the Caucasus by Sháh 'Abbás, some Ṭálish families from the coast near Lankurán, and a few Tát (a Persian tribe) and Gúdar families.

Ashraf in 1859 numbered 845 houses and 70 shops, 4 quarters,

4 *madrasas*, 5 warm baths, 5 mosques, 5 *takyas*, and 1 *Imámzáda*. To-day it has 7 quarters, viz.: Naqqásh Maḥalla, Bázár Maḥall, Gurjí Maḥalla, Farrásh Maḥalla including Chashmasar and Bágh-i-Sháh, Ṭálish Maḥalla, a second Ṭálish Maḥalla or Gálish Maḥalla, Giraylí Maḥalla. The total number of houses is said to be over 1000, but many of the inhabitants only live here during the winter. There are 3 bazaars, 150 shops, 4 caravanserais, 6 baths, 10 mosques, to wit: Jámi', Báshí, Gulshan, with a *madrasa*, Chál, Ákhúnd, Dáru'sh-Shifá, Gurjí, Sarábdang, Arbáb with a *madrasa*, and Náṣir Khán (92), 6 *takyas* (Báshí, Bázár Maḥalla, Qatlgáh, Gurjí, Arbáb, and Náṣir Khán), and 5 *ábanbárs* or water cisterns.

Ashraf and the surrounding country are irrigated by the Barzú stream, the Sárú stream which runs down from 'Abbásábád (93), and the Khalíl Maḥalla and Rubáṭ rivulets which rise in the mountains of Yakhkash. The fields in the immediate vicinity of the town are watered from springs and reservoirs. The plain of Ashraf is especially pleasant in spring when the numerous pastures, such as Basú (Barsú ?), Súzdím, Palhamkútí, Jangdín, Wargakhúsa, etc., are carpeted with every variety of wild flower.

The road from Ashraf to Sháhrúd has five stages: Galúgá, Niyálá, Rádkán, Tásh, and Sháhrúd. The distance is given by natives as 27½ *farsakhs*. From Ashraf to Niyálá the road follows a branch of the famous causeway, after which the country is very mountainous; the road, however, is said to be fairly good on the whole.

Sháhkíla, the port of Ashraf on the Bay of Astarábád, has 50 houses.

On the south the district of Ashraf is bounded by the mountains of Hazárjaríb, on the east by Anazán, on the west by Miyándúrúd, and on the north by the Caspian Sea and the Bay of Astarábád. Ashraf comprises the following *bulúks*: (*a*) Balada; (*b*) Qaráṭughán; (*c*) Kulbád; (*d*) Panj-hazár; (*e*) Yakhkash[1].

Dec. 14th, 14½ miles. We followed Sháh 'Abbás's causeway and after crossing an old bridge over the deep, dry bed of a torrent, we came to a hill about a mile out from Ashraf where there was a village of some 40 houses called Áltappa. The next village is Sárú which has a shrine where Imámzáda 'Abdu'lláh is buried, consisting of a tower surmounted by a cone, with a square, tile-roofed, outer room adjoining. After Sárú we saw about one mile

[1] Villages of Ashraf; see Appendix I, M.

to the right a white *Imámzáda*, that of Áqá Sayyid Ḥasan in Pásand, whilst on our left lay Rán. Then on the road-side was the Imámzáda Dukhtar-i-Imám. The next villages were Walámúzí and Limrásk. Here on the banks of a small brook about 12 miles from Ashraf is the Imámzáda Buland Imám. An inscription dated 873/1468–9 states that the door was made to the order of Sayyid Zaynu'l-'Ábidín b. Sayyid Isma'íl by Ḥusayn b. *Ustád* Aḥmad *Najjár* of Sárí. We passed the village and stream of Siráj Maḥalla, the large village and stream of Talínú, and after passing through the village of Tírtásh, situated on the slope of the hill, came to Khurshídkalá which is 16 miles east of Ashraf and belongs to Kulbád (94).

The small district of Kulbád extends about 1 *farsakh* from Buland Imám on the west to the Jar-i-Kulbád on the east; it numbers some 10 villages. The country here is comparatively open and well cultivated; the mountains are covered with forest whilst the plain has been cleared to a great extent and the sea-shore is entirely free of forest to a breadth of several miles.

The next village on the road was Galúgá, a large one, numbering 600 houses with 5 mosques or *takyas*, to wit: Masjid-i-Mullá 'Abbás, Takya-i-Áqá, Masjid-i-Ḥájjí Faraj, Takya-i-Qúpchí, Masjid-i-Gulshan; and 4 baths. The inhabitants were Imránlú Turks with 9 clans, which give their names to the different quarters of the village.

Blarenberg informs us that, according to the inhabitants, twenty years before his visit in 1836 A.D. the sea covered the whole of the beach here and reached the mound of Qaráduwín, near which Muḥammad Ḥasan Khán Qájár was slain and where Count Voinovitch built a fort in 1782.

There is a mountain path from Galúgá to Sháhrúd, the distance being: over a pass 5000 feet high, 5 miles; Barkalá, 3 miles; Rádkán, 4 miles; Asp-u-Nayza, which is 2 miles south of Ḥájjí-ábád, 8 miles; Tang-i-Lúdyán gorge, 2¾ miles; Burzanday, 6¾ miles; Dú-áb-i-Burzanday, 1¾ miles; Sháh-Kúh-Pá'ín, 2¼ miles; Chalchalyán pass, 8 miles; over the defile of Gandáb to Rubáṭ of Tásh, 7½ miles; Kaláta, 14½ miles; and Sháhrúd, 5¼ miles; total 65¼ miles.

After Galúgá we continued our way for some time through a jungle of all kinds of forest trees and bushes to the Jar-i-Kulbád, which serves as a boundary of the province of Mázandarán. It is a high green rampart of earth with a moat east of it which runs from the base of the mountains through the forest and over the marshy plain to the shore. This rampart was raised a few years before Gmélin's visit (1771 A.D.) by the governor of Mázandarán, Muḥammad Khán of Sawádkúh, to prevent the Turcomans from overrunning Mázandarán. There were 9 forts in the line between the mountain and the sea.

About 4 miles from the Jar-i-Kulbád we reached Líwán, then Ṭulúr, and finally Nawkanda. Nawkanda, the chief place of Anazán, is a large village said to contain 600 houses. The inhabitants are divided into 12 clans: Minúchihrí, Kard, Bú 'Alí, Naẓar, Mullá Khán (to which belong the *Kháns* of the village), Mázandarání, Jahánsháh, Kashír, Shírbatí, Áhangar, Shuháb and Qájár. Ṭulúr and Mazang are part of Nawkanda. The inhabitants of Ṭulúr belong to 4 clans: Áhangar, Rúdgar, Minúchihrí, and Kalákurd; those of Mazang to the Ḥájjí-Bágh, Lur, Sádát, and Súrtijí clans. The forest of Mazang is very fine and is called Malúmarang, that between Nawkanda and Kurd Maḥalla is known as Qarájangal.

A path leads from Nawkanda to Wazwár and thence to Rádkán, a distance of about 10 miles.

Dec. 15th, 4 miles. Crossing the rivers Nawkanda and Jifákanda, we reached Bandargaz (sometimes called Kinára), the port of Astarábád, after an hour and a half's ride through rice and cotton fields[1].

[1] See *Report on the Trade and General Condition of the City and Province of Astarábád*, by H. L. Rabino, Diplomatic and Consular Report, Annual Series, No. 4381, pp. 7-8.

CHAPTER VIII

Bay of Astarábád: Count Voinovitch. Streams. Áshúráda. Gaz. District of Anazán: description. Gaz to Kafshgírí: Kharába-Shahr. Tamísha. Kurd Mahalla. District of Sadan-Rustáq. Streams. Shrine of Rawshanábád. Kafshgírí to Astarábád. Astarábád: origin. Chronicles. Muqaddasí's description. Situation. Walls. Gates. Town-quarters. Public buildings. Masjid-i-Jámi'. Inscription. Governor's palace. Inhabitants.

THE Bay of Astarábád forms one of the most sheltered roadsteads in the Caspian, being protected to the north by the Peninsula of Miyánkala (called by the Russians Potemkin) and the Áshúráda islands. It is some 42 miles long, and its greatest width in the eastern portion is about 8 miles. Its depth decreases rapidly towards the western end, and the Bay itself, I was told, had greatly diminished in area during the last 60 years. From Puschin's account the following rivers and streams flow into the Bay: Qaráṣú, Bághú or Siyáhjú, Sar-Maḥalla, Walafrá, Gaz, Hashtyaka, Jifákanda, Mazang, Nawkanda, Najjárkalá, Líwán, Jar-i-Kulbád, Khurshídkalá, Siráj Maḥalla, Kalákíla, Sháhkíla, Mullákíla, Káẓimkíla, Qarátappa, Bahrám 'Alí kíla, Surgunjakíla ?, Chahár-Imám, Kaftar-khán, and Kupúr-Burún. All these streams rise in the range of mountains to the south; the only two of any size are the Qaráṣú and the Bághú.

Áshúráda, or the island of Áshúr, is composed of three islands, the greater, the middle, and the lesser. The lesser, which is the most easterly of the three, is now the largest, and has 10 to 15 fishermen's huts on its western extremity. The middle one is uninhabited, whilst on the so-called greater, which is really the smallest, is the Russian Naval Station. It was in 1841 that Count Mede, Russian Minister in Persia, obtained from the Sháh permission for Russia to occupy the islands of Áshúráda and use them as a Naval Station with a view to putting a stop to the piratical expeditions of the Turcomans. Already in 1781 Count Voinovitch had been sent in command of a Russian squadron to found a settlement on the south-eastern coast of the Caspian. He chose Ashraf for this settlement, and so certain was he of success that he changed its name to Melissopol, "the town of Bees," and

5—2

obtained from the College of Arms at Petrograd armorial bearings for the new city.

Áqá Muḥammad Khán, however, refused to allow the occupation of Ashraf by the Count, who was, therefore, compelled to change his plans and build instead a fort at Qaráduwín near Galúgá, purposing thereafter to establish a permanent settlement on one of the islands (95) of the bay, which was to be called Melitonis, "Isle of the Bees." How Áqá Muḥammad Khán invited the Russian commodore and his officers to Astarábád, and there detained them in prison until they sent orders to the squadron to demolish the buildings which they had erected, is related by Forster, who passed through Mázandarán shortly afterwards[1].

Gaz lies about 2 miles from the shore of the bay of Astarábád; it belongs to Anazán, and consists of 9 *maḥallas*: Kúykhayl, Tamískánakhayl, Bádkhayl, Kurdkhayl, Báykhayl, a second Kurdkhayl, Maḥalla-i-Sháh, Kúh-Ṣahrá, and Sháhpasand; the last named is in the forest and no longer inhabited. It has about 450 houses. Until some five years ago (about 1904), most of the inhabitants owned horses and worked as *chárwadárs* between Bandargaz and Astarábád. They had found, however, that the cultivation of cotton was more remunerative, and they had, therefore, sold their horses.

Anazán[2] lies to the west of the province of Astarábád, and extends 10 miles from north to south and 12 from east to west. It is bordered on the north by the Caspian, on the north-east by the Yamút country, on the east by Sadan-Rustáq, from which it is separated by the Kurd Maḥalla stream, on the south by Sadan-Rustáq and the Hazárjaríb district of Mázandarán, and on the west by the Jar-i-Kulbád. It is thinly populated, covered with forest to a greater extent than any other portion of Astarábád and Mázandarán, and watered by numerous small streams, which rise in the mountains to the south of the district and flow in deep and muddy beds. These streams are the Nawkanda, Jifákanda, Gaz, Walafrá, Sar Maḥalla, Sarṭáq, Kalafrá, Bághú and Kárkanda. The villages are completely buried in the forest, upon which the cultivated clearings have made little impression. Most of the inhabitants remove to the *yayláqs* of Hazárjaríb for the

[1] Forster, *A Journey from Bengal to England*, vol. 2, pp. 225–227. See also Dorn, *Reise*, pp. 137–140.

[2] Villages of Anazán; see Appendix I, N.

hot season. There is a shrine called Safíd-Cháh, where people usually spend a few days every year.

Dec. 16th, 16 miles. Our road lay along Sháh 'Abbás's causeway. Beyond the dry bed of a torrent called the Rúdkhána-i-Gaz, where Gaz ends, we passed the Líwár stream which flows through Walafrá, forded the Sar Maḥalla, passed the village of Bághú, and crossing the Miyánrúd (which, I believe, is the same as the Kárkanda stream), reached an *Imámzáda* of some pretensions, built on a spot called Kharába-Shahr, or "the ruined city," and surrounded by an extensive cemetery.

An inscription over the door of the *Imámzáda* stated that it contained the tomb of Imámzáda Qásim, and that the edifice was rebuilt, by order of Muhammad Qulí Bayg, under the supervision of Shaykh, by *Ustád* Niyáruk the carpenter. The inscription is dated 1124/1712.

From a close study of the history and topography of Mázandarán, I am of opinion that here stood the former town of Tamísha (96), the residence of Firídún, the ruins of whose palace were still visible in Ibn Isfandiyár's time at a place called Bá-Nasrán, as also the domes and cupola of his bath, with the remains of the moat which he caused to be dug from the mountain to the sea. This moat was to protect Mázandarán against the invasions of the Túrán tribes, and the country east and north-east of it was known as Bírún-Tamísha (*i.e.* outside Tamísha). According to Ẓahíru'd-Dín, Bírún-Tamísha is the same as Astaráḅád. The walls of Tamísha were destroyed by order of Mázyár b. Qárin, but were rebuilt at a later period. The date of the destruction of Tamísha is not known, although there are reasons for supposing that it took place at the time of the Mongol invasion. The Iṣpahbad Bahrám (512/1118-9) besieged his nephew, Rustam b. Dárá, for a whole month at Tamísha, and eventually set fire to the forest to compel him to surrender. Rustam held out until the fire reached the gates and houses of the city, and then fled to Sí-Rustáq and Panjáh-Hazár.

About 100 yards beyond Kharába Shahr is the rivulet of Alwand Kiyá (97). We next crossed the Khushkafal, the wide, dry bed of the Shírdárbun stream, and the Shishdáng rivulet. Kurd Maḥalla, which we pass, is the chief place of Sadan-Rustáq. It is of some importance, containing 700 houses, and is situated half a mile to the north of the road in the midst of a dense forest about 16 miles from Astarábád. It has a small port, known as

Mullákíla, about 3 miles distant, to the north of the Qaráṣú river; it is much frequented by Turcoman boats, which bring naphtha and salt, and carry away charcoal and wood.

The inhabitants of Kurd Maḥalla are divided into 31 clans, namely: Áhangar, Ardashír, Gharíb, Kashír, Máyák, Mu'allam, Sístání, Záhid, 'Aqílí, Dallák, Ghulám, Khíshán, Mázandarání, Najjár, Ṣulbí, Záramrúdí, Alwand Kiyá, Darzí, Ḥabashí, Kiyá, Mahdiyán, Pás, Turk, Zangí, 'Arab, Garshásf, Ḥusayní, Minúchihrí, Misgar, Rashtí, and Yazdí, of which the two most influential are the Kiyá and 'Aqílí (*Sayyids*).

The district of Sadan-Ṛustáq lies to the west of the town of Astarábád, extending from the sea to the foot of the mountains. It is bordered on the west by Anazán and the Caspian; on the east it reaches the Mázandarán gate of Astarábád; on the north it is bounded by the Siyáh-Áb, a tributary of the Qaráṣú, and on the south by the Kútal-i-Jahánnumá, which leads to Hazárjaríb. It measures about 20 miles from east to west, and half that distance from north to south, and consists of a forest-covered, swampy tract, where cotton, rice, and grain are cultivated to a considerable extent. The district is exposed to the raids of the Ja'farbáy Turcomans, who have their encampments on its northern border, and not a week passes without two or three men being killed in encounters between villagers and raiders. The inhabitants are Qájárs, *Sayyids*, Táts and Giraylí Turks. The principal streams from east to west are: Kharába-Shahr, or Alwand Kiyá, Kurd Maḥalla, Alwár, Miyándarra, Yálú or Shaṣtḳalá, and the Áb-i-Kúpán[1].

After Kurd Maḥalla we found ourselves once more on Sháh 'Abbás's causeway. Half way between Kurd Maḥalla and Kafsh-gírí there was a deep ravine, called Siyáh-darra, and beyond it the road continued over the Rúd-i-Bálájáda, through wheat fields belonging to Chahárdih, to the village of Alwár. We next crossed the Dangalán stream and passed the village of the same name on our left, as also a small hill, behind which could be seen Sháhdih.

After negotiating the dry bed of a torrent we reached the *Imámzáda* of Rawshanábád, where there is a large cemetery. The shrine has a dome, which was formerly covered with blue tiles, and now affords a resting-place for large numbers of pigeons. It contains the graves of Ibráhím and Muḥammad, brothers of Imám Riḍá. The doors were of oak, finely carved with inscriptions

[1] Villages of Sadan-Rustáq; see Appendix I, o.

from the *Qur'án*. The wooden sarcophagus over the graves was the work of *Ustád* Ḥájjí 'Abdu'lláh, and bore the date 879/1474–5; the caligraphist's name was Niẓám. The door of the inner chamber was the work of *Ustád* Káẓim b. 'Alí Níshápúrí, and was dated 1 Sha'bán 877/1473. The outer door was made by *Ustád* Naṣru'lláh in 865/1460–1.

From Rawshanábád we followed the small stream of Kafshgírí also called Shaṣtkalá (98) and reached the village of Kafshgírí which numbers some 250 houses.

Dec. 17th, 9 miles. We left for Astarábád about 9 miles distant. We saw to our left the village of Lamisk, with the Imámzáda Panj-Tan, a square building with two rooms. An inscription above the inner door informs the faithful that the shrine known as Panj-Tan was repaired in 1223/1808 by Mullá Shams 'Alí of Lamisk. The inner door is of carved wood, but of much inferior workmanship to what we had hitherto seen. It bore an undated inscription which stated that the door was made by order of 'Alí b. Shamsu'd-Dín and was the work of *Ustád* Muḥammad b. Yádgár Sárawí, resident at Ḥusaynábád. Inside, a large, plain, wooden sarcophagus covered 5 graves.

After Lamisk we passed a spot known as Ṣaḥrá-i-Gáwpíchán, then the villages of Zangí-Maḥalla and Újábun, and, when close to Astarábád, we beheld to our right a high mound, apparently the remains of some ancient fortress, which is called Qal'a-Khandán or, sometimes, Khal'at-Púshán. It lies to the south-west of the town, and its slopes and summits are covered with brushwood, chiefly wild capers. It is approached by a winding path, and rises about 50 or 60 feet above the small and tortuous Khwája Khiḍr stream which flows past at its foot. Between the Qal'a-Khandán and the city stands a small building called Qadamgáh-i-Khiḍr.

Astarábád was known under the early Ṣafawí monarchs as "*Dáru'l-Mulk*"; its present title of "*Dáru'l-Mú'minín*," or "Abode of the Faithful," is probably due to the great number of *Sayyids*, or descendants of the Prophet, residing there.

Ibn Isfandiyár relates that the mule-herds of Gurgín, son of Mílád, and founder of Gurgán, used to graze their charges on the ground where now stands Astarábád, and that the town sprang up to meet their needs, and took its name from their mules, *astar*. When Gurgín destroyed the town of Gurgán, its inhabitants removed to Astarábád.

According to another version, the town was founded on the site of a village named Astarak by Yazíd b. Muhallab, an Arab chief, who commanded the troops of Sulaymán, seventh Umayyad Caliph.

Abu'l-Fidá asserts that the name of the town is derived from that of a man named Astar, whilst in the Jámi'-i-Anbiyá its origin is ascribed to Astara, the wife of Sháhzáda Kay-Khusraw.

No histories of Astarábád and Gurgán (99) have reached us and the general histories of Persia contain but little reference to these cities. The information we have is, therefore, very scanty and incomplete.

Colonel Lovett says that "the site of the town has been selected owing to the natural advantages it possesses as regards water-supply and situation between the passes leading south and the old towns north of the Atrak, long since in ruins, such as Mash-had-i-Miṣriyán for instance."

Writing in the 4th (10th) century, Muqaddasí describes Astarábád as a fine town having the best climate of all the surrounding region, and producing chiefly raw silk. In his day the fortress was already in ruins, for the Buwayhids had ravaged all the country during their wars against the Ziyárids; Muqaddasí adds that the Friday Mosque built at the time of the first Moslem conquest was still standing in the market-place near the city gate.

Amír Walí (754–784/1353–81) had a moat dug round Astarábád, and Pírak Pádsháh (786–809/1384–1406) built a wall round the town and a castle for its protection.

Astarábád[1] is situated about 3 miles from the hills and about 20 miles east-north-east of Bandargaz in an elevated position, and is of irregular form. It is surrounded by a mud wall and ditch, with round towers, formerly tiled, at intervals. The wall has a circumference of about 4 miles, and is so much out of repair that the Turcomans are able to enter the city during the night without difficulty. Near the middle of the eastern wall of the city stands the ruined fort of Muḥammad Ḥusayn Khán Qájár, who was governor of Astarábád in the time of Nádir. Being suspected of nursing an intention to revolt, he was ordered by the Sháh to demolish it.

There are five town gates, all in a more or less dilapidated condition: Basṭám to the east, Chihildukhtarán to the south, Mázandarán to the west, Sabz-Mashhad or Fújird (probably the

[1] Long. 54° 25′ 26″ east, lat. 36° 50′ 52″ north, elevation 377 ft.

former Gurgán gate) to the north, and Dankawán, which is not used. A great portion of the ground within the walls is taken up by gardens, fields, and waste places.

The town has three quarters: Na'lbandán with its subdivisions, Míkhchagarán, Shírkush, Bágh-i-Sháh, Balúch, Pá-yi-Sarw or Hímadúzán; Maydán with its subdivisions, Takya-i-'Abbás 'Alí, Darb-i-Naw, Takya-i-Dúshanbí, Mír-Karímí, Dú-Chinárán, and Gáwbandán; and Sabz Mashhad, formerly known as Súkhta-Takya, including Sar-chashma, Sar-Pír, Dabbághán, Takya-i-Khán, Naqqárchiyán, and Chamandiyán now ruined. The population is about 10,000. There are 40 mosques and *takyas,* 11 shrines, 8 theological schools or colleges, 13 water-cisterns or *ábanbárs,* and 14 public baths.

The mosques are: Na'lbandán, Jámi', Bankashíhá, Áqá Mír Mú'min, Ḥájjí Muḥammad Ḥasan Mi'már, Ḥájjí Muḥammad Riḍá, Gulshan, Dú-Chinárán or Muḥammad Báqir Khán, Bágh-i-Sháh, Safíd, Shírkush, Míkhchagarán, Pá-yi-Sarw, Na'lbaygí, Mír Karímí, Ḥájjí 'Alí, mosque near the house of the *Kalántar,* Kásagarán, Sháhzáda Qásim, Bágh-i-Palang, Mullá Mírzá Ḥusayn, mosque near the house of 'Abbás Qulí Áqá Ghulám-Báshí, Ḥájjí Áqá Muḥammadí, Mullá 'Alí, Daylamíhá or Maqbara, Musallá, mosque and *takya* Bí-Sar, Imám Ḥasan, Sar-Pír, Sar-Chashma, Mullá 'Alí, Dabbághán, Qádí, Kúchik, Naqqárchiyán, Ḥájjí Maḥmúd Áqá, 'Alí Khán, Qájár, Panáhbaygí, and Darwáza-i-Fújird.

The shrines are: Rúbandbarú near the Basṭám Gate, Muḥsin known as Chahárshanba, Sháhzáda Qásim, Qadamgáh-i-Khiḍr outside the Mázandarán Gate, Panja-i-'Abbás 'Alí, Nuh-Tan (١٠٠), Dúshanba in which are buried two sisters, Raḍiyya and Marḍiyya, Bíbí Ḥúr, Bíbí Núr, Murád Bakhsh, 'Abdu'lláh outside the Fújird Gate, Núr or Sháhzáda Is-ḥáq, and Bíbí Sabz in which is buried a daughter of Imám Músạ Káẓim.

The *madrasas* are: Dáru'sh-Shifá, Ḥájjí Mullá Ridá, Sipah-sálár, Ḥájjí Muḥammad Taqí Khán, Áqá Muḥsin, 'Imádiyya or Darwáza-i-Naw, Sádát, and Ḥájji Muḥammad Ṣáliḥ.

The Masjid-i-Jámi', or chief mosque, of Astarábád is remarkable for the number of inscriptions it contains. It has a large inner court with a big tank of water. The *Mihráb* surmounted by a high dome is to the east and not in the proper direction prescribed by *Shí'ah* tradition, a fact due to the mosque having been originally intended as a place of worship for the *Sunní* sect.

The *minbar*, or pulpit, is of wood mosaic and inlet work and bears two inscriptions. The first states that the mosque was begun under the rule of the King of Kings of the Arabs and Persians, Mu'ínu'd-Dín, Abu'l-Qásim Bábur Bahádur Khán, by Bábá Ḥusayn, a descendant of Abí 'Abdu'lláh, and completed during the reign of Sháh 'Abbás-i-Safawí by Quṭbu'd-Dín Aḥmad b. Mullá 'Alí al-Astarábádí. The inscription is dated 15 Sha'bán 1018/1609. The second inscription, dated 1 Dhu'l-qa'da 1157/1745, places on record that the mosque and pulpit were restored under Nádir, Emperor of Persia, India, Turkestan, and Túrán, by Ḥájjí Qurbán Áqá, steward of Muḥammad Ḥusayn Khán Qájár, governor (Bayglar-Baygí) of Astarábád.

The other inscriptions are on slabs of stone and are to the following effect:

(*a*) Restoration of the mosque under Nádir, by order of Muḥammad Ḥusayn Khán, Bayglar-Baygí of Astarábád, by his steward Ḥájjí Qurbán, 1157/1745.

(*b*) *Farmán* of Sháh 'Abbás directing that the inhabitants of the village of Yasáqí (Jamá'at-i-Yasáqí) who, instead of paying a poll tax, were assessed collectively at a sum of 4 *túmáns* and had in consequence abandoned their village, should in future be taxed in proportion to the number of sheep and cattle they owned.

(*c*) On the arrival of Sulṭán Muḥammad Dhú'l-qadar, son of Mír 'Alá'u'd-Dawla, as governor, the inhabitants complained that they could not afford to change the copper currency. This custom, therefore, was abolished, and the person who brought this about was Khwája Sayfu'd-Dín Muẓaffar Tabakchí (101). Date 1 Jumádá II, 937/1531.

(*d*) *Farmán* of Sháh Abu'n-Naṣr b. Sháh Isma'íl II, abolishing the tax paid by slaves on receiving their freedom, 1029/1620.

(*e*) *Waqf-Náma*, dated 25 Dhu'l-qa'da 1042/1633. Khusraw Khán, Governor of Astarábád, directs that the revenue derived from a caravanserai and part of a *qanát*, both in the Shúr-Ájurí square of Astarábád, should, after deducting the cost of their maintenance, be spent on the upkeep and lighting of the 5 mosques, Jámi', Muṣallá, Bázár, Ḥájjí Tabrízí, and Safíd, the fountain of Muṣallá and Panj Imám, and the Minaret on the Maydán-i-Shúr, the keeper of the Masjid-i-Jámi' receiving a monthly allowance of 12 *hazárdínárs* and 10½ *mans* of sesame oil for the lights of his own mosque, and 5 *hazárdínárs* and 4 *mans* of oil for the 4 other mosques, the keeper of the Muṣallá 1 *túmán* a month, and the *mú'adhdhin* of the minaret in the Maydán-i-Shúr 12 *hazárdínárs* a month.

(*f*) The taxes of *Kútwálí* (keeper of the castle), *Qúruqchí Gírí* (guard of the royal preserves), and *Ráhtaráshí* (repairs to roads) levied by former governors are abolished by order of Sháh 'Abbás II, date Sha'bán 1055/1645.

(*g*) Hunters, fishermen, falconers, and artisans engaged in work connected with those callings are, from the beginning of Bárs Íl, exempted from certain taxes which they formerly paid, date Jumádá II 1047/1637.

The other inscriptions we found in Astarábád were: an inscription in the Madrasa-i-Muḥammad Taqí Khán, giving in a chronogram the date of foundation, 1245/1829–30; an inscription in the Imámzáda Chahárshanba stating that the shrine was built in 1224/1809–10 by Naẓar 'Alí Khán; an inscription over the entrance of the *Ábanbár* of the Takya-i-Dabbághán, giving in a chronogram the date of the building of the cistern by Ḥájjí Muḥammad 'Alí, 1010/1601–2; an inscription over the door of the minaret in the cemetery of Sabz Mashhad, known formerly as Maydán-i-Shúr, to the effect that the Minaret was erected in 1055/1645–6 under 'Abbás II by Ḥájjí Muqrí son of Ḥájjí 'Alí Jurjání; an inscription in the Imámzáda Murád-Bakhsh recording that a certain Ghulám Sháh Gúkcha made a *qanát waqf* for the benefit of the inhabitants of Astarábád, date 960/1552–3; an inscription in the Takya-i-Dabbághán, dated 1155/1742–3, stating that Mírzá Muḥammad Báqir made *waqf* a house attached to the *takya* and half a *qanát* in Ḥájjí-ábád known as Qanát-i-Bázíd, the revenue derived from them to go towards the upkeep of the *takya* and the expenses of the keeper; and, lastly, an inscription recording that the same person had assigned the revenue derived from a *qanát* in the village of Gáwzan for the expenses of the passion play in the *takya*.

On the frame of the inner door of the Imámzáda Núr is carved an inscription stating that the door was made by Ḥájjí Muḥammad by order of Amír Jalálu'd-Dín Báyazíd al-Jalílí al-Ḥusayní in Rajab, 857/1453. A similar inscription, written by one Yúsuf, son of Shukrí Darbandí, exists in the Imámzáda 'Abdu'lláh to the effect that the door was made by the order of Kayfarín Sháh b. Shamsu'd-Dín in Dhu'l-qa'da 873/1469. An inscription in plasterwork in the same shrine states that 'Abbás Khán, governor of Astarábád, repaired the building; the date being given in a chronogram.

The governor's palace is in the southern corner of the town and was built by Áqá Muḥammad Khán Qájár; an inscription over the principal entrance, dated 1206/1791–2, relates that all the buildings erected by Áqá Muḥammad Khán and situated near the prison, *anbár*, were made *waqf* and dedicated to the twelve *Imáms*.

There are numerous pious foundations to ensure an adequate supply of water for the wants of the inhabitants of Astarábád; thus Ghulám Sháh Gúkcha Sulṭán in 960/1552–3 gave a *qanát* to the people of Astarábád, whilst Khusraw Khán in 1042/1633 assigned the revenue of a *qanát* (now ruined) which passed through the Maydán-i-Shúr-Ájurí, for the upkeep of certain religious buildings. The most important foundation, however, was that made in Rabí' I 941/1534 by Khwája Sayfu'd-Dawla wa'd-Dín Muẓaffar b. Khwája Fakhru'd-Dunyá wa'd-Dín Aḥmad al-Tabakchí, by which he left 3 *sang* of water out of 18¼ *sang* of the Ziyárat-i-Khwásta-Rúd stream to the city of Astarábád, directing that it should flow from house to house, and thus benefit all the inhabitants alike. Unscrupulous *Sayyids* and *Mullás* have since appropriated these water-rights, with the result that, in summer, the poorer inhabitants are put to much inconvenience through lack of water.

The population of the town is very mixed and consists of *Sayyids*, or descendants of the Prophet, *Búmís*, or natives of the province, *Qájárs*, Turks, and some Balúchís and Kurramís.

The *Sayyids* belong to the Mír Majídí, Baní Karímí, 'Aqílí, Mír-Kamálu'd-Díní, Dirázgísú, Mard Mú'min, Shírangí (from the village of Shírang in Katúl), and Mufídí clans.

The Qájárs, who were brought to this part of Persia by Chingíz, are now much reduced in number. They aggregate no more than 400 families belonging to the following clans: Qawánlú, Dawallú, 'Izzu'd-Dínlú, Qarásánlú, Shámbiyátí, Ziyádlú, Karlú, and Si-pánlú (102).

The Turks consist, apart from the Qájárs, of Ḥájjílar Giraylís from Kabúdjáma, and of Maqṣúdlú Kháns from the neighbouring districts.

The Balúchís have dwindled down to a few families. Some

Kurramís have found their way here from the north-western provinces of India, and belong to the Túrí, Shilawzání, and Zírání clans.

A few families of Daylamís are still to be found here,—descendants, no doubt, of the supporters of the early 'Alíd rulers of Mázandarán and Gurgán.

Lastly, there are the Ziganas (gipsies), known here by the several names of Júkí, Ghalbírband, or Chiginí; they are blacksmiths and farriers and are noted thieves. They may number between 50 and 100 families[1].

[1] For further information concerning Astarábád see H. L. Rabino, Diplomatic and Consular Report, Annual Series, No. 4381.

CHAPTER IX

Province of Astarábád: limits. Description. Districts. Population. Roads. Attacks of tribes. Qizil Álán. Castle of Mubárakábád. Áqá Muḥammad Khán and the Turcomans. District of Sháhkúh and Sáwar. District of Anazán-Rustáq. *Bulúk* of Fakhr 'Imádu'd-Dín. District of Katúl. District of Findarisk. District of Kúhsár. Ḥájjílar. Kabúdjáma. Castles.

THE province of Astarábád[1] lies in the eastern portion of Persia, between latitude 36° 45′ and 37° 20′ and longitude 54° and 56°. It is bounded on the north by the Gurgán river, on the south by the Alburz mountains and the Sháhrúd and Basṭám districts, on the west by the Caspian and Mázandarán, and on the east by the district of Jájarm and the Khánate of Nárdín.

The greatest width of Astarábád, from the Qaráṣú to the borders of Sháhrúd, is about 40 miles, and its greatest length, from Jar-i-Kulbád to the limits of Kúhsár, about 100 miles. Like the other Persian Caspian provinces, it consists of a plain running east and west with a mountainous district bordering it to the south. The plain is covered with magnificent forests through which flow numerous streams, and maintains a uniform width of about 10 miles as far as Nawdih, about 50 miles from the western border. The mountainous section includes the upper course of the Niká river and the mountains of Sháwar, Sháhkúh, Jahánnumá, and Gaz.

The province is divided into seven districts: Anazán, Sadan-Rustáq, Sháhkúh and Sáwar, Astarábád-Rustáq, Katúl, Findarisk, and Kúhsár.

The eastern *bulúks* are inhabited chiefly by Giraylí Turks, whilst the villages of Sangar-i-Ḥájjílar are owned by the Ḥájjílar, a tribe said by some to be a branch of the Giraylís, and by others to be of Balúch origin.

In the western districts the population is mostly Tájík with a few Qájár families and some Maqṣúdlús, the latter having originally come from Qarábágh. At Zangí Maḥalla and Muḥammadábád (near Astarábád) the villagers, at one time, were chiefly Hazára Barbars, immigrants of an early date. Though inferior to the hardy mountaineers of the eastern districts, the inhabitants have a certain reputation for courage and fighting.

[1] For further information regarding the Province of Astarábád see Col. C. Beresford Lovett, Report on Astarábád, March 1882, Consular Reports.

The language and dialects spoken in this province are Persian, Turkí, Turcoman, Tát, and Mázandaráni. All the inhabitants are *Shí'ahs* with the exception of the Turcomans who are *Sunnís*.

The roads in the plain are swampy, and those in the hills stony and abrupt. Sháh 'Abbás's causeway, which traverses the whole province, is still used by *chárwadárs* between Bandargaz and Astarábád, although it is much out of repair.

The principal passes over the mountains are:

(*a*) From Gaz to Sháhrúd, via Kútal-i-Dúk, to Barkalá 12 miles, Yánisar 16 miles, Mullá 'Alí 16 miles, Tajar 20 miles, Sháhrúd 16 miles; total 80 miles according to native information.

(*b*) From Nawkanda to Rádkán and thence to Sháhrúd.

(*c*) From Gaz to Ustúnábád 6 miles, Rádkán 20 miles, Sháhkúh 20 miles, Basṭám 28 miles, according to native information.

(*d*) From Astarábád to Sáwar via the Jahánnumá pass, which I believe to be the same as the Sar-Darwáza pass, and thence to Chahárdih.

(*e*) From Astarábád to Tásh, via Ziyárat; Ziyárat, 11 miles; Siyáh-khánpay, Shahrbut, Lara mountain (9200 feet), Chahárbágh valley, Sháhkúh-Bálá (8200 feet), 16½ miles; Chalchaliyán pass and Tásh, 14 miles; thence to Sháhrúd 19½ miles; total 61 miles.

(*f*) From Astarábád to Sháhrúd via the Quzluq pass. By way of Númal to Khayrát (1040 feet), 10 miles; Garmdasht, Rubáṭ-i-Quzluq, Buland-Sufála (5200 feet), 15 miles; summit of Quzluq pass (7200 feet), Chahárbágh (6700 feet), ruins of 'Alí-ábád (7300 feet), Jilínbirín pass (8000 feet), to Haft Chashma, 10 miles; Qabr-i-Safíd, Kútal-i-Wíjmanú (9000 feet), Tásh (7700 feet), 9 miles; Rubáṭ-i-Tajar, Kaláta (5510 feet), Sháhrúd (5000 feet), 19¼ miles; total 63¼ miles.

(*g*) From Astarábád to Jájarm: Nawdih, 13 miles; Kinára, ruined, 2 miles; Píchák Maḥalla, 11 miles; Katúl, 3 miles; Namtalú, 8 miles; Findarisk, 2½ miles; Rámiyán 11½ miles; Nawdih, 12½ miles; Abr-Rúd stream running down from Abr, 8 miles; Pársiyán-i-Qánchí, 11 miles; Chináshk (whence a path leads to Basṭám), 10 miles; Gulistán, 2 miles; Túlbín, 3 miles; Nárdín, 8 miles; and over the Sang-i-Súrákh pass to Jájarm, 30 miles. The pass from the Nawdih valley to Jájarm or Mayáma is said to be the easiest of the whole Alburz range, from Ṭihrán to Herát.

(*h*) From Astarábád to Gurgán, the Gurgán defile to Isfará'ín in the Juwayn plain. The stages according to Muqaddasí were: Rubáṭ-i-Ḥafṣ; Gurgán; Dínárjárí; Amrúbáw (Amrúbalú); Ajgh (now called Ashk); Sangkhwást; Isfará'ín. An alternative route from Astarábád to Gurgán went via Rubáṭ-i-Wizára, whilst a third passed through the forest and was called Hashtádíl (103).

(*i*) From Bastám to Gurgán the stages according to Ḥamdu'lláh Mustawfí were: Kíj (Kaláta-Khíj) passing Nardabán Páya on the way, 28 miles; Mílábád, 24 miles; Músá-ábád, 20 miles; Gurgán, 20 miles. Total 92 miles.

From time immemorial Astarábád has been exposed to the attacks of the tribes settled to the north of the province.

To protect Gurgán and the surrounding country, Anúsharwán built the great wall of Qizil Álán. With the invasion of Persia by the Caliphs' armies a new danger threatened Gurgán, and the city of Astarábád was more than once looted and destroyed by the contending parties. The province fared no better under the Ziyárids and the Buwayhids, and was overrun by the Mongols when they invaded Mázandarán. During the reign of the early Ṣafawís it was for some time under the rule of the Úzbaks. Sháh 'Abbás the Great rebuilt Mubárakábád, which had been founded by Sháh Ṭahmásp, and there stationed a strong contingent of Qájárs. These, however, soon entered into friendly relations with their neighbours over the border, and it was amongst the Turcomans that Muḥammad Ḥasan Khán, father of Áqá Muḥammad Khán Qájár, always sought refuge when in difficulties. As a reward for the assistance they had always given him and his father, Áqá Muḥammad Khán allowed the Turcomans to remove from the barren banks of the Atrak to the rich plain of Gurgán, and gave them as *tuyúl* the villages on the banks of the Qaráṣú, such as Újábun, Qal'a Maḥmúd, Laladuwín, Ḥaydarábád, Atrakchál, etc., since when a continuous state of war has existed between the wild tribesmen and the inhabitants of the Atak villages, that is, the villages along the Astarábád border, facing the Turcoman steppe.

The district of Sháhkúh and Sáwar[1] includes the whole mountainous tract south of Astarábád as far as Sháhrúd and Basṭám. It has now only a few inhabited villages, but there were over 30 at one time, and its green valleys bear ample evidence of former cultivation.

Tásh, the principal village of the district, is about 20 miles from

[1] Villages of Sháhkúh and Sáwar; see Appendix I, P.

Sháhrúd at the junction of the two roads from Astarábád—the one via Ziyárat, and the other over the Quzluq pass. Near Tásh the Sháhkúh has the local name of Sháhkúh Gukshán.

Astarábád-Rustáq[1] lies to the north and east of the town of Astarábád, which forms its western limit. It extends to the village of Mír Maḥalla on the east, on the north to the river Qaráṣú, on the further bank of which dwell the Atábáy Turcomans, and to the Quzluq pass on the south. From east to west it measures 12 miles, and from north to south 20 miles. There is some open ground and pasture land towards the Qaráṣú, but the greater portion of the district is forest. The surface of the country is slightly higher and less swampy than the *bulúks* to the west.

The *ním bulúk*, or so-called "half district," of Fakhr 'Imádu'd-Dín, is now accounted part of Astarábád Rustáq. It is bounded on the east by the Karak stream, on the west by that of Mír Mahalla, on the north by Qárí-áb and Ílghártappa, and on the south by the mountains of Nawkúh and Lalagandú. It measures from north to south 24 miles, and from east to west 12 miles. It was formerly a flourishing and independent district, but most of its villages have since been destroyed by the Turcomans. The inhabitants are mostly Turks, amongst whom are a considerable number of *sayyids*. The governor resides at Miyánábád.

The district of Katúl[2] lies to the south-east of Astarábád and to the south of Astarábád-Rustáq. It extends from the mountains to the open plain held by the Turcomans. It is bounded on the west by the river Karak and the plain of Kumálán, on the east by the stream of Surkh-Maḥalla (which separates it from Findarisk), on the north by the Dawají territory, and on the south by Mayghán in Basṭám. It measures about 10 miles from east to west, and 30 miles from north to south. The country is covered with forest for the most part, but has several grass-covered plains.

The Wál-i-Qúsh-Kuprí, called by the Turcomans Qaráṣú, rises in the mountains behind Katúl, and joins the Gurgán near Sáliyán Tappa. It is formed by the following streams: the Áb-i-Dahana-i-Katúl, also called Karak or Áb-i-Bakhshán; the Áb-i-Surkhán-Maḥalla, which runs down from the Zarríngul gorge and waters part of Findarisk and Katúl; the Áb-i-Kabúd-Wál, which rises in the forest of 'Alí-ábád, and the Áb-i-Qájár, which rises at Baraftán in Katúl.

[1] Villages of Astarábád-Rustáq; see Appendix I, Q.
[2] Villages of Katúl; see Appendix I, R.

The inhabitants are mostly Giraylís and are a fine, hardy race, of good physique, and for the most part well armed.

Findarisk[1], which includes the small district of Rámiyán, is bounded on the west by the Surkh-Maḥalla stream, and extends to Sangar-i-Kabúd-jáma, east of which lies the Gúklán country. On the north it borders on the territory of the Aymír, Kúchik, Qujuq and Tátár Turcomans, and on the district of Kúhsár on the south. It measures 36 miles from east to west, and 32 miles from north to south. It includes the whole belt of forest as far as Naẉdih, and the lower slopes of Ḳhúsh-Yayláq.

It is traversed by several large streams, all tributaries of the Gurgán: Áb-i-Findarisk, which flows down from the Dárkalá gorge and joins the Gurgán at Band-Aymír; the Áb-i-Shírábád, also called Chaqallí, which passes through the village of Khánbibín and the plain of Qaráṭughán, and then crosses the Qujuq territory; the Áb-i-Rámiyán, which waters the greater part of Findarisk, and flows east of the Qujuq territory; the Áb-i-Alláh Qulí and the Khurmárúd, which are to the east of Rámiyán, and flow through the Qányukhmaz and Qujuq territories; and the Áb-i-Sangar-i-Ḥájjílar, which flows through the Qányukhmaz territory. There are two other streams, the Áb-i-Gulchashma and the Rúd-i-Marzar, about which I have no information. The Údarwa Rúd must be one of the streams mentioned above under another name.

The level ground in the valley is cleared and closely cultivated, but dense forest encircles the clearing, meeting above and below it. The men are fine, active, well armed, and skilled in woodcraft; they are more than a match on their own ground for any over-venturesome Turcoman on raiding bent. I was informed that there were many Kurds, Daylams, and *sayyids* in Findarisk. The inhabitants of Rámiyán are divided into seven clans: Yazdarí, Rajablí, Sádiqlí, Kághadhlí, Qawánlí, Báy, and Bayglarí. The principal village of the district is Zarríngul, but the governor resides at Shírábád. The hereditary *kháns* are descendants of Mír Abu'l-Qásim Findariskí, known as Mír-i-Findariskí, a celebrated physician and philosopher who died in Iṣfahán in 1050/1641.

The district of Kúhsár[2] is described as a fine plateau lying to the south-east of the *bulúk* of Findarisk, about 30 miles in length and 10 to 12 miles in width. It is bounded on the north by Shír-

[1] Villages of Findarisk; see Appendix I, S.
[2] Villages of Kúhsár; see Appendix I, T.

ábád and Kabúd-jáma, on the east by Nárdín, on the south by Abr in Basṭám, Kaláta Khíj, and Mayáma, and on the west by the *yayláqs* of Katúl.

The Kúhsár stream rises in the Wámanán mountain, which stands between Kúhsár and Gulistán of Nárdín. It waters many of the rice fields of Sangar-i-Ḥájjílar, and forms to the east of Gunbad-i-Qábus marshes which drain towards the Gurgán river. The Khurmárúd rises in the Abr mountain of Basṭám; it then passes Nawdih-i-Isma'íl Khán and Nawdih-i-Ḥájjí-Sharíf, and reaches Waṭaná 10 miles from its source. Four miles further on it divides into two branches, one flowing south (called Áb-i-Waṭaná), and the other flowing east towards Fársiyán and Qánchí. Eight miles below Qánchí the eastern branch passes Chináshk, and then reaches Wámanán and Gulistán of Nárdín. Here it divides into two further branches, one of which flows south of Wámanán and joins the Áb-i-Tílawá, which runs down from the Zardawá mountain. From the junction of these two streams to Kaláta-Khíj of Basṭám is about 16 miles.

I have seen the Khurmárúd called Fírang and found mention of the Chilchá stream.

Kúhsár comprises four *maḥalls*: Kúhsár, Chináshk, Qánchí and Ḥájjílar. The inhabitants are a fine, hardy race, chiefly Giraylí Turks, and the climate is said to be very good. Thanks to its mountainous nature, Kúhsár is comparatively secure from Turcoman raids. The principal villages are Dúzín and Qal'a-Káfa, but the governor of Kúhsár, being also governor of Findarisk, resides in the latter district at Shírábád.

The Ḥájjílar, who have given their name to the small district they inhabit, are remnants of the Giraylí tribe, and inhabit the precipitous glens descending from the plateau north of the Gurgán river. Naṣíru'l-Kuttáb relates that Muḥammad Ḥasan Khán Jaláyír made himself master of the Gurgán valley, and declared himself independent. He retired to the castle of Máránkúh (104), whence he defied the troops sent against him by the Sháh of Persia. One of his confidants, a certain Ḥájjí, was bought over by the Persians, and betrayed his master, receiving as a reward Máránkúh and the neighbouring district. The Ḥájjílar villages are inhabited by his descendants, whence their name of Ḥájjílar.

The people of Chináshk and Qánchí, though living in a narrow, pent up, abundantly watered valley, and cultivating little but rice, are tall, robust, and healthy looking,—in every respect a finer looking race than the inhabitants of the dry highland glens about Nárdín.

Kabúd-Jáma (105), now known as Ḥájjílar, is described by Mustawfí in the 8th (14th) century as a district producing much silk, and abounding in corn land and vineyards. It had been a very rich country, but was entirely ruined as a result of Tímúr's march into Mázandarán at the close of the 8th (14th) century. The city of Rú'ad or Rúghad, which is also mentioned as passed by Tímúr on his invasion of Mázandarán, probably belonged to the Kabúd-Jáma district. It was, says Mustawfí, a fair-sized town, being 4000 paces in circumference, and standing in the midst of many fertile lands, where much corn and cotton, besides various fruits, were grown in abundance.

Muqaddasí says that travellers going from Basṭám to Gurgán city across the mountain pass stopped at Juhayna, which is described by Ibn Ḥawqal as a fine village on a river. Juhayna, which is often mentioned in local histories, must have been a castle of some strength as it was the refuge of the rulers of Kabúd-Jáma when attacked by the governors of Khurásán or the *Ispahbads* of Mázandarán.

There are three castles of Chináshk: Síbchál, Wálamán (Wá-manán), and Káshídár. The first two are not very important, but Káshídár, which stands on the crest of a mountain now called Dashlí and below the Qal'a-i-Tanbat-Barzín, was of very great strength. It is impossible to say which of these three castles of Chináshk is the one in which Qábús b. Washmgír was imprisoned after being dethroned

The castles of Humáyún and Kajín or Kachín were apparently in or near Kúhsár. Kachín remained in good repair from the time of Shápúr Dhú'l-Aktáf until the time of the Ispahbad Ardashír b. Ḥasan (568—602/1172—1205-6), who ordered it to be destroyed lest it should fall into the hands of Tukush b. Íl-Arslán.

CHAPTER X

Astarábád to Gunbad-i-Qábús: Sultán Duwín. Sháhmarz. The Qarású. Áq-Qal'a. Founding of Mubárakábád. Qızıl Álán wall. The Gunbad, or dome of Qábús. Climate of Gurgán. City of Gurgán: its origin. History. Ibn Hawqal's description. Mustawfí's description. Ábasgún. Ním-Mardán. Former villages of Gurgán. The river Gurgán. Ruins of Gurgán. Shrine of Qarangí Imám. Dahistán: laid waste by successive invasions, desolate and uninhabited at the present day.

DEC. 22ND, 24½ miles. We left Astarábád by the Fújird gate and proceeded north-north-west to Áq-Qal'a, 10½ miles over flat country. About a mile from the town-gate we passed the shrine of Karímábád to the left of the road, and, shortly afterwards, the ruined villages of Ja'farábád and Amírábád on the right and left of the road respectively. On a hill to the left stands the tomb of a Turcoman chief who died 40 years ago. It goes by the name of 'Imárat-i-Músá Khán. Beyond and on the same side of the road are the mound and shrine of Ya'qúb Payghambar, "the Prophet Jacob," and beyond these Áqzakalám, a hill near which flows the Yaka-Mázú stream. On the right are the hills of Fújird, Shigháltappa, and Bájtappa, and further on Gultappa and Sultán Duwín, the latter a favourite winter-residence of Mírzá Abu'l-Qásim Bábur. Four miles from Astarábád we crossed the Sháhmarz, a ditch, now nearly filled up, which, we were told, runs from below the Qarású to Rámiyán, and serves as a boundary between the Turcoman settlements and the Atak villages of Astarábád. It was probably dug by order of Amír Nizám, the first Prime Minister of Náṣiru'd-Dín, who caused towers to be built at regular intervals in the jungle from Astarábád to the sea, and garrisoned each with a detachment of 50 men. The tower of Khwája-Nifis in particular was, so Eastwick informs us, a great check on the Turcoman marauders, but when the Amír was put to death (in 1851) all these places went to ruin.

We had now left the settled country of Astarábád and entered the steppe, where the only landmarks are mounds of varying heights indicating the sites of the numerous settlements which at one time dotted the Gurgán plain[1].

[1] Many of these mounds are marked on de Morgan's map. See J. de Morgan, *Cartes des Rives Méridionales de la Mer Caspienne*, Mission Scientifique en Perse, Paris, 1895.

At $6\frac{1}{4}$ miles from Astarábád we crossed by a brick bridge of many arches the Qaráṣú river, or Siyáhbálá as it is called by the Persians. This river rises in the mountains to the south of the district of Katúl, about 30 miles east of Astarábád. It flows at first in a north-westerly direction, and then west for 40 or 50 miles, finally falling into the Caspian 6 or 7 miles south of Khwája-Nifis.

The site of the former citadel of Mubárakábád is marked by low mounds. At its northern extremity on the bank of the Gurgán are the ruins of the fort of Áq-Qal'a, through which we passed in order to reach the four-arched bridge over the Gurgán.

According to local tradition, Áq-Qal'a was known in the time of Qábús as Ispí-Diz, a name which the Turcomans translated into Áq-Qal'a. The fort of Áq-Qal'a was built under Náṣiru'd-Dín Sháh to keep the Turcoman country under observation, but the soldiers stationed here were practically prisoners within the walls of their fort, and could not even ensure the safety of their communications with Astarábád, although within sight of the town.

Mubárakábád was first founded by Sháh Ṭahmásp I the Safawí, who instructed the governor of Astarábád to remove to the new city so as to be able more effectively to guard the province against the incursions of the Turcoman tribes, who owed allegiance then to the King of Khwárazm. In 1007/1598–9 Sháh 'Abbás I came to Astarábád and gave orders for the fort to be rebuilt. Its walls were completed in 12 days. He then transferred a large section of the Qájár tribe to this city where they remained until compelled to abandon it on account of terrible brawls which broke out between the Yúqáríbásh and Ashághíbásh sections of their tribe.

Shortly after Áq-Qal'a we reached the Qizil Álán wall, which was first erected by Alexander the Great as a protection against the incursions of the wild tribesmen of the east. It was rebuilt by Núsharwán, the Sásánian monarch (530–578 A.D.), and consisted apparently of a deep moat, behind which was a solid wall of masonry with guard-houses at more or less regular intervals. A low embankment with a mound here and there is all that can now be seen of this formidable rampart which ran from near Gumish-Tappa to Gukcha in the Gúklán country. In some parts there seems to have been an inner moat or canal backed by a second wall. On the other side of the river was Sáliyán Tappa.

We crossed to the left bank of the Gurgán by the Muyút-Gashan ford and stopped for the night at a small *'ubba* or camp of Bahlaka *chárwás*.

Dec. 23rd, 24½ miles. For three miles we followed the left bank of the river, then crossed to the right bank at the Sangar-Suwát ford. An hour before reaching Gunbad-i-Qábús we passed a mound (Qaráwáy Tappa) standing at an angle of the Qizil Álán wall, at a point where the bricks of the latter seemed to me to be of a more recent date than those we had hitherto seen. Away to our right could be seen Bíbí-Sharwán, a mound about 4 miles west-north-west of Gunbad-i-Qábús, which bears the name of a wife of Núsharwán. Crossing by a wooden bridge the Gurgán river, which flows here between very steep banks, we reached Gunbad-i-Qábús, which is about 50 miles east-north-east of Astarábád, about a mile away from the river, and 2 miles north-east of the ruins of the former town of Gurgán.

The *Gunbad*, or dome, of Qábús is a ten-sided brick tower on a mound 60 feet high. The tower is circular at the base and has a conical roof. Its shape somewhat resembles that of a lighthouse. There are no signs of any steps either inside or out. The door faces east and there is a small window in the roof. In the centre of the floor is an oblong opening now filled with earth, in which no doubt was placed the coffin of Qábús b. Washmgír, king of Jurján. The tombstone has disappeared. An inscription runs round the building above the door and is repeated under the eaves of the roof. Its translation is: "In the name of God the Merciful, the Compassionate. This is the lofty Palace of Amír Shamsu'l-Ma'álí, Amír son of Amír, Qábús son of Washmgír. He ordered it to be built during his lifetime. Year 399 lunar and year 375 solar." Report has it that the tower was half cut through by Nádir, who, weary and thirsty after a long day's march, decided, on perceiving the tower, to rest under its shade, but was so incensed at the distance he had to cover before reaching it that he gave orders for it to be destroyed to prevent others being deceived in like manner. According to another version, a Gúklán chief, under the belief that a treasure was hidden in its roof, ordered the tower to be undermined all round so as to bring it down, and only desisted from his barbarous design when informed that the tower would probably kill all the workmen in its fall.

The following are the measurements of the tower: outer circumference 210 feet; inner circumference 95 feet; height of tower 168 feet; height of roof 42 feet; the total height of the tower, therefore, is equal to its outer circumference[1].

The Gurgán plain is very hot in summer, but in the afternoons there is usually a breeze from the north, so that on the whole the climate is healthy, although insects, and especially sand flies, cause one much annoyance. The winter is mild, and a few pieces of fuel are sufficient to warm a tent. There is little, if any, snow. Torrential rains are of frequent occurrence except in summer. From February to April the plain is covered with narcissi and other flowers. Game is found in plenty.

Gurgán, the Vehrakána of the Avesta, and the Hyrcania of the Ancients[2], consisted for the most part of the broad plains and valleys watered by the Gurgán and the Atrak. It was at first considered part of Ṭabaristán (Sykes says that Gurgán corresponded with ancient Hyrcania and Parthia).

For centuries after that Gurgán was held to be a province by itself, though dependent on Khurásán, but, after the changes brought about by the Mongol invasion, it was annexed politically to Mázandarán. It comprised Tamísha, Astarábád, Ábasgún, and Dahistán. It is no longer mentioned under the Ṣafawís, when the authority of the governor of Astarábád seems to have extended no farther than the Gurgán river.

Muqaddasí writes that Gurgán, being rich in streams, its plains and hills were covered with orchards producing dates, oranges and grapes in abundance. His mention of dates is no doubt due to a mistake; *khurmá* in Mázandarán is the name of the wild-pear and not of the date.

The capital of Gurgán was the city of the same name, founded, so we are told, by Gurgín, the son of Mílád. Its early rulers bore the title of *nahapits* of Súl. In the year 18/639 Suwayd b. Muqarran conquered Basṭám, and wrote to the King of Gurgán (a name which the Arabs changed into Jurján), Rúzán b. Ṣúl, inviting him to make his submission. This Rúzán did, agreeing also to pay a yearly tribute to the Arabs.

Masqala b. Hubayra took Gurgán on his way to Mázandarán, but he was killed after waging war for two years with Farrukhán

[1] See E. Diez, *Churasanische Baudenkmaler, mit einem Beitrage von Max van Berchem*, Berlin, 1918, Bd I, pp. 39–43 and 100–106.

[2] For Hyrcania see Strabo, B. XI, ch. VII, para. 2 and 3; also Rawlinson, *History of Herodotus*, London, 1858–1860, vol. IV, p. 200. For Gurgán see Marquart, *loc. cit.*, pp. 72–74.

the Great. In 98/716–7 Yazíd b. Muhallab defeated Ṣúl the Turk, ruler of Gurgán, and took his capital. Leaving 'Abdu'lláh b. 'Ámar there, he advanced towards Ṭabaristán. 'Abdu'lláh was attacked by the inhabitants and had to retire to a fortified place until relieved by Yazíd, who had been compelled to pay a large sum to the *Ispahbad* of Ṭabaristán to be allowed to retire with his army. After a siege of seven months, the *marzubán* of Gurgán, who had retired to a mountain fastness, surrendered and was put to death, and Yazíd ordered a general massacre of the inhabitants of Gurgán.

Ibn Ḥawqal in the 4th (10th) century describes Gurgán as a fine town, built of clay bricks, and enjoying a far drier climate than Ámul, for less rain fell in Gurgán than in Ṭabaristán. The city consisted of two parts, one on either side of the Gurgán, which was here crossed by means of a bridge of boats. Gurgán was more properly the name of the eastern half of the town, whilst on the western bank lay Bakrábád the suburb; the two parts of the city together, according to the description of Ibn Ḥawqal, who had been there, were nearly as large as Ray. The fruit from the gardens around was abundant, and silk was produced in great quantities. The main quarter of Gurgán, that on the eastern bank, Muqaddasí calls Shahristán; it had handsome mosques, and markets where the pomegranates, olives, water-melons, egg-plants, oranges, lemons, and grapes of the neighbouring gardens were sold cheaply, notwithstanding their superlatively fine flavour. The town was intersected by canals, spanned by arched bridges or by planks laid on boats. A *maydán*, or public square, faced the governor's palace, and this quarter of the town had nine gates. The defect of Gurgán was the great heat of its climate, whilst flies were very numerous as well as other insects, especially bugs of a size so large as to be punningly referred to as "wolves" (*gurgán*). Bakrábádh, as Muqaddasí spells the name, was also a populous city with its own mosques, and the buildings occupied a considerable frontage along the western bank and extended back from the river no small distance.

When Qazwíní wrote in the 7th (13th) century, Gurgán was famous among the Shí'ahs by reason of the shrine called Gúr-i-Surkh "the red tomb," which was said to be that of one of the descendants of 'Alí, whom Mustawfí identifies as Muhammad (died 203/818–9) son of Ja'far aṣ-Ṣádiq, the sixth *Imám*. Mustawfí reports that the city had been rebuilt by the grandson of Malikshâh the Saljúq, and that its walls were 7000 paces in circumference.

Sháh Ardashír of Mázandarán rebuilt the walls of the city by order of Sulṭán Tukush, but destroyed them again shortly afterwards.

In the 8th (14th) century, when Mustawfí wrote, the town lay for the most part in ruins, never having recovered from the ravages of the Mongol invasion. He praises, however, the magnificent fruit grown here, and, in addition to the varieties enumerated above, mentions the jujube-tree as bearing so freely here that trees which were only two or three years old gave good fruit twice in a season. The population was entirely Shí'ah in his time, but was not numerous. In the year 795/1393 Tímúr, who had devastated all Mázandarán and the neighbouring country, stopped at Gurgán and built for himself here on the banks of the river the great palace of Shásmán, which is especially referred to by Háfiẓ Abrú[1] (106).

I find that there was a mosque at Gurgán called Garzín. In addition, there was a quarter of the town near the rampart called Jamájú (written Jamáján), and another near the Bábu't-Ṭáq was called Shúsh. Allusion is also made to a gate known as Bábu'l-Yahúd. Dá'í'l-Kabír was buried outside Gurgán in the village called Rawshanákhura, and the headless body of Sayyid Muḥammad b. Zayd, who was defeated and killed in 287/900, two miles from Gurgán, was buried in a place which became known as Gúr-i-Dá'í, the Propagandist's grave.

The port on the Caspian for both Gurgán and Astarábád was Ábasgún, given as one day's march from the latter and three from the former city (Maníní says 16 miles from Astarábád and 56 from Gurgán), but the site would appear to have been submerged during the 7th (13th) century, soon after the Mongol invasion. Iṣṭakhrí and Ibn Ḥawqal, writing in the 4th (10th) century, describe Ábasgún as a considerable market for the silk trade, being the border station at that time against the Turks and Ghuzz, and the chief port for the coasting-trade with Gílán. It was protected by a strong castle built of burnt brick, and there was a Friday mosque in the market-place. Muqaddasí writes of it as "the great harbour of Gurgán," and the Caspian itself, according to Yáqút, was often called the Sea of Ábasgún. In history Ábasgún is celebrated as having been the final refuge of Muḥammad, the last reigning Khwárazm Sháh, who, fleeing before the Mongol hordes, died here miserably in 617/1220. Ibn

[1] See Le Strange, pp. 377–378.

Serapion states that the town of Ábasgún stood on the banks of the Gurgán river, near where it flowed into the Caspian (107).

The most important river of the province is that generally called by its name, the Gurgán river; Muqaddasí refers to it as the Ṭayfúrí, whilst he makes no mention of the river Atrak. In the 8th (14th) century Mustawfí gives the name as the Áb-i-Jurján, and says that it rose in the valley of Shahr-i-Naw, and flowed through the plain of Sulṭán Duwín and past the city of Gurgán, entering the Caspian near the island of Ábasgún in the bay of Ním-Mardán (108). According to this writer, the stream was deep and almost unfordable throughout its course, so that travellers were often drowned in attempting to cross it; in flood-time its waters were carried off by channels and used up in irrigation, though much always ran away to waste.

The Gurgán rises at the foot of the Qulí Dágh, at a point where three streams flowing from springs unite, the Yallí Chashma, another stream 1½ miles higher up, and the Dilmá half a mile beyond. The river next receives the united waters of the Káy and Is-háqí streams on the left, then the Ṣáríṣú on the right and the Áb-i-Shúr 12 miles lower down on the same side. Near the ruins of the former city of Gurgán, the river receives from the south the Khurmárúd (109), also called the Nawdih or Sumbar. Other tributaries from the south are the Kuwanchí Mullá, probably the same as the Qujuq, the Aqríkul (3 miles from Yárimtappa), the Albakulí or Almakánlí (6 miles from Yárimtappa), the Chaqallí, the Qúshkuprí, the Aqírajár, and the Gurp streams. According to von Bode the Is-ḥáqí Ṣú, also called Qaráwul Cháy and Dúgh-ulúm, receives on the left the Suwásína and on the right the Qarasli.

The Gurgán river has a course of over 100 miles. Its mouth was formerly near Básh Yúzkha, a little to the north of the Qaráṣú, and in 1854 the Persians tried unsuccessfully to divert the river to its former course. After that the river continued to flow in two channels, the principal one to Gumishtappa and the other to Khwája Nifis, until about 1886 when the former branch ran dry.

There are five bridges across the river, one of wood at Gunbad-i-Qábús, one of stone at Áq-Qal'a, and three other wooden ones at the camp of Mullá Qilíj Khán, at Unchalí, and at Khwája-Nifis respectively.

We went to visit the extensive mounds which mark the site of the former town of Gurgán[1]. To the north-west of the town was the citadel which included a palace, bazaar, and bath, the latter in a fairly good state of preservation. The citadel stood on the right bank of the Qarangí Imám or Khurmárúd stream, a tributary of the Gurgán, which was formerly spanned here by a brick bridge, traces of which could still be seen. Stone channels carried water to the city, from the Gurgán and the Qarangí Imám, which formerly flowed at a much higher level than they do now. Outside the city of Gurgán stood the shrine of Qarangí Imám (110), an old, domed mausoleum mostly under ground. The distance from the top of the dome to the floor, where stands the tomb of the saint, is about 15 yards. As there is no inscription it has been impossible to identify it. It is generally believed to be the tomb of Imám Yaḥyá b. Zayd, who was slain in battle outside the city in about 125/742–3, and whose body was buried by his enemy, Abú Muslim.

Before closing a chapter dealing chiefly with the province of Gurgán, it may be of interest to give a short summary of the little that is known about Dahistán, formerly a part of Gurgán, which was so completely desolated and laid waste by successive invasions as to be still, at the present day, without a fixed population, cultivation, or settlements of any description, being only visited for brief periods by wandering nomadic tribes.

Dahistán is believed to be the country of the Dahae[2]. It lay four marches from Gurgán city and had but small villages and a sparse population. The chief settlement was Ákhur which Muqaddasí refers to as a city surrounded by 24 villages, the most populous of all the Gurgán province. To the eastward of Ákhur was ar-Rubáṭ on the desert road to Khwárazm. Yáqút mentions the villages of Kharṭír, Farghúl, Habaztan, and Habrathan, but adds no details. Four stages from Dahistán, on the road to Khwárazm, stood the city of Afráwa which is supposed to be identical with the modern Qizil Arwat, a corruption for Qizil-Rubát, "the Red Guard-house[3]."

From Gurgán to Dahistán it was 23 *farsakhs*, the stages being Yázar-Rúd, 9 *farsakhs*; Muḥammadábád, 7 *farsakhs*; Dahistán, 7 *farsakhs*. From Dahistán to Faráwa the stages were: Rubáṭ-Gazíní, 7 *farsakhs*; Rubáṭ-i-Abu'l-'Abbás, 9 *farsakhs*; Rubáṭ-i-Ibn-Ṭáhir, 7 *farsakhs*; Faráwa or Afráwa, 7 *farsakhs*.

[1] See Col. P. M. Sykes, "A sixth Journey in Persia," *J.R.G.S.*, Vol. XXXVII, January, 1911, p. 15.
[2] See Strabo, B. XI, Chap. VIII, para. 2, also Chap. IX, para. 3.
[3] See Le Strange, pp. 379–380.

CHAPTER XI

Gunbad-i-Qábús to Unchalí. Unchalí. The Band-i-Amír. Khwája-Nifis. Persian Turcomans: intertribal feuds. Authority of Persian Government. *Sarkardas*. Ihtishámu'l-Wizára's account of the Turcomans. Marriage. The Yamút. Country. *Chumúr* and *Chárwá*. Cultivation and industries. Business honesty. Sharaf and Chúní. Permanent settlements. Relations with the Atak villagers. Raids. Possible pacification. The Gúklán. Country Relations with the Yamút and other neighbours. Tradition as to origin of name. Astarábád to Rádkán. Kútal of Jahánnumá. Caravanserai of Rádkán. Tower of Rádkán. Inscriptions. Descent to the Caspian.

DEC. 26TH, 27 miles. Leaving Gunbad-i-Qábús we passed the Qarangí Imám shrine and crossed the stream by a wooden bridge. Next we reached the deep Taglí-Qaráṣú stream and came to the hill of Áqnáwur on the left bank of the Kuwanchí Mullá stream, which we crossed. To our right stood the hill of Tandurlí. The path now led across the Albakulí stream. Our next obstacle was the dry stream or canal of Karatkán, on the banks of which grew pomegranate and other thorny bushes: to our right were some marshes fed by the Chakdalí stream, two arms of which we crossed before reaching the main branch which, although dry at this time of the year, has a very deep bed. An hour from our starting-place we came to the Qúsh-Kuprí stream. Farther on were some large mounds called Allahkarak, which mark the boundary-line between the Dáz and Dawají settlements. We spent the night at the camp of Túqdárí Dáz.

Dec. 27th, 17 miles. We crossed the Qárí-áb, then the Agíra-jár stream and later the muddy Gurp stream. Passing through the ruins of Mubárakábád we reached the Russian Astarábád-Chikishlar telegraph line, which is the boundary between the Ja'farbáy and their neighbours, the Atábáy. After an hour's ride we came to a walled enclosure, called Qal'a-i-Ílgaldí Khán; another three miles brought us to the Gurgán, over which was a substantial wooden bridge of planks, and soon after we entered Unchalí, the most important Turcoman settlement we had yet seen. It numbers in summer 300 tents and there are here 40 *tams*, or wooden shanties, with stores attached.

Dec. 28th, 25 miles. We proceeded over a flat and swampy plain to Gumishtappa, 10 miles from Unchalí, on the old branch of the Gurgán.

In his *Voyages en Turcomanie et à Khiva*, 1823, Muraview informs us, that, according to the Turcomans, the hill of Gumishtappa had been an island until quite recently before his visit (1814–5), and Voinovitch also mentions that he saw an island at Gumishtappa. We were told that there were 1000 families of Turcomans at Gumishtappa. It has already been mentioned that Gumishtappa is situated on the banks of the Gurgán's original channel, about 1½ miles from where it flowed into the sea. In 1307/1889–90, during his governorship of Astarábád, Naṣru's-Salṭana (later Sipahdár-i-A'ẓam) constructed a dam across the Gurgán to divert the river into its former course. Two thousand men were employed in driving poles into the river and throwing earth over them, but the dam was swept away on the day of its completion. The site of the dam is still called Band-i-Amír. The inhabitants have since dug a canal from Khwája-Nifis to Gumishtappa, but levels were unfavourable and the canal is now dry. The prosperity of Gumishtappa has diminished in consequence, and I believe that the people would have deserted it altogether were it not for the expense of moving their shops and sheds.

A ride of 5 miles due south over flat country along the canal brought us to Khwája-Nifis on the banks of the Gurgán, 2 miles from the sea. It consists of 550 houses. We rode to 'Ubba-i-Band, so called from its being near the site of Naṣru's-Salṭana's dam. We crossed the Gurgán by the Unchalí bridge, and an hour later regained the left bank by means of a good wooden bridge, and reached the house of Mullá Qilíj Khán which is about 10 miles from Khwája Nifis, 9 from Astarábád and 6 from Básh Yúzkha.

Dec. 29th, 9 miles. We crossed the Qaráṣú by a wooden bridge called Yaklak-Ḥájjí, the Sháhmarz ditch and then a small tributary of the Qaráṣú, called Yaka-Mázú, after a solitary walnut-tree which stands here. Leaving Qal'a Maḥmúd south of us, we reached the Russian telegraph line, whence it is 4 miles to the Fújird gate of Astarábád.

The Persian Turcomans belong to two great tribes, the Yamút and the Gúklán, which are divided and subdivided into clans, and sections of clans, and these again into smaller divisions[1]. They have no constituted authority, although each section has an *áq-saqal* or "grey beard." His position, however, confers no authority and is simply attained by virtue of his age, experience, and personal influence.

[1] See Col. C. E. Yate, *Khurasan and Sistan*, London, 1900, pp. 212–281, and H. L. Rabino, Diplomatic and Consular Report, Annual Series, No. 4381, pp. 23–33.

The intertribal feuds which prevail amongst the Turcomans are due to this want of a central authority or of some supreme chief to keep the various sections under control.

The degree of influence or authority of the Persian Government extends to the imposition of tribute, but leaves the movements of the people free, and does not admit of the punishment of offences by the supreme power. This authority is submitted to or resisted at the caprice of the people or their leading men, and is increased or diminished as the action of the local governor is strong and resolute or weak and vacillating.

The tribute is paid to certain agents, or *sarkardas*, appointed by the Central Government, who are responsible for its collection as well as for the quota of horsemen which the various sections of the tribe are supposed to furnish when called upon to do so.

The post of agent became practically hereditary in certain families, so that the holders of those posts soon abused their position and entered into partnership with the Turcomans to plunder the unfortunate villagers of Astarábád. They supplied rifles and ammunition and, being also in command of the Astarábád militia, effectively contrived to thwart all punitive expeditions undertaken by the governor of Astarábád.

It was under directions from the *sarkardas* that, after the bombardment of the National Assembly, the Turcomans advanced towards Astarábád, burning the villages that lay on their route. That the town was not sacked was solely due to the efforts of the Russian Consul and of the Russian Commissioner, who brought about the immediate withdrawal of the Turcomans.

When the ex-Sháh was deposed, the inhabitants of Ḳatúl plundered the house of their governor, 'Alí Muḥammad Khán, Mufákharu'l-Mulk, who was *sarkarda* of an important section of Yamúts and had acquired great wealth. The governor fled to the Turcoman steppe, and three persons, sent by the Local Assembly of Astarábád to induce him to return to town, failed to do so. Their visit, however, said a Persian newspaper, was not without result, as the Mufákhar died the very same night.

Mír Sa'du'lláh Khán Findariskí, Sálár-i-Muqtadir, was undoubtedly the most influential district governor and *sarkarda* of the province of Astarábád. On hearing that the Nationalist troops had entered Ṭihrán, he fled to the Atábáys, where he remained many months until, receiving assurances as to his personal safety, he, unfortunately for himself, decided to return to town. Accused of intrigues in favour of the ex-Sháh, he was, by order of the new Cabinet, sent to Ṭihrán. He died on the first stage, and his death was attributed in official circles to want of opium, whilst rumour had it that he had been strangled not far from the Quzluq pass and buried at the caravanserai of Rubaṭ-i-Safíd.

In a small work by Naṣíru'l-Kuttáb dealing with the Gurgán plain I find the following letter addressed by the Iḥtishámu'l-Wizára, a former Persian Commissioner at Gunbad-i-Qábús, to the Persian Government: "Probably no one will believe me, and what I say may cast doubts on anything I may say in future, yet it is my duty to inform the Persian Government that the Yamút and Gúklán are loyal subjects of H.I.M. the Sháh and are always ready to serve him. If they have such a bad reputation, it is due to the fact that they have never had a representative at Court to remove misunderstandings. Governors and persons in authority, in the interest of their own pocket and to increase their reputation, have always represented some section or other of Turcomans as being in open rebellion, and the Persian Government has immediately sent instructions for the punishment of the rebels. I myself have often seen innocent tribes ruthlessly plundered. The chiefs and grey-beards more than once informed me that they dislike becoming Russian subjects, but that the governor of Astarábád forces them to rebel. Thus the Gúklán are represented as having refused for the third year to pay their taxes and as having thrown off their allegiance, yet they have often informed me that they were ready to pay these taxes and were well disposed towards the Persian Government."

Naṣíru'l-Kuttáb continues: "Turcomans despise Persians for calling at every moment on God or the Prophet to witness the truth of what they say. A Turcoman never swears by God and he will seldom take an oath. Such is his respect for the name of the Almighty that he will often abandon a claim of, say, even ten camels or one hundred sheep, rather than support it by oath. He will also, when brought before a court of inquiry for raids and murders, tell the truth even to his own disadvantage. It would be difficult in the whole of Persia to find a good Muḥammadan who would do such a thing."

The age for marriage amongst the Turcomans is usually 15 or 16 for boys, and 9 or 10 for girls. The price paid amongst the Ja'farbáys for a girl is about 300 *túmáns*, of which a half is payable in cash and a half in live-stock. The girl's weight in silver has been paid more than once. After the marriage ceremony the bride remains one, two, or three days with her husband. She then returns to her father's tent to learn all that a Turcoman woman must know, that is, weaving, sewing, cooking, etc. After a few years she returns to her husband. If the husband dies, she returns to her father's tent, but now, should there be a suitor for her hand, it is no longer 300 but 600 *túmáns* that he would have to pay to the father, and a girl who has buried two husbands may fetch as much as 1,500 *túmáns*. Woe to the widowed man who, having lost his wife, cannot afford to pay the price to marry again, for amongst Turcomans a bachelor weds a spinster, and a widower a widow. Such a man is called a *salákh*, and it only remains for him to take his rifle, mount his horse, if he has one, and join parties of marauders, until the proceeds of these forays enable him to remarry.

The Yamút territory is bounded on the north by the Atrak, on the west by the Caspian, on the south by the Atak villages of Astarábád, i.e. the districts of Sadan-rustáq, Astarábád-rustáq, Katúl, Findarisk, and Sangar, the edge of the forest everywhere marking the border, and the open plain beyond being in the undisputed possession of the Turcomans, and on the east by the Harhar and Yástappa (Ilyástappa?) and a strip of neutral ground, which intervenes between the Yamút and Gúklán settlements.

The country near the Gurgán is exceedingly fertile, but that on the southern banks of the Atrak, on account of the saltness of the soil, is unfit for cultivation, although affording good pasture. There are everywhere signs of a former civilization, as well as traces of canals and cultivation, and in good hands this district might be one of the richest in Persia.

The Yamúts are divided into *chumúr* and *chárwá*. The *chumúr*, or the cultivators of the tribe, are practically settled and move their camps but rarely and in a limited circle. The *chárwá*, or nomads, change their camping ground according to the season of the year and the pasture obtainable for their cattle, flocks, camels, and horses. Being unattached to the soil and living for the most part at a distance, the *chárwá* are mostly independent and pay little, if any, tribute.

The Yamúts have their camps on the banks of the Gurgán, and in winter remove to the edge of the forest about 8 miles south of the river.

The *chárwá* keep usually to the north towards the Atrak, and often pass into Russian territory, but they return to the Gurgán and Atrak districts to reap their grain and store it underground.

Apart from barley and wheat, which are largely grown in the Turcoman country, wool and a small quantity of opium are also produced. Yamút carpets are chiefly manufactured by the *chárwá* or nomads. A *gilím* or floor rug called *palás* is manufactured by the Ja'farbáy, Atábáy, and Dáz women. In business, so great is the honesty of the Turcoman trading along the coast, that he can buy large quantities of goods on credit from Mashhadisar and Bandargaz traders without giving any signed document whatever. He always meets punctually his engagements.

The Yamúts number about 7,000 families, of which one third are nomadic and the remainder settled. The Ja'farbáy are the sailors, fishermen, and traders of the tribe, and are the most well-to-do. Then come the Atábáy, Dáz, Dawají, Ílghí, etc., and finally the wild, lawless, and poor *chárwá* of the Qányukhmaz and Ígdir sections, who have nothing but the bare necessaries of life in their camps. The Dáz section cherish a legend, according to which they are descendants of a royal family. They are also considered by their neighbours to be the noblest section of the Yamút tribe.

Turcomans relate that the founder of the Yamút tribe had two wives, a legitimate one, who bore him a son named Sharaf, and a concubine, by whom he had two boys, Chúní and Qujuq. The father on his deathbed left one of his two horses to Sharaf, and the other to Sharaf's two half-brothers. Chúní, however, refused to allow Qujuq to share their common horse, but Sharaf took pity on the boy and mounted him behind him. Thus did Qujuq become attached to Sharaf. The Yamúts are descended from these three boys, and the Sharaf are accordingly considered of higher birth than the Chúní. The Salákh, who are subdivided into Bayrámshálí, Awgaz, and Salákh, and now reside mostly in Russian territory, are accounted Sharaf as they are closely related to the Qujuq.

The various Yamút tribes are settled from west to east in the following order: Ja farbáy, Atábáy, Ílgí, Dáz, Dawají, Bakka, Bahlaka, Badráq, Aymír, Kúchik, Salákh, Qujuq, Qányukhmaz, Ígdir.

The following are some of the permanent settlements of the Yamúts which have not been mentioned :

(*a*) The frontier post of Maráwa Tappa on the southern bank of the Atrak, 72 miles north-west of Bujnúrd and, according to native information, 28 miles west of Bayrám Ulum.

(*b*) The frontier post of Yághí Ulum, 8 miles north-west of Bayrám Ulum.

(*c*) Chátlí, 32 miles from Chikishlar and as many west-north-west of Gunbad-i-Qábús.

(*d*) Sangartappa, near the mouth of the Atrak, 10 miles north-north-east of Táza-ábád.

(*e*) Táza-ábád, 10 miles north of Gumish-Tappa. It has eight or nine houses belonging to Turcoman fishermen, and a small landing-stage.

(*f*) Qarásangar, north of Kurd-Maḥalla and 2 miles north of the Qaráṣú (sometimes called the Sújawál), between Sangar-i-Ním-Mardán and Mullákíla.

(*g*) Áltín Tukhmáq, about 2 miles from the sea, and 8 miles from Unchalí.

(*h*) Gúrak-i-Safíd, 2 miles from Gumish-Tappa and as many from the coast.

The relations between the Yamúts and the Atak villagers are as a rule anything but friendly, and although the *chárwás* are supposed to be responsible for most of the raids, yet the Atábáy and even the Ja'farbáy *chumúr* often take part in these forays, and the villagers of Kurd-Mahalla, whose only neighbours are Ja'farbáy, have to be constantly on the look-out to frustrate the attacks of their hereditary enemies. Not a day passes but what bloodshed occurs, or some plundering foray or retaliatory expedition is undertaken; and the reports of the British Agent at Astarábád during my six years of office at Resht were one long record of murder and robbery.

To guard against these raids many of the Atak villagers pay a Yamút chief an annual quantity of rice, in return for which he is bound to protect them and to make good any losses they may suffer at the hands of the Yamút. This arrangement is termed *sákhlú*.

It is dangerous for a Persian to venture alone on the plain lying between the Atrak and the Gurgán, or for a Turcoman to approach Astarábád. The old hatred between Persian and Turcoman, or, in this case, between the followers of 'Alí and those of 'Umar, has lost none of its fierceness. I must here mention that many inhabitants of Astarábád admitted to me that the

Turcomans received great provocation from the Atak villagers, who often stole their horses and cattle, whilst the governors of Astarábád made an excuse of their so-called punitive expeditions to impose heavy fines on the tribesmen and enrich themselves at their expense.

It would be easy for the Persian Government to pacify this province, as the Turcoman of to-day is much more inclined to agriculture and to settle down than was his father, whilst by the conversion of many of his camping sites, such as Gumish-Tappa, Khwája Nafas, Unchalí, and Básh Yúzkha, into permanent settlements through the erection of wooden shanties and stores, he has rendered himself far more liable to punishment than when he lived under tents, which at the first sign of danger could be removed northwards towards the Atrak.

The Gúkláns occupy a small tract of country at the head of the Gurgán river, stretching from Yás Tappa on the southern bank of the Gurgán river, on the west, to the source of the Gurgán at Yalda Chashma (Yallí Chashma) and to the Dahana-i-Gurgán at Tangirán, on the east, or, roughly speaking, from about longitude 55° to 56° east. The streams watering the Gúklán territory in the Gurgán plain are the Áb-i-Ḥájjílar; Kacha-Qaráshúr, running down from Qal'a Káfa and Dúzín; the Áb-i-Báynal from Wámanán; the Áb-i-Chaqar-Baygdalí from the Dahana-i-Fársiyán-u-Fírang; and the Áb-i-'Ubba-i-Khallí Khán from the Dahana-i-Tangirán.

Gúkláns are cultivators and not nomadic in their habits; they trade with Russia in cattle, sheep, and silk fabrics. They grow the mulberry tree and rear silkworms. They also grow some opium, to the use of which they are much addicted. They are not as industrious as the other Turcomans, and their manufactures consist only of felts, a few coarse rugs, and some silk fabrics.

The soil is excellent and requires no irrigation, but, owing to the want of population, miles and miles of fertile land lie waste.

The Gúkláns live in constant dread of the Yamúts, but those of the Khwája section, by reason of their sanctity as descendants of the Prophet, are never molested by the Yamúts and go unarmed to and from the tribes as they like. The Gúkláns are also on bad terms with the Kurds of Bujnúrd, the Ḥájjílar of Kabúdjáma, and the other inhabitants of the neighbouring district of Astarábád. Raids and counter-raids are of frequent occurrence. They are lightly taxed, and the revenue is collected by a *Sarkarda*, usually one of the district governors of Astarábád. The Gúkláns number about 2000 families.

According to Turcoman tradition the Gúkláns at the time of the Mongol invasion were called Qáy, from Qáy Khán, son of Gún Khán, son of Ughuz Khán, son of Qará-Khán, the first Khán of the east. During the reign of Sultán Símjúr they removed to their present country. After the destruction of Mashhad-i-Miṣriyán and the dispersal of its inhabitants, some Ígdir and Bahlaka Yamúts settled near its ruins and had to drink water from the marshes, as the Atrak had been diverted near Chát by an exceedingly solid dam, in the construction of which much lead and pitch had been used. Whilst engaged in vain attempts to destroy the dam, the Turcomans saw a man riding a lame horse of the colour known in Persia as *kabúd* (grey). The stranger advised them to light a mighty fire behind the dam in order to melt the lead and pitch, and then to loosen the stones with their spears so as to allow the water to find a passage, when it would have no difficulty in carrying the dam away. The Turcomans always referred to this man as "he of the lame grey horse" *Kúklángallí*, which was abbreviated into the present Gúklán.

Dec. 31, 18 miles. We left Astarábád for the Jahánnumá pass and Rádkán. We followed the foot of the hills until we reached Sa'dábád, a prosperous looking village of 200 houses. After the Sa'dábád stream and the Kinársar pasture-grounds, we passed a mound called Gundul Tappa on our right, and entered a magnificent forest. We next crossed the deep, boulder-strewn bed of the Áblú stream, and later the Áb-i-Chárwá and the Shaṣtkalá stream. The ascent of the pass was most precipitous and led in zigzags up to an outcrop of rock called Ṣandúqa or Gachyán, the most dangerous part of the ascent. As it was snowing we had perforce to spend the night in the *yayláq* of Jahánnumá, which is on a plateau at the top of the pass and consists of some 45 wooden huts, where the inhabitants of Sa'dábád spend the summer (111).

January 1st, 1910, 14 miles. Our progress over the snow-covered plateau of Jahánnumá was very slow. After two hours we descended abruptly over frozen and extremely slippery ground to a valley, which led us to the Maqasí stream and a little further on to the *Rubáṭ* of Maqasí, said to be 8 miles distant from Jahánnumá and 32 miles from Astarábád. The *Rubáṭ*, or station consists of extensive caves excavated in the clayey soil of which the sides of the mountains are composed, and can accommodate about 30 horses; it is used by small *chárwadárs* plying between Chahárdih (112) and Astarábád. We soon reached the Chaman-i-Sáwar, a fine grazing-ground about two miles wide, where many of the inhabitants of Astarábád spend the summer months in tents or in small stone huts.

An hour and a half's ride from Maqasí brought us to the caravanserai of Rádkán.

The Míl-i-Rádkán is a round, brick-built tower, about 40 yards high, with a conical spire. The outer circumference is 31 *dhirá'* and the inner 16½; the inside diameter measures 6¼ *dhirá'*. The tower stands on the side of the mountain and is visible from a great distance. An inscription runs round the top of the tower, and another once existed over the door, but has been removed or destroyed, an act of vandalism attributed by the inhabitants to a former Russian Consul. From the inscription over the door, a sketch of which is given in Hommaire de Hell's "*Voyages en Turquie et en Perse*, 1856–1860," pl. LXXXV, we learn that it is the mausoleum (*qaṣr*) of the Ispahbad Abú Ja'far Muḥammad b. Wandarín Báwand, date Rabí' II, 407/Sept.–Oct. 1016. The inscription round the top says that the shrine (*mashhad*) was built under the Ispahbad Abú Ja'far Muḥammad b. Wandarín Báwand and that it was begun in 407/1016, and completed in 411/1020. A third inscription comes immediately after the second and states that the building was completed in 411 A.H. by Ahmad b. 'Umar[1].

Another tower stood to the west of this one, but nothing now remains of it except the foundations, the bricks having been used in the construction of the *takya* of Rádkán.

I find in Ibn Isfandiyár's history of Ṭabaristán a "Qasr-i-Dádaqán" which was midway between Tamísha and Sárí and was founded by Ispahbad Khurshíd's father. This, however, cannot be a copyist's error for Qasr-i-Rádkán, as the situation given does not tally with that of Rádkán, unless we substitute "on the mountain road" for "mid-way."

The village of Rádkán lies hidden by trees above the Niká stream on the side of the mountain to the right of the road. It

[1] See Ernst Diez, *Churásánische Baudenkmaler*, mit einem Beitrage von Max Berchem, Berlin, 1918, Bd. I, pp. 36–39 and 87–100.

has a good mosque and a *takya* built by Badí'u'z-Zamán Mírzá, Ṣáḥib-Ikhtiyár, a son of Muḥammad Qulí Mírzá Mulkárá and a grandson of Fatḥ 'Alí Sháh. The mountains around Rádkán are: Mishkzár on the north, Zirishk-Khúní on the south, Diyáriyán on the south-east, Zirishkchál on the east, and Khákistar Dála on the west.

According to native information Rádkán is 32 miles from Astarábád, 16 from Kurd Maḥalla, 20 from Gaz, and 4 from Barkalá. The distance from Astarábád was given as follows: Astarábád to Sa'dábád, 4 miles; Sa'dábád to Jahánnumá, 14 miles; Jahánnumá to Rubát-i-Maqasi, 8 miles; and thence to Rádkán, 6 miles, thus giving a total of 32 miles.

January 2nd, 20 miles. On leaving the caravanserai we ascended the hill-side by a steep path known as Kútal-i-Qal'a-sar. At the top of the *kútal* were a few stone walls, the remains of the former village of Sarqal'a. We passed the stream of Dihdarra, at a point where once there stood a village of the same name. The caravanserai of Barkalá could be seen at our feet on the road from Ashraf to Rádkán, surrounded by well-cultivated fields and patches of forest and woodland.

The path we were following led us to Kundáb, a village of some 30 or 40 houses, the majority of the inhabitants of which spend the winter in the plain of Astarábád. We next saw some ruined houses known as Bálá Barkalá, a ruined hamlet formerly belonging to Barkalá, a village of Hazárjaríb. From here we continued uphill to Lawsar, a spot on the divide at the summit of the pass to Bandargaz. The forest, which is very thick on the northern side of the mountain, begins here. The road down the pass was simply abominable, consisting of a succession of holes, full of water and mud, formed by the constant passing of horses and mules over soft and slippery soil, so that the animals have to slide down from hole to hole. We passed places called Áblú, Mír-Sharíf, and Kúlanga, and went down a steep descent into the wooded glen of Áwdarra, through which flows a small stream. This glen is said to be half way between Rádkán and Bandargaz. We came to a place called Kúkúwarsar, and then to Dídwán, where, as the name indicates, there is a fine view of the plain of Ashraf, Anazán, and the Turcoman steppe far away to the east. The plain is covered with forest, with a few scattered, cultivated spots, that mark the vicinity of villages, which, however, are completely hidden from view. At Afrá-Humám a giant *palat* tree, or sycamore, which stood in solitary splendour on a small mound, had recently been ringed by some ruthless woodsman. We next saw the spring of Sháhpasand, or Shúpasan as it is called locally, and came on to the plain about 2 miles from Gaz. The forest here is called Bandbun. Further on we crossed Sháh 'Abbás's causeway leading from Nawkanda to Kurd Maḥalla. We entered Gaz soon after and proceeded to Bandargaz, whence we sailed the next day for Kraznovodsk and Baku.

APPENDIX I

VILLAGES AND LOCALITIES OF MÁZANDARÁN AND ASTARÁBÁD

A. Tunakábun. B. Kalár-rustáq. C. Kujúr. D. Núr. E. Ámul. F. Láhiján. G. Sawádkúh. H. Mashhadisar. I. Bárfurúsh. J. Farahábád. K. Sárí. L. Hazárjaríb. M. Ashraf. N. Anazán. O. Sadan-rustáq. P. Sháhkúh and Sáwar. Q. Astarábád-rustáq. R. Katúl. S. Findarisk. T. Kúhsár. U. Localities unidentified or not otherwise mentioned[1].

A. TUNAKÁBUN

(*a*) Balada*: Balada*.

(*b*) Gulayján*: Akhúnd Maḥalla; ‘Alíábád; ‘Amúghlí Maḥalla; Barashí*; Bázár Maḥalla; Búrámsar; Chalúsar; Chinárbun; Faqíh Maḥalla; Garákúh; Gulayján*; Harátbar (a *gálishnishín*); Karátkutí; Karímábád; Karjíkúh* (whence the former district of Karjiyán probably took its name. Sháh Yaḥyá, governor of Tunakábun and brother of Sulṭán Muḥammad of Láhiján, died in 884/1479, and was buried in Karjiyán at a place called Siyasar. Ẓahíru'd-Dín also mentions Shiyarúd or Siyarúd and Wáchak in Karjiyán); Kashkúh; Khalkhálí Maḥalla and Táza-ábád; Kúkaláya; Lashtú*; Látkinár; Límák* with Ásiyábsar and Gálish Maḥalla; Marzánkand*; Mázúlanga; Miyánrúd; Mullá Ḥájjí Maḥalla; Nasiya Maḥalla; Rafí‘ábád; fields of Razpat*; Riḍá Maḥalla; Rúdbárkinár; Shírrúd* (divide into Shírrúd comprising Charwarsar, Gurgrúd, Kulámasar, Lapasar, Niyása, and Shushtá; and Chalkrúd comprising Aḥmadsará, Basalkúh and Larasar, Kaláyabun, Mázíkulám, Miyándaj Maḥalla, and Nurdí Maḥalla); Ṣúfí Maḥalla; Sulaymánábád; Wáchak (where was buried in 823/1420 Sayyid ‘Abdu'l-Ḥay, son of Naṣíru'd-Dín b. Kamálu'd-Dín Mar‘ashí); Zangí Sháh Maḥalla.

Ishkawar* is included in the revenue list of Gulayján. The *yayláqs* of Ishkawar are: Ákana; Ífí; Kayd; Kaláya; Laj; Míj; Nadak; Narna; Súparda; Tamal or Tumul; and Yázín.

Ẓahíru'd-Dín mentions the village of Dímrún in Gulayján.

(*c*) Langá*, including the subdistricts of Jírband* and Júrband*: ‘Abbásábád; Ardarúd; Aspchín*; Ayúb; Bá'új Maḥalla*; Dárasará; Galakúh; Girdáb; Gísá; Ḥaydarábád; Káẓimkalá; Kharábasar; Kurdkalá; Mashhadísará; Mashkalá; Muḥammad

[1] Names marked with an asterisk appear in the official revenue list.

Ḥusaynábád; Palangkalá; Parchawar or Kúrzayl; Sarlangá; Sartakúsará; Sayyid Maḥalla; Shálaka; Shál Maḥalla; Shírkalá; Umíchkalá; Ziyáratbar. The *yayláqs* of Langá comprise: Bábrúdbár; Gazdarra; Gú'ígala; Kalasará; Kalb; Kúskúh; Máziyachál; Máziyasar; Nashkaján; Rikápushta; Síchkání; Taliyán; Wíragardan.

(*d*) Nishtá*: Subdistrict of Nishtá: Chikádih; Faqíhábád, Hangaw; Izrúd*; Káẓimkalá; Khushkbur; Lúladíh; Makárúd, Máránkúh; Nishtá or Nishtárúdsar*; Palangábád; Palasará, Pasanddih; Píshdákúh; Qal'a; Ruwár Maḥalla; Síbun; Ṭálish Mahalla; Túbun. Subdistrict of Zawár*: Álúkalá; Habíbábád, Hasanábád; Intithárábád; 'Ishratábád; Katkalá; Kútara; Mázúbun; Palatkalá; Qulí-ábád; Rúdpusht; Sarburd; Ṭálish Maḥalla; Zawár.

(*e*) Sakhtsar*: Ákhúnd Maḥalla; Dariyápushta; Futúk*; Halakalá; Kandasar; Karkat Maḥalla; Lamtar; Lát Maḥalla; Lazarbun; Ma'áf*; Manḥala; Manshalak; Miyánband; Nárinjbun; Purdasar; Pusht-i-Júb; Raḍí Maḥalla; Ramak* or Garmrúd with Saráb-i-Garm and Salmrúdsar; Rúdkhána; Sádát Maḥalla; Shaykhu'l-Islámí*; Shúrábsar; Ṭálish Maḥalla; Tangdarra*; Túbun; Turkrúd; Túsastán; Uskanakúh; Zakín Maḥalla; Zír Márkúh.

(*f*) Sarḥadd*, subdivided into Rúdbárakí* and Kalárábád*: Aṣgharábád (on the site of the village of Tamúshkalá which was destroyed by the troops of Sa'du'd-Dawla in 1890 at the time of the rebellion of Sayyid 'Álamgír, a chief of the 'Alí-Iláhí sect); Charaz; Dániyál; Garjıyasará; Gulúr; Jamshídábád; Jísá; Kalárábád; Khájakasar; Khushámiyán; Náranjbandán; Palatkalá; Sístán; Táza-ábád; Tílkinár; Tílrúdsar; 'Uthmánsará.

(*g*) Siyáh-rustáq* (in the district of Ránikúh in Gílán; it is given as part of Tunakábun as it is under the jurisdiction of the Sipahdár-i-A'ẓam to whom it belongs): Bálá Maḥalla*; Bíbálán*; Da'wísará; Gizáfrúd*; Isṭalkhbijár*; Kalmázíbun*; Lát*; Límúnjú*; Máyistán*; Mírak Maḥalla*; Pata or Púdih; Sáram; Sháh Murád Maḥalla*; Siyáh-rustáq-i-bálá*; Siyáh-rustáq-i-Pá'ín*; Ṭalábun; Talam.

(*h*) Tawábi'*: 'Abdu'lláh-ábád; Aghúzkalá; Akbarábád; Akúlasar; Ásiyábsar; Gíla Maḥalla; Gulayj*; Ḥabashabur (comprising Aghúzdárkútí or Amínábád, Barashabur, Ḥabashabur, Karakúh or Amírábád, Shántarásh, Táza-ábád or Naṣrábád); Ḥajjí Maḥalla; Ḥasankaláya; Isṭalkhsar; Kárdgar Maḥalla; Kınársar;

Khúbánrazgáh; Khurramábád; Lashkarak with the ruins of Qal'a Khandán; Mazardasht* (comprising Kabúdkaláya*, Karaf, and Shabkhuskútí); Mazarak; Mázúbun; Mír Shamsu'd-Dín; Miyánkúh; Miyán Maḥalla; Miyansará; Naẓarabad; Paskaláya; Qawí-Ḥiṣárlú*; Rúdpusht; Sabz Maydán; Salaf*; Sangarmál; Sangsará; Sháhsuwár; Shírajkhayl; Shíraj Maḥalla; Shírakraz; Shírwán Maḥalla; Siyáhwaraz or Sádát Maḥalla and Kiyawaz; Tílpurdasar*; Túshkún*; Walí-ábád; Walímarz; Zamínkín.

The revenue list of Tawábi' comprises the *yayláqs* of Dú-Hazár*, divided into Dú-Hazár and Sih-Hazár. Dú-Hazár: Aghúzdárbun; Áqá Sayyid Qásim; Asal Maḥalla; Balas; Barasa; Chálakúh; Gulistán; Gulkhánasar; Halúdarra; Ishkarbun; Jazmá where is buried Abu'l-Qásim b. al-Mú'ayyad bi'llah; Karkarachál, Kilíshum; Kúhistán; Lát; Madrasa; Miyánkúh; Naras; Píladárbun; Sardábá; Ustúj; Yághdasht. Sih-Hazár: Áb-i-Garm; Arúd; Dákúh; Dáriján*; Gáwbar; Gulzarúd*; Khániyán; Márán*; Miyánrúd; Píchabun; Qádí Maḥalla; Salambar; Shahristán; Sír; Yaj.

In the old chronicles Sih-Hazár is written Sí-Hazár. The castle of Sí-Hazár was rebuilt in 916/1510-11 by Sulṭán Aḥmad Khán of Láhiján. It had twelve towers and took three years to rebuild.

The following names are also mentioned as those of villages in Tunakábun: Aghúzdárkalá; Alpara; Bálán; Búrdatán; Falakdih; Gulpushta; Kachkan; Kaláta-Ispí; Lúlí Maḥalla; Miyánladak; Paramaz; Qal'a Pushta; Rajú; Rújayna; Siyáhband; Súlak; Sútak; Takala; Tamíjána; Tárík Mahalla; Túsakalá; Túsakulám. In the *Táríkh-i-Khání* we find Shahristán of Tunakábun. Ẓahíru'd-Dín mentions the castle of Karzmánsar somewhere between Karjiyán and Namakábrúd. The mountain district of Tanhiján was probably in Tunakábun.

B. KALÁR-RUSTÁQ

(*a*) Bírún Bashm*, subdivided into Bírún Bashm and Miyán Bashm. Bírún Bashm: Aghúzdárbun; Asawlat; Bábúdih; Banafsha; Barár; Chinas; Garkalá; Garmáwak; Harsí or Haris; Kalák; Kawítar; Khushkdarra; Marzánábád; Míchakar; Murádchál; Razán; Sayyidábád; Shahristán; Sharí; Síragáh. Miyán Bashm: Dihchar; Másál; Sannar; Túdí.

(*b*) Dasht: 'Abbáskalá; Ábrang; 'Alíábád*; 'Alídiráz*; Awíjdán*; Bázársar; Darárkash; Dárkalá*, Darzídih; Dímú; Dizgarán; Gílakalá*; Gurámaján*; Hardakalá*; Imámrúd*; Isfankalá; Kalnú; Kapar; Katasarkalá*; Kaláján*; Kharáb; Kulama; Kurdíchál; Lapáwak* or Farajábád; Largum; Marzándih*; Najjárkalá*; Páykalá; Píshambur; Rúdbárak; Samá; Sardih* (or Pírdih); Sarká; Shagarkúh; Síbdih*; Tabkalá; Túlíchál; Tursú; Újábayt; 'Ulwíkalá*; Wáha; Walad; Walí-ábád; Walwal.

(*c*) Kalárdasht*: 'Abbásábád; Áhangarkalá; 'Ayshabun; Akbadár?; Alifkalá; 'Arabkhayl; Búrasar* (on the Búrrúd stream); Diráz-Zamín; Dármúshkalá; Dújamán; Dúsagar; Faqíhábád; Ḥasankayf* or Pá-Takht; Ízad*; Karímábád; Kark*; Láhú*; Majal*; Maká*; Marsadih; Miyándih; Miyánkí; Muḥammadábád (in ruins); Namakábrúd; Nís-alwár?* (Písh-Alwár); Nawdihak; Nawrúdsar; Salímábád; Túydarra*; Wájí; Zawát.

(*d*) Kúhistán*: Western: Bíjnú; Dalír; Fashkúh; Ílat; Kútil; Maras; Nátir; Palatkúh; Tuwár. Eastern: Alámul*; Aland*; Angúrán*; Avír; Dúná; Haraján*; Hazárcham; Hiká; Ín*?; Jiríndih; Kamarbun; Kandawán (a caravanserai); Makárúd; Walíábád.

Kiyákalá is also in Kalár-rustáq, and Ẓahíru'd-Dín mentions Samangán, a village of Chálús.

The *yayláq* of Piyázachál[1] was between the village of Dízán in Ṭálaqán and that of Almír in Kalár-rustáq. Demorgny mentions Fírúzábád as the chief place of Kalár-rustáq.

C. KUJÚR

(*a*) Balada* and Kúrshídrustáq* (written by Ibn Isfandiyár Gúrishbard, Gúrishjird; Gúrshír; Gúshírd, and Júrishjird. Ẓahíru'-d-Dín mentions the village of Kúrshíd).

(*b*) Angás*: Angás; Angil; Badí'khayl; Chumúrkúh; Farazan; Gangar; Hazárkhál (where stands the shrine of Sayyid Ṭáhir and Sayyid Muḥammad built by Malik Kayumarth of Rustamdár who was subsequently buried in it in 857/1453); Kháchak; Kumchák; Naytal; Píchalú; Ṣáliḥán* (here stood the shrine of Sayyid Muḥammad b. Ibráhím, a man of great piety, asceticism and virtue. The people of Rúyán, groaning under the tyranny of Muḥammad b. Aws, came to this *sayyid* and begged him to receive their oaths of allegiance. He referred them to his brother-in-law, Ḥasan b. Zayd, who later became ruler of Mázandarán. The tomb of that holy *sayyid* was known as Ziyárat-i-Sayyid

[1] For a description of Piyázachál see Zahíru'd-Dín, *History of Gílán*, p. 348.

Muḥammad Kiyá Dabír Sáliḥání, but the inhabitants called him Sultán Kímdúr); Sháhnajjár; Sarwídih; Walígán; Washkan.

(*c*) Bandpay*: Bandpay; Najjárdih; Nasrábád.

(*d*) Chalandar*: 'Alíábád; 'Alíábád-i-Aṣghar Khání or Táza-ábád; Amzídih; Anárwar; Chalandar; Chálak; Duzdak or Duzdakarúysar; Hawḍkútí; Mulkár; Sangsará.

(*e*) Fírúzkalá* and 'Ulwíkalá*: 'Alamkalá; Fírúzkalá; 'Izzat; Kábúlaj; Lashkinár; Minúchihrkalá; Miyának; Miyánshahr; Mullákalá; Munawwal; Pímat; 'Ulwíkalá; Wázak; Wázawár or Waziyamál.

(*f*) Girán: 'Alíábád or 'Alíábád-i-Buzurg; Bíntásí?*; Dihgirí*; Ḥabíbábád or Khwáchak; Halúsán; Ḥasanábád; Ḥusaynábád; Khayrasar; Kúlksará*; Kurkrúdsar*; Majídábád; Músá-ábád*; Nírang*; Pálújdih*; Sa'd-dih; Sangtijin*; Sharí'atábád; Shu-kríkalá*; Táza-ábád.

(*g*) Kacharustáq*: 'Alamdih; Bázígarkalá; Buljakán; Falí-marz; Falzíkalá; Ḥasanábád; Hindúmarz; Ḥusaynábád; Kacha-rúd or Kacharúysar; Nawdih; Siyáhrú; Zarrínkalá.

(*h*) Kálíj*: Bún; Dankúh; Dajaj; Kálíj; Kásagar Maḥalla; Kulangrúd; Lazír; Nashú; Pasparas; Qal'a-sar; Sangnú; Táchakí; Turkdih; Tuská. On the way from the castle of Najú (Nashú) to that of Kalár was Qal'a Walíj.

(*i*) Kalúrúdpay*: Hazártíza; Kahír; Náranjbun; Páshákalá; Ṣaláḥu'd-Dín-kalá*; Wanúsh or Wanúshdih (formerly Banafsha-gún).

(*j*) Khayrrúdkinár*: Ábbandának; Aspsumdih; Darzíkalá; Khayrrúdkinár; Latangán; Márgírdih; Marúrdí; Sa'ádatábád; Shabkhuskaj; Sham'járán; Sulṭán 'Alí Kiyá Sulṭán.

(*k*) Kúhpar*: Aldarra; Awíl*; Báfchál*; Bálú*; Chár*; Chúran*; Hayrat; Kunnizkalá; Kúshkak*; Láshak*; Lásh-kinár; Nímawar; Pásang*; Samúr*; Walasp; Wísar.

(*l*) Panjak-rustáq*: Bastam; Bindar; Chatam; Dasht-i-Náẓir; Fírúzábád (at the foot of Kuh-i-Palar); Ḥasanábád; Kíkú; Munjir; Nayras; Samá.

(*m*) Ránús-rustáq*: Ástánakrúd*; Dawangasí; Gatapusht*; Gílkalá*; Kandalús with Míkhsáz and Mullákalá; Khúshal*; Kínj*; Kiyákalá; Kúsh; Laktar; Largán*; Lazúr; Míng; Mullá*; Na'l*; Níjkúh*; Paydih*; Ránús*; Sás*; Sítuk; Úṭáq-sará.

(*n*) Zandrustáq.

The following names also appear on de Morgan's map: Amírábád; Furanábád; Gulandarú; Kurutkalá; Líkash (in Rúyán, where took place the fatal combat between Rustam and his son, Suhráb); Pá'ínsará; Saraway; Siyáhsangar; Walama.

Ẓahíru'd-Dín passed Ábbandánkúh, Khúratáwarúd, and the village of Walígán on his way from Hazárkhál to Láwíj. In 867/1462–3 he went from Gílán along the sea-shore to Kúrshíd-rustáq, whence by way of Kunusánaband he reached the castle of Kujúr. He mentions Gáwzanakaláta between the Khayrrúd and the Namakáwarúd, the village of Amíra Mankás, and the castle of Lúrá which was built by the Assassins on the summit of a mountain. Demorgny gives Ṣáliḥábád as the chief place of Kujúr.

D. NÚR

(*a*) Balada*.

(*b*) Kamarrúd*: Bardún; Baṭáhirkalá*; Kamar*; Kuliyak*; Sarást*.

(*c*) Kúp*: Halúpushta*; Kúp*.

(*d*) Miyánband*: Balwíj*; Dirázdih*; Gatábsar*; Katiyá*; Khatíbkalá; Máliyakalá*; Miyánrúd*; Núrámak-kalá*; Qal'a-kash*; Qálíbáf*; Sangtáb*; Zarkiyá*.

(*e*) Nayjkúh*: *Maḥall* of Bandpay*; Gaznasará; Íl*; Kata-lagardan; Katúl* and Alwá*; Kangalachál; Khudádád; Kúrí*; Langúr*; Nayj*; Rúdbárak; Tíránkalá.

The following clans are assessed in the revenue list of Ná'íj*, no doubt the same as Nayjkúh: Akhí-Nápalár*; Akhí-Paydarra*, Ankatárúdí*; Barnájí*; Dúz*; Ḥaddád*; Ḥaydariyya*; Kal-wad; Kárdgar*; Kárdgar-i-Alíshrúd*; Kurd-i-Mullá-Ya'qúb*, Kurd-i-Sháhrúdbár*; Láwíjí*; Sayf-i-Zargar*; Ṣayqal-i-Áqá Bábá Bayg*; Ṣayqal-i-Dúst 'Alí*; Sháh-Ḥusayn-i-Ḥaydar Dariyá-ábádí*; Shaykh-Ṣayqal*; Wází*; Yahshum*.

(*f*) Namárustáq*: 'Abdu'l-Manáf; Amra; Dárkinár; Kafá-kalarí; Nasal; Namár; Pulúriyya; Sihlur; Saja Maḥalla; Shaykh Maḥalla; Suwa.

(*g*) Nátilkinár*: Afrásiyábkalá* and Rúnajkalá*; Anárjár*; Darásta*; Dárjár*; Gandiyáb*; 'Izkhurdih*; Júrkalá*; Khákistarkhúní* or Galínkhúní*; Kíkabun*; Nátil* and Hardúrúd*; Shahrkalá* and Dún*; Suladih*. Also 'Abbásá; Dárkandán; Khariya; Mardú; Saliyákútí.

(*h*) Nátilrustáq*: 'Abbáskalá*; Abdáldih*; 'Abdu'lláh-ábád; Áhúdasht*; Annádih*; Bághbánkalá*; Chumástán*; 'Izdih* (comprising Bázársar*, Ulká Maḥalla*, and Sárúj Maḥalla*),

Kamálkalá*; Karátkútí*; Karkchaspán*; Kurdábád*; Marzándih*; Mahdísará*; Mughándih*; Nánwákalá*; Nayzawarán*; Nawdih*; Sáldih*; Sangchálak*; Sangíndih*; Sáraldih*; Sayyidkalá*; Shaykh Qulíkalá*; Siyáhkalá*; Wátáshán; Yalápán*. Also 'Arabkhayl; Farsíkalá; Ispíkalá; Jalílkul; Kurdílkalá; Largsarí; Mardínkalá; Ni'matábád; Nisfján; Shahrkalá; Shálíkalá; Shahrband; Sharafdih; Sírakalá.

(*i*) Rúdbár-i-Suflá*: 'Alí-ábád* and Hashwá*; Bútadih*; Dalírgán*; Fúládkalá*; Gílándih*; Harat*; Kachaldih*; Kachagáh*; Kíshkalá* and Sarí*; Mashkíndasht*; Nay*; Safíddárdasht*; Tarmazar*; Tújánbkalá*; Úchkádih*. Rúdbár-i-Suflá formerly included Tákar and Míng and apparently the whole upper valley of the Núr river.

(*j*) Rúdbár-i-'Uliyá*: Chál* or Chal; Dúwílát*; Mazíd*; Tákar*; Waláchíd*; Zardkamar; also Fiyúl; Ítá; Íwa; Kal; Núj.

(*k*) Tatarustáq*: Áqá Sayyid Níkí (in ruins); Karsí; Kiyákalá (mentioned by Ẓahíru'd-Dín); Razán; Rustamrúd*; Tatarustáq*.

(*l*) Úzrúd*: Angarúd*; Gulbángáh*; Hajay; Kám*; Kalák*; Khajírkalá*; Míng*; Níknámdih*; Nisin*; Núhyá*; Píjdih*; Píl*; Úrsúsí*; Úz*; Úzkalá*; Walama*; Yásil*; Yúsh*. Ẓahíru'd-Dín mentions the mountain of Kangal-Áb-Raja on the way between Amír Mankás in Kujúr and Míng in Rúdbár-i-'Uliyá.

(*m*) Yálúrúd*: Khaṭír*; Kúshkak; Marj*; Míra; Palang-Darwáza; Warzan*; Yálú*.

On the way from the castle of Núr to Ṭálaqán was a place called Siyáhbísha. One day's march, or five leagues, to the west of Ámul, in the plain near the coast, was the town of Nátil (which Ẓahíru'd-Dín calls the capital of the plain of Rustamdár), and a like distance further to the west of this was Chálús. Laythám the Daylamite had built over the Shímrúd, which flowed east of Nátil, a bridge which was known as Pul-i-Laythám. Near it was buried Bakr b. 'Abdu'l-'Azíz b. Abí Dulaf al-'Ijlí who was appointed in 279/892–3 governor of Rúyán and Chálús by Sayyid Muḥammad b. Zayd, and who, on his arrival at Nátil, was poisoned with some sherbet. The country around Nátil was called Nátilrustáq. Above the village of Khusrawábád, which in Ẓahíru'd-Dín's time was called 'Adúldih and belonged to the district of Nátilrustáq, there stood a large oak tree at a spot called Sháh Mází-bun. Under this tree Afrásiyáb pitched his tent for 12 years until he concluded peace with Minúchihr, the son of Íraj, the son of Firídún. Near Nátil was a village called Mandúr, and in the same district was another village called Nigáristán, both mentioned by Ibn Isfandiyár[1]. Ẓahíru'd-Dín mentions Tamishánsar, east of Kacharúdbár near the Ámul border, and Kamál-kaláta, which was the residence of the Shíráya Kiyás. When the rule was wrested from the hands of the family of Mu'ayyad bi'lláh, his descendants went to reside at Shíráya-kaláta, where they remained until Sayyid Rikábzan, Kiyá's grandfather, rebelled and seized Tunakábun and part of Daylamistán including Shírrúd and Dú-Hazár.

After having conquered Rustamdár, Sayyid Fakhru'd-Dín b. Qiwámu'd-Dín Mar'ashí chose Wátáshán in Nátil as the seat of his government and, collecting men from Sárí and Rustamdár, had a deep moat dug round the town, and built a residence and a bath for himself, and a bázár and a mosque for the people.

In the *Táríkh-i-Khání* mention is made of Qal'a Dúk which was in ruins and repaired by Áqá Rustam of Mázandarán. This Dúk is probably identical with Dún in Nátilkinár. We also read of the castle of Dárná, a stronghold of the rulers of Núr.

E. ÁMUL

(*a*) Balada*.

(*b*) Ahlamrustáq*: Áhan Maḥalla; Ahlam*; Ázádmán*; Búndih*; Charíndih*; Dárkalá*; Gálishpul; Harapay; Juníkála; Karchak*; Kaládih; Kalúdih*; Khishtsar; Khúrdúnkalá*; Kílápay; Maḥmúdábád; Mír 'Alamdih; Muláram; Námúsdih; Qal'amarz; Sharuftí* and Parchíndih*; Shúrustáq*; Siyárkalá*; Súrákh Mázú*; Talíkasar*; Tarsí-Áb*; Tijinak*; Túlindih*; Yúsufábád.

(*c*) Chuláb*: Banafa; Chamabun*; Dawránsar*; Jángudár Maḥalla*; Kaluband* and Lúbá*; Kandábád*; Kangaraj Maḥalla* and Ispúrdasht*; Lahásh*; Míla* and Shahnakalá*; Miyánrúd*; Namalú; Párádíma*; Parasp (a roadside station); Páshákalá*; Tiyáf; Ṭíbár?*; Újákalá*.

(*d*) Dábú*: Áhangarkalá* and Kabúdkalá*; Askárkalá*; Bánsarkalá*; Bárík Maḥalla*; Bínamad*; Dífarí*; Dihsará*; Díma*; Díwkalá*; Dúnajkalá*; Faríkinár*; Farímún*; Gámíshbuna; Gílkalá*; Hájjíkalá*; Hashtádíl*; Húdakán*; Ispáhíkalá*; Izbárán*; Jazín*; Kachap*; Kalúsá*; Kamángarkalá*; Kárdgarkalá*; Kulangsar*; La'lkiyádih*; Maríj Maḥalla*; Marzangúr*; Mu'allamkalá*; Mullákalá*; Qarákalá* and Qará

[1] Ibn Isfandiyár, p. 40.

Maḥalla* or Bámarkalá*; Sangbast*; Saríján*; Sháhkalá* and Kalá Maḥalla*; Sháhkalá-i-Gulayj*; Shahnákalá*; Sírjárán*; Súrak*; Surkhrúd*; Tamask*; Tasíkalá*; Tufangá (formerly Tamangádih and Faríḍa-i-Tamangá. Near Tamanjádih was the plain of Kázar); Túlasará-i-Bínamad*, Újáq-i-Sádát*; 'Ulwíkalá*; Wánkas*; Wazrá Maḥalla*; Zangíkalá*; Zardáb*.

Ẓahíru'd-Dín mentions Dúngá in Dábú as the residence of Abu'l-Faḍl Dábú.

(*e*) Dashtsar*: Absaraft*; Áhangarkalá*; Búránkalá*; Buzmínán*; Chumázkalá; Fírúzkalá*; Gálishkalá*; Hárúnkalá*; Hárún Maḥalla*; Hindúkalá*; Kamángarkalá*; Kámkalá*; Katapusht*; Khúrdúnkalá*; Kúbíjkalá*; Kuhnadún*, Mahdíkhayl*; Mullákalá*; Páshákalá*; Rachakalá*; Rúdbárdasht*; Sharámakútí*; Surkhakalá*; Turkkalá*.

(*f*) Garmrúdpay*: Áhangarkalá*; 'Atáyán*; Changmiyán*; Hájjíkalá*; Lúrán*; Madras*; Tamask*; Wusṭákalá*. Garmrúdpay is probably identical with Ẓahíru'd-Dín's Garmábarúd.

(*g*) Harhazpay*: Alamdih*; Alamtútzár*; Armakkalá*; Bánúdih*; Bíshakalá*; Chahár-afrá*; Dábaqadih*; Dariyásar*; Iskanadih*; Gálishkalá*; Gúrak*; Iram*; Jawzákalá*; Kalíkán*; Kahlírd*; Mutwaríj*; Nawkalá*; Páshákalá*; Rúdpusht*; Újíábád*; Urínadasht*.

(*h*) Lítkúh*: Akárja*; Alámasar*; 'Alíjangal*; Anchapul*; Angushtar* and Mushtagán*; Ankasí*; Anṣárí Mahalla*; Bazham-i-'Abbáskútí*; Bárkútí (Márkútí)*; Bídár*; Bútagarán*; Darándih*; Darkápay* and Warkádih*; Darmakalá*; Darzínkalá*; Haní*; Ja'farkalá*; Jingár*, Halúmasar; Kabútargáhdih*; Kalhúdasht*; Kárchakalá*; Kásmindih*; Katakhwástkútí*; Kalák*; Kalán*; Khalíj*; Khásakalá* and Darárán*; Kúkdih*; Kúshazar*; Marzúnkalá*; Míjrán*; Pardamakalá*; Qádíkalá*; Qájár*; Rawáparinda*; Razdaka; Razkíbasta*; Rúdbárkash*; Rúdkash*, Sardáy Mahalla*; Sarhangkútí*; Sháhíkalá*; Sháh Maḥalla*; Sháh Zayd*; Sútakalá*; Tijinjár*, Tijinjár-i-Láriján*; Walísadih* and Yásmínkalá*; Yásmínkalá-i-Sháyakh*; Yásmínkalá-i-Warzí*.

The following are also in the district of Ámul: Abu'l-Ḥasanábád; Afrásará; Afrátakht; Aḥákalá; Ahmadábád; Alarb; Awurtasht; Bajakalá; Bakhtiyárkútí; Barjandih; Bázyárkalá; Chandar Maḥalla; Chawarí; Chawsar Maḥalla; Dangpáya; Dútíra; Dúd Mahalla; Ijbárkalá; Iskú Maḥalla; Ispanat; Ispanj; Ispiyárbun; Farrásh; Garmsar Maḥalla; Ghiyáthkalá; Ḥájjí-ábád;

Halakash; Halíchál; Halisunkash; Kamarband; Kapí; Kharkún; Khiḍr; Khurna; Khushwásh; Kunasí; Kunusamarz; Kunusapá; Kursíkalá; Lankaj; Largasarí; Líwaján; Mákhúrán; Mangal; Marzaband; Miyándih; Murídchar; Nardinkalá; Palamkútí; Parasang; Pílak; Pushta; Qal'abun; Ruḥkalá; Sa'du'd-Dín kalá; Sagarchí; Sar Maḥalla or Ḍiyárúd; Sayyid Maḥalla; Sharmkalá; Shírkalá; Takhtband; Ṭúlakalá; Turkarán; Tuskábun; Útáqsaráchál; Wákatán (mentioned by Ẓahíru'd-Dín); Walík; Zághdih.

In the time of Farrukhán the Great there stood a castle at Fírúz-Khusraw, later known as Fírúzábád, 2 *farsakhs* from Ámul. Ẓahíru'd-Dín mentions Falás, half a *farsakh* from Ámul on the road to Daylamán. He also mentions Míránábád on the western border of Ámul, Miyánrúd further east, Marándíh a village near Ámul and to the west of it, and Míránádih near which was Karkapáydasht. Of Máhánasar, which later became a stronghold of the Mar'ashí rulers of Mázandarán, Ibn Isfandiyár wrote: "A king called Máhiyasar (Máhanasar?) dwelt in a place four parasangs from Ámul, called now Así Wísha, and his palace was in a village which still exists and is called Wílír. Between the villages of Kílankúr and Shírábád is a great forest, thick and high, which is still called Máhiyasarí Diz, and near it is a deep moat or dyke filled with water covered with duck-weed into which anything which falls disappears for ever[1]."

F. LÁRIJÁN

(*a*) Amírí* or Pá'ín Láriján: Aḥá*; Akhúnzí; Alzam (pastures) Anárbun*; Anjí (pastures); Bághchúpán*; Díṇán; Haftachál*; Ilís; Kalpáshá*; Lashalwár; Qal'a-Dargáh*; Sháhándasht*; Shangaldih (113); Wána.

(*b*) Bálá Láriján*: Abhí*; Amráb*; Angamár; Ask*; Azú; Bandqurfa*; Barfábpay*; Bastak*; Garmábsar* and Bahmanábád*; Garná*; Gazana; Gazának*; Gílás*; Írá*; Kandalú*; Kuffárulká*; Lasan*; Lazúrak*; Malárd*; Malikábád*; Malhár*; Mún*; Nawá; Niyák*; Pá'ínkúh; Pulúr*; Qarangúm*; Rína* (near which stood the castle of Lawandar); Sa'ámak*; Shásbpar*; Siyáhkatú; Ziyár*.

(*c*) Bıhrustáq*: Afnasar; Báyján*; Bu'l-kalám*; Darkás*; Hafttanán*; Hulba*; Kaládúsh; Kháf; Kúzak; Lúshlú'í*; Lúṭ*; Maḥmúdábád or Talínú; Maríján*; Mihkatán*; Nawsar*; Pan-

[1] See Ibn Isfandıyár, pp. 37–38.

jáb*; Pardama*; Sárúghápay*. The pastures are Fíksara; Haḥrán; Irnís; Latapasht; Nay; Nayrín; Nuqlabán; Nuqlasar; Shírasal; Siyáhkamarband; Zardal; Zarzamín.

(*d*) Daylá-rustáq*: Dizán*; Fara*; Ḥájjídílá*; Ḥarmún*; Jawchár*; Kaharrúd*; Kiyán*; Kurf*; Lahír*; Malamuttaká*; Mándar*; Miyándih*; Nunnal*; Sardasht*; Tína ; Warká* (where was born Firídún).

(*e*) Lár valley; *Yúrt* or pastures: Chashma-i-Sháh; Chihil-Chashma; Gilurdak; Imámzáda Ibn Imám Músá; Khán Aḥmad; Khánlar Khán; Kharsang; Lataband; Sihdarra; Sháh. The caravanserais of Surkhak; Bastak (8500 ft.), and Safíd-Áb are on the Ṭihrán-Balada-i-Núr road via Lashkarak. The hamlet of Namakjáh is also in the Lár valley.

Minúchihr, Marzubán of Láriján, made of Qal'a Kuhrúd, later known as Kárú (compare Kaharrúd), such a prosperous place that men of all trades from India, Egypt and Syria had settled there. The castle was taken in 783/1381–2 by Sayyid Fakhru'd-Dín Mar'ashí and remained in ruins until rebuilt by Malik Kayúmarth. Ẓahíru'd-Dín mentions the castle of Fulúl in Láriján and Ibn Isfandiyár the village of the same name, Dih-Fulúl. A path led from Áram in Hazárjaríb to Pardama in Láriján via Anjadán and Ábbandánkúh.

The following are also names of localities in Láriján: Siyúwaja or Siyáhwásha (between the Lahásh bridge and Parasp on the Ámul-Ṭihrán road); Zardabán; Chashta Hárún; 'Alí-ábád and Pasangíkáh.

In Daylárustáq are the road-stations of Buryá; Aḥyú (a number of caves); and Aḥmadábád.

G. SAWÁDKÚH

(i) Rástábpay*.

(*a*) Dú-áb-Bálá*: Arfadih or Arfarúdbár; Gúr-i-Zaynu'l-'Ábidín-Khayl (Gúrzaldínkhayl); Milird; Sangsarak; Surkhachál; Urím.

(*b*) Khánqáh*: Anáram; Asa; Dihmiyán; Kúh-Iṣtabl; Raja.

(*c*) Khánqáhpay*: Arim; Azrúd; Báyakalá; Fulurd; Girdásiyáb; Kumrúd; Kurmaz; Yarnat.

(*d*) Rástábpay-i-Kúchik: Azanrúd; Kumrúd; Miyárkalá; Shúrmást; Tala.

(*e*) Surkhrubáṭ*: 'Abbásábád*; Atarkalá; Bímdarra; Maliyadarra; Wandachál; Warask.

(ii) Walúpay.

(*a*) Alásht*: Alásht; Kúlisán; Larzana; Línad; Sabukrúd; Sarín; Sawádrúdbár.

(*b*) Anand: Anand; Bímdarra; Dúráh-Isṭala; Gulbághcha; Kákarán; Paland; Shishrúdbár; Wala; Wasiyakash.

(*c*) Chirát*: Chirát.

(*d*) Karmazd*: Asal, Karmazd; Námashí*; Shírkala.

(*e*) Kasliyán: Amírkalá; Atú; Bahmanán*; Kajíd; Kasliyán* and Maláḥim*; Lúlak; Lúbiyúr; Matakalá; Pasákalá; Pír Na'ím; Sangnishát; Sípí; Sútasara; Wakasar; Walúkash.

(*f*) Kiláríján* and Kamandayn: Awat; Dú-áb; Íratbun; Kamand; Kiláríján; Mímajíkhayl; Pína-aram; Talím; Zankiyán.

(*g*) Zíráb*: 'Aliyakalá; Charsún; Chundilá; Díwlaylam; Kalíj-kalá; Kalá; Khwájakalá; Khalílkalá; Khurmandachál; Kurdá-bád; Nakhkalá; Nargisjár; Shírdarra; Surkhakalá*.

Paríján*, Shúndí*, and Fará*, and the Áhangar*, Káwá*, Khunnáz*, and Máshakh clans are also mentioned in the revenue list.

The following are also given by Melgunof as in Sawádkúh: Imámzáda Hasan, Imámzáda Safíd, Ispí-Chashma, Shaykh Mahalla, Shúrkúh. I'timádu's-Salṭana mentions Sarkalá and Bunkalá as villages passed on the road between Díwlaylam and the bridge of Kasliyán, and adds that the country to the west of the road belongs to the district of Dábú.

The Anasárán (Stahl has Asárán) valley on the road from Fírúzkúh to Fúlád Mahalla is, I believe, part of Sawádkúh. It is cultivated in parts and the wheat crops are fine. The Anasárán pass leading from the Jashn or Jash valley to Mázandarán is reported to be rough and difficult. Salash, the Rusiyá spring, Kúh-i-Qadamgáh, and the village of Chashma are all near the stream called Kúryá on Lovett's map, which I take to be the Kumrúd. This stream receives a tributary from the south, the Jashn stream.

The Walárúd (or Wálárúd) mentioned by Ẓahíru'd-Dín is the stream that waters the district of Walúpay.

H. MASHHADISAR

(*a*) Balada* comprising 'Arabkhayl, Bábulpusht, Báqirtanga, Bázár Maḥalla, Káẓimábád, Miyándasht, Qal'a, and Safí Mahalla.

(*b*) Bánṣarkalá*: Bahnamír*; Bíshasar*; Chumázdih* and Gílúr*; Kalándún*; Muqríkalá* and Kabútardún*; Rawshandún*.

(*c*) Pázwár*: Áhangarkalá*; Armíjkalá*; Armíjkalá-i-Marí*; Bábá-Bayg-Kamángar*; Dalwkalá*; Darzíkalá* and Muqríkalá*; Fúkalá*; Ḥájjí 'Abdu'l-'Aẓím Kamángar*; Hájjí Sa'íd Kamángar*; Kafshgarkalá*; Kalbast*; Kurdkalá*; Láríkalá*; Malikkalá*; Mírbázár*; Muẓaffar*; Naqíbkalá*; Riḍákalá*; Sayyidkalá*; Shihábu'd-Dín kalá*; Sulaymánkalá*.

(*d*) Rúdpusht*: Gáwzan Maḥalla*; Isfandiyár Mahalla*; Jámabázár*; Kúhír Maḥalla*; Lárí Maḥalla*; Mírzád Maḥalla*; Qáḍí Maḥalla*; Sádát Mahalla*; Újábụn*; Újáqsar*.

(*e*) Talárpay*: Áhangarkalá*; Akartíjkalá*; Dasta*; Gálishkalá*; Halwá'í kalá*; Junayd*; Kalhúdasht*; Kupúrchál*; Mullákalá*; Najjárkalá*; Rustam-i-Ḥájjí 'Alí*; Rustam-i-Zamán-i-Kafshgar*; Sálarúdkalá*, Sayyid Maḥalla*; Újátálár*.

I. BÁRFURÚSH

(*a*) Balada* and village of Kafshgarkalá*.

(*b*) Bálá Bulúk*: Áqá Malik Diláwar*; Áhangarkalá*; Ala chál-i-Kárdgar*, 'Alízamín*; Bangarkalá*; Darzíkalá* and Kulí* Dúnsar* and Shírsuwárkalá*; Hájjíkalá*; Najjárkalá*; Núsharwán* and Alkán*; Núsharwán-i-Bústání*; Qaṣṣáb-i-Bústání*; Qaṣṣáb-i-Miyándih*; Shaykh*; Sútkalá*.

(*c*) Bálá-Tíjin*: Afrá*; Baykalá*; Dáykalá*; Dizábád*; Findarí-i-Namáwar*; Fúmishkinár*; Ḥájjíkalá*; Ispú* or Hájjíkalá*; Jíjál-Ṭúlkhání*, Kárdgar-i-Khatír*; Kashká*; Káwán Áhangar*; Bálá-Káwán*; Khatírkalá*, Kiyákalá*; Khúrmakalá*; Kurdbarúkalá*; Mání Zargar*; Nawkalá* and Baykalá*; Qulzumkalá*; Ṣan'am*; Súkhtakalá*; Tarsíkalá*; Ṭúlindarrapay*; Zargar*.

Ẓahíru'd-Dín mentions Shírúj Kaláta in Bálá-Tijin.

(*d*) Bandpay*: Aḥmadchál*; Amírdih*; Arí*; Búrá*; Buzrúdpay* and Shánatarásh*; Díwá* and Fírúzcháh*; Díwchál*; Dúlarúdbár*; Fangchál*; Ḥalálkhúr Maḥalla*, Galúgáh*; Ganjkalá*; Garmíkalá*; Kárdgarkalá*; Karakinár*; Kalárúdpay* and Safídtúr*; Káshíkalá*; Kashtalí*; Khúshrúdpay*; Kúpásará*; Kurdrúdbár*; Máshúkalá* and Nargischál*; Muqríkalá* and Afrásiyábkalá*; Náríwarán*; Nawdihak*; Nishál*; Pá'ínrúdpay*; Pústkalá* and Áhangarkalá*; Sahmínkalá*; Sangchál-i-Dádmalá*; Sangrúdpay* with Kárdgarkalá* and Shúrkalá*; Siyáhdih*; Ṣulhdárkalá*; Ṣúrat* and Zarshúrán*; Warzana*; Zawárdih*.

(*e*) Bísha*: Amírkalá*; Ázádkalá*; Bandkhúy*; Bindárkalá*; Chumázdih*; Darzíkalá-i-Ákhúndí*; Darzíkalá-i-Ḥájjí Naṣírá*; Díwdilá*; Ḥájjíkalá*; Ḥájjíkalá-i-Kárdgar*; Hatakápusht*; Ḥaydarkalá*; Kamángarkalá*; Kashtalí-i-'Azíz-'Alamdár*; Khayrábád* and Lágharzamín*; Kuhnadasht*; La'lzan-i-Kiyá-kalá*; Mákarkalá*; Manṣúrkanda*; Maríkanda*; Naqíbdasht*; Náṣirábád*; Qádirkalágar*; Qarákhayl*; Sirájakalá*; Sayyid Káshí*; Sháhkalá Maḥalla*; Shihábu'd-Dínkalá*; Úshíb*; Walíkdún*; Waríkanda*.

(*f*) Jalál-Azrak*: Árdkala*; Baṣrá*; Bíjá*; Bíjíkalá*; Darkhí* (Archí?); Faram*; Kalíká*; Kalárasí*; Karímkalá*; Laylam-dasht*; Marzbál*; Marzúnábád*; Míka*; Múzúraj*; Nawdihak*; Qáríkalá*; Qúshchí*; Razakinár*; Ridákalá*; Rukun*; Sára*; Sardúrqádí*; Sarúmamiyán*; Sayyid 'Azíz Gashtasb*; Shaykh Dhakiyá*; Surkháb*; Súta* and Mahalistán*; Tahnadar*; Tajrí-Aspshúrpay* or Kárdgar-i-Namáwar* (near it is Mashhad-i-Sabz, 12 miles from Bárfurúsh on the road to Ámul. Close by are traces of former walls and moats, overgrown with moss and bushes, which mark the site of the former Shahr-i-Tajrí, a city the circumference of which was four miles. Dorn says it is in Bandpay and that on its site stands the shrine of Naw-Imám); Táju'd-Dawla*; Ṭughán* and Khurshíd*.

(*g*) Lafúr*: Azádgún; Dihún; Lafúr; Lafúrak; Nafṭchál; Maḥalla-i-Ḥájjí Ja'far; Tangsará. Ibn Isfandiyár mentions Mawujakúh, a village of Lafúr.

(*h*) Lálábád*: Aḥmadchálapay*; Aymánábád*; Alshá*; An-dakalá*; Bázyár*; Chinárbun*; Chumázdúnkalá*; Darzíkalá* or Ṭaraqchí Maḥalla*; Dáwudkalá*; Garmishkalá* or Garmíjkalá*; Gílkalá*; Ḥájjíkalá*; Ispúkalá*; Kamángarkalá*; Karúkalá*; Khása-i-Bábulkán*; Khaṭíbkalá*; Lalúk*; Mardumánkalá*, or Qal'akash*; Marzkinár*; Mínaskalá*; Muzaffarkalá*; Násirkalá*; Nawá'íkalá*; Ramanat* and Dáwudkalá*; Rangríz*; Rikájkalá*; Rúdpusht*, or Darwíshakhák*; Shamshírzan-i-Abu'l-Muḥammad Bayg*; Shamshírzan-i-Muḥammad Hádí Bayg*; Surkhakalá*; Tárí Maḥalla*; Yághíkalá*; Záhidkalá*.

(*i*) Mashhad-Ganjúrúz*: Abu'l-Haṣanábád* (with the shrine of Imámzáda Muḥammad, in which there is a wooden sarcophagus made by order of Muḥammad Káẓim, carpenter Muhammad Taqí b. Muḥammad Yúsuf Damáwandí, inscription by 'Abdu'l-'Azíz Mahdí); Járí* and Káwán-Áhangar*; Armak-i-Alarúdbár*; Dalwkalá*; Darúnkalá*; Ganjúrúz*; Gatáb* with Jilawdár Maḥalla*; Júbpusht*; Kashtalí*; Kalchúb*; Kalárúdpay*; Marznák*; Mírkalá*; Mírshab*; Rawshanábád*; Ṭulút*.

(*j*) Sásíkalám*: Áqá Muḥammad; Alarúdbár or Gáza Maḥalla; Darwísh Maḥalla; Díwbandkalá; Ispígarkalá; Kalágarkalá; Kurdkalá (probably the Kurdkalá mentioned by Ẓahíru'd-Dín which was known formerly as Lákábbandán); Kurdpay; Matíkalá; Mullá Muḥammad; Naqqárachí Maḥalla; Qumíkalá; Ruwárkalá; Tírkalá; Turk Maḥalla.

Ẓahíru'd-Dín mentions Qárinábád-dasht in Sásíkalám. The following villages are also in Bárfurúsh or in the immediately neighbouring districts of Mashhadisar and Faraḥábád: Aḥmadkalá; Andawar; Archí; Arzlú-Hájjíkalá; Asírkalá; Áwa; Azarband; 'Azízkalá; Bághasht; Bálá Khánasar; Balifkalá; Bamtú; Barbaríkhayl; Barsamín; Bázárgáh; Chahár; Chumázán; Chumázkalá; Darkádasht; Darzí Maḥalla; Dashtsar; Dih Mullá; Dirázkalá; Díwdasht; Durdín; Galiyá; Gamíshkalá; Gardanbarí; Gáwlangar; Gúrántálár; Hajírkalá; Halíkanda; Haliyasht; Ibn Núh; Iskanadih; Ispíkalájí; Isríkalá; Janafkalá; Jana; Kalamí; Káẓimbaygí; Káẓimkalá; Kabriyákalá; Kalárakalá; Kharábdih; Khardamard; Khasínkalá; Khushkrú; Kíkhá; Kuch; Kúchání Mahalla; Kushnábád; Ladar; Langúr; Lamiskalá; Maydánsar; Maykalá; Malafa; Malikakhayl; Malikkalá; Malik Sháh Maḥalla; Masí Maḥalla; Mahdíkalá; Naṣír Maḥalla; Nishúnkalá; Núdíkalá; Pádsháhmírkalá; Paríkalá; Rahkalá; Raḍiyakalá; Sangapúsh; Sarádárkalá; Satadih; Saras; Shabkalá; Shaftakalá; Sháhkútí; Shamíkalá; Shaykh-Kadír; Shaykh Músá; Shírdárkalá; Shúrak (Súrak); Síb-bágh; Siyáhdargáh; Siyáhkalá Maḥalla with Ḥaydarkalá, Shírazak and Kundakalá; Súrabun; Talárpusht; Talíkarán; Tamtamakalá; Taras; Tijinak; Tírkhání; Tírúnshíkalá; Turágil; 'Ulwíkalá; Walwand.

The district of Sawádkúh is often given as a subdistrict of Bárfurúsh. Shírgáh is sometimes counted as part of Sawádkúh.

J. FARAHÁBÁD

(*a*) Balada and Dázníkanda.

(*b*) Andarúd*: Ábbandánkash*; Ábbandánsar*; Asram* (Sálim of Farghána was slain by Wandá Ummíd at Harsamál three *farsakhs* from Ámul, but some say that this incident took place at Asram at a place called subsequently Híhí Kiyán);

Ázádgala*; Bálú Maḥalla*; Barárdih*; Chúkalá* with Karámak* and Rází*; Dangsarak*; Dárábkalá*; Darín* with Máh* and Parwín*; Hásiyatábád*; Haywalá*; Isfandiyár Maḥalla*; Jám-khána*; Kalmá*; Kalák*; Kúkbágh*; Lákdasht*; Malikábád*; Marzúd*; Marmat*; Mu'allamkalá*; Panbachúla*; Qádíkalá*; Ṣahibíwíshkalá*; Samiskanda*; Shahriyárkanda*; Súrak*; Ṭá-hirdih*; Zughálchál*.

(*c*) Gílkhwárán*: Bihistán*; Díwchál*; Díwkalá*; Fútam*; Írinábád*; Isma'ílkalá*; Júbar*; Kurdkalá* and Chapukrúd*; Miyándih*; Pahnkalá* and Kúkanda*; Sarwkalá*; Sirájkalá*; Shíb-Ábbandán*; Súrká*.

(*d*) Miyándúrúd*: 'Alíkanda*, Báblúr*; Báykalá*; Buzmíná-bád*; Chamán*; Darrapushtán*; Ispúkalá*; Kalá* and Táji-kalá*; Kalbistan*; Mákrán*; Niká*; Nawdihak* and Gílábád*; Súrím*; Ṭabaqadih*; Újákalá*; Walatúr*; Warandán*; Zayt* (or Zayd).

(*e*) Rúdpay*: Ábmál*; Ákand*; Fírúzkanda*; Kalmar* or Qájárkhayl*; Máhfírúz Maḥalla*; Panbazarkútí*; Ṣaláḥu'd-Dín Maḥalla* and Píchakalá*; Sayyid Maḥalla*.

(*f*) Shahrkhwást*: 'Alíwak*; Álúkanda*; Chumázak*; Dám-sar*; Darík*; Dímtúrán*; Diráz Maḥalla*; Díwkútí*; Dúnak* and Samandak*; Gíladún*; Gílnishín*; Isfandán*; Khárамiyán* and Miyáncháh*; Khárík*; Múrídár*; Sulaymán Maḥalla*; Táju'd-Dín Maḥalla*; Tijinak*; Zargarbágh*; Zarrínkalá*.

The following villages also belong to Farahábád: Gílchálasar; Kawsarkanda; Kumshyán; Láktaráshán; Malígula.

K. SÁRÍ

(*a*) Baladá*.

(*b*) 'Alí-ábád*: *Bázár* of 'Alí-ábád* (Sháh 'Abbás had a palace built and a garden laid out here and his famous causeway passed through the village. Ẓahíru'd-Dín mentions a shrine here which was a great place of pilgrimage for the people of this district. The shrine still exists)· Chumázkútí*; Darzíkalá* with Mujáwar Maḥalla* and Iskandarkalá*; Kafshgarkalá* with Matíkalá* and Paríjákalá*; Khamírkanda* and Karwá*; Kúshksará*; Qádíkalá* and Sárúkalá*; Wáskas*, Wústákalá* and Sarwkalá*.

(*c*) Bíshasar*: Áhangarkalá*; Chabí*; Gul-afshán*; Maráta'*; Míla* (the site of an ancient settlement) and Parchínak*; Ríkanda*, Taháram*.

(*d*) Isfíward* and Shúráb*: Azdárak*; Báríkábsar*; Bíjkalá*; Gílakalá*; Gurjíkalá*; Laylákalá*; Máfrúzjak*; Malik*; Páshákalá*; Rúdpusht*; Salúkalá*; Shamladún*; Sharafdárkalá*; Surkhakalá*; Zardíchál* (Zarwaján?); Zarrínábád-i-Bálá*.

Zahíru'd-Dín mentions the village of Dizádún on the Tijinrúd, not far from the village of Shúráb.

(*e*) Gulayján Rustáq*: Ahídasht*; Amrí*; Áqá Mashhad*; Bindárkhayl*; Dálistán*; Darwár*; Dizá*; Gardishí*; Garmístán*; Garmrúd*; Gulchíní*; Húlár*; Kalúrd*; Khán 'Abbásí*; Kúlá* (on the top of Darband-i-Kúlá, near the road to Áram, there was a palace, since known as 'Á'isha Kargílí Dizh, where the Ispahbad Khurshíd left his wives and family when the Muslim army invaded Ṭabaristán. Later, when the Caliph's general Firásha invaded Ṭabaristán, the Ispahbad Wandá Hurmazd retired to Darband-i-Kúlá and constructed near it at Gawázúnú, two great dykes, one above and one below. At the foot of the castle of Kúzá, above the village of Tálpúr, the people of Kúlá, with those of Mount Qárin, built for Suhráb, the son of Báw, a palace, hot bath, and *maydán*, and the buildings were afterwards enlarged by the Ispahbad Sharwín, and were still visible in Ibn Isfandiyár's time); Lármá*, Nawdihak*; Pahnkalá*; Pul-i-Gardan*; Sangtaráshán*; Salím-Bahrám*; Salím-Shaykh*; Shilírkanda*; Warakí*; Warand*.

(*f*) Kárkanda*: Abaksar*; Afrápul*; Alamshír*; Arán*; Chártábun*; Dínárgúshí* (Dínárkútí?); Dawlatábád*; Ḥájjíkalá*; 'Ísákhandaq*; Khúsháb*; Máchakpusht*; Tírkárkalá*.

(*g*) Kiyákalá*: Az; 'Azízak; Bacha-Chálasar; Darwísh 'Alambází; Díwkalá*; Dúk; Garwasdih; Jaziya-Salámíkhayl; Ruknkalá; Sangtú; Sihrúz-i-Bálá; Sayyidábád; Sháhzád.

(*h*) Mishkábád*: Darkásar*; Kalírd*; Lárím*; Markúra*; Pahnáb*; Rúdpusht-i-pá'ín*; Talárak*; Warsúkalá*.

(*i*) Nawkandaká*: Afrá-kash*; Áhangarkalá*; Lamúk*; Rikábdárkalá*.

(*j*) Sárí-Rúdpay*: Ashraf Maḥalla*; Ajwarsar*; Asárúpay* and Bálú Maḥalla*; Bijlú*; Gul-afshán*; Istalkhsár*; Kalá; Najjárkalá*; Qúruq*; Rukundasht*; Sarwínabágh*; Sharafábád*.

(*k*) Sawádkúh*, already dealt with separately.

(*l*) Shírgáh*: Áhangarkalá; Arsinján; Búrakhayl; Cháhsar; Íwa*; Kilíj; Manḥal; Músákalá; Púládkalá; Ráhdárkhána; Sháh Maḥalla; Shírgáh.

The following villages were also mentioned to me as belonging to Sárí: Adrustáq; Afrábágh; Afrákútí; Anjílasán; Arata; Asadábád; Ásiyábpísh; Ásiyábsar; Atíkalá; Bálákalá; Bandafurúsh; Barúḥasar; Bashal; Bínasúnak; Biríján; Chálapul; Chálazamín; Charáhar; Chúlí; Dangaladih; Darúpay; Dashtmiyán; Dinjakalá; Harmíná; Ḥasanábád; Ḥusaynábád; Ispíwáshí; Ispúrízí; Jámnú (or Chamanú. Ẓahíru'd-Dín informs us that it is a village of Sárí with a shrine where some *sayyids* are buried and which is a place of pilgrimage. In Siyáhrúd, near Jámnú, in the village of Danakí there was a whirlpool or eddy called Ganjgirdáb mentioned by Ibn Isfandiyár); Khanar Maḥalla; Khánqallí Maḥalla; Kharchang; Khushksarí; Kurdkhayl; Kútísar; Kútísardasht; Lúlat; Mashkhhíkalá; Mihrúnkalá; Nadáfkhayl; Naqqárachí Maḥalla; Nargiskútí; Na'lbandán; Nawdasht; Nawmal; Pá'ínkalá; Píchákalá; Qal'asar; Qaríb Maḥalla; Rustamdárkalá; Sadpay; Sa'íd Mahalla; San'akhayl; Sangríza; Santí; Sarkat; Shírkatá; Siyáh-anárbágh; Siyáhchinár; Siyáhkalá; Sír; Talíbágh; Talíkalá; Tarsíkalá; Waláshit (with a tumulus called Tappa Múrandín); Warat; Wastún; Záhid Mahalla; Zarríndih; Zawár Maḥalla. Ibn Isfandiyár mentions Dawlatábád near Sárí.

L. HAZÁRJARÍB

(i) Dúdánga.

(*a*).........[1]: Alasar*; 'Alí-ábád*; Arzam*; Ast Mír Muḥammad*; Atíní*; Aylál*; Balada*; Chahárdihrúdbár*; Chálúd*; Darbíb* and fields of Shahmírzád*; Fítask* (on the Rasúm Rúdbár, an upper branch of the Tijin); Fítask-Áhangar*; Fúlád Maḥalla*; Gáward*; Gawhardih*; Gílkhwárán*; Híkú*; Húlá*; Jásham*; Jásham-i-Tangsar*; Kalímkhwája*; Karkám*; Kharíd*; Khurramábád*; Kiyádih*; Kít* and Yasram*; Kulí*; Kulídar*; Kust*; Lálá* (given by Demorgny as the chief place of Hazárjaríb); Nawdih*; Pá'índih*; Pájí*; Pardakalá*; Parkinár*; Purwar*; Rawshanáb*; Rúdbárak*; Salí*; Sangchashma*; Sarúk*; Shalímak*; Siyáhdasht*; Siyáhwushkalá*; Surkhadih*; Talájím*; Tamám*; Tanbalá*; Tarázdíh*; Tílabun*; Tílak*; Warmazábád*; Wáwsar*.

(*b*) Niyáft*: Áhangarkalá*; Áyaksar*; Aysás*; Balárak*; Bíshakalá*; Dámádkalá* and Kuhnadih*; Dáwudkalá*; Dúmarkalá*; Gulgul*; Ja'farkalá*; Kalíjkalá*; Margáw* and Páshákalá*; Mírázdih*; Nawdihkalá*; Pahmawar* and Darwár*;

[1] The name is illegible in my notes.

Parakúh*; Pahpusht*; Sangchál*; Sangdih*; Shahrdasht*; Shahriyárdarra*; Sútakalá*; Ṭabaqakalá*; Taqí-ábád*; Talá-ram*; Walíkbun*; Walíkchál*; Wáwdarra*; Wizmalá*.

(ii) Chahárdánga*.

(*a*) Achrustáq*: Áhangarkalá* and Isṭalkhsar*; Andín* and Sáq Maḥalla*; Burná*; Díwá*; Kalágar Maḥalla* and Kurd Maḥalla*; Khwájakalá*; Limrad*; Lawjanda*; Mashbúkalá* and Arsam*; Mutakázín*; Qaríb Maḥalla*; Samachúl*; Súrak*; Tárasam*; Zírband-i-Sahlpul*.

(*b*) Anazánkúh*: Afṭalat*; Aláraz-i-Búm*; Aláraz-i-Shúráb*; Andarát*; Astáram*; Azrat*; Bádila*; Chinárbun*; Chínparch*; Dáwud Maḥalla*; Gatakash*; Gatarúdbár*; Gáwsálár*; Giwá*; Haftlab*; Halúchál*; Ḥulrum*; Istájnán*; Istí Mahalla*; Kamarbun*; Kaláram*; Kalwaz*, Kháragat*; Malik Mahalla*; Pársá*; Páytú*; Pítanú*; Pushtrúdbár*; Sangdih*; Shiyám*; Shíldarra*; Wahí*; Waywá*; Wanasht*; Yalmá* and Kalwár*.

(*c*) Bálárustáq*: 'Ábidínkhatír*; Aghúzbun-i-Ispú*; Astúrúá-i-Gíl*; Astúrúá-i-Kafshgar*; Gílkash Maḥalla*; Kaliyá-i-Khaṭír*; Káfíbáfí*; Kúshk-i-Nadáf*; Kurddasht Maḥalla*; Land-Ispú* (Naw and Kuhna); Landrúdbár*; Marand-i-Kashal*; Míká Maḥalla*; Sarmard*; Sarúkbun-i-Ḥájjí Kafshgar*; Sayyidak Maḥalla*; Siyáh-balú-i-Tamár*; Súta-i-Nadáf*; Tímúy-lang*; Yánisar-i-Bargír*.

(*d*) Bard* (114): Bard* and Tilmádarra*; Agra; Bádilakúh; Siyáhpara; Surkhdih.

(*e*) Barkár*: 'Abdu'lláh Maḥalla*; Áram*; Bághbán Maḥalla*; Ilyás Maḥalla*; Isma'íl Maḥalla*; Kalágar Maḥalla*; Kurd Maḥalla* or Kurdkalá*; Maydának*; Rízúsham*; Safídkúh*; Sulaymán Mahalla*; Wasam*.

(*f*) Chálú*: Chálú*; Chirkat*; Guljárí*; Halwír*; Manzil-darra*; Túsa*; Úrasht*; Wana*.

(*g*) Darká*: Ajúrd*; Andarácham*; Burmárúdbár*; Darká*; Darúk*; Gárpám*; Kalágar Mahalla*; Sang*; Túlit*; Zarríná-bád*.

(*h*) Ghulámí*: 'Abdu'lláhí*; Ghulámí*; Kalá*; Malú*; Muṣay-yib Maḥalla*; Párch*; Shal*; Shalar*; Wímá*; Zangat*.

(*i*) Kúhsár*: Áqá Zamán*; Aghúzdarra*; Anármá*; Ardár-síra*; Bíshaband-i-Mu'íní*, Bíshaband* and Karáb*; Chashma-bun*; Daram* (Aghúzdarra)*; Garnám*; Hímaján*; Katarúd-bár*; Kalápaydarra* (Rúdbár); Kiyásar*; Kúhistán-i-Andarún-Tanga*; Kúhistán-i-Garnám*; Níward*; Rúdbár-i-A'lá*; Shálá*

(Niyálá?); Súta Aghúz*; Túskáchashma*; Wazwár*; Walásara*.

(*j*) Kuyúsar*: 'Alamdárdih*; 'Alamdárpay* and Darmántarak*; Dihdú*; Daylamrúdbár*; Diyájim*; Kaním*; Kasúb*; Kharkám*; Kuyúsar*; Lamsúkalá*; Mádúrustáq*; Nawkanda-i-Dárúb*; Rízsardih*; Shayldarra* and Kirát*; Shawílásht*; Túmlaj*; Úlít*.

(*k*) Láy*: 'Aybchín; Arazk; Kalárúdbár; Mullákhayl; Rúdbár; Sayyidkhayl Maḥalla; Ziyáratkalá.

(*l*) Mawáẓi'*: 'Alamkúh*; Ázádsafídkúh*; Darbíb-i-Shihábu'd-Dín*; Ḥalmí*; Harla*; Kísná*; Láktarásh*; Máram*; Shabkalá*; Shúráb*; Siyúr*; Warpám*.

(*m*) Miyánsí*: Bargírkalá*; Barúm* and Rúkatam*; Ḥaná*; Katakash*; Kaláft*; Lárak*; Lármá*; Malwá*; Ma'súmábád*; Miyánsí*; Nakarán*; Palúr Maḥalla*; Sírjárí*; Turk*; Turkdasht*; Úmár*.

(*n*) Payraja*.

(*o*) Sa'ída*: Ardashír Maḥalla*; Bálákalá*; Gandak Mahalla*; Járchiyán*; Khúrt*; Kút*; Miyándarra*; Ním*; Qádíkalá* and fields of Bardam*; Qádí Mahalla*; Sábiq Mahalla*; Sangá Maḥalla*; Siráj Maḥalla*; Sayyidgúr*; Súḥalmá*; Turk Maḥalla*; Wármí*; Warpám*; Yakhdum*.

(*p*) Sartíka*: Ayúl*; Bulkhás*; Kaláracha*; Kurdamír*; Kirát*; Qatárma*; Sartíka* or Pishirt*.

(*q*) Tírkár*: Chálú*; Khása-i-Ramadání* (including Azdársíra, Gurgtáj, Láypasand, Láktásh, Shírkalá, Shít); Límúndih*; Nawdih*; Núríbun*; Rúzkiyádih*; Tarkám*; Úland*; Warmazár*; Waswá*.

(*r*) Wardíma*.

(*s*) Wilwíma* and Warí*: Warí*; Wilwíma*.

(*t*) Zárimrúd*.

The reading of many of the above-mentioned names is uncertain. The following were also given me as being in Hazárjaríb: In Dúdánga: Afráchál; Aghúzgula; Angapám; Aḥmadábád; Darzíkalá; Dhakírkalá; Dínasar; Istílasar; Gandalak; Jamálu'd-Dín-kalá; Kamarkalá; Karasim; Katrum; Khishtistán; Khúshrúdbár; Khulrat; Kurchá; Maydánsar; Maskúpá; Muḥammadábád; Mulládih; Mutají; Paráh; Parchawá; Rasgat; Sarkám; Sayyidábád; Sayyidkalá; Siyáhkúh; Súámara; Talúkalá; Zanbíní In Chahárdánga: Áhangar Mahalla; Báláband; Bárkalá; Bídar; Buznám; Chinárbíní; Chínapul; Chumázdih; Dabbágh; Dúkal;

Ispíkúh; Ḥusaynábád; Jandakulí; Kaftarkár; Kachap Maḥalla; Katchashma; Kat Maḥalla; Kuhnagún; Kuhnakúh; Kudmínú; Latakúma; Masháni; Maṣaf; Parímag; Páwand; Pírkalá; Ramadánkhayl; Sádát-i-Badábsarí; Sangrúj; Siyáhkhání; Sútakhayl; Ṭa'ífa-i-Palang; Tájirkhayl; Talúkalá; Wilú; Wínabun.

M. ASHRAF

(*a*) Balada* with Qádíkiyáb* and Ra'yatkhayl*.

(*b*) Qaráṭughán*: Dawránasar*; Ḥájjí Mahalla*; Kalít*; Kúsán-i-Búmí*; Kúsán-i-Gurjí*; Miyánkalá* (pastures); Nawdihak* and Niká*; Nímcháy*; Qal'a-Zaynawand* and Qal'a-Ḥusaynábád*; Qal'a-Náṣirábád*; Qarátappa*; Rustamkalá*; Shahzádkalá*; Shúrábsar*; Siyáhwáshkalá*; Turújan*; Walínábád*.

In the *Táríkh-i-Khání* we find Ibráhím-kútí and Míránarúd in Qaráṭughán.

(*c*) Kulbád: Áblúr etc., Galúgá; Khurshíd; Khurshídkalá; Lawaskanda; Limrásk.

(*d*) Panjhazár: Awrán; Báqirábád; Kalák; Pásand; Qal'apáyán; Rán; Rikáwand; Rubáṭ and Khalíl Maḥalla; Sárú and Áltappa; Sháhkíla; Walamázú; Zírwán.

(*e*) Yakhkash: Awárt; Bijat; Bíkhbun; Chálish Maḥalla; Dalároz; Gharíb Maḥalla; Páram; Shaykh Maḥalla; Shírdárí; Walam.

The Ispahbad Khurshíd had a general named Qárin, after whom was named the village of Qárinábád in Panj-hazár. Námina and Yahúdiyya were also in Panjáh-hazár.

N. ANAZÁN

Bághú; Banafshatappa; Dashtkalá with Watanå and Ustúnábád; Gaz and Bandargaz; Hashtiyaka; Jifákanda; Kárkanda and Kharába-Shahr; Kuhna Kulbád; Líwán; Nawkanda; Sar Maḥalla; Sartáq; Sútadih; Walafrá.

O. SADAN-RUSTÁQ

Alang; Alwár; Anjíláb; Ázád Maḥalla; Bákar Maḥalla (fields); Bálájáda; Bánu'mán; Chahárdih; Chaqqar; Chálakí; Dankalán; Dúrúd Maḥalla; Galú; Gurjí Maḥalla; Háshimábád; Ḥaydarábád; Ispú Maḥalla; Kafshgírí; Kalámú; Kalá Sangiyán; Kharába-Mashhad; Kulájan-i-Qájár; Kulájan-i-Sádát; Kurd Maḥalla; Laladuwín; Lalafan (pastures); Lámílang; Lamisk; Mihtarkalá;

Miyándarra; Mufídábád; Náman; Naw-Chaman; Nawdíja; Pashínkalá; Qal'a-Maḥmúd; Qalandar 'Aysh; Qalandar Maḥalla; Qásimábád; Sa'adábád; Sadan; Sarkalá; Sayyid-Mírán; Sháhdih; Shahráshúb (fields); Shamúshak; Shúryán and Táza-ábád; Tukhshí Maḥalla; Túshan; Újábun; Warsan; Yisáqí; Zará Maḥalla; Zangí Maḥalla; and the ruined villages of Atkaram; Bunkaláta; Ja'farábád; Khurúsábád; Qal'a (near Mihtarkalá); Rawshanábád; Ṣadrábád; Túgilbágh; 'Ulúfan; Waláshkí; Yájíní; and Yálú.

Yálú is said to have been a *bulúk* of 35 villages, amongst others Bálájáda; Galú; Lalafan; Lamisk; Qásimábád; Sadan; Sayyid Mírán; Túgilbágh; 'Ulúfan; Yájíní; and Yálú.

The mountains of this district are: Astarakúh; Galúkan; Gáwpá; Jahánnumá; Manzúlak; Pashtú; Sháhpasandkúh; Tábkún; Tarktá; Ṭulúr.

P. SHÁHKÚH AND SÁWAR

Ḥájjíábád; Jahánnumá (*yayláq*); Kundáb; Rádkán; Rasúlábád or Rubáṭ-i-Safíd; Sháhkúh-Bálá including Yúrt-i-Áqá Riḍá, Chahárbágh (115), Chálkhána, Jirín-Birín, Yúrt-i-Shárak; Sháhkúh-Pá'ín; Tásh.

Rádkán was formerly a district containing over 30 villages, all of which, with the exception of Kaláta, Kundáb, and Ḥájjíábád, are now in ruin and uninhabited. The names of these villages were: 'Abbás Khaṭírí; Ámadkhayl; Búdúsará; Bústamín; Chíristán; Dídarra; Dúkabun; Gáwkúh or Gúkúh; Gazanasará; Haftchashma; Ḥájjíábád; Ḥaydarkhayl; Ispanjárí; Kalmíshkíjá; Kaláta or Rádkán; Karkasá; Kháksardila; Khánasarí; Kúldín; Kundáb; Lísagú; Maqasí-Sarpích; Mázíbun; Púlád Maḥalla below Kaláta; Sarkalá; Tamartáshkhayl; Walár; Wazma; Zakwár; Zirishkchál.

Mountains and *yayláqs* of Sháhkúh and Sáwar: Ashtás; Aspchar; Asp-u-Nayza; Bahárak; Bahrám Khán; Bandnard; Báríkáb; Chálasará; Chaman-i-Dárá; Chandarsítkhayl; Chinárbíní; Fúzakalá; Garmábadasht (near the Quzluq pass); Gáwsang; Gurgpá; Haftchashma; Jájuglí; Júlíkhán; Kabúdchála; Kalúkáy; Khúshámad; Kutchashma; Landakúh; Larakúh; Lílásar; Miyándúrú; Miyányúrt; Naqdyúrt; Nayrúdbár; Pá'ízbun; Pá'ízsar; Pusht-Girdúkúh; Qabrán; Quzluq (116); Rusúl (a green glen at the foot of the Tang-i-Shamshírbur); Rítú; Rízáw; Sangbun; Sang-Imám; Sangkalán; Sardarwáza (a hill nine miles south of

Astarábád); Sarmákhúrda (a forest in the plain of Sáwar); Sárú Chashma; Sáwar 'Uliyá; Shaliyár; Shúr-Chashma; Surkhchádih; Sútasar; Takht-Míl; Tappa-i-Sarw (at the foot of the Quzluq pass); Turkchál; Turk-Maydán (6800 ft., 25 miles from Chahárdih and 11 from Ziyárat) (117); Yúrt-i-Chinára; Zalabán.

Q. ASTARÁBÁD-RUSTÁQ

Áhangar Maḥalla; 'Alí-ábád; Álúkalá; Amírábád; Atrakchál; Bágh Gulbun; Chahárchinár; Chúplání; Dúdánga; Fayḍábád; Fújird; Iṣfahánkalá; Ja'farábád; Jilín or Jirín; Karímábád; Khayrát (only a little pasture); Kumásí; Maryamábád; Marzánkalá; Ma'ṣúmábád; Mír Maḥalla; Muhammadábád; Mú'minábád; Naṣrábád; Nawdih-i-Niẓámu'd-Dín; Númal; Pul-Khúrda; Qarnábád; Rustamkalá-i-'Abbás Bayg; Rustamkalá-i-Sádát; Shamsábád; Siyáhtalú; Surkhánkalá; Sulṭánábád (east of which is Sangar-i-Aḥmad-'Alí Khán, built as a protection against the Turcomans); Tawshan; Turangtappa; Úzína; Walíkábád; Ziyárat-i-Khwástarúd commonly called Ziyárat-i-Khásarúd (117); and the ruined villages of Dabbághkul; Gultappa (a former city); Kharasgilú; Maḥmúdábád; Nárinjbágh and Rawshankalá; Písh-áhang or Shúrkalá; Qal'a Siyáhbálá; Rabí'Kaláta; Simárú; Ṭálibú or Waláshábád; Újátúk; Ẓahírábád.

The villages of Fakhr 'Imádu'd-Dín are: Dawlatábád or Kinára; Ḥusaynábád-i-Malik; Ja'farábád; Miyánábád; Qulí-ábád; Taqartappa; Taqí-ábád; and the ruined villages of Áhúsará: Anda'ábád; Chihilgísú; Gawzan; Gulbágh or Qal'a-Ḥasan; Ḥaydar Maḥalla and Burbar; Jahánábád; Káfirduwín; Khusrawábád; Máránkalá; Misgar Maḥalla; Nirsá; Qiz-Qal'a; Shahristántappa; Talúkalá.

In an old *Waqf-Náma* dated 989/1581, now in the possession of the Shírang *Sayyids* who were to receive the revenues derived from them, we find mentioned the following villages of the district of Fakhr 'Imádu'd-Dín: Agra; 'Aláman; 'Alázamín; Álústán; Anda'ábád; Andashírábád; Anúshtanga; Bawána; Dizgáh; Dúqabrán; Gáwá'í Maḥalla; Girá'i Maḥalla; Gulbun; Gúní Maḥalla; Ḥájjí Yádár; Kamál Gharíb; Kamál Khán; Máránkaláta; Misgarán; Nírgán; Píchák Maḥalla; Qará-Ágháj; Qarákul; Qárluq (upper and lower); Sangchashma; Sangduwín; Shírang; Thúr-Kaláta; Ṭabarsá; Ṭawá; Zargarán. The following villages, said to be about 12 miles east of Astarábád, are also mentioned in this document: Amírdih; Garmábasará; Kashta;

Marzubán Kaláta; Muḥibbábád; Mushtak-i-Quṭbu'd-Dín now called Shawkatábád; Nafṭú; Qaranjamín; Rawshaná'í Maḥalla; Rubáṭú; Talúkaláta.

Peaks and localities in the mountains of Ziyárat-i-Khwástarúd: 'Arúsíkalá; Birinjyakí; Farímán (ruins of a castle); Garmdasht (2100 ft., name of a portion of the valley south of Ziyárat), Gulachál; Kal-Yayláq; Kharú; Kurmatú; Lútiyá; Marsang; Mázúkash; Murád Chashma; Nawkalá; Nawmarú; Úlangdarra; Qulílá; Sartakhta; Shahrbut (said to be the site of an ancient city); Surkh-chashma; Takht-i-'Umar; Ṭalábakht; Talamiyár; Ṭálú; Zarmishkúh; Zíla.

Ruins are found in the forest of Ziyárat at the following spots: Anjílúkhayl; Ispandiyár Maḥalla; Jírú; Malásh; Úlangdarra, Qal'a-Ḥasan; Takht-i-Díká; Takht-i-Khusraw.

R. KATÚL

'Aláman; 'Alázamín; 'Alí-ábád formerly Qádirábád; Álústán; Baraftán (clans Palang and Dánkúh); Basísar; Chajáh; Chalí; Ganú; Gharíbábád; Hájjíábád; Jangaldih; Kardábád; Khárkalá; Khúlíndar; Kumálán (with the Imámzáda Dú-qabrán); Márán-kalá; Máyán; Mazra'a; Muhammadábád; Nawdih; Nírgán; Nirsú; Nuṣratábád (formerly Sangduwín); Píchák Mahalla; Qúsh-Kuprí; Ríg-Chashma; Sáwarkalá; Siyáhmarkúh; Tábar.

S. FINDARISK

(i) Findarisk: Áqá Muḥammadábád (formerly Lalabágh); Chínú; Dárkalá; Darra-i-Malik-Sulaymán; Kalúkan; Khánbibín; Mashú; Ma'ṣúmábád; Mázú-arám; Namtalú; Naqí-ábád; Sa'ad-ábád; Shafí'ábád; Shírábád; Zarríngul.

(ii) Rámyán: Gulchashma (formerly Darrawiya); Ispirinján; Jawzchál; Kabúdchashma; Khándúz; Kúmyán; Lírú; Mír Maḥalla; Nargischál; Nawdih-i-Isma'íl Khán (118); Nawdih-i-Mír Sa'du'lláh Khán; Páqal'a; Pulrum; Rámyán (in a glen enclosed by two forest-covered spurs of the Khúshyayláq mountain); Razí; Sayyidkalá; Súkhtasará; Túrán; Watan.

The mountains of Rámyán are: Ásmyán, in which is Qal'a Púrán; Nílakúh, south of Chakúr, half way between which two places is the mound of Takht-i-Rustam. The mountain is variously called Máránkúh and Ílángurgán. Qal'a Márán is in the midst of meadows, and the path which leads to it is easily defensible against any number of assailants.

T. KÚHSÁR

(*a*) Chináshk: Aytarjlú; Chilín; Chináshk (4 miles from Tulbín); Darra-i-Qadamgáh; Dúrúk; Garfang; Ḥusaynábád or Síná; Káshídár; Narráb; Qishláq; Rúdbár or Chaman-i-Qishláq; Síbchál; Wálamán or Wámanán (Ẓahíru'd-Dín mentions Walabun in Shahr-Duwín).

(*b*) Qánchí: Balánjarak; Dújuz; Fársiyán-i-Qánchí; Tílawá (probably Dílábád); Zardwá.

(*c*) Kúhsár: 'Alí-ábád; Birín; Birinján; Birinjbín; Chakarchál; Chamaní; Dahana-i-Kalásangiyán; Dihjúlí; Dúkhar; Dúdrajan or Qal'a-Sayyidhá; Dúzín; Fársiyán-i-Fírang (the stream running from Pársiyán towards the Gurgán basin is called Tará); Fírang; Gulistán; Gulsará; Isfirinján; Kandakhar; Khándúshar; Khurramábád; Mahdí-ábád; Qal'a Káfa; Qal'a-sará; Qulítappa; Sálá; Sáyir; Sih-Hír; Sihrú; Shaydán; Surung; Taqí-ábád; Tarsa; 'Ubba-i-Khallí Khán; Warchashma; Zarrínkaláta; Zímsháh.

(*d*) Sangar-i-Kabúdjáma or Sángar-i-Ḥájjílar: Áhangar Maḥalla; Khúrda Aymúqlí; Pisarak; Sangar; Siyúmák; Talang-sará; Tígha-Zamín; Zindánchál.

U. LOCALITIES UNIDENTIFIED OR NOT OTHERWISE MENTIONED[1]

Abkhama, a city in the mountains of Ṭabaristán [a]; Anáristán, near Marznák on the way to Sárí [b]; Anúshadádhán [a], perhaps the same as Wanúshadih; Arán and Sharán, two cities of Ṭabaristán [c]; Ardal [b], in the district of Bábulkinár; Ardashírábád [a], where, in the 8th (14th) century, stood a palace of the Kings of Mázandarán; Arz, a small town in the mountains of Ṭabaristán towards Daylamán [c]. Abú Sa'd Manṣúr says that it was one of the strongest and greatest fortresses in the world. The products not required locally were all exported to Awdiya. After passing the town of Arz one enters the mountains of Wandá Hurmazd and thence those of Sharwín; Ashíládasht [a], near Ámul in the plain of Líkání; Awájan [b]; Áwdiz, in the neighbourhood of the castle of Núr; Bahrámkaláda [b]; Bálá'ín [a], probably between Ámul and Sárí; Baráz, a castle in or near

[1] (*a*) Ibn Isfandiyár.
(*b*) Zahíru'd-Dín.
(*c*) Yáqút.
(*d*) 'Abdu'l-Fattáh Fúmaní
(*e*) 'Alí b. Shamsu'd-Dín Láhijí.

Núr; Báshír [a], near Ámul; Bakanda, a village on the banks of the Bábul river; Bíjúrí or Machúrí [a]; Kúh-i-Bínár, a magnificent, scarped hill in Astarábád, seen to the left of the Chilcháliyán pass on the road from Sháhrúd to Sháhkúh; Bundárakalá [b], in or near Shahriyár Kúh; Dúlár [b], near the coast not far from Ámul; Fírú'íz, a village in Astarábád [c]; Plain of Ganjína and Ispíd Dáristán [a]; Gawd-i-Názir, a plateau 4 miles west-north-west of Rúdbár on the road from Fírúzkúh to Fúlád Maḥalla, 4½ miles west-south-west of Fúlád Maḥalla; Girdzamín [a], 4 *farsakhs* from Sárí; Ghulámaráh, probably south of Rustamdár; Gúshwárakúh, on the Sháhrúd or Dámghán border [b]; Ḥarandáb, a mountain of Barlúr [d]; Harján; Harsamál [a], 3 *farsakhs* from Ámul; Ḥázimazar or Ḥázimadiz [b], compare with Ibn Isfandiyár's Kharmazar near Ámul; Ilyání, a narrow glen in the Astarábád district through which passes the Astarábád-Sháhrúd road, 24 miles from the latter town; Injír [a]; Jaláyin [a]; Jahannamdarra, north of Chuláw where the Harhaz was spanned by a bridge in 806/1403–4; Jawzistan [b]; Jind, a city in Ṭabaristán founded by Qubád b. Fírúz b. Yazdijird the Sásánid; Jurbast, a village in the mountains of Ṭabaristán. The roads leading to it are narrow and difficult [c]; Júrpushta; Kalam, a castle dating from the time of Khusraw. It was in the mountains of Astarábád and was one of the strongholds of the Assassins; Kandar; Karkam [a]; Káwadán and Káwardán [c], villages of Astarábád; Kashfal, a village of Ámul; Kawíj; Kaywán Bazham [b]. Sultán Muḥammad b. Malik ordered it to be besieged and had it destroyed; Khúr suflaq, a village of Astarábád [c]; Kílárján [a]; Kimnán [a]; Kúladarra [e], on the confines of Fírúzkúh; Kúláwíj [b]; Kútí Ibráhím Kárdgar [e], to the east of Ámul; Landar or Land, on the way from Farím to Gulpáygán, identical with Landakúh; Lankúrkhán [a]; Lariz, probably Lazúr, a village of the district of Ámul, better known under the name of Qal'a-Lariz. It was two days' distance from Ámul; Latrá [a]; Lícham [a]; Madú [a]; Mahastiya or Quhsibah (reading uncertain) or Tís [a]; Má'múní villages (300 villages in the mountain and plain of Mázandarán, which Wandá Hurmazd was compelled to cede to Má'mún, the son of Hárúnu'r-Rashíd, were known under the name of Má'múní); Mankúl [a]; Marzubánábád [b], a village in the plain, probably not far from Qal'a-Dárá; Maskán or Mashkán [b], a village probably in or not far from the district of Miyánrúd, north-west of Ámul; Mazrak; Míl or Milla, 3 or 4 square miles of grass 4½ miles north of Fúlád Maḥalla; Míla[b], 3 *farsakhs* from Ámul; Mírwandábád [a], a village of Gulpáygán; Mír Wazán, name given to the various spots where the coffin of Mír Qiwámu'd-Dín was laid down when on its way from Bárfurúsh to Ámul for burial. These spots were called Ziyárat-i-Mír-Wazán; Muḥammadábád [b], near Chináshk; Muyassar [b], between Khayrrúdkinár and Lasha-Lazúr; Bazham Músá [b], a peak near Lawandar; Naftakútí, a low mound on the mainland west of the peninsula of Miyánkala; Námina, a city 20 miles from Sárí, in the district of Panjáh-Hazár; Náwasar [b]; Níshávwur: according to Dimishqí Mázandarán was also called Níshávwur and was distinct from Ṭabaristán; Nawrúzábád (Nawdharábád?) [a]: we read that Hasan b. Zayd, advancing from Ámul, went to Tarícha and thence to Jámnú, when, hearing that Sulaymán b. 'Abdu'lláh, the Ṭáhirid Governor of Sárí, had sent his general, Asad b. Jandán, with an army from Sárí to a place called Dúdán on the road to Tújí, he turned aside and marched by way of Zarmíkhwást to Nawrúzábád by the village of Fútam, where his ally the Masmughán had camped; Nusrat Sang (at the death of Sulṭán Tukush in 596/1199–1200, Sháh Ardashír of Mázandarán seized the castles of Bálaman and Juhína, the whole country from Gurgán to Ray and the castle of Fírúzkúh, and built the castle of Nuṣrat Sang in Bírún Tamísha) [b]; Palang [e], a castle probably in Tunakábun; Parustáq [e], a castle in Sawádkúh or Hazárjaríb; Pásgah-i-Mír Marḥúm [e]; Pázwar, a shepherd camp in the southern border of Mázandarán. It lies north of the Khing plateau, and about 12 miles west of Fúlád Maḥalla; Pír Girdú Kúh, a mountain in the Astarábád district, south of Astarábád, and a few miles north of Tásh. From this peak a good view of Astarábád and surrounding peaks is to be had; Qaṭarí-Kaláda: in the time of the tyrant Ḥajjáj b. Yúsuf, the Khárijites who were made prisoners at Samnán by the Ispahbad Farrukhán-i-Buzurg were brought to Mázandarán, where traces of their encampment were still visible in Ibn Isfandiyár's time at a place called Qaṭarí-Kaláda; Qádíkaláya, a village of Astarábád; Rúdbárpích [a]; Rú'yín [b], a castle in Bírún Tamísha. It was taken and destroyed by the Ispahbad Najmu'd-Dawla Qárin (501–508/1107-8–1114). It is the same as the castle of Rúhín mentioned in Ibn Isfandiyár; Ṣafúḥ [a], near Ámul; Salash, 8600 ft., a pasture of a few acres between Fírúzkúh and Chásham in Mázandarán. It is visited annually by the shepherds of the Sangsar tribe who inhabit during the cold season the large village of the same name close to Samnán. Salash is probably the same as Ẓahíru'd-Dín's Shalas Kúh, which he informs us was formerly called Silsila Kúh. We also have Silsití Kúh, formerly known as Silsila Kúh; Sha'búdasht [a]; Shádkúh [c] or the mountain of joy, name of a locality near Gurgán; Shaláb [a], on the confines of Sawádkuh where pasture is abundant and the people live by cattle-farming; Biyábán-i-Shalíb [b]; Shiman [c], a village of Astarábád; Shirriz [c], a mountain of Daylam where the *Marzubán* of Ray took refuge when that town was taken by 'Uttáb b. Warqá: probably Shírrúd; Siyáhrúdpay [e], a stronghold in Mázandarán which had never been taken. Kamízdasht [e] was in the vicinity of this stronghold; Surkhkamar [b], near Kujúr; Suráb and Surnú or Surna, villages of Astarábád; Tálániyán [a]; Tamashkídasht [a]; Tapar [b]; Taricha or Turícha: the name was originally Túránchar, as it marked the site of a massacre of the Turks by the Ispahbad Farrukhán the Great [a]; Tújí: on the way from Ámul to Sárí one passed first Tújí and then Jámnú. The castle of Tújí, notwithstanding the desperate resistance offered by Kiyá Wishtásp-i-Jalál and his sons, was taken by Sayyid Kamálu'd-Dín and levelled with the ground. It was rebuilt, but Tímúr destroyed it when he invaded Mázandarán. Sayyid 'Alí b. Kamálu'd-Dín began rebuilding it, but it was never completed, and in Ẓahíru'd-Dín's time, i.e. 880/1475–6, it was a heap of ruins; Úfar [a]; Walajúy [a], near Sárí; Walabun [b]: Qal'a Walabun was a castle in Shahr Duwín, built by Mu'ayyad bi'lláh and destroyed by Sháh Ardashír of Mázandarán; Wamạd or Wabád [a]; Wárfú [a]; Wariyán [b]; Wázakúh [b] in or near Rustamdár; Walíkán [a], a plain on the way from Sárí to 'Amul; Wínábád [a], a large village near Sárí; Zangí Kaláta [b], a village in Rustamdar; Záyigán [e], a castle in Mázandarán; Zínwán [a], a village a *farsakh* from Sárí.

For names of localities, which are presumed to be in Mázandarán or Astarábád, appearing in Greek and Latin authors, see Dorn's *Reise*, pp. 156–161, and A. F. v. Stahl, "Notes on the March of Alexander the Great from Ecbatana to Hyrcania," *The Geographical Journal*, Vol. LXIV, No. 4, October 1924, London.

APPENDIX II

RULERS OF MÁZANDARÁN[1]

I. House of Gushnasp. II. Kayús. III. House of Zarmihr. IV. The Súkhrániyán or Qárınwand. V. House of Dábúya (Dáhuwán) VI. House of Báwand. VII. Governors of Mázandarán: Caliphate, Ṭáhırıd, Caliphate, Ṣaffárid, Caliphate, Sámánıd, Buwayhıd, Salj̇úq, Khwárazmsháhs, Mongols, Tímúrıd, Ṣafawıd. VIII. 'Alíd Rulers. IX. Asfár b. Shírúya. X. House of Kákí. XI. House of Zıyár. XII. Kıyás of Chuláw. XIII. Kiyá-ı-Jalál. XIV. Mar'ashí Sayyıds. XV. House of Rúzáfzún. XVI. Díw. XVII. Murtadá'í Sayyıds of Hazárjaríb. XVIII. House of Pádúsbán. XIX. Vassals: Tamísha, Amír-Ká, Mıyándúrúd, Láriján, Mámṭír, Landak, Lafúr, Kabúdjáma, Gulpáygán or Gúshwára, Lesser Báwands and others, Tunakábun.

I. HOUSE OF GUSHNASP

Gushnasp, a contemporary of Ardashír Bábakán (119), ruled over Ṭabaristán, Gílán, Rúyán, and Damáwand. His ancestors had been rulers of the same provinces since the time of Alexander the Great (330 B.C.), and the sovereignty remained in the hands of his descendants until about the year 529 A.D. when Kayús the son of Qubád was sent to govern Ṭabaristán.

II.

Kayús, 7 years (529–536).

III. HOUSE OF ZARMIHR

The rule of the House of Zarmihr lasted 110 years, beginning in the reign of Núsharwán (531–578), who sent Zarmihr as governor to Ṭabaristán after the death of Kayús, and ending about 685 A.D. when Ádhar-Walásh relinquished his government to Gíl Gáwbára in the 35th year of the new era which the Persians had lately inaugurated.

The rulers of the House of Zarmihr are:

Zarmihr, 23 years; Dázamihr b. Zarmihr, 17 years; Walásh b. Dázamihr, 25 years; Mihr b. Walásh, 20 years; Ádhar-Walásh b. Mihr, 25 years. Walásh who slew Báw and himself reigned for eight years belonged to this family, as also did the Masmughán Walásh of Miyándúrúd.

[1] For further information on individual rulers of Mázandarán see Browne's *Ibn Isfandıyár*. For rulers and governors of Astarábád see note (120).

IV. THE SÚKHRÁNIYÁN OR QÁRINWAND

This dynasty ruled in the mountains of Ṭabaristán for about 274 years, beginning with the grant of Shahriyár Kúh and Kúh-i-Qárin to Qárin b. Súkhrạ, about 50 years before the *Hijra* and ending with the death of Mázyár in 224/839. They bore the title of Kings of the Mountains, "*Jar-Sháh,*" or "*Maliku'l-Jibál*" and that of *Ispahbad*(121).

The rulers of the Qárinwand dynasty are:

Qárin b. Súkhrá, 37 years; Álandá b. Qárin, 52 years; Súkhrá b. Álandá, 65 years; Wandá-Hurmazd b. Álandá (or b. Súkhra), 50 years; Qárin b. Wandá-Hurmazd, 40 years; Mázyár b. Qárin, 30 years.

These are the reigns attributed to the Qárinwand rulers by Ẓahíru'd-Dín. They cannot be relied upon as we know that Wandá-Hurmazd died in the reign of Má'mún (813–833), that his son Qárin had a very short reign, and that Mázyár was put to death in 839 A.D.

V. HOUSE OF DÁBÚYA (the DÁBUWÁN) (also called House of GÁWBARA)

The House of Dábúya is said to have reigned in Ṭabaristán for 104 years, but from the evidence of coins[1] its rule only lasted 46 years, beginning with the accession of Dábúya at the death of his father, Gáwbara, in 50*/700 and ending with the death of Khurshíd in 116/766.

Farrukhán and his descendants bore the title of *Ispahbad.* The rulers of this house are: Dábúya (or Khurshíd) b. Gíl, 50–66*/700–716; Farrukhán-i-Buzurg b. Dábúya, 66–83*/716–733; Dázamihr b. Farrukhán-i-Buzurg, 83–88*/733–738; Sárúya b. Farrukhán-i-Buzurg, regent for eight years during the minority of his nephew Khurshíd; Khurshíd b. Dázamihr, 88–116*/738–766.

VI. HOUSE OF BÁWAND

The House of Báwand ruled in Mázandarán from the year 45/665–6 when the people of Ṭabaristán gave Báw absolute power, even to life and death, over them, to the year 750/349, when Fạkhru'd-Dawla Ḥasan was assassinated by the Chulábís.

[1] Colonel Allotte de la Fuye very kindly allowed me to examine his collection of Tabaristán coins from which I gathered very valuable information.

* New Sásánian era beginning in 650 A.D. These dates are taken from coins.

The Báwands were known at first as "Kings of the Mountains," and bore the title of *Ispahbad*. Their rule was supreme in Mázandarán for a long time, and, although they lost the plains, they always maintained to a certain extent their authority in the highlands.

This dynasty may be divided into three branches:

(*a*) Kayúsiyya, from 45/665-6 to 397/1007, when Qábús put the Ispahbad Shahriyár b. Dárá to death.

1. Báw, 45-60/665-680, 15 years.—2. Suhráb b. Báw, 68-90/687-8-716-7, 30 years.—3. Mihr Mardán b. Suhráb, 40 years[1].—4. Surkháb b. Mihr Mardán, 20 years.—5. Sharwín b. Surkháb, 25 years.—6. Shariyár b. Qárin b. Sharwín, 28 years.—6[a]. Shápúr b. Shahryár; a very short reign.—7. Ja'far b. Shahriyár, died in 250/864-5, 12 years.—8. Qárin b. Shahryár, 30 years.—9. Rustam b. Surkháb b. Qárin, died 282/895, 29 years.—10. Sharwín b. Rustam, 35 years.—11. Shahriyár b. Sharwín, 37 years.—12. Rustam b. Sharwín. His reign is only known to us through a coin struck at Farím in 355/966, bearing the names of the Caliph al Mutí' bi'llah, the Buwayhid Ruknu'd-Dawla, and the Ispahbad Rustam b. Sharwín.—Al-Marzubán the son of Rustam wrote the *Marzubán-náma* and the *Níkínáma*, both in the *Ṭabarí* dialect. Shírín, a daughter of Rustam, was the mother of Majdu'd-Dawla Rustam the Buwayhid.—13. Dárá b. Rustam, 8 years.—14. Shahriyár b. Dárá, died 397/1006-7, 35 years. He had two sons Rustam and Surkháb. Qárin the latter's son died in 466/1073-4.

(*b*) Ispahbadiyya, from 466-606/1073-1210, when Shamsu'l-Mulúk Rustam was assassinated and the Mongols overran the country.

1. Ḥusámu'd-Dawla Shahriyár b. Qárin b. Surkháb b. Shahriyár, 37 years.—2. Najmu'd-Dawla Qárin b. Shahriyár, 8 years.—3. Shamsu'l-Mulúk Rustam b. Qárin, 4 years. His son Sayfu'd-Dín 'Imádu'd-Dawla Farámurz was the protector of the poet 'Imádí'.—4. 'Ala'u'd-Dawla 'Alí b. Ḥusámu'd-Dawla Shahriyár 21 years.—4[a]. Bahrám b. Ḥusámu'd-Dawla Shahriyár.—4[b]. Rustam b. Dárá b. Ḥusámu'd-Dawla Shahriyár.—5. Nuṣratu'd-Dín Sháhghází Rustam b. 'Alí, died 558/1163, 24 years.—6. Sharafu'l-Mulúk ('Alá'u'd-Dawla) Ḥasan b. Rustam, 9 years.—7. Ḥusámu'd-

[1] Ibn Isfandiyár says that Mihr Mardán only had a brief reign and was succeeded by his grandson Sharwín b. Surkháb. See Browne's *Ibn Isfandiyár*, p. 237.

Dawla Ardashír b. Ḥasan, died 602/1205-6, 34 years.—8. Naṣíru'd-Dawla Shamsu'l-Mulúk Sháhghází Rustam b. Ardashír, died 606/1210, 4 years.

(*c*) Kínkhwáriyya, from 635-750/1237-8-1349, when Fakhru'd-Dawla Ḥasan was assassinated.

1. Ḥusámu'd-Dawla b. Ardashír b. Kínkhwár b. Shahriyár b. Kínkhwár b. Rustam b. Dárá b. Ḥusámu'd-Dawla Shahriyár, died 647/1249-50, 12 years[1].—2. Shamsu'l-Mulúk Muḥammad b. Ardashír, died 663/1264-5[2].—3. 'Alá'u'd-Dawla 'Alí b. Ardashír, died 663/1264-5[3].—4. Táju'd-Dawla Yazdijird b. Shahriyár b. Ardashír, died 701/1301-2.—5. Nasíru'd-Dawla Shahriyár b. Yazdíjird, died in 714/1314-5.—6. Shams'l-Mulúk Muḥammad b. Shahriyár, died in 714/1314-5.—7. Ruknu'd-Dawla Sháh Kay Khusraw b. Yazdijird, died in 728/1327-8, 14 years.—8. Sharafu'l-Mulúk Rustam b. Kay Khusraw, died in 734/1333-4, 6 years.—9. Fakhru'd-Dawla Hasan b. Kay Khusraw, died 750/1349, 16 years.

VII. GOVERNORS OF MÁZANDARÁN

(*a*) *Governors of the Caliphs.*

'Umar (634-644).

Suwayd b. Muqarran, 18 or 22/639 or 642-3.

'Uthmán (644-656).

Sa'íd b. al-'Áṣ, 29/649-650.

Mu'áwiya (661-680).

Masqala b. Hubayra ash-Shaybání.—Muḥammad b. al-Ash'ath.

'Abdu'l-Malik (684-705).

Muhallab b. Abí Ṣufrá, 78 or 79/697-8 or 698-9.—Qaṭarí b. al-Fujá'at al-Mázíní.

Sulaymán (714-717).

Yazíd b. al-Muhallab, 98/716-7.

Manṣúr (754-775).

Abu'l-Khaṣíb Marzúq as-Sa'dí, 140-142/757-8-759-60.—Abú Khuzayma, or Kh) Kházim b. Khuzayma al Tamímí, 143-144/760-1-761-2 (122).—Abu'l-'Abbás Ṭúsí, 1 year.—Rúḥ b. Ḥátim b. Qayṣar b. al Muhallab.—Khálid b. Barmak, 116-

[1] 15 years. Ibn Isfandiyár. [2] 665/1266-7. Zahíru'd-Dín.

[3] According to Ibn Isfandiyár, but Zahíru'd-Dín gives him a reign of 10 years.

119*/766–769.—Ḥasan b. Ḥusayn?—'Umar b. al-'Alá, 7 years, 120-125*/771–776.

Mahdí (775–785).

Sa'íd b. Da'laj, 125–128*/775–778. 'Umar b. al-'Alá, 127–129*/777–779.—Yaḥyá b. Mikhnáq, 129–130*/779–780.—'Abdu-'l-Ḥamid Maḍrúb, 2 years.—Rúḥ b. Ḥátim.—'Umar b. al-'Alá.—Taym b. Sinán.—Yazíd b. Marthad.—Ḥasan b. Qaḥṭaba?

Hárún (786–809).

Jarír b. Yazíd, 135–137*/785–787.—Mu'ádh, 136*/786.—Sulaymán b. Músá, 8 months, 136–137*/786–787.—Hádí b. Hání, 137–138*/787–788.—Muqátil, 139*/789.—'Abdu'lláh b. Qaḥṭaba, 139–140*/789–790.—Ibráhím, 141*/791.—'Uthmán b. Nahík.—Sa'íd b. Muslim (or Salm) b. Quṭayba b. Muslim.—'Abdu'lláh b. 'Abdu'l-Azíz Ḥammád, 10 months, 177/793–4.—Muthanná b. al-Ḥajjáj, 1 year and 4 months, 177–179/793-4–795.—'Abdu'l-Malik b. Qa'qá', 1 year, 179–180/795–796.—Fadl b. Yaḥyá.—'Abdu'lláh b. Ḥázim.—Maḥmúd and Músá b. Yaḥyá b. Khálid b. Barmak.—Yahyá b. Yaḥyá?—Jahḍam b. Khabbáb.—Khalífa b. Sa'd b. Hárún al-Jawharí.—'Abdu'lláh b. Sa'íd al-Jurayshí, 4 months, 187/803.—'Abdu'llah b. Málik.

Má'mún (813–833).

'Abdu'lláh b. Khurdádba, 201/816–7?—Muḥammad b. Khálid.—Músá b. Ḥafṣ.—Muhammad b. Músá b. Ḥafṣ.

Mu'taṣim (833–842).

Bundár b. Múní, 224/839.

(*b*) *Ṭáhirid governors.*

Ḥasan b. Ḥusayn, 3 years, 4 months and 10 days. Died in Dhu'l-hijja 228/Sept. 843.—Ṭáhir b. 'Abdu'lláh b. Ṭáhir, 1 year and 3 months.—Muḥammad b. 'Abdu'lláh b. Ṭáhir, 7 years ending in Safar 237/Aug. 851. Sulaymán b. 'Abdu'lláh b. Ṭáhir, 3 years ending in 240/854–5.—Muḥammad b. Músá b. 'Abdu'r-Raḥmán.—Músá b. 'Ísá b. 'Abdu'l-Ḥamíd.—Sulaymán b. 'Abdu'lláh b. Ṭáhir; he retired to Khurásán in 252/866.

(*c*) *Mu'tazz* (865–869).

Muflih, recalled in Jumádá II 255/May–June 869.—Aḥmad b. Muḥammad as-Sakaní.—Shárí (governor of Gurgán).

(*d*) *Ṣaffárid governors.*

Ya'qúb b. Layth, 4 months, 260/874–875.

(e) *Mu'tamid* (870–892–3).

Ráfi' b. Harthama, 272–282/885-6–895.

(f) *Sámánid governors.*

Muḥammad b. Hárún, 18 months, 287–288/900–901.—Ismá'íl b. Aḥmad the Sámánid, 288–289/901.—Abu'l-'Abbás 'Abdu'lláh b. Muḥammad b. Núḥ b. Asad, 289–296/902–908.—Salám the Turk, 9 months and 22 days, 297/910.—Abu'l-'Abbás Aḥmad b. Núḥ, died in Safar 298/October 910.—Muḥammad b. Sa'lúk, fled from Ṭabaristán in Jumádá II 301/January, 914.—Muḥammad b. 'Abdu'l-'Azíz, 40 days.—Ilyás b. Ilísa', in 301/914.—Qarátakín the Turk.—Aḥmad Ṭawíl.—Abú 'Alí b. Aḥmad b. Muḥammad al-Muẓaffar, governor of Gurgán, 7 months beginning in Muḥarram 328/Oct.-Nov., 939.—Subuktigín.

(g) *Buwayhid governors.*

Ruknu'd-Dawla Ḥasan.

'Alí b. Káma, about 350/961–2.—Ḥasan b. Fírúzán, governor of Gurgán in 337/949.

'Aḍuḍu'd-Dawla Fanákhusraw.

Ispahbad Sharwín, 371/981–2.—Mu'ayyadu'd-Dawla the Buwayhid, governor of Gurgán and Ṭabaristán, 7 years ending in 983.

Fakhru'd-Dawla.

Ṣáḥib, i.e. Ismá'íl b. 'Abbád, 377/987–8.—Ḥusámu'd-Dawla Abu'l-'Abbás Tásh, governor of Ámul and later of Astarábád, Gurgán, Dahistán and Ábasgún, died in 379 or 381/389–90 or 991–2.—Ustád Abú 'Alí Jurjání, governor of Gurgán.—Fá'iq and Abú 'Alí Símjúr, governors of Gurgán.

Majdu'd-Dawla Rustam.

Naṣr b. Ḥasan b. Fírúzán, governor of Gurgán.—Rustam b. al-Marzubán, governor of Shahriyárkúh.

(h) *Saljúq governors.*

Malik Aḥmad b. Sulṭán Muḥammad b. Malik Sháh the Saljúq.—Mardawíj b. Basú, appointed governor of Gurgán in 433/1041–2.

(i) *Governors of the Sháhs of Khwárazm.*

'Alí Sháh b. Sulṭán Tukush, governor of Gurgán and Dahistán.—Fírúz, governor of Bírún-Tamísha.—Náṣiru'd-Dín Mankalí, 606/1210.—Amínu'd-Dín Dahistání, 607/1210–1.

(*j*) *Mongol governors.*

Júrmághún, 617/1219–20.—Jintímúr, 630–633/1232-3–1235-6. —Núsál, 633-637/1235-6–1239-40.—Gúrgúz, 637–643/1239-40–1245-6.—Arghún, 643/1245–6.—'Imádu'd-Dín Maḥmúd.—Húlágú, 654/1256–7.—Amír Mú'min.

(*k*) *Tímúrid governors.*

Iskandar Shaykhí, governor of Ámul, 795–805/1393–1402-3.—Jamshíd b. Qárin Ghúrí, governor of Sárí, 795–805/1393–1402-3. —Shamsu'd-Dín Ghúrí b. Jamshíd, governor of Sárí, 805–809/1402-3–1406.

(*l*) *Ṣafawid governors.*

Sharafu'd-Dín of Bitlís, governor of Tunakábun, 7 years, 974–981/1566-7–1573-4. Sulṭán Ḥusayn Mírzá b. Sulṭán Muḥammad Khudábanda Ṣafawí, left Mázandáran in 985/1577–8.—Sharaf Khán, governor of Tunakábun, 1003/1594–5.—Farhád Khán, 1005/1596–7.—Alwand Sulṭán.—Ibn Ḥusayn Khán Fírúz Jang, governor of Tunakábun, 1006/1595–6.—Ḥaydar Sultán Qawí Ḥiṣárlú, governor of Tunakábun, 1004/1595–6, and also in 1038/1628–9.—Ibráhím Bayg, governor of Rustamdár, 1003/1594–5.—Mírzá Muḥammad Shafí' Mírzá'yi-'Álamiyán, *wazír* of Mázandarán, fell into disgrace in 1018/1609–10.—Mír Abu'l-Qásim Khurásání, *wazír*, 1018/1609–10.—Mírzá Muhammad Taqí, *wazír*, 1021–1031/1612-3–1622.—Mírzá Háshim, *wazír* in 1675.—Mírzá 'Alí Aṣghar on behalf of Ṭahmásp II (123).

VIII. 'ALÍD RULERS

The 'Alíd rulers first established themselves in Mázandarán in 250/864, when Ḥasan b. Zayd took Ámul, and came to an end somewhere about the year 337/949, when Ath-Thá'ir Abu'l-Faḍl Ja'far, having quarrelled at Ámul with the Ustundár, went to Gílán where he took up his abode, and eventually died and was buried. We know that the descendants of Náṣiru'l-Kabír reigned for a long while in Gílán and Daylamán, but we have very little information about them (124). The 'Alíd rulers are divided into Ḥasanid and Ḥusaynid.

The Ḥasanid are: Dá'í'l-Kabír Ḥasan b. Zayd, 20 years, 250–270/864–884.—Abu'l-Ḥusayn Aḥmad b. Muḥammad, known as al-Qá'im, 10 months, 270–271/884.—Dá'í ila'l-Ḥaqq Abú 'Abdu'lláh Muḥammad b. Zayd, 16 years, 271–287/884–900.—Ḥasan b. al Mahdí b. Muḥammad b. Zayd.—Dá'í'ṣ-Ṣaghír Ḥasan b. Qásim, 12 years, 304–316/917–928-9.

The Ḥusaynid are: Dá'í Náṣiru'l-Kabír Abú Muḥammad Ḥasan b. 'Alí b. Ḥasan, 3 years, 301–304/914–917.—Abú'l-Qásim Ja'far b. Náṣiru'l-Kabír, 306–307 and 311–312/918-9–919 and 923–925.—Abu'l-Ḥusayn Aḥmad b. Náṣiru'l-Kabír, known as Ṣáḥibu'l-Jaysh, 311/923.—Abú 'Alí Muḥammad b. Aḥmad b. al-Ḥasan, 312–313?/924–925?—Abú Ja'far Ḥasan b. Aḥmad b. al-Ḥasan, known as Ṣáḥibu'l-Qulansuwa, 313–317?/925–929?—Isma'íl b. Abu'l-Qásim Ja'far b. Náṣiru'l-Kabír, 317?/929?—Abú Ja'far Muḥammad b. Aḥmad an-Náṣir, ruled at Amul somewhere between 325 and 328/936–939.—Ath-Thá'ir Abú'l-Faḍl Ja'far b. Muḥammad b. Ḥusayn b. 'Alí, known as Sayyid-Abyaḍ, 331?–337?/943?–949?—Abú Ṭálib Hárún Ath-Thá'ir b. Muhammad b. Ḥusayn b. 'Alí.

Another Ḥasanid branch established itself in Daylam: Abú'l-Ḥusayn al-Mu'ayyad bi'lláh Aḍudu'd-Dawla b. Ḥusayn b. Hárún b. Ḥusayn, died 421/1030—An-Náṭiq-bi'l-Ḥaqq Abú Ṭálib Yahyá b. Ḥusayn b. Hárún b. Ḥusayn, died 422/1031.—Abu'l Qásim b. al-Mu'ayyad bi'lláh.—Rikábzan Kiyá, a descendant of al-Mu'ayyad bi'lláh, who was ruler of Tunakábun, 750–769/1349–1367-8.

Hazárfann mentions Abu'l-Qásim Zayd b. Abú Ṭálib Muḥsin b. Zayd, who ruled over part of Daylam and took the title of Musaddad-bi'lláh.

IX.

Asfár b. Shírúya of Lárijáñ and of the Wardadáwand clan, beheaded in 319/931.

X. House of Kákí

The House of Kákí were rulers of Ishkawar in Gílán. At first they helped the various Dá'ís to subdue Ṭabaristán, but later themselves aspired to the government of that and the neighbouring provinces.

Kákí b. Nu'mán, 220/835.—Kákí b. Nu'mán and Fírúzán b. Nu'mán, slain in 289/902.—Laylá b. Nu'mán, slain in 308/920–1.—Mákán b. Kákí; he brought the whole of Ṭabaristán under his control, slain in 329/940.—Ḥasan b. Fírúzán.—Naṣr b. Ḥasan b. Fírúzán, died a prisoner in the castle of Ustúnáwand.—Fírúzán b. Ḥasan b. Fírúzán, ruler of Daylamán in 371/982–3.—Kinár b. Fírúzán, one of the leading men of Daylamán in 388/998.

XI. HOUSE OF ZIYÁR

Ziyár was a descendant of Arghash Wahádán[1], who was governor of Gílán in the time of Kay Khusraw. His family were always in Gílán, although from time to time the governorship was wrested from their hands. The rule of the House of Ziyár over Gurgán and Ṭabaristán began with Mardáwíj in 319/931 and ended with Sharafu'l-Ma'álí Anúsharwán b. Qábús in 471/1078-9. Already the year before during the reign of Gílánsháh b. Kay Ká'ús, Ḥasan b. Ṣabbáḥ had dealt the final blow to the fortunes of the House of Ziyár by subduing the mountainous districts.

The rulers of this House are: Abu'l-Ḥajjáj Mardáwíj b. Ziyár, 319-323/931-935.—Abú Ṭálib Washmgír b. Ziyár, 323-356 or 357/935-967.—Ẓahíru'd-Dawla Abú Manṣúr Bísutún b. Washmgír, 357-366 or 367/967-977-8.—Shamsu'l-Ma'álí Abu'l-Ḥasan Qábús b. Washmgír, 367-371 and 388-403/977-982 and 998-1012-3[2].—Falaku'l-Ma'álí Abú Manṣúr Minúchihr b. Qábús, 403-421/1012-3-1030.—Dárá b. Qábús, 403-404/1012-3-1013-4.—Sharafu'l-Ma'álí Núshirwán b. Minúchihr b. Qábús, 421-423/1030-1032; according to Bayhaqí he was poisoned by his maternal uncle Bákálánjár in 423[3].—Bákálánjár, 424-441/1033-1049-50.—'Unṣuru'l-Ma'álí Kay Ká'ús b. Iskandar b. Qábús, author of the *Qábús-náma*, 441-462/1049-50-1069-70.—Gílánsháh b. Kay Ká'ús, 462-471/1069-70-1078-9.—Sharafu'l-Ma'álí Anúsharwán b. Qábús, 471/1078-9.

XII. KIYÁS OF CHULÁW

The Kiyás of Chuláw were the rivals of the Kiyá-i-Jalál, consequently when Fakhru'd-Dawla Ḥasan put to death Kiyá Jalál b. Aḥmad-i-Jál, he was compelled to ally himself with the Kiyás of Chuláw who murdered him in 750/1349, a deed which secured

[1] Querry has Farhádwan. See A. Querry, *Le Qabous-namé*, Paris, 1886, p. 16.

[2] The date of his death is also given as 424 and 426/1033 and 1034-5. Querry mentions Sharafu'l-Ma'álí Iskandar b. Qábús as the successor of Minúchihr b. Qábús and ascribes to him a reign of 16 years 424-441/1033-1049, *loc. cit.* p. 168.

[3] Huart says that Abú Kálánjár (Bákálánjár) b. Wíhánu'l-Qúhí ruled over Gurgán from 424-433/1033-1041-2. In the latter year Mardáwíj b. Basú was appointed Governor of Gurgán by Tughrul Bayg, and Núsharwán b. Minúchihr retired to a castle where he died in 441/1049. See Cl. Huart, *Les Ziyârides. Extrait des Mémoires de l'Académie des Inscriptions et Belles-Lettres*. Tome XLII. Paris. Imp. Nat. 1922.—Yáqút says that Núsharwán died in 435/1043-4 and was succeeded by his son Jastán or Hisán. Professor Browne mentions that Mas'úd the Ghaznawid took Tabaristán and Gurgán from the Ziyárid prince Dárá b. Minúchihr in 426/1034-5. See *A Literary History of Persia*, London, 1906, vol. II, p. 169.

the rule of Ámul to Kiyá Afrásiyáb. He remained in power for ten years.—Iskandar Shaykhí b. Afrásiyáb, governor of Ámul, 795–805/1393–1402-3.—Luhrásp b. Ḥusayn b. Iskandar ruled over Ṭálaqán, 880/1475–6.—Amír Ḥusayn Kiyá, b. ‘Alí b. Luhrásp, ruled over part of Rustamdár and was compelled to surrender to Sháh Ismá‘íl Ṣafawí in 909/1503–4.

XIII. KIYÁ-I-JALÁL

The Kiyá-i-Jalál were of the nobles of Ṭabaristán and held important posts in Sárí. At the death of Fakhru'd-Dawla Ḥasan in 750/1349 Kiyá Fakhru'd-Dín Jalál and Kiyá Wishtásp became rulers of Sárí, the former residing in that city and the latter at the castle of Tújí. Kiyá Fakhru'd-Dín was killed in battle near Bárfurúsh by the Mar‘ashí *Sayyids* and Kiyá Wishtásp at the siege of Tújí in 763/1361–2.

XIV. MAR‘ASHÍ *SAYYIDS*

The rule of the Mar‘ashí *Sayyids* in Mázandarán began with the rebellion of Qiwámu'd-Dín against Kiyá Afrásiyáb Chuláwí in 760/1359, and ended with Mír Murád b. Mírzá Khán, who was dispossessed of his government by the Ṣafawís towards the end of the 10th (16th) century. The rulers of this dynasty are: Qiwámu'd-Dín b. ‘Abdu'lláh b. Ṣádiq, known as Mír-i-Buzurg, 760–763/1359–1361-2.—Kamálu'd-Dín b. Qiwámu'd-Dín, 763–795/1361-2–1393. He was besieged by Tímúr in the castle of Máhánasar near Ámul, taken prisoner and sent to Káshghar where he died in 801/1398–9.—‘Alí b. Kamálu'd-Dín, 806–812 and 813–820/1403-4–1409-10 and 1410-11–1418.—Murtaḍá b. Kamálu'd-Dín, 812–813/1409-10–1410-11. Murtaḍá b. ‘Alí b. Kamálu'd-Dín, 821–837/1418–1433.—Muḥammad b. Murtaḍá, 837–856/1433–1452.—‘Abdu'l-Karím b. Muḥammad, 856–865/1452–1461.—‘Abdu'lláh b. ‘Abdu'l-Karím, 865–872/1461–1467.—Kamálu'd-Dín b. Muḥammad took over the government from ‘Abdu'lláh b. ‘Abdu'l-Karím but was unable to maintain himself in Sárí.—Zaynu'l-‘Ábidín b. Kamálu'd-Dín b. Muḥammad, 872–897/1467–1491-2.—Ghiyáthu'd-Dín Muḥammad b. Jalálu'd-Dín ‘Abdu'l-Wahháb b. Ghiyáthu'd-Dín b. Kamálu'd-Dín b. Qiwámu'd-Dín; in 873/1468–9 he obtained from Ḥasan Bayg the *firmán* of the government of Mázandarán, but we do not know whether he was ever installed at Sárí as ruler of Mázandarán.—Shamsu'd-Dín b. Kamálu'd-Dín b. Muḥammad, 897–905/1491-2–1499-1500.

—Kamálu'd-Dín b. Shamsu'd-Dín succeeded his father in 905/1499–1500 but was killed by Áqá Rustam Rúzáfzún, who annexed all his dominions. 'Abdu'l-Karím b. 'Abdu'lláh b. 'Abdu'l-Karím, 917–932/1511-2–1525-6.—Mír Sháhí b. 'Abdu'l-Karím, 932–939/1525-6–1532-3.—Mír 'Abdu'lláh Khán b. Mír Sulṭán Mahmúd b. 'Abdu'l-Karím, known as Khán-i-Kúchik, 939–969/1532-3–1561-2; his daughter, Khayru'n-Nisá Baygum, was the mother of Sháh Sulṭán Muḥammad Khudábanda Safawí.—Mír Sulṭán Murád b. Sháhí, 969-972/1561-2–1564-5. Mír 'Abdu'l-Karím b. 'Abdu'lláh Khán, succeeded his father as ruler of part of Mázandarán ; he took poison and died in Shawwál 972/1565.—Mír 'Azíz Khán b. Mír 'Abdu'lláh was entrusted with that part of Mázandarán to which he was heir, but fell from the favour of Sháh Ṭahmásp I and was cast into prison. Sulṭán Maḥmúd b. Sulṭán Murád, known as Mírzá Khán, succeeded his father as ruler of part of Mázandarán. At the death of Sháh Ṭahmásp the whole of Mázandarán came under his sway. When the daughter of Mír 'Abdu'lláh Khán became Dowager Queen of Persia, she summoned Sulṭán Murád to Qazwín, but he refused to come, and retired to the castle of Fírúzaját. The Sháh's officers, who were sent to besiege the castle, gave him assurances for his safety, whereupon he agreed to come to Qazwín, but he was treacherously murdered by the Queen-Dowager's minions.—Sulṭán Muḥammad b. Sulṭán Murád is only known to us by a letter written to the Queen-Dowager of Persia, from a castle in which he had taken refuge, wherein he implores her not to revenge herself on him for the death of her father (who was assassinated, by order, it is said, of Sulṭán Murád), as he was a child when that event took place.—Mír 'Alí Khán b. Sulṭán Maḥmúd b. 'Abdu'l-Karím, uncle of the Queen Dowager of Persia. After the death of Mírzá Khán, this 'Alí Khán was appointed by the Queen Dowager governor of Mázandarán.—After his death at an early age, a period of anarchy prevailed in Mázandarán.—Mír Murád b. Sulṭán Maḥmúd (Mírzá Khán) was ruler of Mázandarán in 990/1582.

XV. HOUSE OF RÚZÁFZÚN

Áqá Rustam, independent ruler of Sawádkúh, 897–917/1491-2–1511-2.—Áqá Muḥammad b. Rustam, 917–923/1511-2–1517.

XVI. DÍW

Mírak Díw was *wakíl* of Sulṭán Ḥusayn Mírzá Ṣafawí, governor of Mázandarán in the time of Ṭahmásp I. He was assassinated by order of the Prince, who, however, was obliged, as a result of the disturbances that ensued, to leave Mázandarán soon after the death of the Sháh.—Shamsu'd-Dín Díw; it was due to his efforts on the death of Sháh Ṭahmásp I (984/1576) that the whole of Mázandarán was brought under the rule of Mírzá Khán.—Alwand Díw was ruler of Sawádkúh and part of Mázandarán. He surrendered to Sháh 'Abbás I in 1007/1598–9.

XVII. MURTAḌÁ'Í *SAYYIDS* OF HAZÁRJARÍB

'Imád became independent ruler of Hazárjaríb about 760/1359. —'Izzu'd-Dín was ruler of Hazárjaríb in 809/1406–7.—Mír Ghaẓanfar, 892/1487.—Ḥasan, 923/1517.

I find the following account of the *Sayyids* of Hazárjaríb in I'timádu's-Salṭana's *Kitábu't-Tadwín fí Aḥwál-i-Jibál-i-Sharwín* (1311). The founder of the dynasty was Sayyid 'Imád, who was confirmed by Tímúr in the government of Hazárjaríb. His descendants were divided into two branches, the Raḍí'u'd-Díní and the Jabrá'ílí. The last ruler of the Raḍí'u'd-Díní branch was Sayyid Ḥusayn, who was put to death in 929/1522–3 by order of Sháh Ismá'íl Ṣafawí. Of the Jabrá'ílí branch, Sayyid Rúḥu'lláh died in 927/1520–1, and his son Sayyid 'Abdu'lláh in 934/1527–8. Between the latter date and 973/1565–6, the following members of the Jabrá'ílí family ruled over Hazárjaríb: Hárún, Mu'ínu'd-Dín, Háshim, and Ḥasan.

On the death of Mír 'Alí Khán b. Sulṭán Maḥmúd Mar'ashí, Sayyid Muẓaffar b. Ḥusayn Murtaḍá'í divided Mázandarán with Alwand Díw. He died in 1005/1596–7.

XVIII. HOUSE OF PÁDÚSBÁN

The members of this House ruled over Rustamdár, Rúyán, Núr and Kujúr, the country situated between Gílán and the district of Ámul, from about the year 45 of the *Hijra* (665–6) to the year 1005 (1595–6), when Sháh 'Abbás did away with the various princes of this house.

After the death of Malik Kayúmarth in 857/1453, Rustamdár was divided between his two sons, Ká'ús and Iskandar, the founders of the branches of Baní-Ká'ús, or rulers of Núr, and Baní-Iskandar, or rulers of Kujúr.

The rulers of the House of Pádúsbán first bore the title of *Ispahbad*, then that of *Ustundár*, which is said to signify "ruler of the mountains," and finally they all adopted the prefix of *Malik*.

1. Pádúsbán b. Gíl, 30 years.—2. Khúrzád b. Pádúsbán, 30 years.—3. Pádúsbán b. Khúrzád, 40 years.—4. Shahriyár b. Pádúsbán, 30 years.—5. Waṇdá Ummíd b. Shahriyár, 32 years.—6. 'Abdu'lláh b. Wandá Ummíd, 34 years.—7. Áfrídún b. Qárin b. Surkháb b. Namáwar b. Shahriyár, 22 years.—8. Pádúsbán b. Áfrídún, 18 years.—9. Shahriyár b. Pádúsbán, 15 years. 10. Harúsandán b. Tídá b. Shírzád b. Áfrídún, 12 years. 11. Shahriyár b. Jamshíd b. Díwband b. Shírzád b. Áfrídún, 12 years.—12. Shamsu'l Mulúk Muhammad b. Shahriyár, 12 years. —13. Abú'l-Faḍl b. Muḥammad (125), 14 years.—14 Husámu'd-Dawla Zarrínkamar b. Farámurz b. Shahriyár, 35 years.—15. Sayfu'd-Dawla Báḥarb b. Zarrínkamar, 27 years.—16. Ḥusámu'd-Dawla Ardashír b. Báharb, 25 years.—17. Fakhru'd-Dawla Namáwar b. Naṣíru'd-Dawla Shahriyár b. Báḥarb, 32 years.—18. 'Izzu'd-Dawla Hazárasf b. Namáwar, 40 years.—19. Shahrnúsh b. Hazárasf, 19 years.—20. Kayká'ús b. Hazárasf, died in 560/1164–5, 37 years.—21. Hazárasf b. Shahrnúsh, 26 years.—22. Husámu'd-Dawla Zarrínkamar b. Jastán b. Kayká'ús, died in 610/1213–4, 24 years.—23. Sharafu'd-Dawla Bísutún b. Zarrínkamar, died in 620/1223–4, 10 years.—24. Fakhru'd-Dawla Namáwar b. Bísutún, died in 640/1242–3, 20 years.—25. Husámu'd-Dawla Ardashír b. Namáwar, died in 643/1245–6, 3 years.—26. Fakhru'd-Dawla Shahrákím b. Namáwar, died 671/1272–3, 31 years, including the rule of his brother Ardashír. —27. Fakhru'd-Dawla Sháhghází Namáwar b. Shahrákím, died in 701/1301–2, 30 years.—28. Sháh Kaykhusraw b. Shahrákím, died in 711/1311–2, 11 years.—29 Shamsu'l-Mulúk Muhammad b. Kaykhusraw, died in 717/1317–8, 5 years.—30. Nasíru'd-Dawla Shahriyár b. Kaykhusraw, murdered in 725/1325, 7 years.—31. Táju'd-Dawla Ziyár b. Kaykhusraw, died in 734/1333–4, 10 years.—32. Jalálu'd-Dawla Iskandar b. Ziyár, died in 761/1359–60, 27 years—33. Fakhru'd-Dawla Sháhghází b. Ziyár, died in 780/1378–9, 20 years.—34. 'Izzu'd-Dawla Qubád b. Sháhghází, 2 years.—35. Sa'du'd-Dawla Ṭús b. Ziyár was ruling Rustamdár in 794/1391–2—36. Jalálu'd-Dawla Kayúmarth b. Bísutún b. Iskandar, died in 857/1453, 50 years.

BANÍ-KÁ'ÚS

1. Ká'ús b. Jalálu'd-Dawla Kayúmarth 857–871/1453–1467.—2. Jahángír b. Ká'ús, 871–904/1467–1498-9.—3. Ká'ús b. Jahángír, heir to his father, slain in 904/1498–9 by his brother Bísutún.—4. Bísutún b. Jahángír, 904–913/1498-9–1507.—5. Bahman b. Bísutún, 913–957/1507–1550.—6. Kayúmarth b. Bahman succeeded his father.—7. 'Azíz b. Kayúmarth.—8. Jahángír b. 'Azíz.

BANÍ-ISKANDAR

1. Jalálu'd-Dín Iskandar b. Jalálu'd-Dawla Kayúmarth, 857–881/1453–1476-7.—2. Táju'd-Dawla b. Iskandar, 881–897/1476-7–1491-2.—3. Ashraf b. Táju'd-Dawla, 897–913/1491-2–1507-8, died in 921/1515–6.—4. Ká'ús b. Ashraf, 913–950/1507-8–1543-4.—5. Bísutún b. Ashraf, 950/1543–4.—6. Kayúmarth b. Ká'ús, 950–963/1543-4–1555.—7. Jahángír b. Kayúmarth, 963–975/1555–1567-8.—8. Sulṭán Muḥammad b. Jahángír, 975–984/1567-8–1576-7.—9. Jahángír b. Sulṭán Muḥammad, 984–1006/1576-7–1597-8.

XIX. VASSALS

We have but scanty information about the Vassals of Mázandarán. Some of them belonged to branches of the ruling Houses of Báwand, Qárinwand, and Ustundár, whilst others mentioned by Ibn Isfandiyár were the *Nahapits* of Ṣúl, the *Nahapits* of Sárí, the Surḥánwand, Láriján, Waláshán, Sa'ídúhá, Úlán-Mihán, Marzubán, Dábuwán, Gulayj, Amír-Ká, Kabúdjáma, and the following vassals of the *Ustundár* mentioned by Ẓahíru'd-Dín: the *Ispahbads* of Kalár, Namíwand, Shírazílwand, Khúrdáwand and Karjí.

(*a*) *Lords of Tamísha.*

Farshwád, about 218/833.—Hurmazd-Káma (b. Yazdánkard?), about 297/909–10.

(*b*) *The Amírs Ká.*

Amír Ká b. Wardásf, 312/925. Ibn Amír-Ká, a contemporary of Qábús b. Washmgír.

(*c*) *Lord of Miyándúrúd.*

Masmughán Walásh, of the House of Zarmihr, was *Marzubán* in the district of Ṭayzana-rúd (126), or Miyándúrúd as it is now called. His daughter married the Ispahbad Farrukhán-i-Buzurg.

(*d*) *Lords of Láriján.*

Fadl b. al Marzubán, 252/866.—Sahl b. al-Marzubán held Lariján. He constructed a road through the country, which, before his time, was impassable both in summer and winter.—Abú Isḥáq b. al-Marzubán constructed, out of his own pocket, most of the roads and bridges of Ṭabaristán and Rúyán.—Muḥammad b. Faḍl.—'Abdu'lláh b. al Ḥusayn b. Sahl, known as Tájí Duwayr.—Ispahbad Parwíz, grandson of the Ispahbad Rustam b. Sharwín b. Qárin, was Lord of Láriján in 287/900.—Abú'l-Husám, *Marzubán* of Láriján, 512/1118-9. He had a son named Shírzád.—Amír Báḥarb of Garmábarúd, 512.—Minúchihr, *Marzubán* of Láriján, a contemporary of the Ispahbad Sháh Ghází Rustam.—Báḥarb b. Minúchihr (127); he left a son Kínkhwár, a year old, and the Ispahbad 'Alá'u'd-Dawla Ḥasan (558-567/1163-1171-2), who was Kínkhwár's maternal uncle, took possession of Láriján.—Ispahbad Abú Ja'far Ásarb, 568/1172-3.

(*e*) *Ispahbads of Mámṭír.*

Khurshíd b. Abú'l-Qásim, 512-540?/1118-9-1145-6? He had three brothers, Qárin Tábaryábí, Suhráb and Shírzád.—Táju'd-Dín Shahriyár b. Khurshíd, 568/1172-3.

(*f*) *Ispahbad of Landak.*

Fírúz b. al-Layth, 512/1118-9.

(*g*) *Lords of Lafúr.*

Pádúsbán b. Girdzád, 250/864.—Ispahbad Amír Mahdí Qárinwand, 500/1106-7.—Amír (Abú) Isḥáq, 512/1118-9.—'Alí Namáwar b. Ispahbad Ziyár, 512.

(*h*) *Lords of Kabúdjáma.*

Rustam was contemporary with the Ispahbad 'Alá'u'd-Dawla 'Alí (512-533/1118-9-1138-9).—Fakhru'd Dawla Garshásf.—Nuṣratu'd-Dín Muḥammad was put to death by 'Alá'u'd-Dín Muḥammad Khwárazmsháh in about 600/1203-4.—Fakhru'd-Dawla Mas'úd b. Muḥammad was a poet of some merit.—Ruknu'd-Dín, a nephew of Nuṣratu'd-Dín Muḥammad. He joined the Mongols against the Sháh of Khwárazm in order to avenge the death of his uncle.—Nuṣratu'd-Dín was named in 630/1232-3 by Qá'án ruler of the district extending from Kabúdjáma to Bírún Tamísha and Astarábád.

(i) Lords of Gulpáygán, or Gúshwára.

Ispahbad Pádsháh Mubárizu'd-Dín Arjásf b. Fakhru'd-Dawla Garshásf; at the accession of Ḥusámu'd-Dawla Ardashír (568/1172) Mubárizu'd-Dín received an appointment at Ámul, and was replaced as ruler of Gúshwára, to which post Sharafu'l-Mulúk Ḥasan had appointed him, by his cousin, Khurshíd b. (Kay) Ká'ús. This caused great enmity between the two cousins.—Qárin b. Garshásf, in 521/1127, defended the castle of Rúhín against Bázghásh, a general of Sanjar.—'Izzu'd-Dín Garshásf, Sipahsálár of Gúshwára and one of the great noblemen of Ṭabaristán, 560/1164–5.—Páshá 'Alí, a grandson of Fakhru'd-Dawla Garshásf. He was appointed governor of Rúyán and Daylamán in 586/1190–1, and was slain by the inhabitants.—Kay Ká'ús b. Fakhru'd-Dawla Garshásf, brother of Mubárizu'd-Dín Arjásf. He was given Gurgán by Sulṭán Tukush of Khwárazm.—Hizabru'd-Dín Khurshíd b. Kay Ká'ús, appointed governor of Gúshwára in succession to his cousin, Mubárizu'd-Dín Arjásf.—Fakhru'd-Dawla; thrown into the Bábul by order of Ḥusámu'd-Dawla Ardashír (568–602/1172–1205-6).—Siráju'd-Dín Zardustán b. Fakhru'd-Dawla Garshásf. He was given Chináshk by Sulṭán Tukush of Khwárazm. By order of Ḥusámu'd-Dawla Ardashír, Nuṣratu'd-Dín Kabúdjáma invited him to a banquet and put him to death. The king of Mázandarán subsequently gave Gúshwára to Amír Sábiqu'd-Dawla Rustam.—Táju'd-Dín Túránsháh b. Zardustán, ruler of Chináshk.—Ibn Táju'd-Dín Túránsháh was kept as hostage in the castle of Aylál and put to death by Sháh Ghází Rustam.—Ispahbad Rustam Búrkala was governor of Gúshwára after Amír Sábiqu'd-Dawla Rustam.

(j) Lesser Báwands and others.

Ispahbad Abú Ja'far Muḥammad b. Wandarín Báwand, whose mausoleum is the tower of Rádkán which was begun in 407 and completed in 411, 1016–1020-1.—Abú Ja'far Báwand, killed by the Assassins towards 500/1106–7.—Ispahbad Majdu'd-Dín Dárá, king of Daylamán, 558/1163.—Ispahbad Kay Khusraw of Ámul, 500/1106-7.—Amír Bákálánjár b. Ja'far of Kúlá or Kúláwíj, about 508/1114–5.—Amír Ḥasan Bahá'u'd-Dawla, governor of Ámul towards the end of the reign of Sháh Ghází Rustam (558/1163).

GOVERNORS OF TUNAKÁBUN

Sayyid 'Alí Kiyá, of Láhiján, wrested Tunakábun from Sayyid Rikábzan Kiyá and gave that district to his own brother Sayyid

Hádí Kiyá b. Amír Kiyá Maláṭí. The latter on becoming ruler of Biyapísh gave Tunakábun to his son Sayyid Yaḥyá Kiyá. Sayyid Yaḥyá Kiyá was succeeded by his brother Sayyid Dáwud Kiyá b. Hádí, who in 833/1429 was replaced by Kárkiyá Muḥammad Kiyá b. Yaḥyá. In 868/1463–4 Kárkiyá Muḥammad Kiyá relinquished the rule to his son Kárkiyá Yaḥyá Kiyá, who was dismissed in 887/1482–3 and replaced by his brother Kárkiyá Mír Sayyid. Sulṭán Háshim, brother of Mírzá 'Alí of Biyapísh, was appointed governor of Tunakábun in succession to Kárkiyá Mír Sayyid. In 910/1504–5 he rebelled against his brother Sultán Ḥasan who had usurped the rule of Biyapísh, and was defeated and replaced by Mír Ḥusayn b. Kárkiyá Yaḥyá Kiyá. In 912/1506–7 Sulṭán Háshim tried to seize Tunakábun but was taken prisoner and put to death by Sadíd, the *wazír* of Sulṭán Aḥmad Khán of Biyapísh, who also cast into prison Mír Ḥusayn and gave the command of the troops of Tunakábun to Bráhím Kiyá b. Ḥájjí Muḥammad Ishkawarí Sipahsálár of Karjiyán, and that of the troops of Karjiyán to his own brother Bú Nasr. Sulṭán Ḥamza b. Sulṭán Háshim was living in Tunakábun; he was killed by people of Biyápish in 984/1576. His son Kárkiyá 'Alí was killed during an insurrection in 1002/1593–4.

GOVERNORS OF KARJIYÁN (128) AND GULAYJÁN

In 820/1417–8 when Sayyid Radí Kiyá, *wálí* of Biyapísh, seized Gulayján and Karjiyán, he gave those districts to Sayyid Amír Kíya b. Hádí b. 'Alí Kiyá Maláṭí. The latter was replaced by Sháh Yaḥyá, son of Sayyid Náṣir Kiyá, *wálí* of Biyapísh, who was deprived of his governorship in 845/1442–3 in favour of Kárkiyá Muḥammad Kiyá Tunakábuní. Twelve years later we find Sháh Yaḥyá mentioned as governor of Karjiyán and Gulayján. He died in 884/1479 and Kárkiyá Sulṭán Ḥusayn, brother of Mírzá 'Alí, *wálí* of Biyapísh, was appointed in his stead. The latter died the same year and was replaced by Kiyá 'Alí Ishkawarí, whilst Mír Ẓahíru'd-Dín, the historian, was given the command of the troops of Karjiyán and Gulayján, a post which he held from 887 to 890/1482–1485. In 907/1500–1 Mírzá 'Alí gave Karjiyán and Gulayján to his brother Sultán Ḥasan. When Sulṭán Ḥasan usurped the power in Biyapísh in 910/1503–4, Sulṭán Háshim obtained from Sháh Ismá'íl I an order for him to be placed in possession of Karjiyán, but he was defeated by Sulṭán Hasan and retired to Mázandarán.

NOTES

(1) Farshwádgar is probably identical with Strabo's Parachoathras. "The northern parts of this range (the mountains which the Greeks call Taurus) are occupied by Gelae, Cadusii, and Amardi, as we have said, and by some tribes of Hyrcanians; then follow, as we proceed towards the east and the Ochus, the nation of the Parthians, then that of the Margiani and Arii, and the desert country which the river Sarnius separates from Hyrcania. The mountain, which extends to this country, or within a small distance of it, from Armenia, is called Parachoathras." *The Geography of Strabo*, B. XI, ch. viii, para. 1 and 2. *Bohn's Classical Library*, London, 1912.

(2) According to Yáqút Ṭabaristán extended from Tamísha, 6 *farsakhs* east of Sárí, to Daylam. The cities of Nátil, 15 *farsakhs* west of Ámul, Chálús, Kalár-rú-pay, Sa'ídábád, and Rúyán, were in Daylam.

(3) The restricted application of the name Mázandarán is well defined by Ẓahíru'd-Dín when he mentions that Sháh Ghází Rustam (6th/12th century) collected troops from Gíl, Daylam, Rúyán, Láriján, Mázandarán, Kabúdjáma, Astarábád, and Qaṣrán, and marched towards Dahistán.

(4) Under the Mongols Mázandarán was divided into seven *túmáns*: Gurgán, Múrdistán or Múrustáq, Astarábád, Ámul and Rustamdár, Dahistán, Rúghad, and Sáristán.

(5) The great fortress stronghold of the Qárinwands in the Jabal-Qárin, which they held since Sásánian times, was at Farím, and the chief centre of population was the town of Sihmár (or Shihmár) where there was the only Friday Mosque of all this region. See Le Strange, p. 372. For Shihmár we also find Shimhár. Ibn Isfandiyár mentions Parím and Kamímnám.

(6) Yáqút mentions the town of Tamár on the Khurásán border, then Sharaz and Dahistán. Beyond Alázd (compare Alázd with Kúh-i-Alárd) was Wandád-Hurmazd Kúh and then Kúh-i-Sharwín.

(7) I enquired about a mountain of this name but could obtain no information on the subject until one day, when travelling along the beach in Ránikúh, we perceived a snow-capped mountain towering above the wooded hills to the north of the road, and I asked our guide the name of the mountain; he replied: "Sumám Múz." "You mean Kúh-i-Sumám," said I. "Well, of course," was the reply, "in our country we call a mountain *múz*."

(8) Gmelin in 1771 mentions 13 districts, adding Bandpay and 'Alí-ábád. Tunakábun was at that time part of Gílán, and Mashhadisar part of Bárfurúsh. Sam. G. Gmelin, *Reise durch Russland zur Untersuchung der drei Naturreiche*, 4 vols., 1770–1784.

(9) "Du haut du Demavend dont les fumées volcaniques, à près de 6000 mètres, couvrent le dernier pic, quatre ou cinq régions se succèdent: Entre 6000 et 4800 mètres, il n'existe pas la moindre trace de végétation; entre 4800 et 4400, on rencontre quelques rares lichens, très petits et collés sur le rocher; au-dessous, des graminées; à 4000 mètres commencent les herbes épineuses jusqu'à 3000 mètres environ où quelques broussailles et de petites

conifères viennent rompre la monotonie des rochers volcaniques ; au-dessous, une large zône de pâturages ; enfin vers 1000 mètres d'altitude, les forêts composées d'abord de conifères et de chênes, puis de charmes, de hêtres, de sycomores, jusqu'aux marais caspiens où les mimosas, les buis, les arbres fruitiers sauvages se mêlent avec les vignes et les lianes de toute sorte." J. de Morgan, *Mission Scientifique en Perse*, 1889–1891, 5 vols., Paris.

(10) After the Salmrúd Mackenzie mentions two branches of the Sayyid Maḥalla, then Shúrábsar, Sígárúd, and Baríshrúd.

(11) The Ráhpushta and Zawárkíla are mentioned by Mackenzie between the Tílpurdsar and Izarúd, also the Nírúd between the Chashmakíla and the Tílpurdsar.

(12) Holmes has the Kalárábád after the Palangrúd. W. R. Holmes, *Sketches on the Caspian Shores*, London, 1845.

(13) Called by Mackenzie Armanij.

(14) According to a list which was communicated to me by the Lionozoff Fisheries the distances in *versts* between the principal streams and rivers from Safíd Tamísha to Ámul are: Safíd Tamísha, 0; Sakhtsar, 3; Salmrúd, 4; Ramak, 2; Sayyid Maḥalla (brackish), 5; Baríshrúd, 2; Nísarúd, 3; Chalkrúd, 1; Shírrúd, 6; Áwsiyárúd, 2; Nasiyarúd, 2; Karímábád, 1½; Mazar, 2; Chashmakíla, ½; Muḥammad-Ḥusaynábád or Sangar, 2; Hájjí Maḥalla, 2; Walí-ábád, 3; Tílpurdsar, 3; Izarúd, 3; Nishtárúd, 1; Káẓimrúd, 10; Aspchín, 5; Kharrakrúd, 2; Tílrúdsar, 2; Gulúr, 2; Palangrúd, 2; Namakábrúd, 2; Nawrúsar, 2; Ḥacharúd, 3; Sardábrúd, 2; Chálús, 5; Kurkrúsar, 3; Kháchak, 4; Mashalak, 3; Khayrrúd, 4; Duzdak, 16; Nawrúdbár, 14; Bazawár, 14; Alamdih, 7.

(15) This is not quite exact. Forster, who passed through Mázandarán in January 1784, says: "crossed a fordable stream (2½ *farsakhs* from Sárí) which runs to the left or north-west, and falls into the Mázandarán river. The carriers were stopped at the passage, and ordered to convey on their horses a quantity of stones, and place them in certain swampy parts of the great road, leading from Sárí to Bárfurúsh, which, it is said, was first constructed by Sháh 'Abbás, and appears to have been cut through the forest....Though deep ditches are extended on each side, and drains cut across, to carry off the extraordinary moisture of the soil, we proceeded with much difficulty and hazard. The carriers, at certain stations, were required to deliver their respective portions of stones, and the defaulters were detained by the officers of Government." G. Forster, *A Journey from Bengal to England*, 2 vols., London, 1808, Vol. II, pp. 227–8.

(16) Rubáṭ-i-'Ishq is in the midst of the Dasht-i-Rubáṭ, N.W. of Sangkhwást in Khurásán. Rubáṭ-i-Qarábil, elev. 4200', is a village 52 miles from Bujnúrd on the Gurgán road to Astarábád. The village consists of 10 houses built near the ruins of an old stone *rubáṭ*. The original *rubáṭ* was founded by the Ispahbad Shahriyár b. Sharwín. See Dawlatsháh's *Tadhkiratu'sh-Shu'ará*, or *Memoirs of the Poets*, edited by E. G. Browne, London, 1901, pp. 54–55.

(17) "The Tapyri are said to live between the Derbices and the Hyrcani. Historians say that it is a custom among the Tapyri to surrender the married

women to other men, even when the husbands have had two or three children by them." Strabo, B. XI, ch. ix, para. 1. "The Tapyri have a custom for the men to dress in black, and wear their hair long, and the women to dress in white, and wear their hair short....He who is esteemed the bravest marries whom he likes." Strabo, B. XI, ch. xi, para. 8.

(18) Fraser is not of the same opinion. He says: "It must not, however, be supposed that the Mázandaránís are a wretched, puny, and diseased-looking race, with frames enfeebled and little energy either of body or mind: this is far from being the case."

(19) A poet has said:

Mulk-i-Ṭabaristán ki dar ú fisq u fujúr
Shámil báshad bi ḥál-i burná u dhukúr
Dání zi chi dár-i mumin-ash míkhwánand
bar 'aks nihand nám-i-zangí Káfúr.

(20) These *Imámzádas*, or *Ma'ṣúmzádas* as they are called in Mázandarán, consist usually of a round, square, hexagonal, or octagonal tower, of varying height, surmounted by a conical roof or cupola. To this tower has generally been added at a later date an outer room used as a sort of antechamber by pilgrims visiting the shrine. Many fine wooden doors and sarcophagi beautifully carved are found in the shrines of Gílán, Mázandarán, and Astarábád.

(21) Of the great ruling clans of Mázandarán mentioned in Ibn Isfandiyár's history, such as the Báwand, Qárinwand, Surḥánwand, Láriján, Marzubán, Ustundár, Dábuwán, Kúlá'ij, Waláshán, Sa'ídúhá, Úlán-Mihán, Amír-Ká, and Kabúdjáma, we find no trace at present in Mázandarán. At the time of Ibn Isfandiyár, the nobles of Lafúr and Astarábád and the people of Qárinwand represented the descendants of Qárin, the son of Sukhrá.

The Ustundár Jalálu'd-Dawla Iskandar (731–761/1333-4–1359-60) transferred to Rustamdár many of the inhabitants of Qazwín as well as many of the Turkish tribes settled in Ray and Shahriyár, such as the Tabakí, Qapcháq, Kharlásh, Bahrámán, Qarábúqá, Qawlí-Tímúr, Sartízí, Sárútí, Tarkhání (descended from the rulers of Tarkhán), and Mírán.

In 809/1406-7 Mírzá 'Umar brought 2000 families of Mongols from Ray to Mázandarán. All these tribes, however, seem to have been absorbed by the aborigines.

(22) For this dialect see: A. Chodzko, *Specimens of the Popular Poetry of Persia*, London, 1842.—B. Dorn and Mírzá Muḥammed Shafí', *Beiträge zur Kenntniss des Iranischen Sprachen*, Theil I, Mazanderanische Sprache, Theil II 1 u. 3. Lieferung, Die Gedichtsammlung des Emir-i-Pasewary, St Petersburg, 1860 and 1866.—G. Melgunof, "Essai sur les Dialectes de Mazendéran et du Ghilan, d'après la prononciation locale," *Zeitsch. des deutschen Morgenl. Ges.*, T. xvii, 1868, pp. 195–224.—J. de Morgan, "Recherches sur les dialectes de la Perse et de l'Asie Centrale," *Études de linguistique publiées dans sa Mission Scientifique en Perse*, in 4° (Notices grammaticales et vocabulaires des dialectes mazandéranis, guilékis, talyches et kurdes, afghan d'Astérabad, juif de Kourdestan, etc.)

(23) A Christian tribe (of Ṭabaristán, says Ẓahíru'd-Dín) called the Banú Nájiya is mentioned by Ibn Isfandiyár as having reverted to Christianity

during the Caliphate of 'Alí b. Abí Ṭálib. They were attacked and destroyed and their women and children sold as slaves. In Assemani (T. III, ii, p. 425) we find that the Apostle Thomas, and later Agaeus, preached the Gospel to the Hyrcanians and that still later (778–820 A.D.) an endeavour was made to bring back to Christianity those that had apostatized. Subkhal Jesus was named metropolitan of Gílán and Daylam (*loc. cit.* p. 478). There were two bishoprics for Daylam and two for Ray and Ṭabaristán. Kardagus was bishop of Gílán and of the mountains (Jabalhá).

(24) Ḥamdu'lláh Mustawfí Qazwíní in the *Nuzhatu'l-Qulúb* says that it was built by Fírúz the Sásánian and that its length was 50 *farsakhs*, whilst Dawlatsháh, in his *Memoirs of the Poets*, states that it extended from Ámul to Abíward and Marw and the other side of the Jayḥún to the borders of Farghána and Khujand.

Sykes calls the great wall "Sadd-i-Sikandar" or Barrier of Alexander.

(25) Holmes mentions the Manzarúd, Síkararúd, and Ḥusaynábád. Concerning the Manzarúd I could obtain no information; the other two must be the Siyáhkalarúd and the Qásimábád.

(26) De Morgan mentions the Laparúdbár and the Shayza.

(27) Some of the *yayláqs* of Sakhtsar are: Agrasar, Garlaspasar, Pá'ín-Mázú, Salamál, and Jandarúdbár. The latter place as well as the castle of Sardábasar were part of the former district of Karjiyán.

(28) The district traversed by the Shírrúd was known formerly as Shírján.

(29) Mackenzie mentions Cháwush Maḥalla on the right bank of the Áwsiyárúd, a few hundred paces from its mouth. No one there, however, has heard of the name.

(30) The meaning of Tunakábun is "below Tunaká." Tunaká was a city which was already destroyed in 789/1387. At that time a castle called Diz Tunaká stood on the site of the former city. An Englishman who had seen the ruins of a city in the oak forests of Tunakábun was unable to explain to me their exact location, and I could obtain no information on the subject. In the revenue list the village of Balada still appears as the chief place of Tunakábun.

(31) Mountains of Dú-Hazár: 'Á'ishabar; Chákhúní; Chalakí; Daryásar; Dúgúr; Gáwkul; Girdgú; Gúcha; Guldast; Habana; Hiyán; Íjar; Iriya; Jál; Jáldarra; Kangalcháh; Khánabun; Kulacháh; Kultalasar; Kúrasar; Lakrí; Láktaráshán; Laylán; Niyárdarra; Núshá; Nuwártala; Píshkúh; Rábar; Rásh; Sargalchák; Sarjasará; Siyáhgala; Siyáhgáw; Siyáhguda; Siyáhkul; Siyáhlan; Túlídasht; Zalam; Zardsar.—Mountains of Sih-Hazár: Siyáhkúh; Takht-i-Sulaymán; Yatímkush.—Mountains of Ishkawar: Áb-anbárkash; Chákhání; Dúrán; Ispiyabuna; Ispiyachan; Khánakiyán; Khashachál; Khushksal; Lazar; Nachíkúh; Nafṭachák; Palímdasht; Shají; Sháh-Safíd-Kúh or Miyánkúh; Siyáhpulasará; Tanúrkash; Turangsar; Zarú.

(32) Mullá Fattáḥ Tunakábuní, author of the *Kitáb-i-Ḥakím Mú'min* and the *Tuḥfa-i-Ḥakím*, two works still consulted by native physicians in Persia, belonged to the Kalántariyya clan. In the *Ta'ríkh-i-Khání* of 'Alí b. Shamsu'd-Dín the Marashtáwand and Chalíndán clans of Tunakábun are mentioned. Ẓahíru'd-Dín speaks of Kákú Ardashír, one of the great Kákús of Tunakábun

az jumla-i-Kákuwán-i-buzurg-i-Tunakábun, who towards the end of the 8th (14th) century made his submission with his clan to Sayyid 'Alí Kiyá. Kákú Ḥusám, *khalábar* and *rastar* of Karjiyán, is mentioned in 897/1491-2 in the *Ta'ríkh-i-Khání*, and Kákú Dáráy Amíra in 912/1506-7.

(33) Gmelin in 1771 says that, until the year before, Tunakábun had been for six years under Ibráhím Khán 'Amárlú. It was then taken by Hidáyat Khán from Rustam Khán 'Amárlú, and, with Karím Khán Zand's approval, added to Gílán.

(34) Mackenzie mentions the Nírúd, the Ḥájjí Maḥalla, the Tílpurdsar, the Ráhpushta and the Zawárkíla.

(35) Near Aspchín was a place called Dúládár. See Ibn Isfandiyár p. 221.

(36) The castle of Isparúz is said to have been built by the legendary Díw-i-Safíd. It was repaired in 867/1462-3 by Malik Iskandar. Between it and Chalandar grew a very thick forest, called Warnábád. I have not been able to locate the exact site of the castle of Isparúz or Ispírúz (Ispíríz). From the castle of Kujúr a route to Qal'a Ispírúz passed Chinárbun and Cháhsar This Chinárbun was on the way from Ṭálaqán to Ṣáliḥán. The Isparúz is probably the same as the Ispídjúy which, according to Ibn Isfandiyár, could be reached by sea in an hour from Chálús with a good wind.

(37) Mackenzie mentions the Imámrúd, the Marzánkíla, the small hamlet of Nawdikak, the Sardábrúdsar, the *Maḥalla* of Gúramaján, and the large village of Áwrang which is a mile from the sea. I take the Sardábraja mentioned by Ẓahíru'd-Dín to be the same as the Sardábrúd.

(38) Al-Kabíra is the Kawír mentioned by Ẓahíru'd-Dín. He informs us that Iskandar, the brother of Malik Ḥusámu'd-Dawla Ardashír b. Namáwar, at his father's death (640/1242), ruled over Nátil and the neighbouring districts, and that he himself saw the name Iskandar b. Namáwar engraved on the pulpit of the mosque of Kadír, which at that time was called Kawír.

(39) Kajja, Kacha, Kajú, Kajúya, or Kachú was a town in the district of Rúyán. It is in error that Barbier de Meynard says it is also called Kalár. Ibn Isfandiyár mentions that Maṣqala b. Hubayra, who waged war with Farrukhán-i-Buzurg for two years, was killed on the road between Kajú and Kandasán and buried in the village of Chahársú, where his tomb, during the author's time, was ignorantly visited by the common people under the false impression that its occupant was one of the Prophet's companions.

(40) The town of Kalár was at 3 days' distance from Ámul and 2 from Ray on the border of the country of the unbelievers, i.e. Daylam. It was the residence of the Ustundár Shahriyár b. Pádúsbán Gáwbara. In 780/1378-9 the castle of Kalár was in ruins. Ibn Isfandiyár mentions the village of Dilam near Kalár, and adds that no one born there survives his twentieth year.

Ẓahíru'd-Dín says that Kalár-rustáq reached the zenith of its prosperity under Naṣíru'd-Dawla Shahriyár b. Kay-Khusraw (717–725/1317-8–1325), who built a palace, a town and a bazaar at Gurgú, which can but be Kurkú

In 850/1446-7 the residence of Malik Uways b. Kayúmarth was at Kurgú-Gardan, no doubt the same place as Kurkú or Gurgú.

(41) Mackenzie mentions the Tizkalá after the Gandábrúd.

(42) The mountains south of Chalandar are: Hashtád-Tan; Qal'a Gardan, Chúmásán, and Talúkútí. The villagers of Chalandar retire during the summer to the *yayláqs* of Barkán and Bín.

(43) The inhabitants of Warzan are of Turkish descent. They were brought here from Turbat-i-Ḥaydarí by Fatḥ 'Alí Sháh.

(44) Sa'ídábád was founded by Sa'íd b. Da'laj, who was sent by the Caliph Manṣúr to replace 'Umar b. al-'Alá as governor of Ṭabaristán. Sa'íd b. Da'laj did not remain long enough to finish the town. This was done by his successor, 'Umar b. al-'Alá, who had been re-appointed. At the time of the general massacre of the Arabs in Ṭabaristán, the life of 'Umar b. al-'Alá, who was in disgrace with the Caliph al-Mahdí, was spared. The mound at Sa'ídábád is the site of his palace. In the history of Khwája 'Alí Rúyání we find that the grave venerated by the inhabitants of Sa'ídábád was that of 'Umar b. al-'Alá although the inscription on the sarcophagus stated that it was the tomb of 'Abdu'lláh b. 'Umar b. al-'Alá b. 'Abdu'l-Muṭṭalib. Sa'ídábád was destroyed by the deputy of 'Abdu'lláh b. Ḥázim, governor of Mázandarán.

Sa'ídábád was passed on the way from Ḥasankayf in Kalár-rustáq to the village of Kiyákaláta near Laktar. See also Ibn Isfandiyár, p. 39, ll. 24–28.

(45) The Sarkíla and another stream are mentioned by Mackenzie as between the Kulírúd and the Kunusarúd.

(46) Mackenzie mentions the Tanashún stream with a stony bed, between the Suladih and Rustamrúd.

(47) This stream, which forms the boundary between the districts of Núr and Ámul, is called Alíshrúd farther inland.

(48) Ibn Isfandiyár relates that Minúchihr, when compelled to flee before Afrásiyáb, escaped by way of Láriján to the forest of Tamísha and thence to Rustamdár. Ẓahíru'd-Dín surmises that the forest of Tamísha was in the district of Ahlam.

(49) Ámula was the daughter of Ashtád. Her father and his brother, Yazdán, came from Daylam and settled near Ámul where the one founded the hamlet of Ashtád and the other the village of Yazdánábád. At Yazdánábád the Ispahbad Khurshíd built a lofty palace on the sea shore for his first and favourite wife, Ramja Harúya. For the village of Ashtád, Ẓahíru'd-Dín has Ashtád-rustáq. See Ibn Isfandiyár, pp. 20–21 and 115.

(50) This is the same as the Dar-i-Júr gate or "upper gate."

(51) 'Umar b. al 'Alá, when sent the second time to Ṭabaristán by the Caliph, to the district of Dábú, built there a village, situated near Wanabun, which he named 'Umarkaláta, and where he erected a palace and a *bázár*. He also built another town called 'Umarábád which was on the way from Ámul to Chálús.

(52) Qasrán was probably the name of the valley of the Jájrúd river. 'Alí b. Káma, the lieutenant of the Ispahbad Shahriyár b. Sharwín b. Rustam, built a castle at Qasrán on the banks of the Jájrúd, and that valley was

therefore known as Kúshkdasht, and the ruins which were to be seen there five centuries later were the ruins of 'Alí b. Káma's castle.

(53) This old mosque contained a fountain which drew its water from the mountain of Wandád-Ummíd.

(54) Apart from the names of quarters or buildings of Ámul already mentioned there were: Gázargáh or the "washing-place" and Kúshk-i-Jáwalí, a palace which was razed to the ground by Sháh Ardashír (end of thirteenth century). There was also the Maydán-i-Rúdbár-i-Báqilí-Pazán.

(55) Gmelin, who visited Ámul in 1771, says: "On s'apercoit qu'Amol a été mieux fortifiée qu'aucune autre ville de la Perse; car son enceinte est encore pourvue de bons bastions, et ses remparts, qui la rendent presque partout susceptible de défense, sont en bon état."

(56) This bridge was built originally by a former Shaykhu'l-Islám of Ámul towards the beginning of the eighteenth century and was rebuilt towards the beginning of the nineteenth century by Mírzá Shafí', the *Wazír* of Mázandarán.

(57) Maḥalla-i-Gúrak, Bághbán Maḥalla, Khushwásh Maḥalla, Úrdasht Maḥalla, and Gálish Khayl, which are mentioned by Melgunof, are no doubt part of one or other of the above quarters. The Maḥalla-i-Tijinajár, in which was the Masjid-i-Gulshan built by Sayyid Zabdar?, was unknown to my informants. Gmelin in 1771 says that Ámul had eight quarters, namely: Mashá'í Maḥalla, Rúdgar Maḥalla, Chinárbun, Kuhna-Masjid, Áhangar Maḥalla, Kárdí Maḥalla, Darzí Maḥalla, and Bájilú.

(58) The original mausoleum over the grave of Mír Qiwámu'd-Dín was razed to the ground by Iskandar Shaykhí whom Tímúr appointed governor after the sack of the town in 795/1392-3. Sayyid 'Alí, who was governor of Mázandarán from 806–820/1403-4–1418, gave orders for a temporary structure, which had been erected on the emplacement of the former mausoleum, to be replaced by a domed building. The latter was either in ruins or considered unworthy of its occupant when Sháh 'Abbás, a descendant of Mír Buzurg in the female line, erected the shrine which exists to this day. Sayyid 'Alí of Ámul, who died at Zághsará in Tunakábun in 825/1422, was buried near his father. Many other descendants of Mír Qiwámu'd-Dín were buried either near him or in other burial-grounds around Ámul, but their tombs are no longer to be seen.

(59) A descendant of this *darwísh*, Sayyid Sharafu'd-Dín, was contemporary with Ibn Isfandiyár and did much to check the Zaydí and propagate the Imámí doctrines in Mázandarán His tomb was in the college of Sayyid Imám Khaṭíb, opposite Mashhadisar.

(60) In 315/927-8 Dá'í'ṣ-Ṣaghír was slain at the bridge near the 'Alí-ábád quarter of Ámul and was buried in the house of his daughter in the said quarter.

(61) This is no doubt identical with the old cupola surrounded by trees, in the centre of Ámul, mentioned in the *Haft Iqlím* by Aḥmad-i-Rází, in which was said to be buried Íraj, the son of Firídún.

(62) The new road, which was built in 1878, runs along the left bank of the river Harhaz. The old road, traces of which are still to be seen, ran along the

rocky precipices at a height of 200 feet in places and had been built out from the cliff instead of cut in. At a place called Tufangá, near Wana, on the new road, a bas-relief of Náṣiru'd-Dín Sháh surrounded by his courtiers has been carved on the rock.

In the *Kitábu'l-Masálik wal-Mamálik* the stages from Ray to Ámul are given as: Bámahin, 8 *farsakhs*; Pulúr, a stage; Kalázil, a stage; Qal'a Alárd, a stage; Farasp, 6 *farsakhs*; Ámul, a stage;—and those from Ámul to Gurgán as: Míla, 2 *farsakhs*; Túji, a stage; Sárí, a stage; Námina, a stage; Limrásk, a stage; Tamísha, a stage; Astarábád, a stage; Rubáṭ-i-Ḥafṣ, a stage; Gurgán, a stage.

(63) Other mountains of the Lár valley are: 'Uthmánkúh; Yánisar; Kamardasht; Surkhak (north of Khushkrúd); and Surkhkamar. Mountains of Láriján appearing on the maps of Stahl and de Morgan are: Hanasán; Más; Bazham; Miyánrúd; Taramúmaj; Kúh-i-Sard; Bámsar; Buzkúh; Giyábandán; Gumadasí; Malakhábád; Maryár; Siyáhband; Uzunkúh; Zardakúh.

(64) In 784/1382-3 there stood a strong castle at Lár, and Sayyid Fakhru'd-Dín b. Qiwámu'd-Dín Mar'ashí, unable to reduce it, ordered a second castle to be constructed near it so as to dominate it. The besieged were thus soon compelled to surrender.

Wells speaks of the ruins of a small fortress or castle which commands the pass out of the Lár valley near Wardagar, and of the remains of a stone rampart which formed a barrier right across the Lár valley at Chashma-i-Safíd.

(65) Safíd-Áb is no doubt the same as Ẓahíru'd-Dín's Ispí-Áw.

(66) At the Yálú gorge the Núr cuts at right angles through an enormous mass of basalt forming a rocky defile. The valley is rugged and picturesque the whole way down to Balada, and the river contains trout. At Balada the Núr, passing through a defile, turns sharply east to join the river Harhaz at Panjáb.

(67) In Sásánian times a king named Saliyán took refuge in Ṭabaristán and built himself a residence at a place called Kísaliyán, the meaning of *Kíya* in the Ṭabarí dialect being "house." This building was still standing in the time of Ibn Isfandiyár. The castle of Gíliyán mentioned by Ẓahíru'd-Dín is a mistake; it should be the castle of Kasliyán.

(68) I take Kalíp to be a scribe's error for Kilís. The pass of Kilís, Darband-i-Kilís or Tanga-i-Kilís, led from 'Iráq to Kurdábád in Sawádkúh and is identical with the Gadúk pass.

(69) The names of the quarters, mosques and *madrasas*, *takiyas* and shrines of Bárfurúsh are:

Quarters: Abú Maḥalla; Áqárúd; Áhangar Maḥalla; 'Arab-khayl; Ástána; Astarábádí Maḥalla; 'Aṭṭár Maḥalla; Báb-i-Báqir-i-Náẓir; Bághbán Maḥalla; Bakhshí Maḥalla; Biyákalá; Bídábád; Bíjináji Maḥalla; Bísar Takiya; Chahárshanba; Chúbáq Maḥalla; Dabbághkhánapísh; Darb-i-Shuhadá; Darzíkútí; Darwísh-khayl; Darwísh Táju'd-Dín; Díw Maḥalla; Gulshan; Ḥamzakalá; Ḥaṣír-Furúshán; Hataká-kalá; Hazárbun; Ispit Takiya; Kásagar Maḥalla; Kaláj-Mashhad; Khiyábán-i-Ḥaram; Kúrasar; Lílak Maḥalla; Masjid-i-Jáma; Miyándasta; Miyánqaṭ'; Míchgáh Maḥalla; Mírzá Kúchik; Murád Bayg; Nakhíbkalá; Nafṭí Maḥalla; Panákalá;

Panjshanba-Bázár; Qádiriyya Maḥalla; Qarákalá; Qaṣṣábkalá; Qáḍíkútí; Raḍiyakalá; Rúdgar Maḥalla; Sar-i-Ḥammám-i-Áqá-Ḥasan; Sabz-Maydán; Sayyid Jalál; Sayyid Zaynu'l-'Ábidín; Sháhkalá; Sháh Zangí; Shamshírgar Maḥalla; Sha'rbáf Maḥalla; Takiya-Arbáb; Ṭúqdárbun; Turk Maḥalla; Újábun; Yahúdí Maḥalla; Zargar Maḥalla.

Mosques and *Madrasas*: 'Allámа with *madrasa*; Astána, or Áqá Shaykh Ḥusayn 'Andalíb; Astarábádí Maḥalla; Chál; Gulshan; Ḥájjí Ḥusayn; Ḥájjí Ja'far; Ḥájjí Mírzá Hidáyat; Ḥájjí Sayyid Ḥasan Mawláná, with *madrasa*; Haṣírfurúshán; Jáma; Káẓimbaygí with *madrasa*; Mashhadí Muḥammad Khurásání; Mullá Majíd; Nakhíbkalá; Panákalá; Qádiriyya with *madrasa*; Qahháriyya with *madrasa*; Qarákalá; Qaṣṣábkalá; Rúḥiyya with *madrasa*; Sayfu'l-Islám; Saqqá; Thiqatu'l-Islám; Újábun or Mullá Ḥusayn 'Alí; Zargar Maḥalla or Shaykh 'Abdu'l-Rasúl; and the *madrasas* of Ḥájjí Ibráhím, Ṣadr, and Mírzá Zakí.

Takiyas: Abú Maḥalla; Áhangarkalá; Áqá Sayyid Rabí'; Astána; Báb-Báqir; Bíjinájí; Bísar-Takiya; Chahárshanbapísh; Darb-i-Shuhadá; Darwísh-Khayl; Gulshan; Haṣír-furúshán; I'timád-i-Díwán; Lílak Maḥalla; Mírzá Hádí; Murád Bayg; Nakhíbkalá; Nafṭí Mahalla; Naw 'Alam or Qarákalá; Panákalá; Qaṣṣábkalá; Raḍiyakalá; Rúdgar Maḥalla; Sabz-Maydán; Sar-i-Ḥamám; Sayyid Jalál; Sháh Zangí; Shamshírgar Maḥalla; Ṭúqdárbun; Újábun; Zargarhá.

Shrines or *Imámzádas*: 'Abdu'lláh, in Chahárshanbapísh; Abu'l-Ma'ṣúm, in Báb-Báqir-i-Náẓir; Bíbí Ásiya Khátún; Haft Tan, south of Bárfurúsh; Ma'ṣúm; Qásim; Rikáb-i-Amír; Sayyid Jalálu'd-Dín; Shuhadá, in the *Bázár*; Yaḥyá, in Kásagar Maḥalla.

(70) The port of Ámul, where its river flowed into the Caspian, was the small town of 'Aynu'l-Humm, a name generally written Ahlam. The port was of no great size. The *Sayyids* of Ahlam were descended from Fakhru'd-Dín b. Qiwámu'd-Dín Mar'ashí.

(71) The village of Lárím is 2½ miles from the mouth of the Siyáhrúd or Lárím river. The village is divided into two by a stream which is crossed by a good serviceable bridge for men and horses. Between the village and the sea shore is the small Imámzáda Maḥmúd. *Íliyáts* of the Jánbáz tribe of Sawádkúh descend with their flocks and cattle to the neighbourhood of Lárím in winter. Mackenzie mentions that the Jánbáz tribe numbered 1000 houses.

(72) Dorn mentions that a mountain path from Fírúzkúh to Bárfurúsh over the Tang-i-Wáshí, or Sú-Wáshí, passes over that part of the Alburz chain known as Lapút or Lafút, and he believes this Lapút or Lafút to be the Labos or Laboutas of the ancients and the locality whence Amír Muḥammad b. Sulṭán Sháh Láwadí and Sulṭán Ḥasan Láwadí take their names.

(73) It was in this district at the village of Máwujkúh that Firídún spent his boyhood. Lafúr, according to Ẓahíru'd-Dín, is on the slope of the Sawádkúh mountain and its inhabitants spend the summer in the *yayláqs* of Sawádkúh where their cattle and horses are sent to graze. Similarly the inhabitants of Sawádkúh spend the winter at Lafúr where they own pastures for their sheep. The Kiyás of Bísutún, who were notables of Sárí, owned property in Lafúr and Sawádkúh and resided there. Ibn Isfandiyár mentions Fírúzábád in Lafúr.

(74) Faraḥábád, formerly known as Tabúna, was founded by Sháh 'Abbás in 1020/1611-12.

(75) Mackenzie says that on leaving Faraḥábád the road lay along the left bank of the Tijin. To his right was Ḥamídábád which was inhabited by Kurds of the Jahánbayglú tribe, to his left a place called Súta and another called Isfandín where there was a mound or tumulus. He then came to the village of Ábmál and the *maḥalla* of Ákand.

(76) In the shrine here is buried Sulṭán Muḥammad Ṭáhir, son of Músá Káẓim. An inscription, dated 875/1470-1, places on record that the building was erected by Amír Murtaḍá al-Ḥusayní (son of Sayyid 'Alí and grandson of Sayyid Kamálu'd-Dín, the son of Mír Qiwámu'd-Dín of Ámul), and after him by his son, Muḥammad, and then by the latter's sons, 'Abdu'l-Karím and 'Abdu'r-Raḥím, and was completed under Amír Raḍí'ud-Dín al-Ḥusayní. The name of the *ustád* is Mawláná Shamsu'd-Dín, son of Naṣru'lláh al-Muṭahhar.

(77) Ẓahíru'd-Dín mentions the shrine of Imám Dádras which was near Sárí on the way to Ámul. The shrine was on an island and could only be reached by boats.

(78) I believe Sih-Gunbad to be identical with the Gunbad-i-Chahár-Dar or "four-doored dome," which, according to Ibn Isfandiyár, stood opposite the palace of the Báwands and was included by King Ardashír in his private garden. It was originally built by Minúchihr, but fell into dilapidation in the time of the Ispahbad Khurshíd Gáwbara. It was then repaired, and was so strong that it was impossible to detach a single brick from the fabric.

(79) The mosques of Sárí are: Masjid-i-Jámi' with *madrasa*; Sulaymán Khán with *madrasa*; Dar Masjid; Imámiyya with *madrasa*; Riḍá Khán; Sháh Ghází; Chál; and the *madrasas* Mádar-i-Sháhzáda and Nawwábiyya. Melgunof mentions the mosque and *madrasa* of Ḥájjí Muṣṭafá Khán. The *Takiyas* are: Chahár-Takiya outside the Bárfurúsh gate; Takiya-i-Naw, or Bísartakiya; Shukrábád; Na'lbandán; Mír Mashhad; Muḥammad Taqí Khán; Bayrámtar; Sháh-Ghází-bun; 'Abbás Khání; Shipishkushán; Mullá Áqá Bábá; Ḥájjí-ábád; Maḥalla-i-Iṣfahání; Sar-i-Darwáza-i-Astarábád; and the Takiya-i-Anbár-i-Naw.

(80) Ẓahíru'd-Dín mentions that Sayyid Kamálu'd-Dín, who was ruler of Sárí from 763–795/1361-2–1393, and who died in exile in Máwará'un-Nahr, was buried at Sárí, and that a fine mausoleum was erected over his grave. Ghiyáthu'd-Dín, his son, was buried later in the same mausoleum. Sayyid Yaḥyá b. Qiwámu'd-Dín and Sayyid Ashraf b. Kamálu'd-Dín were also buried at Sárí, but their graves were not known to our informants.

(81) Ibn Isfandiyár mentions the tomb of Sindí b. Sháhak, a Shí'ite leader under the Caliph 'Abdu'lláh al-Má'mún, which was at Sárí in the place since called Bá Naṣrí Mashhad. Melgunof mentions the ruined shrine of Khurram-sháh in the plain of Sha'bán, to the west of Sárí.

(82) Ibn Isfandiyár mentions the *Maydán*, and Ẓahíru'd-Dín the river, of Atrábun (Afrábun) outside the walls of Sárí. Ibn Isfandiyár also mentions the Maydán-i-Tápán of Sárí. No one had heard of these places which belonged to the former city of Sárí.

(83) To these should be added the Záyandarúd, a small *bulúk* on the banks of the Niká river. This river is practically dry below the Pul-i-Niká, but farther down it springs forth again and is known as the Záyandarúd. It falls into the Caspian in three branches, the most westerly being named Muḥammad Kíla and the middle one Gawhar-Bárán.

(84) This stream is no doubt the Dár-Rúd (Dárá-Rúd) mentioned by Napier as 6½ miles west of Pul-i-Niká. Mackenzie mentions Nawdihak as a village of 40 houses inhabited by Giraylís and Mázandaránís and situated near the road between Dárábkalá and the *Imámzáda* of Niká.

(85) The spits of land between these arms are from west to east Naftachál (i.e. *Namak-chál*); Sháṭirlanga; Jannakútí; Ya'qúblanga; Miyángula; Yághígúrak; etc.

(86) This fort was built to prevent any surreptitious occupation of Miyánkala by the Russians. It was commenced about 1860 and completed about 1873.

(87) Napier says the length of the peninsula is 12 *farsakhs*, which is reckoned as three stages from Qal'a Palangán: Zardí, Muqím, and Sartúk. At Qal'a Rúsiyán, four miles west of Sartúk, along the shore, is a spot marked by the ruins of a Russian fort, which is either the place where Stenka Razin in 1668 made his last stand before leaving Persia, or the fort erected by Count Voinovitch in 1781. Dorn says the name is Urús Qal'a and that the place was formerly an island.

(88) Chahár-Imám is identical with the *fariḍa* or harbour town of Chármán or Chahármán, formerly called Shármán or Shármám, where Walásh slew Báw.

(89) At Dhághmarz we were told that Surkhdím was the name of certain pastures near which were two mounds, Sangtappa and Badiyántappa.

(90) The village of Kúsán on a stream of the same name is 4 miles west of Ashraf. Ibn Isfandiyár mentions that Kúsán was at the foot of the castle of Áb-Dárá. This castle is no doubt identical with Qal'a Dárá and Diz-i-Dárá. Near Qal'a Dárá was the village of Marzubánábád. It is said that Ṭús-i-Núdhar, who was commander of the troops of Kay Khusraw, built a town in Panjáh-Hazár, in the locality known as Kúsán, and named it Ṭúsán. The site of a castle built by him was still visible in the time of Ibn Isfandiyár, at a place called Lúman Dún. Kayús, the grandfather of Báw, had founded a fire-temple here. Kúsán in the 9th (15th) century was the residence of the Bábulkáni *Sayyids*.

(91) Gmelin says that Northern Persia does not produce oranges and lemons and that the trees seen at Ashraf were probably imported from India by Sháh 'Abbás. It is known, however, that sweet oranges from Mázandarán are mentioned in the time of Naṣr b. Aḥmad the Sámánid (died 330/942), whilst Bayhaqí speaks in 426/1036 of the numerous orange and lemon groves to be seen in Mázandarán.

(92) To these may be added the ruined mosque of Mírzá Mahdí Ashrafí and the *madrasa* Aḥmad-i-Mullá Ṣafar 'Alí. In the Masjid-i-Jámi' there is an edict of Sháh Sulṭán Ḥusayn dated Shawwál 1106. It is practically identical with those found in the *Masjid-i-Jámi's* of Láhiján and of Ámul.

(93) At 'Abbásábád, 6 miles from Ashraf, there is a royal residence of Sháh 'Abbás little known to travellers in this part of Persia. There is here a large artificial lake which feeds the Sárú and Sháhkíla streams.

(94) Mackenzie mentions the following villages between Pásand and Khurshídkalá: Khalílkhayl, Rikáwand, Kalák, and Qal'a-Páyán.

(95) At that time there were three islands, a large one, which, already in 1840, had become part of the peninsula of Miyánkala, and two smaller ones. The Russians called the larger island Orest, and the two others Eugenis and Ashik.

(96) In his history of Mázandarán Ẓahíru'd-Dín mentions Tamísha-i-Kútí-Bá-Naṣrán and Tamísha-i-Bá-Naṣrán.

(97) There was formerly a village called Alwand Kiyá, east of Kharába-Shahr. Some of its inhabitants were killed by the Turcomans and the others dispersed, some settling at Sarkalá, 2 miles distant.

(98) The village of Shaṣtkalá whence Minúchihrí, court poet of Falaku'l-Ma'álí Minúchihr, who survived till 1041 A.D. or later, takes his name, no longer exists.

(99) We know of the following histories of Astarábád and Gurgán: History of Astarábád by Abú Sa'íd 'Abdu'r-Rahmán b. Muḥammad al-Idrísí (died 405/1014–5); History of Astarábád by Ibn al-Káẓim Ḥamza b. Yúsuf as-Sahmí al-Jurjání (died 427/1035–6); History of Jurján by the same author; and History of Jurján by 'Alí b. Aḥmad al-Jurjání al-Idrísí. All these histories seem to have been lost.

Zadracarta, according to Arrian, was opposite the waggon-track across the range and is possibly Astarábád, which is situated to the south of the best and easiest pass across the great Alburz range. The termination *carta* is probably the same as the Persian *gird*.

(100) Muḥammad Kátibí Turshízí, a contemporary of Báysunghur Mírzá, was buried at Astarábád outside the shrine of Imámzáda Ma'ṣúm, which was known by the name of Nuh-Gúrán. See Dawlatsháh, *Memoirs of the Poets*, ed. E. G. Browne, p. 390.

(101) It was the custom for every new governor to change the copper currency of his predecessor, which suffered forthwith a depreciation of 50 °/₀.

(102) Astarábád may be called the cradle of the present dynasty of Persia. Fatḥ 'Alí Khán, who was put to death by Sháh Ṭahmásp II at the instigation of Nádir, was from Astarábád, and his son Muḥammad Ḥasan Khán made it his capital (1752–1762 A.D.). Ḥusayn Qulí Khán, after his father's death, retired to Rámiyán, where he was practically independent for six years, when he was murdered by his own men at Surkhdasht. Áqá Muḥammad Khán was born at Astarábád in the house of Sayyid Riḍá Mufídí, which has since been known as Mawlúd-Khána.

(103) Sykes relates that from Bujnúrd he went to Samalqán and camped at Sháhábád, the chief place of the valley. Proceeding he reached the valley of Chálbásh. Qaráṭughán, some five miles from Dasht, is on the edge of the forest. From Dasht he marched down the Dahana-i-Gurgán and camped at Isḥáqí, half-way down the pass. Near a place called Tang-i-Ráh is the site of what appears to have been a fortress. It is called Takht-i-Sulaymán.

Shaghál Tappa is a mound near a stream. Close to Chakúr, the chief centre of Gurgán, as the Gúklán country is called, are the important ruins of Shahrak (Shahr-i-Naw and Shahrak-i-Naw). He camped at Khár, close to which lie the ruins of Paras, 14 miles from Gunbad-i-Qábús. See P. M. Sykes, "A Sixth Journey in Persia," *J.R.G.S.* January 1911, Vol. XXXVII, No. 1, pp. 9–14.

(104) Sykes claims to have identified Qal'a Márán with the second Parthian capital which was founded by Tiridates and termed Dárá—the Dareion of the Greeks.

(105) 'Awfí informs us that the Kabúdjáma were a tribe that resided between Astarábád and Khwárazm. They had a city named Shahr-i-Naw or Shahrak-i-Naw, the ruins of which are still to be seen in the Gúklán country. Tímúr in 792/1390 marched from Gurgán to Samalqán by way of Shahr-i-Naw and Ḥúrḥábád. Kúhsár was part of Kabúdjáma, as the village of Dilábád (the present Tílawá) in Kúhsár is mentioned by Dawlatsháh as being in Kabúdjáma. Gulpáygán was very probably part of Kabúdjáma. Mustawfí says that Kabúdjáma included the whole of Gurgán after that district had been completely devastated.

(106) In 761/1360 Abú Bakr Shásmání was governor of Shásmán on behalf of the Sarbadáls. He is said to have built 40 Mongol soldiers into the walls of the castle which he had erected here. Later, Tímúr built a palace at this place and there spent the winter of the year 795/1392.

(107) The following are the names of some of the villages of the former district of Gurgán: Ábbandán; Barkám; Jarkán; Júghán; Juwángán; Másúrábád; Rushín; Rúk; Rú'ín; Zabaḥ near the city; Zú'ín; Sulaymánábád near the city; Salína, described as 120 miles from Sárí by the mountain road and of which the inhabitants were mostly from Gurgán, only a few families being from Ṭabaristán; Fírúzkand; Kash (Kaj or Jaṣ), 12 miles from Gurgán, on a mountain; Maṣqalábád; Máqláṣán; Mihr Jamín; and Mísha, all near Gurgán; Wazdúl; Wasaskar, 28 miles from Gurgán and belonging to Júrdistán; Násir or Násirúdh; and Hyán. Bayhaqí in 426/1035 mentions Muḥammadábád near Gunbad-i-Qábús.

(108) The Bay of Astarábád is described by Mustawfí under the name of Ním Mardán. "The settlement here was very populous in the 8th (14th) century and was a harbour for ships from all parts of the Caspian. The port was but three leagues distant from Astàrábád, and the town behind it which carried on a brisk trade was called Shahrábád" (Le Strange, p. 375). It succeeded no doubt the port of Ábasgún when the city of that name was submerged at the beginning of the 8th (14th) century. There exists at the present day a ruined village called Amínábád-i-Ním Mardán. It is part of Kurd Maḥalla.

(109) The Khurmárúd, which joins the Gurgán near the ruins of the ancient city of Gurgán, is formed by three streams: that of Pisarak in Ḥájjílar, which rises in the Kúh-i-Nílí and is known as Chihilgísú or Chihilјáy; the stream (Tara?) which runs down from the Chináshk and Qánchí or Pársiyán valley; and the Nirṣú, which, according to local tradition, was the property of Naríman, the ancestor of Rustam, whence its name Narímanṣú, which has in course of time become Nirṣú, a name also given to a mountain in this vicinity. A canal brought water in olden days for a distance of four miles from the

Khurmárúd to the gardens of Gurgán. This information is at variance with that already given on page 91.

(110) Qarangí Imám, in Turcoman, means black *Imám*. There are two other shrines held in equal veneration by the Turcomans, viz.: Qizil Imám, or the Red *Imám*, near Qárí-Qal'a in Russian territory, and Áq Imám, or the White *Imám*, on the summit of a hill near the village of Nílí, in Findarisk. These three *Imáms* are said to have been brothers.

(111) The Jahánnumá peak (8900 ft.) is the highest point between the ridge of Sháhkúh (13000 ft.) and Nizwár (13000 ft.) far away to the west, the highest point of the range save Damáwand. The mountain is formed of sandstone and limestone and its slopes are covered with a thick forest of oak. The plateau is 6500 ft. high and is crossed by the road from Astarábád to Chahárdih *viâ* the Ṣandúqa Pass.

(112) Chahárdih (6500 ft.) is a group of four villages in Dámghán, 12 miles south of Chashma 'Alí. The four villages are disposed in a cluster, their names being Kasha, now known as Kharábdih as it was destroyed by an earthquake, Zardawán, Warzan, and Qal'a.

(113) "Above Shangaldih a torrent precipitates itself down the side of a conical red rock crowned with the ruins of an old castle, ascribed to Jamshíd." Stuart, *Journal of a Residence in Persia*, p. 284.

(114) Bard is on the southern slopes of the range of mountains which forms the border of Mázandarán, and to the west of Dámghán at 6 *farsakhs* from that city. The Sar-Tang valley runs north-west to south-east from Bádila to Fúlád Maḥalla. On the north of this valley is a gorge called Tang-i-Shúráb. Lovett has on his map to the north of the Sar-Tang mountain, Wulna, Tilma, Kirát, Ḥawát, Qal'a-sar, Rús, Súrí, and Bádila. Qal'a-sar is situated on a low hill on the east side of the Sar-Tang valley. It contains at least 80 houses and from 300 to 400 inhabitants. There is a good deal of cultivation about, every favourable spot being under the plough.

(115) Chahárbágh (7100 ft.), in a valley hemmed in by the Lara and Landa mountains to the north, and by the Sháhkúh range to the south.

(116) Quzluq: a ruined village and pass 14 miles from the town of Astarábád on the road to Sháhrúd. Regarding the pass Lovett gives the following account: "the actual ascent begins at an elevation of 3453 ft. from the wide commons of Ziyárat. The march from Ziyárat to the pastures of 'Alí-ábád, three miles from the water-shed (7600 ft.), is very long; and it is best to break the journey at Buland Sufála. At an elevation of 4700 ft. a stratum of gypsum is met with; and a little higher a small serai called Rubáṭ-i-Quzluq. Buland Sufála, where there is a spring, is reached at 5200 ft. Just before reaching the summit of the pass another *rubáṭ* is reached, very useful for travellers during the winter, when great cold and deep snow prevail."

(117) Ziyárat: a village about 15 miles south of Astarábád. North-east of it is the Qal'a Gardan peak, 6000 ft.; south, the Siyáhkhání, 7200 ft.; south-west, the Landa peak, 9000 ft.; and east, the Zabala peak.

(118) Three openings lead from Nawdih to the Yamút plain, the southernmost by Khándúz, the middle one is called Qarátappa, and the northern one the

Sádiqánlí pass. A path leads from Nawdih to Mayáma on the Tiḥrán-Mashhad road, passing up the Khurmálú defile and emerging on the Zardwá plain.

(119) Ardashír Bábakán, says Mas'údí, divided Mázandarán between four *Ispahbads*, under whom was a *Marzubán*. The Múbad Ways and Rámín governed Khurásán and Mázandarán on behalf of Bírí son of Gúdarz b. Balásh of the Ashghániyán dynasty.

(120) Rulers and Governors of Astarábád: Ṭughá Tímúr ruler of Astarábád was murdered by Yaḥyá Karábí, and 'Alí Bu'l-Qalandar was appointed governor of that province by Pahlawán Ḥasan. Amír Valí, son of Shaykh Hindú, independent ruler 754/1353. He submits to Tímúr in 784/1381 and is put to death two years later. Pír Pádsháh b. Luqmán b. Ṭughá Tímúr 786–809/1384–1406. Shamsu'd-Dín 'Alí b. Jamshíd-i-Qárin 810/1407–8. Amír Hindúká 840–853/1436–7/1449–1450. Bábá Ḥusayn who was appointed governor at the death of Bábur was slain in battle near Nasá in 862/1457–8. Mírzá Jalálu'd-Dín Sulṭán Mahmúd on behalf of his father Sulṭán Abú Sa'íd 864–5/1460–1. 'Abdu'r-Raḥmán Arghún on behalf of Mírzá Sulṭán Ḥusayn 865/1460–1. Amír Shaykh Záhid Ṭárumí 873/1468–9. He is succeeded by Ḥasan Shaykh Tímúr. Khwája Aḥmad Findariskí on behalf of Shaybak Khán 914/1508–9. Zaynal Khán 933/1526–7, Ṣafawid governor. 'Abdu'l-Azíz Sulṭán on behalf of his father 'Ubayd Khán of Khwárazm 935/1528–9. He is replaced by Rínash Bahádur. Sulṭán Muḥammad Dhú'l-Qadar b. Amír 'Alá'u'd-Dawla, Ṣafawid governor 937/1531. Ṣadru'd-Dín Khán Ustájlú in 944/1537–8. He was followed by Sháh 'Alí Sulṭán Ustájlú who died in 957/1550. Kachal Sháh Vardí Sulṭán Ustájlú was replaced in 962/1554–5 by Gúkcha Sulṭán Qájár. Ibráhím Khán Dhú'l-Qadar 965/1557–8. Khalíl Khán was governor later than 973/1565–6. Murtaḍá Qulí Khán Parnák and Badr Khán Afshár were at various times governors of Astarábád during the reign of Muḥammad Khudábanda and at the beginning of that of Sháh 'Abbás I. Consequent upon a general rising of the province 'Uliyár Bayg Aymír was appointed governor by Sháh 'Abbás. He was followed by his son Muḥammad Yár Khán who was slain by the Turcomans and replaced by Qilíj Khán his brother. Farhád Khán was then given Astarábád, which after his death was entrusted to Ḥusayn Khán Ziyád-uglú Qájár. Alláhyár Khán governor of Astarábád died in 1007/1598 and was succeeded by his son Muḥammad Yár Khán. Farídún Khán Charkas died in 1031/1621–2 after having governed the province for 18 years. Khusraw Khán. Ḥusayn Khán Bayglar Baygí died in 1051/1641–2 when Mihráb Khán was appointed in his stead. Ḥájjí Minúchihr Khán is replaced in 1071/1660–1 by Jamshíd Khán. In 1086/1675 Muḥammad Khán is governor. Later Fatḥ 'Alí Khán Qájár seized Astarábád which he held until 1139/1726 when he was put to death by Sháh Ṭahmásp II at the instigation of Nádir. Raḥím Khán Giraylí on behalf of Nádir was followed by Muḥammad Ḥusayn Khán Qájár, and Muḥammad Zamán Bayg the latter's son, who was governor in 1157/1744. Bábá Ṣádiq, for a very short period, on behalf of Muḥammad Ḥasan Khán Qájár. Muḥammad Ḥusayn Khán Qájár on behalf of Nádir. Muḥammad Ḥasan Khán Qájár, independent 1160/1747. Ḥusayn Qulí Khán Qájár, independent. Áqá Muḥammad Khán Qájár, independent 1779.

Governors of the Qájárs: Fatḥ 'Alí Khán (later Sháh) in 1206/1791-2. Muḥammad Zamán Khán 'Izzu'd-Dínlú died in 1229/1814.—Muṣṭafá Khán is replaced in 1238/1822 by Badí'u'z-Zamán Mírzá Ṣáhib Ikhtiyár.—Ardashír Mírzá Mulk-Árá, 1250/1835.—Faḍl 'Alí Khán, 1251/1836.—Imám Qulí Khán Qájár and his son 'Abbás Khán Bayglar Baygí.—Sulaymán Khán Khán-Khánán, 1256/1840.—Muḥammad Naṣír Khán.—Muḥammad Taqí Khán, Ẓahíru'd-Dawla.—'Abbás Khán, Bayglar Baygí.—Sháhrukh Khán.—Amír Músá Khán.—'Abbás Khán, Bayglar Baygí.—Aḥmad Mírzá.—Muḥammad Raḥím Khán of Bujnúrd. His brother Ja'far Qulí Khán Ílkhání replaces him in 1273/1856-7 and dies on the return from an expedition against the Turcomans.—'Abbás Mírzá Mulk-Árá.—Muḥammad Valí Khán Qájár, 1277/1861.—Anúsharwán Khán, 'Aynu'l-Mulk 1280/1863-4.—Muḥammad Valí Khán Sardár, 1281/1864-5.—Mírzá Muḥammad Khán Sipahsálár, 1283/1866-7, is replaced during the same year by Ḥájjí Kayúmarth Mírzá.—Anúsharwán Khán, I'tiḍádu'd-Dawla, Khánsálár.—I'timádu'd-Dawla son of I'tiḍádu'd-Dawla, 1285/1868-9. He is followed by Sulaymán Khán Sartíp, Ṣáhib Ikhtiyár, who built the bridge over the Gurgán at Áq-qal'a.—Ḥusayn Qulí Khán is appointed in 1292/1875 but dismissed shortly afterwards and replaced by Ṣáhib Ikhtiyár.—Jahánsúz Mírzá, 1293/1876.—Muṣṭafá Khán Mírpanj, 1296/1879.—Muṣṭafá Qulí Khán is replaced by Ḥabíbu'lláh Khán, Sa'du'd-Dawla, in 1298/1881.—Yár Muḥammad Khán, Sahmu'd-Dawla of Bujnúrd, 1303/1886.—Vajíhu'lláh Mírzá, Sayfu'l Mulk, 1305/1888.—Muḥammad Valí Khán Tunakábuní, Naṣru's-Salṭana, 1307/1889.—'Abdu'lláh Mírzá, Ḥishmatu'd-Dawla, Naṣru's-Salṭana, 1309/1891-2.—Mírzá 'Abdu'lláh Khán, Intiẓámu'd-Dawla, 1310/1893.—Kayúmarth Mírzá, 'Amídu'd-Dawla.—Vajíh-u'lláh Mírzá, Amír Khán Sardár, 1312/1895.—Jahánsúz Mírzá, Amír Núyán, 1315/1898.—Sa'du'd-Dawla, 1316/1898. Aḥmad Khán Qájár, 'Alá'u'd-Dawla, 1317/1900.—Ḥájjí Muḥammad Ṣádiq Khán Shámbiyátlú, Amír-i-Túpkhána, 1318/1901.—Ḥájjí Sulṭán Muḥammad Mírzá, Sayfu'd-Dawla, 1322/1904.—Muḥammad 'Alí Khán, Sardár-Afkham, 1322/1904.—Nuṣratu'lláh Mírzá, Amír Khán Sardár, 1324/1906.—Naṣru's-Salṭana, 1325/1907.

(121) The Qárinwand was one of the seven most honourable stocks of Sásánian Persia, the members of which were called the *Ahlu'l-Buyútát* by the Arab historians.

(122) Abú Khuzayma settled garrisons at the following places: Tamísha; Rúdbár, 2 *farsakhs* from Tamísha; Kúsán; Asrámíl; Sámta; Kúsán; Zírwán in Panjáh Hazár; Dú-Áb; Mihrawán; Aṣram; Azdarra; Awsarzín; Awrárábád above Parícha; Rawá; Sárí; Aratá; Chapukrúd; Khurramábád; Chamanú; Farím; Yazdánábád; Kúlá; Mámṭír; Sáliyán near Lafúr; Níshápúriyya; Ṭábarán; Isfandiyár; Tarícha; Fatḥ Faṣlab; Jábarán; Masla (Míla) Zarrínkúl; Ámul; Gílánábád above Ránikúh; Pá-yi-Dasht; Haláwán; Nátil; Bahrámdih; Qaráṭughán of Báláráh; Wáláshjird; Kajú; Júrishjird-i-Sa'ídábád; Kalár, the beginning of Daylam; Kúhistán-i-Dú-Bazham; as-Sa'ídí.

(123) Subsequent governors of Mázandarán were: Mírzá 'Alí Aṣghar on behalf of Nádir.—Muqím Khán on behalf of 'Ádil Sháh and Ibráhím Khán.—Muḥammad Khán Qawánlú on behalf of Muḥammad Ḥasan Khán Qájár.—Naẓar Khán on behalf of Karím Khán.—Muḥammad Khán Dádú of Sawádkúh

and his son Mahdí Khán on behalf of Karím Khán.—Ḥusayn Qulí Khán Qájár, independent.—Zakí Khán on behalf of Karím Khán.—Murtaḍá Qulí Khán Qájár, independent.—Áqá Muḥammad Khán Qájár, independent.—Khán Abdál Khán on behalf of Áqá Muḥammad Khán Qájár.—Áqá Muḥammad Khán Qájár, independent.—Then follow the governors regularly appointed by Áqá Muḥammad Khán Qájár and his successors.

(124) The following are the only names I have found: Náṣir 'Alawí, came to meet Amír Mas'úd b. Sulṭán Maḥmúd Ghaznawí at Ámul in 426/1035.—Mahdí 'Alawí surrendered the castle of Alamút to the Assassins in 483/1090.—Kiyá Buzurg, Dá'í ila'l-Ḥaqq Hádí, helped Sháh Ghází Rustam with 5000 Daylamites in 521/1127, when Sulṭán Mas'úd, the nephew of Sanjar the Saljúq, invaded Mázandarán.—Kiyá Buzurg, Dá'í ila'l-Ḥaqq Riḍá b. Hádí, to whom the Ispahbad Ardashír (568–602/1173–1205-6) assigned the district of Daylamán.—Sayyid Ḥusayn-i-Náṣir buried at Rúdisar.

(125) I attribute to Abú'l-Faḍl the coin struck at Ámul in 343/954–5 with the name of Ruknu'd-Dawla Abú 'Alí Buwayh on the reverse and that of *al-Ustundár* on the obverse, which is in the possession of the British Museum.

(126) "Whenever the Ispahbad Farrukhán went on a hunting expedition in this direction, he used to stay a few days there to drink and make merry at Tanparast under Tarduwíní, where the ruins of the palace of the Ispahbads Farrukhán and Khurshíd are still visible. He presently asked and obtained in marriage the Masmughán's daughter, for whom he built a residence in this place, which he connected by a canal with the sea; but later he was offended with his father-in-law, beheaded him, and annexed all his domains as far as Dárán." See Ibn Isfandiyár, p. 101. The district of Miyándúrúd extended from the Darkalárúd to the river Mihrabán, which became known as Mírbán. It was part of Sárí, the eastern limit of which was Qarátughán. See Ẓahíru'd-Dín, *History of Mázandarán*, p. 42. Mihrawán was a district situated in a plain in the mountains at 10 *farsakhs* from Sárí. It contained a town of the same name. The Mihrawán-river, Júy Mihrawán, is certainly the present Niká river, and Dú-Áb must have been a village at the junction of the Asp-u-Nayza and Sar-Tang streams, south of the present bridge of Niká.

(127) There was a place near the Harhaz river known as Darband-i-Shínúh, so called because Báharb, when fleeing from the men sent in pursuit of him by his father Minúchihr, the *Marzubán* of Láriján, leaped his horse into the river, which runs like a mill-race at this spot.

(128) Bahmanshír was founded by Ardashír Bábakán. It was known later as Karjiyán. See Ḥamdu'lláh Mustawfí Qazwíní, *Ta'ríkh-i-Guzída* (Gibb facsimile), p. 105, l. 5.

OTHER WORKS BY THE AUTHOR OF THIS BOOK

Report on the Trade and General Condition of the City and Province of Kermanshah. 1903. *Dipl. and Cons. Reports*, Misc. Series, No. 590.

Report for the year 1902–3 on the Trade of Kermanshah. *Dipl. and Cons. Reports*, Ann. Series, No. 3043.

Report for the year 1903–4 on the Trade of Kermanshah and District. *Dipl. and Cons. Reports*, Ann. Series, No. 3189.

Report for the year 1904–5 on the Trade of Kermanshah. *Dipl. and Cons. Reports*, Ann. Series, No. 3420.

Report from March 20, 1903, to March 20, 1907, on the Trade of the Consular District of Resht and Astarabad. *Dipl. and Cons. Reports*, Ann. Series, No. 3864.

Report from March 21, 1907, to March 20, 1909, on the Trade of the Persian Caspian Provinces (Consular District of Resht and Astarabad). *Dipl. and Cons. Reports*, Ann. Series, No. 4398.

Report from March 21, 1909, to March 20, 1911, on the Trade of the Persian Caspian Provinces (Consular District of Resht and Astarabad). *Dipl. and Cons. Reports*, Ann. Series, No. 4628.

Report on the Trade and General Condition of the City and Province of Astarabad. *Dipl. and Cons. Reports*, Ann. Series, No. 4381.

Report for the year 1910–11 on the Trade and General Condition of the City of Barfurush and the Province of Mazanderan. *Dipl. and Cons. Reports*, Ann. Series, No. 4812.

Report on the Production of Rice in the Provinces of Ghilan, Mazanderan and Astarabad. See *Board of Trade Journal*, April 25, 1907, p. 185.

Silk Culture in Persia. *Board of Trade Journal*, June 6, 1907, pp. 455–459.

Mineral Prospecting in Persia. *Dipl. and Cons. Reports*, 1910.

Openings for British Trade in Morocco (French Zone). *Board of Trade Journal*, Dec. 1917–Jan. 1918.

Notes on Lur-i-Kuchik and Pusht-i-Kuh and Pish-Kuh Tribes. Govt. Central Press, Simla, 1906.

Gazetteer of Kermanshah. Govt. Central Press, Simla, 1907.

Report on Kurdistan. Govt. Monotype Press, Simla, 1911.

Coins of the Shahs of Persia:

I. Silver. From Ismail I Sefavi to the reform of the Currency by Nádir; 1499–1737 A.D. *Numismatic Chronicle*, Fourth Series, Vol. VIII, London, 1908.

II. Silver Coinage from the reform of the Currency by Nádir to the accession of Náṣiru'd-Dín Sháh; 1737–1848 A.D. *Loc. cit.* Vol. XI, London, 1911.

III. Addenda. IV. Copper Coinage; 1502-1877. *Loc. cit.* Vol. XV, London, 1915.

A Journey in Mazanderan (from Resht to Sari). *The Geographical Journal, R.J.S.* Nov. 1913, pp. 435–454.

Rulers of Láhiján and Fúman, in Gílán, Persia. *J.R.A.S.* Jan. 1918, pp. 85–100.

Rulers of Gílán. Rulers of Gaskar, Túl and Náw, Persian Tálish, Túlam, Shaft, Rasht, Kúhdum, Kúchisfahán, Daylamán, Ránikúh, and Ashkawar, in Gílán, Persia. *J.R.A.S.* July 1920, pp. 277–296.

Les Provinces Caspiennes de la Perse. Le Guilan. *Revue du Monde Musulman*, Vol. XXXII. Paris, 1915–1916.

Les Provinces Caspiennes de la Perse. Le Guilan. Illustrations. Paris, 1917.

Les Anciens Sports au Guilan. *Revue du Monde Musulman*, Vol. XXVI, pp. 97–110.

Coins of the Shahs of Persia. Denominations of Persian Coins. *Loc. cit.* pp. 111–127.

Quelques Pièces Curieuses Persanes. *Loc. cit.* pp. 128–132.

Une tentative de réformes en 1875. Tanẓímát-i-Hasaneh. *Loc. cit.* pp. 133–139.

Une Chanson guilek. *Loc. cit.* Vol. XXVIII, pp. 222–229.

Kermanchah. *Loc. cit.* Vol. XXXVIII, pp. 1–40.

La Réorganisation des Habous au Maroc. *Loc. cit.* Vol. XXXIX, pp. 53–97.

Une Lettre Familière de Fath Ali Chah. *Loc. cit.* Vols. XL–XLI, pp. 131–135.

Hamadan. *Loc. cit.* Vol. XLIII, pp. 221–227.

Le Kourdistan. (In preparation.)

Lettres inédites de Dupleix (en Persan). *Loc. cit.* Vol. LVII, 1ère section, pp. 168–172.

Les Tribus du Louristan. } *Collection de la Revue du Monde Musulman.*
Médailles des Qadjars. } Paris, 1916.

Ta'ríkh-i-Gílán wa Daylamistán of Ẓahíru'd-Dín. Persian Text, followed by the Letters of Khán Aḥmad Khán Gílání. Rasht, 'Urwatu'l-Wuthqá Press, 1328/1911.

Jaráyid-i-Írán. In Persian. Rasht, 'Urwatu'l-Wuthqá Press, 1329/1911.

Fúman. In Persian. Rasht, 'Urwatu'l-Wuthqá Press, 1330/1912.

Carte de la Province du Guilan, d'après les notes de reconnaissances exécutées par M. H. L. Rabino, Vice-Consul d'Angleterre à Recht, de 1906–1912, et d'après les renseignements donnés par l'Agence à Recht de la Société Lyonnaise Séricicole et Soies d'Extrême Orient, dressée et dessinée par le Capitaine Faure du 3e Zouaves, publiée par la Société Lyonnaise Séricicole et Soies d'Extrême Orient, Lyon, 1914.

Contribution à l'histoire des Saadiens. *Archives Berbères.* Paris, 1920.

La Réorganisation des Habous au Maroc. *Gazette des Tribunaux du Maroc.* Casablanca, 1922.

Situation légale des Détenteurs de Biens Makhzen dans les Villes du Maroc. Le Caire, MDCCCCXXIV.

Les dynasties Alaouides du Mazandéran. *Journal Asiatique*, Avril—Juin, 1927, pp. 253–277.

La dynastie des Bávands du Mazandéran. (In preparation.)

La dynastie de Pádousbán du Mazandéran. (In preparation.)

La dynastie Ziyáride du Gourgán. (In preparation.)

Histoire d'Astarábád de 750 à 1317 de l'hégire. (In preparation.)

Notice généalogique : famille Pagès. (In preparation.)

" " maison de Voisins. (In preparation.)

" " famille Belliard. (In preparation.)

" " famille Rabino. (In preparation.)

WORKS BY THE AUTHOR AND D. F. LAFONT

L'Industrie Séricicole en Perse. Montpellier, 1910.

La Culture du Riz en Guilan. *Extrait des Annales de l'École Nationale d'Agriculture de Montpellier.* Montpellier, 1911.

Culture du Tabac en Guilan. *Extrait du Progrès Viticole.* Montpellier, 1911.

Culture de la Gourde à Ghalian en Guilan et en Mazandéran. *Revue du Monde Musulman,* Vol. XXVIII, Sept. 1914, pp. 232–236.

Culture de la Canne à sucre en Mazandéran. *Loc. cit.* pp. 237–243.

Contribution à l'étude de la Flore du nord de la Perse. (In preparation.)

INDEX OF NAMES OF AUTHORS AND OTHER PERSONS

Agaeus, 153
Allotte de la Fuye, Colonel, 134
Anet, Claude, xvii
Arrian, 161
Assemani, 153
Baker, V., xvii
Barbier de Meynard, C., xvii, 154
Bauer, xvii
Bell, Dr C. M., xvii
Berchem, Max, xvii, 88, 102
Blarenberg, 65
Bode, von, xvii, 91
Browne, E. G., xvii, 2, 14, 41, 133, 135, 141, 151, Persian text 6
Brydges, Sir Harford Jones, xvii
Buhse, Dr F. A., xvii
Chardin, Sir John, xvii, 49
Chodzko, A., xvii, 152
Curzon, Hon. George N., xvii
Darmesteter, J., xvii, 1, 30
Demorgny, G., xvii, 13, 108, 110, 122
Diez, Ernst, xvii, 88, 102
Dorn, B., xvii–xviii, 1, 3, 38, 68, 118, 132, 152, 158, 160
Dorn, B. and Mírzá Muḥammad Shafí', xviii, 152
Drouin, Ed., xviii
Eastwick, E. B., xviii, 85
Eichwald, Ed., xviii
Ethé, xxiii
Falconer, W., xxi
Ferté, H., xviii
Forster, G., xviii, 54, 68, 151
Fortescue, Captain L. S., xviii
Fraser, J. B., xviii, 4, 5, 6, 8—11, 54, 152
Gasteiger Khán, 7
Gmelin, Sam. G., xviii, 46, 54, 62, 63, 66, 150, 154, 156, 160
Grewingk, Dr C., xix
Haentsche, Dr J. C., xix
Hamilton, H. S., xxi
Hanway, Jonas, xix, 37
Herodotus, xxi, 88
Holmes, W. R., xix, 6, 17, 151, 153
Hommaire de Hell, X., xix, 102
Huart, Cl., xix, 141
Jaubert, P. Amédée, xxi
Kardagus, 153
Khanikoff, N., xix
Lafont, D. F., Preface, xx–xxi, 10
Lee, Sir Richard, xxiii
Le Strange, Guy, xix, 1, 2, 27, 35, 41, 52, 53, 90, 92, 150, 162
Lionozoff, 151
Lovett, Col. C. Beresford, xix, 31, 72, 78, 116, 163
Mackenzie, Captain F., 6, 13, 17, 18, 20, 23, 27, 29, 62, 151, 153–155, 159–161
Malcolm, Sir John, xix
Marquart, J., xix, 1, 27, 30, 33, 41, 88
Mede, Count, 67
Melgunof, G., xix, 19, 39, 41, 54, 116, 152, 156, 159
Mordtmann, A. D., xix
Morgan, J. de, xix, 48, 61, 85, 109, 151–153, 157
Moses Xorenac'i, xix, 1
Muraview, xix, 93
Napier, Hon. G. C., xx, 160
Necrasof, A., xxiii
Noel, Captain J. B., xx
O'Donovan, E., xx
Olshausen, Justus, xx, 5
Ouseley, Sir William, xx
Poslawski, General, xx
Puschin, Captain, xx, 67
Querry, A., xx, 141
Rabino, H. L., xx–xxi, 10, 11, 13, 32, 36, 45, 46, 54, 56, 66, 77, 94
Rawlinson, George, xxi, 88
Rehatsek, E., xxi
Ries, P., xxi
Rollin, Charles, xxi
Schindler, A. H., xxi, 41
Seidlitz, xxi
Sheil, Sir Justin, 12, 13
Sheil, Lady, xxi, 12
Stenka Razin, 45, 46, 49, 160
Stahl, A. F. von, xxi, 116, 132, 157
Stickel, J. G., xxi
Strabo, xxi, 88, 92, 150, 152
Stuart, General Charles, xxi, 37, 43, 55, 163
Subkhal Jesus, 153
Sykes, Brigadier-General P. M., xxi, 88, 92, 153, 161, 162
Thomas, apostle, 153
Tiridates, 162
Todd, E. d'Arcy, xxi
Trezel, Colonel, xxi
Voinovitch, Count, 65, 67, 94, 160
Wells, Lt.-Col. H. L., xxii, 29, 157
Yate, Col. C. E., xxii, 94

INDEX OF NAMES WHICH DO NOT APPEAR IN THE PERSIAN INDEX

Amardi, 150
Arii, 150
Ashik, 161
British Museum, 166
Cadusii, 150
Dahae, 92
Dareion, 162
Derbices, 151
Don Cossacks, 46, 49
Ecbatana, 132
Eugenis, 161
Gelae, 113, 150
Hyrcania, 88
Hyrcanians, 132, 150, 151, 153
Kraznovodsk, 104
Labos, 158
Laboutas, 158
Margiani, 150
Marseilles, 10
Melissopol, 67
Melitonis, 68
Milan, 10
Niniva, 123
Orest, 161
Parachoathras, 150
Parthia, 88, 150
Petrograd, 68
Phanaca, 51
Potemkin, 67
Sarnius, 26
Syrinx, 51
Tapuri, Tapyri, 1, 51, 152
Taurus, 150
Vehrkana, 88

سفرنامهٔ

مازندران واستراباد

با شرح بلاد و نقشهٔ جغرافی آنها

تألیف

ه . لوی رابینو دی برگوماله

بسعی واهتمام

مولّف حقیر

در مطبعهٔ اعتماد در قاهره مصر بطبع رسید
سنهٔ ١٣٤٢ هجری مطابق سنهٔ ١٩٢٤ میلادی

مقدّمه

در جلد سی ویکم مجلّهٔ عالم اسلامی Revue du Monde Musulman وضعیّت گیلان یعنی ایالتی‌را که از غرب به آستارا در سرحدّ روسیّه واز شرق برودخانهٔ سرخانی محدود است بیان نموده‌ام در این کتاب از مازندران واستراباد که از غرب برودخانهٔ سرخانی واز شرق برودخانهٔ اترك محدود هستند صحبت خواهم نمود.

از سال ۱۹۰۶ تا سال ۱۹۱۲ میلادی شش سال در رشت بوده‌ام. درآن اثنا در سال ۱۹۰۸ و ۱۹۰۹ دوبار بمازندران سفر کرده وکلیّتاً شانزده سال در بارهٔ مازندران بجمع آوری اطّلاعات صرف اوقات نموده‌ام.

مازندران از حیث حسن طبیعت وآب وهوا از بهترین نقاط ایران است. فردوسی در ستایش آن چه نیکو گفته است:

که مازندران شهرما یاد باد
همیشه بر وبومش آباد باد
که‌در بوستانش همیشه گل است
بکوه اندرون لاله وسنبل است

هوا خوشگوار وزمین پرنگار
نه سرد ونه گرم وهمیشه بهار
نوازنده بلبل بباغ اندرون
گرازنده آهو براغ اندرون
گلاب است گوئی بجویش روان
همی شاد گردد زبویش روان
دی وبهمن وآذر وفرودین
همیشه پر از لاله بینی زمین
کسی کاندر آن بوم آباد نیست
بکام از دل وجان خود شاد نیست (۱)

برای آنانکه شیفتهٔ تاریخ ایران هستند تاریخ مازندران یك جاذبهٔ مخصوصی دارد. اگرچه بعد از فتح اسلام تاریخ مازندران موقّتاً مدّتی از تاریخ بقیّهٔ ولایات ایران جدا میشود لکن در اوایل قرن یازدهم هجری شاه عبّاس صفوی بقعهٔ مازندران را از سلالهٔ قدیم امرای ساسانیان منتزع نموده دوباره بسایر ایالات ایران ملحق نموده است.

بعد از فتح اسلام زبان وخطّ پهلوی در مازندران بیشتر از

(1) Shâhnâma, ed. Turner Macan, Vol. i, p. 231.

سایر نقاط ایران متداول و مستمرّ بوده چنانکه مدّتها بعد از آنکه در سکّه های تمام بلاد ایران خطّ عربی جایگیر خطّ پهلوی شده بود هنوز در سکّه های مازندران خطّ پهلوی باقی بوده است

بالجملة گرگان و مازندران غالباً در تاریخ ایران اثرات کلّی ودر روابط و مراودات شرق باغرب أهمیّت مخصوصی داشته اند زیرا که این دو ایالات بدبختانه در معبر ایلات غارتگر و جنگجوی آسیائی که ازشرق بغرب هجوم آور میشدند واقع بوده ازصدمات این جزر ومدّ بسی سختیها کشیده وخرابیها دیده اند .

در این کتاب اسامی بعضی از دهات را از تألیفات وسفر نامهای اسلاف اخذ نموده ام . چون شخصا نتوانسته ام آن اسامی را یك بیك تحقیق وبحقیقت واقع تطبیق نمایم دور نیست بعضی ازآنها غلط یامکرّر شده باشد . تصحیح آنهارا بأخلاف خود که درآن نواحی مسافرت خواهند نمود وا گذار مینمایم .

چون درچاپ کردن این کتاب از مراعات صرفه وقناعت نا گزیر بودم بأین سبب اطلاعاتیرا که در بارهٔ استراباد و مازندران تحصیل کرده ام لا بدّا در این کتاب بأختصار گنجانیده ام

صورت کتابه هائی را که در ابنیه آثار مازندران واستراباد موجود هستند حتی الأمکان استنساخ کرده در جزؤ مخصوص این کتاب درج نموده ام .

امیدوارم در آینده نیز از ایرانی وغیر ایرانی اشخاصی پیدا بشوند که در بارهٔ دیگر ایالتهای ایران بتحصیل اطّلاعات تاریخی واثری وغیره صرف اوقات نموده در سایهٔ همّت وزحمت ایشان دوستداران ایران جمال طبیعی آن مرز وبوم وجلال تاریخ وکیفیّت طبایع ایرانیان را بهتر بشناسند .

بدوستان گرامی وحکّام واعیان آن سامان که در هنگام مسافرت واقامت مورد مهربانی ومساعدتم داشته اند از دل وجان شکر گذار وبجناب پروفسر براون که در تصحیح قسمت انگلیسی این کتاب وبجناب میرزا فرج الله خان مستنصر السّلطنه که در تصحیح قسمت فارسی آن زحمت کشیده وهمراهی نموده اند مخصوصاً سپاسدارم .

ه . ل . رابینو

در قاهرهٔ مصر روز ۲۸ رجب سنهٔ ۱۳٤٤

رحمت حقّ بر سر بنده بود
عاقبت جوینده یابنده بود

صورت کتابه هائی که در گیلان ومازندران واستراباد موجود است

صورت کتابهٔ صندوق مقبرهٔ سیّد علی در تجن گوکه

کلّ شیء هالك إلاّ وجهه — امره الواثق الغنی محمّد بن علی الحسینی فی سنة احد وتسعین وثمانمایه — عمل استاد محمد یادگار بن حاجی مسافر تبریزی

صورت کتابهٔ سنگی در مسجد جامع لاهجان

هو السلّطان المتعال - حکم جهان مطاع آنکه وزیر گیلان بیه پیش بشفقت شاهانه سرافراز گشته بداند که چون هنگامی که مهرهٔ انجم بر تختهٔ زرنگار فلك آبگون سیماب نمون بدست قضا چیده وکعبتین عاج نیّرین جهت تحصیل نقد سعادت کونین بنقش شش جهة گردیده گنجور گنجینهٔ وجود بمؤدی حقّانیّت اقتضای قول اللّهم مالك الملك تؤتی الملك من تشاء وتنزع الملك ممّن تشاء وتعزّ من تشاء وتذل من تشاء بیدك الخیر انّك علی کلّ شیء قدیر درهم ودینار

تمام عیار دولت واعتبار ده وزردهی پادشاهی وفرماندهی عرصهٔ
روزگاررا جهت این دودمان خلافت وامامت وخاندان نبوّت
وولایت در مخزن هستی در کمال تردستی محفوظ ومضبوط داشته
جهة سپاس این نعمت بی قیاس واداى شکر این عارفهٔ محکم اساس
در این عهد سعادت مهدکه عذرای دولت روزافزون در آغوش
وایلای سلطنت ابد مقرون دوش واوّلین سال جلوس میمنت
مأنوس واوان شکفتگی گلشن امال عامّهٔ نفوس است همت صافی
طویت معدلت گستر وظمیر منیر مهر اضائت شریعت پرور بحکم
ایهٔ وافی هدایهٔ الّذین مکّنّاهم فی الارض أقاموا الصلوة وآتوا
الزکوة وأمر بالمعروف ونهی عن المنکر واجرای اوامر ونواهیٔ
خالق وعقل کل خاتم انبیا ورسل بفحوای صدق انتمای اطیعوا الله
واطیعوا الرسول لعلّکم تفلحون معطوف ومصروف داشته امر
عالم مطیع شرف نفاذ یافت که بمضمون بلاغت مشحون قل إنّما
حرّم ربی الفواحش ما ظهر منها وما بطن پرده کیان پرده گشا
پرده نشین وشاهدان چهره نما خلوت گزین بورده بأنامل عصیان
نقاب بی شرمی از رخسار عفّت ابراز ننموده دامن زن آتش غضب
وادار بی نیاز نگردیده ساکنان خطهٔ ایمان ومقیمان دار السعادهٔ
ایقان به مضمون حقیقت نمون یا أیّها الّذین آمنوا انما الخمر والمیسر
والانصاب والازلام رجس من عمل الشیطان فاجتنبوه لعلّکم

تفلحون دست بأساس دراز نکرده قبل ازآنکه شطرنجی روزگار ایشان‌را در روز ممات مات وفیل بند حیرت وهیمان هنگامهٔ عرصات ساخته معلوم شود که آنچه نرده در باخته اند سالك طریق اجتناب بوده بهیچوجه پیرامون آن عمل شنیع نگردند وکلّ وجوه بیت النُطف وقمارخانه وچرس فروشی وبوزه فروشی ممالك محروسه‌را که هر سال مبلغهای خطیر میشد بتخفیف وتصدّق فرق فرقدان سای اشرف مقرّر فرمودیم ودر این ابواب صدور عظام وعلمای اعلام وفقهای اسلام وثیقه وانیقهٔ علیحدهٔ مؤکّدهٔ ابدی وطعن سرمدی که موشّح ومزیّن بخط گوهر بنان همیون ماست بسلك تحریر کشیده اند می باید که آنوزارت پناه بعد از شرف اطلاع بر مضمون رقم مطاع لا زال نافذاً فی الأقطاع والأرباع مقرّر دارد که در کلّ محال ضبطی خود ساکنین ومتوطّنین بقانون ازهر شریعت غرّا وطریق اظهر ملّت بیضا ناهج منهج صلاح وسداد بوده مرتکب امور مذکور نگردیده وبدکاران‌را درحضور اهالی شرع شریف وکلانتران وریش سفیدان محلّات توبه داده مرتکبین محرّمات مزبوره‌را تنبیه وتأدیب والتزام بازیافت نموده هرگاه شخصی اشتغال بان افعال ذمیمه نماید یا بر نهج شنیعهٔ دیگری مطّلع گشته اعلام ننماید آن شخص‌را بنوعی تنبیه نماید که موجب عبرت دیگران گردد وآن وزارت پناه بعلّت وجوهات مزبوره چیزی

بازیافت ننموده نگذارد که آفریدهٔ بدانجهة دیناری طمع وتوقّع نماید وخلاف کننده از مردودان درگاه الهی ومحرومان شفاعت حضرت رسالت پناهی وائمهٔ طیّبین صلوات الله علیهم اجمعین ومستحقّان لعنت ونفرین ملائکهٔ آسمان وزمین باشد واهالی واوباش را نیز از کبوتر پرانی وگرگ دوانی ونگهداشتن گاو وقوچ وسایر حیوانات جهة جنگ وپرخاش که باعث خصومت وعناد وموجب انواع شورش وفساد است ممنوع ساخته سدّ آن ابواب را از لوازم شمرند ودقیقهٔ در استحکام احکام مطاعه واشارت واجرای اوامر شریفه فروگذاشت نه نماید واز جوانب بر این جمله روند ورقم قضا شیم معدلت مضمون را بر عموم خلایق خوانده برسنگ نقش ودر مساجد جامعه نصب نماید ودراین ابواب غدقن داشته هر ساله رقم مجدّد طلب ندارند ودر عهده شناسند تحریراً فی شهر شوّال ۱۱۰۶

أیضاً صورت کتابهٔ سنگی دیگر

در زمان فخر شاهان جهان سلطان حسین

وارث ملك سلیمان خسرو مالك رقاب

روی همّت از رسوم کارداریها که تافت

عدل جو دستور صاحب رای طاهر انتساب

با دل شاد از خرد تاریخ او کردم طلب
گفت دارد دادگر عار از رسوم بیحساب

۳

صورت کتابهٔ صندوق مقبرهٔ سیّد رضی در بقعهٔ شیخانبر

کلّ شیء هالك الاّ وجهه هذا المرقد المنوّر والمضجع المعطّر للسيّد المكرّم والشّيخ المعظّم السيّد رضى بن مهدى الحسينى الباشكجانى وانتقل فى شهر الله المبارك رمضان سنة اربع وثلثين وثمانماية عمل استاد محمود بن شهاب الدّين دروگر

قد كان صاحب هذا القبر لؤلؤة
عزّ لقد صاغها البارى من اللّطف
عزّت ولم تعرف الأيّام قيمتها
فردّها غيرةً منها الى الصّدف

أيضاً صورت كتابهٔ در بقعهٔ مزبور

عمل استاد يادگار دروگر سنة خمس وثلثين وثمانماية

أيضاً صورت كتابهٔ در ديگر

أمر . . . . هذا الباب الفقير سيّد رضى بن مهدى الحسينى الباشكجانى سنة اثنى وعشرين وثمانماية

براين درگاه اين در ياد گاراست زاستاد احمد واز ياد گاراست

أيضاً صورت كتابهٔ صندوق مقبرهٔ شيخ زاهد در بقعهٔ مزبور

كلّ شىء هالك الاّ وجهه — له الحكم واليه ترجعون — هذا المرقد للسّالك فى مسالك المعارف ذى الرّياضة المرضيّة العارف العابد الشّيخ الزّاهد وتاريخ وفاته بعد العصر من يوم الثلثاء أربع وعشرين ربيع الثانى سنة احدى عشر وسبعماية تاريخ وفات شيخ فاضل ومقتدى الكامل شيخ الزّاهد المرحوم طاب ثراه وجعل الله فى الجنّة مثواه آخر روز سه شنبه بيست وچهام ماه ربيع الاخر سنهٔ احدى عشر وسبعمايه — عمل عبد الله دروگر

٤

صورت كتابهٔ در امامزاده ابراهيم در آمل

قفل درب الكعبه بكشا يا مفتّح الابواب هذه الرّوضة المقدّسة أنّهم الابرار العالم ابو محمّد ابراهيم الملقّب بالاطهر والكاظم واخيه المعالى يحيى وامّهما سلام الله عليه وعلى ابو محمّد ابراهيم ابن امام الهمام الموسى حجّة الله بن امام ابو جعفر محمّد التقى بن الامام

الشّهید الغریب المدفون بارض طوس الامام علی بن موسی الرّضا
فی شهر شوّال سنه ۹۲۵

أیضاً صورت کتابهٔ صندوق امامزادهٔ مزبور

السلام علی أولیاء الله واصفیائه السّلام علی أمناء الله وأحبّائه السّلام علی انصار الله وخلفائه السّلام علی محال معرفة الله السّلام علی سلالة رسول الله السّلام علی سلالة امیر المؤمنین ولی الله السلام علی ذریّة المخصّین فی طاعة الله السّلام علی المتقرّبین فی مرضات الله اشهد یا مولای ابراهیم ابن مولای موسی ابن جعفر الکاظم انّك عشت سعیداً ومتّ مظلوماً والتقیت بآبائك الطّاهرین واجدادك المعصومین فاز متّبعك ونجی مصدّقك خاب وخسر مکذّبك والمتخلّف عنك اشهد لی بهذه الشهادة لان اکون من الفائزین ولعنة الله علی اعدائکم ومن یبغضکم اجمعین الی یوم الدّین فیالیتنی کنت معکم فافوز فوزاً عظیما العمل العاصی شیخ حاجی اقا ۱۱۸۷

ایضاً کتابهٔ دردیگر

عقد هذا الباب علی امر امام واجب التعظیم امامزاده ابراهیم ابن امام الهمام موسی کاظم علیه السّلام والصّلوة

صورت کتابهٔ سنگ مقبرهٔ امامزاده سه‌تن درآمل

فی شهر الله شعبان المبارك سنة اربعة عشر وخمس مایة

بسم الله الرّحمن الرّحیم لا اله الاّ الله محمّد رسول الله الملك لله العزّة لله الحمد لله

هذه قبر الامام السّعید قاضی القضاة تاج الدّین فخر الاسلام ابو القاسم بن الامام الشّهید فخر الاسلام ابو المحاسن الرّویانی قدّس الله روحه

صورت کتابهٔ در امامزاده مزبور

امر بعمارة هذه البقعة الشریفة . . . . سیّد عزیز الدّین ابن سیّد بهاء الدّین آملی

صورت کتابهٔ سنگی در مسجد کاظم بیگی در بار فروش

بسم الله الرّحمن الرّحیم

محمّد خان ان سرور نیکبخت

کزو یافت امر حکومت نظام

همان مظهر عزّ وشان وشرف

که شد حاملِ شرع خیر الانام

چو نوشیروان شد باو عدل ختم
چو حاتم دراو گشت همّت تمام
بر آمد زفیض سحاب عطاش
نهال امید خواص وعوام
نموده نهالی که در وصف او
خرد خوانده ثانی بیت الحرام
زاقبال بانی والطاف حقّ
چه در ملك ودین یافت عزّ تمام
خرد بر حسین گفت وتاریخ شد
شود ثانی کعبهٔ حقّ بنام

أیضاً صورت کتابهٔ سنگ دیگر

قصر خیررا بانی کاخ جودرا معمار
قبلهٔ خردمندان کعبهٔ نکوکاران
ملك وعقل‌را حاکم شهر وشرع‌را رونق
نور بخش هفت انجم شمع بزم برایوان
صبح گلشن دولت مهر مشرق قاجار
گلبن حلاوت را نیك بود محمّد خان

با دل صفا پرور طرح مسجدی افکند
کز شکوه او شد نیک راه خیر بر کیوان
معبدی که هر طاقش جفت گنبد گردون
مسجدی که محرابش رشک ازفری خوبان
کرد امر سرکاری بر او صاف خان تفویض
هریکی گل دیگر در حدیقهٔ احسان
فخر صدر دین داری زبده شیخ الاسلامی
کز قدش برازنده گشت خلعت ایمان
گلشن قضا پرور خاصه قاضی عسکر
کز نسیم خلق او گل شکفت در بستان
شد چو این بنا برپا از توجّه بانی
سر بر آسمان کردن گشت خلق را آسان
وسعتش ازان افزون کش جهان توان گفتن
رفعتش ازان برتو کش نهم فلك بتوان
شد بنام هر طاعت از ستون آن قایم
شد تمام زارکانش هر نمازرا ارکان
بسکه معرفت خیزاست خاك آن بهشت امن
بسکه طاعت انگیزاست صحن آن فلك سامان

از هوای صحن او تربیت اگر یابد

سجده باز می آرد نخل قامت جانان

چون ز عقل کل طوفان خواست سال تاریخش

گفت قبلهٔ آفاق مسجد محمّد خان

١١٦٩

صورت کتابهٔ سنگ در مسجد جامع بارفروش

در روزگاری همایون که دست ستم در زنجیر عدل بسته بود بفرمان پادشاه جم خدم محمدشاه قاجار عالیجاه فضلعلیخان حاکم مازندران شد اجارهٔ خبازی را بخشید هرکس مطالبه نماید بلعن ابدی گرفتار شود — مشقه محمّد تقی

ایضاً صورت کتابهٔ دیگر

ستوده میر محمد حسین پاک نهاد

کز اوست تولیت این مکان کعبه نشان

بعهد دولت خاقان عصر فتحعلی

چه شد ز زلزله این محترم بنا ویران

زاهتمام تمام کمال سعیش گشت

هزار بار زاول نیکوتر آبادان

(صورهٔ سبّح اسم ربّـك الاعلى . . .)

حرره محمد مهدی فی شهر صفر المظفر ۱۲۲۰

صورت کتابهٔ دری در بارفروش

الله مفتّح الابواب الله ولیّ التوفیق

عمل استاد احمد نجار بن حسین فی التـاریخ محرم سنة سبعین وثمانمایة

ایضاً

عمل سید علی ابن سید کمال الدین آملی غفر الله ذنوبهما

صورت کتابهٔ بردیوار کاروانسرای در بارفروش

خوش است بادهٔ گلرنگ با کباب شکاری

زدست ساقی گلچهره در کنار بخاری سنهٔ ۱۱۱٤

صورت کتابهٔ صندوق مقبرهٔ امامزاده سلطان محمد طاهر

صاحب اختیار هـذه العمارة مشهد منوّر مقدس مطهر امام اعظم سلطان طاهر ابن امام موسی کاظم علیـه التحیة والرضوان وبنـاء العمارة بامر امیر اعظم شاه معظم امیر کبیر خلاصة اولاد

سید المرسلین امیر مرتضی الحسینی طاب ثراه وجعل الجنة مثواه
بعد از شاه مرحوم امیر اعظم امیر محمد الحسینی نوّر الله قبره مدد
دریغ نداشته‌اند وبعد از مغفورین ساختن قبر پر نور از امیر
زاده‌گان اعظام امیر عبد الکریم وامیر عبد الرحیم طاب الله ثراهما
وطاب مثواهما واتمام رسانیدن مشهد مقدس ونهادن قبر پر نور
از امیر زادهٔ اعظم امیر رضی الدین الحسینی خلد الله ملکه
وسلطانه واوضح علی العالمین برهانه حق باریتعالی باذ معمار هذه
المجاور استاد مولانا شمس الدین ابن نصر الله المطهری بتاریخ سنهٔ
خمس وسبعین وثمانمائه

صورت کتابهٔ امامزادهٔ ابو الحسن کلا

عاملها وصانعها محمد تقی ابن محمد یوسف دماوندی بحسب
الفرمودهٔ سیادت پناه محمد کاظم مشهد باز — کاتب الفقیر عبد العظیم
مهدی

صورت کتابهٔ دری درامامزاده ابراهیم ابو الجواب در مشهد سر

امر . . . هذا الباب المزار المتبرک مرتضی الاعظم سید عزیز بن
سید شمس الدین المعروف بیابلکانی — عمل استاد محمد بن استاد علی

النجّار الرازی فی التاریخ شهر محرم سنة احدی واربعین وثمانمایة

ایضاً صورت کتابهٔ دز دیگر

صاحب الخیرات هـذا الباب وعمارة المسماة بی فضّه خاتون بنت امیر صاعد — عمل حسن ابن استاد بایزید نجـار فی التاریخ سـنة خمس وتسعمایة — کتبه تقی الاملی — عمل علی بن استاد اسمعیل نجار الاملی المعروف برازی غفر الله علیهم اجمعین

ایضاً صورت کتابهٔ دیگر

امر . . . هذه العمارة الشریفة سیّد السادات سیّد شمس الدّین بن سید عبد العزیز بابلکانی — عمل استاد محمّد بن استاد علی نجّار رازی فی تاریخ جمادی الاول سنة ثمان وخمسین وثمانمایة

صورت کتابهٔ دیگر

امر . . . هذه العمارة الشّریفة سیّدالسادات الاشراف سیدشمس الدین بن سید عبد العزیز بابلکانی — عمل استاد محمد بن استاد علی نجار رازی فی تاریخ ذیحجه سنهٔ سبع وخمسین وثمانمایه هجریه

صورت کتابهٔ بقعهٔ در مشهدسر

بانی هذه العمارة الشریفة علیا حضرة سیدة بی بی فضّه خاتون
بنت امیر صاعد حرم سلطان الاعظم سلطان امیر شمس الدین
طاب ثراه وجعل الجنّة مثواه — عمل استاد علی بن استاد فخر
الدین بن استاد علی نجار کتبه احمد بن حسین تمت فی شهر محرّم
الحرام سنة ست وتسعمایة هجرة النبویة علیه السلام

صورت کتابهٔ امام زاده زین العابدین در ساری

بنا واتمام یافت این عمارت بسعی واهتمام این بندهٔ درگاه
علاء الدین بن درویش محمد ابو الوفا

ایضاً صورت کتابهٔ در امام زادهٔ مزبور

الله ولیّ التوفیق الله مفتّح الابواب فی التاریخ سنة اربع
وتسعین وثمانمایة

ایضاً صورت کتابهٔ صندوق امام زادهٔ مزبور

صاحب هذه الصندوق والمرقد المبارك الشریف السلطان
الاعظم الاکرم برهان السادات والاشراف المرحوم المغفور السلطان

امیر شمس الدین ابن الامیر کمال الدین الحسینی طاب ثراه تاریخ وفاته یوم الاثنین خامس و عشرین شهر جمادی الثانیـة اربعة عشر خورداد ماه سنهٔ خمس و تسعمایه

صورت کتابهٔ پنجرهٔ امامزادهٔ یحیی در ساری

هذه الرّوضة المبارکة امیر الاعظم صاحب الکرامة و الولایة و الامامة یحیی بن موسی الکاظم علیه السلام و الثانی اخوه حسین ابن الامام موسی الکاظم علیه السلام و الثالث اختهم سکینه بنت الامام موسی الکاظم علیه السلام فی احد عشر شهر ربیع الاولی سنة ست و اربعین و .... مایة عمل استـاد حسین و استاد محمد نجّار گیل

صورت رسالت امام جعفر در بقعهٔ مجد الدین مکّی در ساری

ابو عبد الله صادق   بسم الله الرحمن الرحیم

یا معاشر المسلمین یا زمرة المؤمنین کثّر الله امثالکم اعلموا ان الله تعالی امرکم بالصـلاة و الزکاة و الصّوم و الحج و الجهاد بارتکاب الحلال و باجتناب الحرام و ما قال رسول الله صلی الله علیه و علی آله بامر الله تعالی و تقـدسه فتمسکوا بامره تعالی النجاة فی الآخرة

لتكونوا من المؤمنين ووجب علينا اعلامكم بهذه الاوامر والنواهى مولى الموالى مفخر الصلى والاوالى مولانا مجد الدين مكّى وارسلنا الى مدينتين الآمل والسارى ونواحيها فاسمعوا منه مايقول لكم من جميع اوامر ونواهى وتعزّز وجوده بامره كما قال الله تبارك وتعالى اطيعوا الله واطيعوا الرّسول واولى الامر منكم فى عاشر شوّال سنة ستة وثلثين ومائه

صورت كتابهٔ در اما مزاده عباس در آزادگله

جلّ كلّ حىّ كه هر دم بهر فيض
بر درش روح القدس آمد فرو
مرقد شهزاده عباس شهيد
فقد كاظم انشه باآبرو
در زمان شاه روزافزون لقب
حضرت اقا محمد انك او
خسرو دين پرور است ودادگر
سرور گردون شكوه وعدل جو
بر قرارش ساخت عالى گنبدى
مسجد خاص وعمارات نكو

دین پنــا اقا حسین کہف الانام
تا ابد این نام نیکوماند از او
بہر تاریخش چو پرسیـدم زعقـل
گفت بادا رحمت یزدان براو
عمل بہرام ابن استاد محمد نجّار ساروی سکندان ابادی

ایضاً صورت کتابهٔ صندوق امامزادهٔ مزبور

عمل الصندوق بسعی واهتمام سید مرتضی بن سیـد علی ابن سید شمس الدین بن سید عبد الصمد بن سید شمس الدین — بہرام نجّار — تحریراً فی التاریخ ماه جمادی الاخر سنهٔ سبع وتسعین وثمانمایه

صورت کتابهٔ در اما مزادهٔ نـکاه

من عرف نفسه فقد عرَف ربّه بشّر مال البخیل ذالحارث او وارث الا ینظر الی من قال وانظر الی ما قال الجزع عند البلاء تما لمن لحته هذه الموضع من القریة المبارکـة موسومة بالنـکاه لصاحب الممالك هذه القریة المذکورة المرتضی المعظم والاکرام میر سید عبد المحیط بن (المیرتوانائی) اینـکاد مفخر الفقراء والصلی زین المتورعین درویش سکندر ابن عزّ الدین المعروف با بن الهدا

عمل استاد حسین بن احمد الازاری غرّهٔ محرم الحرام سنهٔ ستین وثمانمایه

صورت کتابهٔ در بقعه بلند امام در گلوگاه

قال النبی علیه السلام الدنیا ساعة فاجعلها طاعة

(امر . . . هذالباب . . . . سید) زین العابدین ابن سید اسمعیل بتاریخ ثلث وسبعین وثمانمایه عمل حسین ابن استاد احمد نجّار ساروی

صورت کتابهٔ منبر مسجد جامع استراباد

قد عمر هذه المسجد فی ایام دولته السّلطان الاعظم ملك ملوك العرب والعجم معین الدین ابو القاسم بابر بهادرخان خلّد الله تعالی ملکه وسلطانه بسعی داعی المبرّات وساعی الخیرات مظفر الدنیا والدین بابا حسین خاندان ابی عبد الله ششم ذی قعده سنهٔ . . .

قد تمّ فی دورة السلطان الاعظم والخاقان المعظم المکرم شاه عبّاس الصفوی الحسینی بهادرخان خلد الله ملکه بر دست بندهٔ کمترین قطب الدین احمد بن ملا علی الاسترابادی فی تاریخ خامس عشر من شهر شعبان المعظم یکهزار وهیجده ۱۰۱۸

ایضاً صورت کتابهٔ دیگر

بسم الله الرّحمن الرّحیم

در زمان دولت وسلطنت خسرو گیتی‌ستان شاهنشه ایران و هند وترکستان وتوران تعمیر این مسجد و منبر نمود اقل عباد الله حاجی قربان اقای ناظر نوّاب عالیجاه محمّد حسینخان قاجار بیگلربیگی دار المومنین استراباد امیـد از فیوضات ابدی و دوات سرمدی بهره‌مند و با نصیب باد بربّ العبـاد فی تاریخ غرّهٔ ذی قعدة الحرام سنهٔ ۱۱۵۷

ایضاً صورت کتابهٔ سنـگ در مسجد مزبور

تعمیر مسجد جامع شریف خجسته نمودند در زمان تاج‌بخش ملوک ممالک هندوستان وتوران نادرشاه نوّاب عالیجاه رفیع‌جایگاه امیر الامراء العظام محمّد حسینخان قاجار بیگلر بیگی دار المومنین استراباد که از رحمت خدا بهره مند باشند بسرکاری حاجی قربان اقای ناظر سرکار عالیجاه معظّم الیه وفّقه الله تعالی فی الدّارین که از ثواب آن فایض باشــند سنهٔ ۱۱۵۷ فی تاریخ سنهٔ الف و مائه و سبع و خمسین من الهجرة النبویّة المصطفویّة والسّلام والا کرام عمل حاجی محمّد رضا خادم مسجد

ایضاً صورت کتابهٔ سنگ دیگر

هو الرّحیم شاه عبّاس الحسینی

مقصود از تحریر این تقریر آنکه مبلغ چهار تومان که مقرّری جماعت یساقی ولایت استراباد داده می شد وداخل جمع ولایت مذکوره بود به طریق سر شمار وخانه شمار از جماعت مذکوره می گرفته‌اند ومراعی ومواشی ایشان منظور نمیشد . . . آن دو معنی موجب تفرقهٔ ایشان گردیده از وطن جدا شده‌بودند بنا بر ترفیهٔ حال ایشان وتصدق فرق همیون مبلغ مذکور بدیشان بخشیده شد که من بعد از ایشان نستانند وآنچه مراعی ومواشی ایشان شود بطریق شمار مال ستانند توقع از حکّام گرام آنکه بر اینموجب عمل نمایند وتغییر دهنده بلعنت خدا گرفتار باد

ایضاً صورت کتابهٔ سنگ دیگر

هو المستعان در تاریخ غرّهٔ شهر جمادی الثّانی ۹۳۷ که حضرت سلطنت سعادی ممالك مداری ملاذی عدالت دستگاهی همیون شاهی سلطان محمد ذو القدر ابن امیر علاء الدوله بایالت وحکومت بلدهٔ استراباد تشریف آورده اند بعضی از صاحبان مستقلات بعرض رسانیدند که آنمعنی در پستی زمان خرج بنوده واین خرج

بدعت است وجمیع مردم شکایت گردش فلوس کردند این هر دورا واللّٰه وباللّٰه خالصاً للّٰه تعالی بتصدّق فرق شاهی التفات فرمودند وتغییرده فلوس شاهی پیوسته بلعنت الهی ... هرکس که این منقوله را تغییر دهد بلعنت خدا ورسول وملائکه معصومین وائمه گرفتار باد این خیر باهتمام حضرت خواجه سیف الدّین مظهّر وتپکجی شد

ایضاً صورت کتابهٔ سنگ دیگر

هو المستعان بسم اللّٰه الرّحمن الرّحیم الحکم للّٰه

شاه ابو النّصر ابن شاه اسمعیل بهادر دوم

وجوه آزادی حسب الحکم نوّاب همیون اعلی در ممالک جهان شرف بخش نفاذ یافتـه وباعلامات کبیر وصغیر مرفوع القلم شد ساداة العظام ووکلاء الکرام ومباشرین وعمّالان وکلانتران بلدهٔ استراباد حسب الحکم عمـل نموده در ولایت مذکوره بملت مزبوره مزاحم نشوند تغییر دهنـده بلعنت خدا گرفتار شود سنهٔ ۱۰۲۹

ایضاً صورت کتابهٔ سنگ دیگر

بسم الله الرّحمن الرّحیم الحمد لله ربّ العالمین والصلوة علی محمّد وآله اجمعین

امّا بعد بتاریخ بیست وپنجم شهر ذی قعدة الحرام سال هزار وچهل ودو هجریه وقف نمود نواب مستطاب معلی الالقاب عالیجناب ایالت وشوکت دستگاه نصفت وعدالت اکتناه ساعی خیرات وداعی مبرّات الموفق بتوفیق الملك المنّان عالیحضرت با رفعت خسرو خان حاکم دار المومنین استراباد همگی وتمامی یکباب کاروانسرا وهمگی وجملگی چهار دانگ ونیم کاریز الواقعتان فی البلدة المذکورة فی میدان شور آجری ینفعهما الله الی یوم النشور بر مساجد خمسهٔ متبرکه مسجد جامع ومصلّی ومسجد بازار ومسجد حاجی تبریزی ومسجد سفید وبر چشمهٔ جاری در مصلّی وپنج امام وبر منارهٔ شور چنانکه حاصل محلّین مذکورین را بعد از خرج ما یحتاج محلّین مزبوره صرف تعمیر وروشنائی وخدمت محال متبرکه شود وخادم مسجد جامع دوازده هزار دینار عراق وبرای روشنائی مقدار ده من ونیم روغن کُنجد خرج چراغ تا بقدر احتیاج خادم مصلّی یتکومان خادم مسجد جامع پنجهزار دینار وروشنائی چهار مسجد هر یکماه چهار من روغن ماءذّن کلدستهٔ

میدان شور دوازده هزار دینار تولیت محاّین از واقف معظّم الیه باشد ثمّ لارشد اولاده الذّکور ثمّ لافضل العلماء واصلح العباد وقفاً صحیحاً شرعیاً تقبل الله تعالی منه عفی الله عنه خلاف کننده در لعنت وسخط باری تعالی وملائکه وانبیاء واولیاء گرفتار خواهد شد

ایضاً صورت کتابهٔ سنگ دیگر

الموفّق ۱۰۱۷ علی   رسالت پناهی ۷۱ لهی

ساداة عظام وارباب ذوی الاحترام واهالی ورعایای بلده وبلوکات دار المومنین استراباد بدانندکه در اینوقت بنا برفاه حال ورعایت احوال جمهور رعایا که بدایع ودایع حضرت خالق البرایااند وبواسطهٔ تحصیل دعای خیر جهت ذات اقدس اشرف همیون وجوه کوتوالی قلعهٔ مبارکه وقورقچیگری وراه تراشی بلوکات را که از زمان حکّام سابق الی الآن مستمر وبر قرار بوده از ابتداء تخاقوی ئیل تخفیف وبتصدّق فرق مبارك اشرف همیون مقرّر نمودیم که من بعد یکدینار ویکمن بار عمّال دیوانی بعلّت وجوهات مذکوره حواله واطلاقی نه نموده تغییر دهندهٔ آن بلعنت وسخط حضرت پروردگار گرفتار ومردود درگاه فلك بارگاه گردد میباید که بشکر این عطیه عظمی بهمهٔ ابواب امیدوار بوده لیلا

ونهاراً بوظایف دعاگوئی دوام دولت بیزوال ابدی الامتثال اشتغال نمایند تاثواب آن بروزگار فرخنده اثار بندگان نوّاب کامیاب اشرف همیون عاید شود دراین باب قدغن دانند تحریراً فی شهر شعبان المعظّم سنهٔ خمس وخمسین والف از بعد نبی صاحب محراب علی است

ایضاً صورت کتابهٔ سنگ دیگر

هو — شاه صفی الحسینی بسم الله الرّحمن الرّحیم

فرمان همیون شد اینکه امراء عظام وحکّام گرام ووزراء وداروغه‌گان وکلانتران وعمّال ومباشرین دیوانی دار المومنین استراباد وتوابع احسن الله تعالی احوالهم بدانند که چون همواره شاه باز همّت بلند وزینت شاهین ارجمند نوّاب همیون در هوای قدس سای عدل واحسان وفضای یزدان ستا بصید دلهای پریشان عجزهٔ زیردستان طیران بوده همگی توجّه خاطر خطیر خورشید نظیر بدان مصروف است که کافهٔ رعایا وعامّهٔ برایا از تشبّث حوادث وتجاّب نوائب نجات یافته در ظل معدلت وکنف حمایت آسوده حال وفارغبال بدعای دوام دولت ابدی الاتصال اشتغال نمایند لهذا شمهٔ از عنایت بی غایت شاهانه شامل حال جمعی از رعایای ممالك محروسه که رسوم میر شکار باشی متوجّه ایشان بود فرموده

از ابتدای پارس ئیل رسوم مزبور را که بدینموجب معمول است و مستمر بود بتخفیف و تصدّق فرق اشرف مقرّر داشته و صیّادان دام گیر و کرم میز و گوه گرد و سلّاخان و ماهی بریزان و ماهی گیران و کبوتربازان و به‌له دوزان و کیسه دوزان و مرغ فروشان و روده فروشان و جیگر بریزان و سایر جماعت متعلق به قوشخانه که در وجه میر شکار باشی مقرّر بوده فرمودیم که مستوفیان عظام این عطیّه را در دفاتر خلود ثبت نموده من بعد یکدینار و یکمن بار حواله و اطلاق ننمایند و میر شکار باشیان عظام امر و سخنان فوق خاصه شمرده بدین علت متعرض احدی نشده و توقّعی ننمایند که باید این حکم همیون لازال نافذٌ فی الربع المسکون بر سنگ نقش نموده در مسجد جامع نصب نمایند و بعد بدین علت از این حواله احدی مزاحمت ننموده و نرسانند نوعی نمایند که دعای خیر جهت نوّاب همیون خواهد شد و آثار ان بروزگار فرخنده آثار گردد باید امیر شکار باشیان عظام گرام حسب المسطور در حالی رسوم مزبور را براطرف داشته در این باب عذر ندانند و بر عهده شناسند فی ششم جمادی الثانیه سنهٔ ۱۰۴۷

ایضاً صورت کتابهٔ سنگ دیگر

یا الله — یا محمّد — یا علی — فرمان همیون شد آنکه چون حکم

جهانمطاع عالی مطیع عزّ اصدار یافته که حکّام وارکان دار المومنین استراباد مزاحمت بحال جماعت درویشان که در بلدهٔ مذکوره به هیمه‌کشی اوقات میگذارنند نرسانند بدعتی سابق بوده که از هر یك از ایشان در هر سال دوازده خروار هیمه بجهت سرکار حکّام میگرفته‌اند منظور بدارند بنا بر این بهمان دستور مقرّر داشته از مضمون حکم مسطور تجاوز ننمایند و بقیمت دوازده خروار هیمهٔ مذکور که سابقاً معمول بوده بهیچوجه من الوجوه طلبی ننمایند واز فرموده تخلّف نورزند وهرساله حکم مجدّد نطلبند وتغییر دهنده در لعنت خدا ورسول گرفتار باشد تحریراً فی شهر ذی حجّه نهصد وهفتاد وشش .... باعث این خیر شد .

ایضاً صورت کتابهٔ سنگ دیگر

الحکم لله — فرمان همیون شد آنکه چون حسب الحکم جهانمطاع مال اصناف وتحرفهٔ دار المومنین استراباد بتخفیف ونصفه مقرّر شده بنا بر این هیچ آفریده بعلت اخراجات وعوارضات خصوصاً درکوچه ازمیرشب وطرح ؟ وبیگار؟ ومردم قلعه وبار وهیمه وکاه وسنگ‌کش ومشتاق فتح واز طالار وطویله بناحق وعلوفه چینان وغیره بهراسم ورسمیکه باشد از رعایا واز

ساخت محزون زبهر تاریخش مصرع فرد اخرین بدعا
کی خداوندگار در محشر جرم بانی بجدّ او بخشا
بسنهٔ ١٢٢٤

صورت کتابهٔ تکیهٔ محلهٔ نعل بندان استراباد

این قصر نیلگون که دم خلد میزنند
روزی که کشته گشته چه سلطان نینوا
این تکیهٔ که شورش او عرش میرود
از نالهای زار محبّان کربلا
طاق رواق همچه سپهرش بدین سیاه
از دود آه شام اسیران کربلا
این قصر زرنگار که گشته سیاه رنگ
از آتش یزید لعین ان سگ دغا
روزی که سرو وش ان شهسوار دین
افتاد در میان بیابان کربلا
زآنروز تا بحال تمامند نوحه گر
در تعزیتسرای شهیدان کربلا
این تکیه گشت باعث بانی گریه هم
چون هست ذرّه پرور سلطان کربلا

یا ربّ گناه صادق محروم ووالدش
بخشا بحق شاه شهیدان کربلا
گفتا خرد نویس هزار ودویست ویك
تاریخ بهر تکیهٔ سلطان اولیا

صورت کتابهٔ سنگ گلدستهٔ محلّهٔ سبز مشهد استراباد

صاحب این خیرات فایض البرکات حاجی مقری بن حاجی علی الجرجانی بسنة الف وخمسة وخمسین

در زمان دولت گیتی ستان جم خدم
انکه از ذاتش سحر خورشید در کسب ضیاست
خسرو انجم حشم عبّاس ثانی کز حلو
از کمین نام خدا کیوان غلام پر بهاست
یادگار مقری نیکوسیر حاجی علی
آنکه کارش دوستی آن علی شیر خداست
صاحب این گلدسته عبّاس نیکو محضری
قربتاً لله صدق تو بر اینمعنی گواست
بهر تاریخش مناسب گفت از این مصرع رحیم
بهر گلبانگ سلیمانی بر این عالی بناست

صورت کتابهٔ سنگی در تکیهٔ دباغان در استراباد

در هزار ویکصد وپنجا وپنج وقف نمود عالیحضرت میرزا محمد باقر در مسجد واقعه در محلهٔ دباغان دار المومنین استراباد عالیحضرت واقف وقف نمود همگی یکباب خانه منقطعه واقعه در جنب مسجد مزبور ونصف یکرشتهٔ قنات واقعه در حاجی اباد که مشهور بقنات بازید است که حاصل ومنافع قنات مزبوره صرف مسجد وخادم مسجد مزبور گردد تغییر دهنده بلعنت خدا گرفتار شود

ایضاً صورت کتابهٔ سنگ دیگر

بسم الله الرحمن الرحیم بتاریخ غرهٔ شهر ذی حجة الحرام هزار ویکصد وپنجاه وپنج وقف نمود عالیحضرت میرزا محمد باقر همگی یکرشتهٔ قنات دایره واقعه در قریهٔ کوزن که منافع حاصل آن صرف تعزیهٔ حضرت امام حسین وامام رضا صلوات اله وامام زاده عبد اله گردد تغییر دهنده بلعنت الهی گرفتار شود

ایضاً صورت کتابهٔ سنگ دیگر

زتوفیق حق بود وبخت سعید برای رضای امام شهید

که حاجی محمد علی کیله کرد

بنا بهر خیرات حوض جدید

که لب تشنگان چون بدانجا رسند

بیاد آورند از حسین شهید

بنوشند آبی ولعنت کنند

بشمر لعین ویزید پلید

قضا بهر تاریخ گفتا بگو

روان لعنت حق بقوم یزید

تاریخ سنهٔ یکهزار وده

صورت کتابهٔ چهارچوبهٔ امامزاده عبد الله در استراباد

اللهم صلّ علی محمد المصطفی وصل علی علی المرتضی وصل علی حسن الرضا وصل علی الحسین الشهید بکربلا وصل علی علی زین العابدین وصل علی محمد الباقر وصل علی جعفر الصادق وصل علی موسی الکاظم وصل علی علی ابن موسی الرضا وصل علی محمد التقی وصل علی علی النقی وصل علی الحسن العسکری وصل علی حجة القائم صاحب الزمان محمد المهدی صلوات الله علیهم اجمعین لقد قال بسم الله الرحمن الرحیم انا انزلناه فی لیلة القدر وما ادراك ما لیلة القدر

دلش بحری است طوفانی که میریزد از آن لؤلؤ
کفش ابری است نیسانی که میریزد از آن گوهر
بنا فرموده است این مدرس زیبای میمونرا
پی خوشنودی حق ورواج دین پیغمبر
چه مدرسه که چون فردوس اعلا سیم گون غرفه
چه مدرسه که چون گردون مینا بیستون مجر
بود هر غرفه اش درجی در او رخشنده گوهرها
بود هر حجره اش برجی در او تابنده اخترها
ملک چون خادمان بهر شرافت از شعف دایم
ستاده بهر خد متکاری این استان بردر
رقم زد کلک مشفق اینچنین از بهر تاریخش
بود این مدرسه میمون علم افروز دین پرور
تاریخ هزار ودویست وچهل ویک ١٢٤١

صورت کتابهٔ سنگی در مسجد قاجارها در استراباد

خان والا نسب امام قلی خان که بهرامش احترام نمود
از شجاعت به تیغ وکرز وسنان رستم زال‌را غلام نمود
یکه رزم از مهابت او شیر نر گم ره کنام نمود

برضای خدا چو ابراهیم　　خانهٔ کعبه‌را تمام نمود
وه چه خانه که بر درش جبریل　　بسجده از بهر احترام نمود
بود محزون بفکر تاریخش　　خردش ختم اینکلام نمود
مصرعی زد رقم بدیحه که خان　　مسجدی وقف خاص وعام نمود

تاریخ هزار ودویست ویازده ۱۲۱۱

ایضاً صورت کتابهٔ سنگ دیگر

خان والا شکوه امام قلی
زانکه شاهیش شد باسکندر
زیب دوران ومفخر ایام
زبده ترک ودودمان قجر
بسکه بافعل نیک مایل بود
بسکه با کار خیر بودش سر
طرفه سقایهٔ در این مأوی
ساخت بر پادشاه تشنه جگر
وه چه سقایهٔ که از رفعت
سوده سقفش بطاق گردون سر
مهر در سایه‌اش گرفته مکان
چرخ اندر بناش جسته مقر

هدایت لم یزلی سعادت سعایت خیرات واشاعهٔ مراسم مبرّات
رفیق حال ومزید اعمال است میر عالیحضرت معالی رتبت گردون
بسطت اعلی منقبت مملکت مدار فلك اقتدار حکومت شعار
معدلت اثار منظور انظار حضرت آفرید گار ناصب رایات
العدل والانصاف صاحب آیات الکرم والالطاف مقرب الصلة
السلطانی اعتضاد الدّولة الخاقانی عون الضعفاء والمساکین مربی
العلماء والفضلاء مقوی الصّلحاء والاتقیاء غیاث الاسلام ومعین
المسلمین المنظور بانظار الملك الاکبر خواجه سیف الدّولة والدّنیا
والدّین مظفّر ابن عالیجناب مرحمت پناه فردوس مکان جنّت آشیان
المغفور المبرور السعید الشهید الواصل روحه الی جوار رحمة الملك
الصمّد خواجه فخر الدّنیا والدّین احمد التپکچی تغمّده الله بغفرانه
واسکنه فرادیس جنانه تا بدیده تحقیق ونظر توفیق مشاهده
وملاحظه فرموده که دولت واقبال این جهانی بر شرف زوال
وعرضهٔ انتقال است مگر آنکه اورا وسیلهٔ تقرّب سازند بحضرت
مهیمن علی الاطلاق که ما عندکم ینفد وما عند الله باقٍ وواسطه
برنجات خود گردانیده اند عقبهٔ عقوبات بموجب کلام بافرجام
سیّد امام علیه وآله الصّلوة والسّلام اذا مات آدم ابن آدم انقطع
عمله الاّ عن ثلث ولد صالح یدعوله بالخیر وعلم ینتفع به وصدقة
جاریة فی سبیل اله ومقرّر است که افضل صدقات که بمرور ایّام

وشهور بر صحایف اعصار ودهور باقی ماند وقف نمودن قنات
ومجاری میاه قنوات است که سبب حیاة وباعث زندگانی هر
موجودات است که ومن الماء کلّ شیء حی بناءً علیهذا عالیحضرت
مشار الیه مدّ ظلّه العالی همّت عالی نهمت بر اشاعت مثوبات مثمر
وافاضهٔ صدقات جاریه مصروف داشته جهة دفع عطش یوم الفزع
الاکبر وقف مخلّد مؤبّد بر دوام فرمود بر جمهور سکنه وعموم
متوطنهٔ بلدة المؤمنین استراباد وحوالی صانه الله تعالی عن الخلل
والزلل والفساد الی یوم التناد از اغنیاء وفقراء وذکور واناث وصغیر
وکبیر ما توالدوا وتناسلوا بطناً بعد بطن وقرناً بعد قرن قربة لله
تعالی وطلباً لمرضاته وهرباً من أليم عقابه وذخيرة ليوم لا ينفع مال
ولا بنون الا من اتی الیه بقلب سلیم از آنچه در قید تملیک وملک
خود داشت از اطیب اموال خود الی یومنا هذا وآن همگی وتمامی
مجرای یک حجر آب است از رود خانهٔ خواسته رود که مشهور
است بمرّ حقّابهٔ قریهٔ مذکوره وایضاً تمامی مجرای یکربع شایع
کامل است از ممر یک حجر آب از میاه رودخانهٔ مذکوره که
مشهور است بمجرای حقّابهٔ مزرعهٔ سیّد اسد که معروف است
وایضاً تمامی مجرای یکدانگ ونیم است از یک حجر آب از میاه
رود خانهٔ مذکوره که مشهور است بحقّابهٔ پادشاه قلیچه که معلوم
است وایضاً تمامی مجرای یکربع شایع کامل از ممر یک حجر آب

از میـاه رودخانهٔ مذکوره که مشهور است بآب فیروز کوهی وایضاً تمامی مجرای یک دانگ ونیم آب است از ممرّ یک حجر آب از میاه رود خانه قریهٔ مذکوره که از جملهٔ حقّابهٔ عزّ الدین بناست که مشهور است وایضاً تمامی مجرای یک حجر آب از رود خانهٔ مذکوره که مشور است بمجرای چهار باغ که تمامیٔ موقوفهٔ مذکوره ممرّ سه حجر آب کامل است از رود خانهٔ مذکوره که واقع است در خارج درب بسطام بلدهٔ مذکوره ومراد آب مذکوره بر هیجده حجر کامل ویک دانگ آب است که قسمت میشود بعرف واصطلاح اهل انجابا جمیع توابع ولواحق ومضافات ومنسوبات از حریم وغیره من المنبع الی المصب که میاه ان ممرّ آب مشروب ومنفع مشار الیهم در بلدهٔ مزبوره میشود وحوالی ان وقفاً صحیحا شرعیاً صریحاً نافذاً لازماً مخلداً مؤبداً الی ان یرث الله الارض ومن علیها وهو خیر الوارثین وشرط کرد حضرت واقف مشار الیه تقبل الله منه که چون این میـاه موقوفهٔ مذکوره جاری گردد در بلدهٔ مذکوره وحوالی ان بخانه ها وحوضها وحمـام برند وبیکدیگر تعلّل نماینـد وبهر موضع که در آید چون محظوظ کردند فی الحال بموضع دیگر گذارند ودر محلّ تنگیٔ آب بر زیاده از ضرورة شرب وصرف نکنند وسعی بلیغ نماینـد که اهل بلده وتوابع از آن محظوظ شوند وشرط کرد ایضاً که بر ممرّ آب

موقوفهٔ مذکوره بهیچوجـه من الوجوه از زمین واجارد وغیره تصرّف نکنند ونفرمایند وبر شرکاء رودخانهٔ مذکوره واجب ولازم است به مقتضای شریعت مطّهره که در حین قسمت نمودن آب ودرک کشیدن آنچه حصّهٔ موقوفه است چیزی قاصی ومنکسر نگردانند واز هول وفزع وعقوبت درک یاد کنند وشرط کرد حضرت واقف مشار الیـه دام ظلّه العالی که باآب مذکورهٔ موقوفه زراعت شالی نکنند در موضع حضرت مشـار الیـه وهیچ جا وا گذارند که بمجاری مذکوره به بلدهٔ مذکوره جاری گردد سبیل قضات اسلام وحکّام عالیمقام وموالیان ذوی الاحترام وکلانتران ذوی الاکرام آنچه بموجب آیهٔ کریمـهٔ انّ الله یامر بالعـدل والاحسان وایتاء ذی القربی ونهی عن الفحشاء والمنکر والبغی الی آخره وبمضمون کلام تمام حضرت سیّـد انام علیه وآله الصّلوة والسلام که من سنّ سنّة حسنة فله اجرها واجر من عمل بها الی یوم القیمة نظر فرموده در استمرار واستقرار موقوفهٔ مزبوره سعی بلیغ نمایند واز مقتضیٔ حدیث صحیح حضرت نبوی علیه وآله الصّلوة والسّلام که من سنّ سـنّة سیّئة فعلیه وزرها ووزر من عمل بها الی یوم القیمة محترز بوده نـگذارند که کسی بتقلّب در مجاریٔ میـاه مزبوره وخلاف شرط حضرت واقف مدّ ظلّه العـالی که بدانند مخالف شرع شریف باشد عمل

نمایند واجر آنرا از حضرت ذو الجلال یوم لاینفع البنون والمال امیدوار باشند فمن بدّله بعد ما سمعه فانمّا اثمه علی الذین یبدّلونه ان الله سمیع علیم ومن غیّره بوجه من الوجوه فهو فی زمرة الملعونین بلعاین الله والملائکة والناس اجمعین وبر تمامیّت وقف ولزوم شرایط آن وصحة وقفیة مذکورهٔ مشروعهٔ مشروحه حکم کرد بعد الاستخاره من الله تعالی قاضی الاسلام نافذ الامر والاحکام مدّ ظلّه بین الانام حکماً صریحاً محکماً وقصاراً بهما ؛ وکان ذلک فی احدی واربعین وتسعمایه فی التاریخ شهر ربیع الاول نهصد وچهل ویک وضح وصح مضمون هذا الوقف الشرعی علی احدی واربعین وتسعمایه وصدر الحکم المذکور بالوقفه الزوم عن العبد الفقیر الی رحمة الله الملک العلام اقل عباد الله غیاث الاسلام عفی عنه وستر عیوبه

(در حاشیه نوشته است) الوقف المذکور علی النهج المسطور صدر عنّی حرّره العبد المذنب العاصی المحتاج الی رحمة الله الهادی مظفّر ابن فخر الدّین تپکچی الاسترابادی غفر ذنوبه وستر عیوبه (محل خاتم شریف واقف رحمه الله)

قطرهٔ زآب رحمت توبس است شستن نامهٔ سیاه همه

صورت کتابهٔ سنگی در امامزاده قاسم در خرابه شهر

هر آنکس را که ایزد بر گزینند
بِبام طارم اعلی نشینند
سعادت چون رفیق یار باشد
به نیکوئی هم کردار باشد
نهاده او بنای اینعمارت
رضای حق رسول با نجابت
بود بر دیدها کحل الجواهر
تراب استانت هست ظاهر
زهر صبح و مسا میدان تو لازم
ثنای مرقد شهزاده قاسم

وبعد یکی از اولاد رفیع القدر عالیشان اچه خدا مقرّب شاهنشهی نیک جهان مردمک محمّد قلی بیک

بعرض حضرت یوسف ستانی
سجلّ رحمت دار الامانی
مقدّس طینتی عالی تباری
معلّیٰ خصلتی احسان شعاری

به طیب خاطرش کرده اشارت

به تجدید بنای اینعمارت

بسرکاری وسعی شیخ کتبه اقابالا عمل استاد نیارک نجار بتاریخ چهار وبیست ویکصد بعد الف از هجرة محمّد

صورت کتابهٔ در امامزادهٔ روشن اباد

(سورهٔ آیة الکرسی تابه کلمهٔ ولا یؤده حفظهما وهو العلیّ العظیم)

شهد اللّه انه لا اله الاّ هو والملائکة والو العلم قائماً بالقسط لا اله الاّ هو العزیز الحکیم اللّهم صلّ علی محمّد المصطفی وامام علی المرتضی وامام حسن الرضا وامام حسین الشهید بکربلا وامام زین العابدین وامام محمّدباقر وامام جعفرالصادق وامام موسی الکاظم وامام علی بن موسی الرّضا وامام محمّدالتقی وامام علی النقی وامام حسن العسکری وامام محمد المهدی صلوات اللّه علیهم اجمعین مشقّه العبد میزان الکاتب عمل استاد حاجی عبد اللّه سنهٔ تسع وسبعین وثمانمایه

ایضاً صورت کتابهٔ در دیگر

(سورهٔ آیة الکرسی) عمل استاد نصر الله سنهٔ خمس وستین وثمانمایه

ایضاً صورت کتابهٔ در دیگر

عمل استاد کاظم بن علی نیشاپوری غرهٔ شهر شعبان المعظّم سنهٔ سبع وسبعین وثمانمایه

صورت کتابهٔ در امامزادهٔ پنج تن در لمسک

نصر من الله وفتح قریب یا محمّد یا علی مالکه وصاحبه علی ابن شمس الدّین عمل استاد محمّد بن یادگار ساروی عاقبت بحسین آباد کتبه علی

ایضاً صورت کتابهٔ سنگی در امامزادهٔ مزبور

به مؤمنین معلوم بودهٔ باشد اینکه ملاّ شمسعلی ساکن قریهٔ لمسک تعمیر معصوم زادهٔ مشهور به پنج امام نمود درسال ۱۲۲۳

صورت لوحهٔ در بقعهٔ چهار پادشاه لاهجان

چون مشهد ودر نو سیّد خوری کیا
ماند بباغ خلد ودر منظر بهشت
واعظ که از لآلیٔ نطق وکلام اوست
گوش زمانه پر زدر وگوهر بهشت
تاریخشان نکرچه مناسب فتاده است
کان روضه گشته وین شده همچون در بهشت
اندر ثنای مشهد ودر گفته قطعهٔ
از لطف عطرآور از او گوثر بهشت

یا غایب مفتح الابواب افتح بخیر هذا الباب اوان دولت السلطان الاعظم فتّاح اقالیم العالم صاحب النسب النبوی والحسب العلوی ابی الفتوح شاه عبّاس الحسینی الموسوی الصفوی دامت دولته فی وزارة صدر الصدور الامجد العظیم الشان مفتاح باب الفضل والاحسان غازی محمّد خان دامت سعادته حسب الاشارة الوالی العالی الدّاعی لدوام دولته المقدّم الباقی العبد الوحید الواعظ ابدّت افادته — کتبه العبد محمد ابن داود کیا سنة ١١٠٥ — اللهم صلّ علی قدوة الانبیاء وقبلة الاولیاء ابی القاسم محمّد المصطفی وصلّ علی سیّد الاوصیاء وسند الاصفیاء علیّ المرتضی وصلّ علی سیّدة

النساء فاطمة الزهرا وصلّ على سبط المصطفى الحسن المجتبى وصلّ على صاحب المحنة والبلاء الحسين الشهيد بكربلا وصلّ على على زين العبّاد وصلّ على البحر الزاخر محمد الباقر وصلّ على الشمس الشارق جعفر الصادق وصلّ على الامام العالم موسى الكاظم وصلّ على الامام ابى الحسن على بن موسى الرضا وصلّ على السيد الجواد محمد التقى وصلّ على الامامين الهمامين المدفونين بسرّ من رأى كاشفى الضر والمحن علىّ النقى والحسن الزكى العسكرى وصلّ على الامام الهمام بقيّة الله فى الانام محمد المهدى الهادى صلوات الله عليه وعليهم اجمعين — نسب السيّد الاعظم الارشد والسند الاكرم الامجد ذى الحسب المنيف الطاهر والنسب الشريف الظاهر السيّد السند السعيد المقبول المعلوم المقتول المظلوم ابى المحاسن السيّد خرّم كيا بن ابى الرضا بن على بن يحيى بن محمد بن على بن محمد بن عبد الله ابن محمد بن حسن بن محمد الطباطبا بن ابراهيم بن اسمعيل ديباج بن ابراهيم بن حسن المثنّى بن الامام الحسن بن على ابن ابى طالب صلوات الله وسلامه عليهم — عمل عبد الفتاح نجار لاهجى

ايضاً صورت لوحهٔ در ديگر

امر بعمارة هذه البقعة الشريفة الحاج خواجه حاجى زنگيشاه

الناظر فی سنة احدی وتسعین وسبعمایة — عمل استاد شهاب الدین بن استاد نظام الدین دروگر قزوینی

ایضاً صورت کتابهٔ صندوقی در بقعهٔ مزبوره

هذا الصندوق المشهد المبارک الامام الهمام الناسک المرحوم الشهید السیّد خور کیا نوّر الله مرقده وانار الله مضجعه — قُتل فی شهر ربیع الاول سنة سبع واربعین وسبعمایة الهجریة -- امر بعمارة هذا الصندوق حاجی علی بن شهاب الدین اللاهجی

ایضاً صورت کتابهٔ صندوق مقبرهٔ سیّد رضی کیا وسیّد ابی تراب در بقعهٔ مزبوره

کل شیء هالک الّا وجهه — هذا المرقد المنوّر والمشهد المطهّر للسیّد المرحوم المغفور المنتقل الی رحمة ربّه الغفور السیّد رضی کیا بن السعید الامام السیّد علی کیا الحسینی نوّر الله تعالی قبره فی اول جمادی الاولی سنة تسع وعشرین وثمانمایة من هجرة خیر البریة —

هذا المرقد المنوّر المشهد المعطر للسیّد المرحوم المغفور المنتقل الی رحمة ربّه الغفور ابی تراب بن رضی بن علی بن امیر بن حسین

ابن حسن بن علی بن احمد بن علی الغزنوی ابن محمد بن ابی یزید بن حسین بن احمد بن عیسی بن علی بن حسین الاصغر بن علی ابن حسین بن علی ابن عم رسول الله صلّی الله علیه وعلی آله وسلّم فی اوّل جمادی الاولی یوم الاثنین سنة تسع وعشرین وثمانمایة —

ندمت الهی علی ما اکتسبت جهالةً
وانت غفور عبدک العفو آمل
تقبّل خضوعی واعف عنّی خطیئتی
فانت کریم عبدک العفو سائل

کتبه حسن بن علی الصالحی الجیلانی

ایضاً صورت کتابهٔ صندوق دیگر

هذا المشهد المنوَّر والمرقد المعطّر للسیّد السعید والامام الشهید المقتول المظلوم . . . . علی بن امیر الحسینی نوَّر الله مضجعه

صورت کتابهٔ صندوق مقبرهٔ بقعهٔ امیر شمس الدین لاهجانی

این صندوق مشهد منوّر معطّر امامزادهٔ واجب التعظیم والتکریم امیر شمس الدین الموسوی علیه الرحمة والمغفرة در سنهٔ

سبعة عشر والف صورت انجام يافت — كتبه سيّد محمد بن داود كيا —

هو العالم بما فى الصدور وناشر الاموات من القبور — هذا مشهد السيّد السعيد امير شمس الدين الحسينى رحمه الله — ووقفت هذا الصندوق خلاصة العفايف خان سلطان بى بى فى زمان تولية فخر المشايخ درويش قاسم فى سنة ١٠١٨ — (آية الكرسى) — كتبه سيد محمد بن داود كيا

صورت كتابه در سر تربت سمام در كيلان

هـذا المشهد المنوّر والمرقد المعطّر للسلطان المغفور المبرور المنتقل من دار الغرور الى دار السرور ذو النسب الطاهر والحسب الباقر الذى ملك مملكت الجيل والديلم بانفاذ الامور الشرعية المصطفويّة ونهى مناكير البدعة الملحديّة اربعين سنة وهو السلطان الاعظم الامجد السلطان محمد بل" الله ثراه بمياه الرحمة والغفران ابن السيّد المعظم مالك الرّقاب الامم مولا ملوك ارباب اصحاب السيف والقلم كاركيا ابن السيّد ناصر كيا ابن سيّد المرحوم المبرور المغفور السيّد محمد ابن السيّد الاعظم الاكرم وهو الذى دعى مع اخيه السيد الفاضل العالم العادل المشهور بالشجاعة والسخاء امام الامة بين الورى

السيّد علی کیا دعوة الحق علی الجمهور وجرحا بالسیف رجاءً لثواب الله یوم البعث والنشور وهما ابنا السیّد المعظم امیر کیا الملاطی ابن السیّد الاجل السیّد حسین ابن حسن ابن علی ابن احمد ابن علی الغزنوی ابن محمد ابن ابو زید ابن حسین ابن احمد ابن عیسی ابن علی ابن الحسین الاصغر ابن علی زین العابدین ابن الامام الحسین الشهید المرحوم بکربلاء ابن علی المرتضی صلوات الله علیه وعلی اولاده الطیبین الطاهرین وقد توفی السلطان المذکور المزبور صبیحة یوم الاربعاء سلخ ربیع الاول مضی سبعة عشر یوماً من ابان ماه القدیم فی سنة مورخة تاریخها ثلث وثمانون وثمانمایة — عمل استاد محمود حجار قزوینی — کتبه العبد المحتاج الی الله محمود بن قطب الدین غفر الله لهما ولوالدیهما

ایضاً صورت کتابهٔ دیگر

هذا المشهد المقدّس النورانی والمرقد المطهّر الصمدانی الروحانی للسلطان الاعدل الاعلم الاکمل السعید السند الشهید المانح التقی الوفی الکریم السنجی المقبول المقتول بالسنان المحیی للقرآن مافیه من النفل والفرض السلطان ظل الله فی الارض المغفور المتصل الی رحمت الله الملك المتعال السلطان کارکیا میرزا علی کیا المغفور الذی قتل

بالواد وهلك بالعاد وبعد القتل والاهلاك دفن كما الفقراء والمساكين في رحبة المسجد الجامع المبارك للنادى الرانكوئى ونبش من بعد ما مضى من اليوم الذى دفن فيه من الايام العرف سنة الهلالية والاسلامية عشرون شهراً فوجد كما دفن ولم تنفصل فيه العظم ولا العضو ولم ينقطع لكل ولى اجمل الاجر ثم ان هذا المشهد المنوّر قد اوصى ذاك السعيد الازلى بذلك فى حال الصحة واوان السلامة وهو ابن السلطان الاكرم السلطان محمد بن السيّد المعظم كاركيا الناصر كيا بلّ الله تعالى ثراه بمياه الرحمة الشاملة ثم هما ابناء السيّد المغفور السيّد محمد ابن السلطان الامجد الاجل الذى دعى مع اخيه السيّد الفاضل العالم المعروف بالشجاعة والسنحاء امام الامة بين الورى السيّد على كيا دعوة الحق وهما ابناء السيّد اميركيا الملاطى وقع ذلك الخطب العظيم والامر الخطير فى يوم الخميس من رمضان المبارك من شهور سنة اثنى عشر وتسعماية هجريّة

ايضاً صورت كتابهٔ ديگر

هذه الروضة المقدسة والتربة المنوّرة الزكيّة التقيّة للحضرة المرحومة المبرورة العفيفة الفالحة الستيرة الصالحة المرتحلة من دار الغرور الى دار السرور المتصلة الى رحمة الله تعالى الرحيم المنان پرى

سلطان بنت السلطان محمد برد مضجعهما ونور مرقدهما انّ واقعة
هذا الموت وقعت سنة ثمان وتسعماية هجريّة

ايضاً صورت كتابهٔ ديگر

هذا المرقد المنور والمنزل المعطر والمقام المطهر والمقر المفخم
للمرحومة المغفورة الستيرة الصالحة العفيفة الصالحة الضعيفة المنتقلة
من الدار الدنياء الى الدار العقبى الباقى المتصلة الى جوار رحمت الرب
الغفور الرحيم العفو الغنى حسنى برد مضجعها ونور مرقدها توفت
المرحومة فى صفر المظفر سنة اثنين وتسعماية هجريّة

ايضاً صورت كتابهٔ ديگر

امر بعمارة هذا المشهد المبارك السلطان الاعظم خليفة المكرم
ووصمه فى الدين والدنيا بين الجيل والديلم السلطان ميرزا على خلد
ملكه ووقف السلطان المذكور لابيه المبرور ولاجله نيلا لثواب
يوم البعث والنشور وقفاً صحيحاً لاصحاب الاستحقاق العبور ولمن
قرأ قرآناً مجيداً فى هذا المقام ليوم الدين المشهور طلباً لغفران
السلطان المسرور ولتعمير المشهد المذكور الضياع والدور والبساتين
والدكاكين والحمامات الى ان يبقى السنة والشهور ليكون ثلثا ثواب

هذه الاوقاف عايداً الى روح مطهر ابيه المغفور وثلثه لاجل الواقف المذبور ونذكر الاوقاف مفصلا انشاء الله الغفور اولا هذا المقام المبارك يقال له كشاجاك وقريه تماجان وقريه كلايه مع توابعها فى ناحية السمام وفى معمورة الرانكو عشر الاف جوف الارض من الاراضى المعمورة يقال لها نقره بجار والحمام الكبير فى رودهسر والحمام فى تيامه جان والحمام فى اللنجرود واثنى عشر دكاكين فى فى لاهجان ومزرعه يحصل منها الاعناب والاثمار فى رودبار المسماة بسلطان آباد لمسرى فى سنة ثلث وثمانين وثمانماية — عمل الاستاد حسين بن على بن احمد المسافر

ايضاً صورت كتابهٔ ديگر

عمل الاستاد الاحد الاستاد حسين بن الاستاد على بن الاستاد احمد المسافر البناء اللاهجانى عفى عليهم فى تاريخ سنة ثلث وثمانين وثمانماية هجرية

صورت کتابهٔ سنگی در مسجد جامع رشت

یا معافی — بتاریخ غرّهٔ شهر شوال المکرّم سنهٔ میمونهٔ توشقان ئیل ۱۲۳۴ باخبار مژدهٔ ورود شاهزادهٔ اعظم اکرم والا محمّد رضا میرزا روحنا فداه وحسب الاشارهٔ مقرب الخاقان معتمد الدّوله وبندگان منجّم باشی پایندگان عموم وکدخدایان بلدهٔ رشت برای دوام دولت سلطان السّلاطین شاهنشاه ایران پناه فتحعلی شاه قاجار ارواح العالمین فداه بدعت غیر مستحسنه از بابت تکالیف دیوانی بهراسم ورسم که بر محلّات ثمانیهٔ رشت اطلاق میشود اهالی بلدان وجمیع ممالك محروسهٔ ایران از صد گونه تکالیف این معاف وبدعت خاص این بلد بود خاصّه بطیب خاطر از کلّ محلّات برداشته موقوف داشته ایم که اهالی شهر من بعد از این مرفّه الحال بدعای ذات خجسته صفات ظلّ اللّهی مشغول گردند ودر این بابت عهد نامه مؤكّد بلعن ابدی وبمهر همهٔ علماء رسانیده بمرقوم برسانند به اهالی شهر سپردیم که چون کاغذجات را دوامی بعلّت مرور سنین وشهور نبوده که باندك مدّتی قارئین این ایهٔ عظیم که در سلطنت عظمی وخلافت کبری به حیّز ظهور وصدور رسیده از خاطرها محو می گشت لهذا برای دوام وبقای این مدّعا که الی قیام السّاعة وساعة القیام مقروع سمع خاص وعام گردد خلاصهٔ مدّعارا در این سخرهٔ

ـنماة مرقوم وبر دیوار مسجد جامع منصوب ساختیم تا از تغییر و تبدیل مصون ماند توقّع از مؤمنین ومقدّسین آنکه چون بر مدّعا واقف بشوند پادشاه اسلام پناه‌را بیاد ابد دعا فرمایند : بنـده گر خدمت کند مزدش حق اقای اوست : چنانچه پس از تاریخ هر ذی نفسی دوباره باعث بدعت صادرات ویا عوارضات گردد انشاء الله الرّحمن بغضب حضرت اله وسخط جناب رسالت پناه وهمدرجهٔ قاتل سیّد الشّهدا باشد : من بدّله من بعد ما سمعه فاعنه الله الی یوم القیامة

صورت کتابهٔ سنگی در بقعهٔ خواهر امام در رشت

السّلطان ابن السّلطان ابن السّلطان ناصر الدّین شاه قاجار — یا حفیظ یا حافظ — پوشیده نماند که حضرت اقدس همیون این فرمان‌را بخواهش فخر العلماء والمجتهدین حاجّی ملاّ رفیع مرحمت فرموده اند — آنکه چون بشکرانهٔ فضل وکرم والانعم خداوند بی مثل ونظیر الّذی لیس له شریک ولا وزیر خوان نعمتش در بسیط زمین گسترانیـده وسایهٔ رحمتش وجود سلاطین بافرّ وتمکین را زیب سریر سلطنت کردانیده دیهیم سلطنت را بوجود همـایون ما مزیّن فرمود وتخت خلافت را بقدوم ما رشک گلشن نمود همواره خاطر خورشید اشراف شاهنشاهی بآرایش بلاد وعباد متعلّق است ورای

پادشاهی را در رعایت رعیّت وولایت توجّه مطلق برشتهٔ همّت ملوکانه برانداخته ایم که سایهٔ رحمت بر کافّهٔ عباد بگسترانیم وعامّهٔ انام را به نعمت رفاهیّت بپروانیم تا ملک از شمول عاطفت آراسته تراز گلشن گردد ودیدهٔ انام بفروغ معدلت خدیوانه روشن شود ووضیع وشریف رعیّت را دعا گوئی بقای این دولت واستدامت این شوکت ورد زبان آید از جمله از قراریکه بعرض مقیمان عتبهٔ خلافت کبری رسید بواسطهٔ مالیاتی که بدکاکین خبّازیٔ دار المرز رشت از دیوان اعلی جمع است اهالی آنجا ازپختن نان در خانه‌های خود ممنوعند واز این رهگذر از سکنه وعابرین از غریب وبومی بعلّت قلّت نان از کثرت عسرت تنگی واقع میشود محض مرحمت شاهانه از هذه السّنهٔ لوی ئیل وما بعدها برای حصول دعای دولت وتوسعهٔ معیشت اهالی از قرار همین فرمان همیون وتوقیع مالیات دیوانی دکاکین خبّازیٔ دار المرز رشت را به تخفیف ابدی مقرّر وصنف مزبوررا از تکالیف دیوانی معاف ومسلّم فرمودیم که از این به بعد هر کس بخواهد دکّان خبّازی در هر جا بگشاید ونان در خانه‌های خود پخته در بازار بفروشد احدی قادر بر اذیّت وازار انها نبوده باشد مقرّر آنکه سلاطین خجسته ائین دولت علیّه واخلاف واعقاب خلافت عظمی از قرار همین فرمان قضا جریان معمول داشته ابد الدّهر دیناری وحبّهٔ مالیات وعوارض وصادر به خبّازان بلدهٔ رشت

وارد نیاورند وخلاف آن را مخالف رضای خدا شمارند مقرّر آنکه عالیجاهان رفیع جایگاهان حکّام ومباشرین حال واستقبال گیلان حسب المقرّر معمول داشته هر ساله بخرج مجری دانند — الحمد لله که اتمام این سنگ بسعی سلالت السّادات العظام اقا میر ابوطالب تاجر رشتی در قزوین خلد ائین انجام گرفته — کتبه ملک محمّد قزوینی فی شهر شعبان ۱۲۷۲

صورت کتابهٔ سنگی در مسجد حاجیّ محمّد خان در رشت

در زمان خسرو دین پرور آموزگار
در قران فرّخ کیهان خدای روزگار
آسمان داد ودین فتحعلی شه آنکه کرد
داد ودین را استوار از یاری پروردگار
پاک دین حاجیّ محمّد خان که آمد از ازل
نیک روی ونیک رای ونیک خوی ونیک کار
دست او دلکش سحابی افتاب آنرا مطر
بخت او فرّخ همائی آسمان آنرا مطار
چون بود از بهر فردوسش ثواب اندر ثواب
چون بود در راه یزدانش نثار اندر نثار

این همایون مدرسه وین نغز مسجد توامان
بهر علم وبهر ایمان کرد در رشت استوار
در جهان ناپای داری دید افکند از خرد
طرح بنیادی کزو ماند بعالم یادگار
حجره اندر حجره از آن صانه الله خلد سان
صفّه اندر صفّه این‌را لوحش الله چرخ وار
هم مدّرس اندر آن ادریس دانا از میان
هم مسبّح اندر این جبریل فرّخ از کنار
الغرض چون از محمّد زیور اتمام یافت
علم وایمان در ابان این همیون روزگار
منشیٔ طبع صبا از بهر تاریخش نوشت
کز محمّد شد بنای علم وایمان آشکار

صورت کتابهٔ در قدیم دار الحکومهٔ رشت

خورشیدی و پیش تو نشستن نتوان جمشیدی و جام تو شکستن نتوان
معمار ازل که ساخت این در گفتا کین باب هدایت است بستن نتوان

صورت کتابهٔ بر گلدستهٔ مسجد ساغری سازان رشت

هو الله تعالی شانه العزیز — وقف مؤبّد نمود این گل‌دسته‌را خیر الحاجّ حاجی علی تاجر شیروانی بتاریخ شهر ربیع الثّانی سنهٔ بارس ئیل ۱۲۰٤ تا ثواب آن در یوم لا ینفع مال ولا بنون الاّ من أتی الله بقلب سلیم عاید او گردد اللّهم اغفر له ولوالدیه بحرمة محمّد وآله الطّاهرین المعصومین

صورت کتابهٔ صندوق مقبرهٔ پیر سلیمان در سلیمان داراب رشت

قد امر بجعل هذا الصّندوق المبارک السّلطان العادل العارف قدوة الامراء العظام انیس الخواقین الفخام المختصّ بعواطف الله الملک العلاّم المؤیّد بتأییدات الملک المنّان سرافراز سلطان خلّد الله تعالی ظلال سعادته ورفعته وجلالته وعظمته واقباله العالی للمرقد المعطّر والقبر المنوّر الشّیخ الفاضل السّالک الکامل المرحوم المغفور والسّالک المبرور وزبدة المشایخ پیر سلیمان بن حمزه دارابی الرّشتی جعله الله تعالی من الآمنین الفائزین الذّین لاخوف علیهم ولاهم یحزنون فی ذیحجّة سنة ثلث وخمسین وتسعمایة تقبّل الله تعالی من السّلطان العادل مدّ ظلّه العالی هذه المبرّات والخیرات ورزقه یوم القیامة

المراتب العظمى والدّرجات الکبری خلّد الله ظلال عظمته وسعادته وجلالته فی الدّنيا علی ما یهواه ویتمنّی وضاعفته الحسنات

صورت کتابهٔ در بقعهٔ فیلده رودبار

گشاده باد بدولت همیشه این درگاه
بحقّ اشهد ان لا اله الاّ الله
شکرها کردم که این درگه میسّر شد مرا
دیده روشن از سجود خاک آدم شد مرا

۱۱۷۷

ایضاً صورت کتابهٔ دیگر

شاهرخ بیمثال نیک خصال　　آن بلند اختر حمیده خصال
در هزار ودویست از هجرت　　غرق گردید او بآب زلال

ایضاً صورت کتابهٔ قبری در فیلده رودبار

هذا المرقد المنوّر للسّلسلة النجیبة السلطان فی العالم بدیع الزّمان میرزا تغمّده الله تعالی بغفرانه واسکنه ببحبوحة جنانه قد توفّی فی خامس شهر جمادی الاولی

چون بدیع الزّمان نیک سرشت

رفت واین دهر بی ثبات بهشت

سال فوتش زعقل چون جستم

گفت میدانش از سرای بهشت

بلبلی خون جگر خورد گلی حاصل کرد

باد غیرت بصدش حال پریشان دل کرد

طوطئ را بهوای قفسش دل خوش بود

ناگهان سیل فنا نقل عمل باطل کرد

ایضاً صورت کتابهٔ قبری دیگر

السّلطان ابن السّلطان شاه منصور تغمّده الله تعالی بغفرانه واسکنه ببحبوحة جنانه ابن عالیجاه اقبال دستگاه شاه ملک اقا ارفع الله تعالی شانه قد توفّی فی التّاریخ عشرین شهر محرّم الحرام

صد حیف نماند شاه منصور

زیر گل تنگ دل ای نوگل خندان چونی

چونکه ما غرقه بخونیم تو بی ما چونی

سلک جمعیّت ما بی تو زهم بگسسته

ما که جمعیم چنینیم تو تنها چونی

صورت کتابهٔ سنگی در مسجد اکبریّه لاهجان

بعهد فتحعلی شاه شهریار عجم
طراز افسر کاوس وزیب مسند جم
شهنشهی که پی خاکبوس درگه او
قد سپهر زبدو وجود آمده خم
حریم حرمت اورا همال میجستم
فتاده وهم در اندیشهٔ حریم حرم
فکنده شمسهٔ چترش چه بر زمین پرتو
گشاده رایت عدلش چه در زمان پرچم
ظلام ظلم بپوشیده روی از گیتی
لوای جور نگو نسار گشت در عالم
زمین درگه او هست بوسه گاه ملوك
رواق حضرت او گشت سجده گاه امم
زطوق طاعت او کرده‌اند زیل رقاب
بطوع تاجوران ترك وتازی ودیلم
سپهر جاه علی اکبر آنکه از نامش
بود علوّ وبزرکی ممهّد ومحکم

به یمن ویسر جهانیش در یمین ویسار
که آفتاب نوال است وآسمان کرم

بریده داد وی از صقر مخلب شاهین
شکسته عدل وی از گرگ پنجهٔ ضیغم

زنیش حادثه هر جا که شد دلی مجروح
نهاده لطف دل آسای او بآن مرهم

کند چگونه زکیفیّتش بیان کامه
کفش بگاه کفایت فزون زکیف وزکم

کمند فکر بقصر نوال او نرسد
بلی بچرخ برین کی توان شد از سلّم

بحکم خسرو عادل بشهر لاهیجان
فراز مسند فرماندهی نهاده قدم

بذات کعبهٔ طاعت بجان مدینهٔ علم
در آن مدینهٔ علم آمداست بیش نه کم

بنا نهاد چنین مدرس وچنان مسجد
که این مدینهٔ علم است وآن حریم حرم

چه مدرس آمده خاکش چو عنبر سارا
چه مسجد آمده آبش چو کوثر وزمزم

حه خاک عالم از او گر کسی بود جاهل
چه آب روشن از او گر دلی بود مظلم
فروغ دانش لقمان در آن بود مضمر
هوای روضهٔ رضوان در آن بود مدغم
زبانی این دو بنا شد چه اکبریّه بنام
بماند نام نکویش همیشه در عالم
نوشت از پی تاریخ هر دو کلک صبا
شده مدینهٔ علم وحرم قرین بهم

کتبه المذنب زین العابدین کاشانی مستوفی دیوان اعلی ۱۲۳۹

غلط نامه

صحیح	غلط	سطر	صفحه
اندرون	اندوون	٤	٤
دوش بدوش	دوش	٦	٨
وامروا . . . . . ونهوا	وامر . . . . . ونهی	١٠	٨
بوده	بورده	١٥	٨
دا دار	وادار	١٧	٨
قدغن	غدقن	١١	١٠
اللّهم صلّ علی ابی	سلام الله علیه وعلی ابو	١٦	١٢
المحصعین	المحصّین	٧	١٣
نیکٔ بو	نیکٔ بود	١٧	١٥
وصاف	اوصاف	٥	١٦
وکمال	کمال	١٦	١٧
ز اوّل نکوتر	زاول نیکوتر	١٧	١٧
سورهٔ	صورهٔ	١	١٨
عظام	اعظام	٤	١٩
بی بی	بی	٣	٢٠
اختهما	اختهم	٧	٢٢
وتقدس	وتقدسه	١٦	٢٢
آن شه	انشه	١١	٢٣
آنکه	انکٔ	١٣	٢٣

صحیح	غلط	سطر	صحفه
الاکرم	الاکرام	١٤	٢٤
الرازی	الازاری	١	٢٥
دولة	دولته	٨	٢٥
کرام	گرام	١٠	٢٧
تپكچی	وتبكچی	٦	٢٨
یك تومان	یتكومان	١٧	٢٩
مؤذّن	ماءذن	١٨	٢٩
جگر	جیگر	٥	٣٢
نافذاً	نافذ	١٠	٣٢
طرف	اطرف	١٥	٣٢
خورشید	حورشید	١٣	٣٤
دم از خلد	دم خلد	٥	٣٦
چو	چه	٢	٣٦
همچه	همجه	٩	٣٦
وش تن آن	وش آن	١٣	٣٦
خلوص	خلو	١٠	٣٧
آل	آن	١٣	٣٧
گلبانگ	بهر گلبابگ	١٧	٣٧
خیر محمّد	محمّد خیر	٢	٣٨
گوزن	کوزن	١٢	٤٠
آن که بهرامش	خان که بهرامش	١٥	٤٤

صفحه	سطر	غلط	صحيح
٤٤	١٦	وكرز	وگرز
٤٤	١٧	يكه	بكه
٤٥	٢	بسجده	سجده
٤٥	٤	بديحه	بديهه
٤٦	٧	زيبدار	زيبد ار
٤٦	١٢	گوسر	كوثر
٥٢	١٥	وافف	واقف
٥٣	٥	نيكوئى	نيكوئيش
٥٦	٢	خورى	خرّم
٥٨	٥	خور	خرّم
٥٨	١٢	السّعيد الامام	الامام السّعيد
٦٠	١١	مملك	ممالك
٦٠	١٥	كاركيا ابن السيّد	ابن السيّد كاركيا
٦٤	٢	المذبور	المزبور

فهرست الرجال والنّساء

ابدال (خان) خان : ١٦٦
ابراهیم : ٤٥ع
ابراهیم : ١٣٧
ابراهیم برادر امام رضا : ٧٠
ابراهیم ابو جواب : ٤٦ ، ١٩ع
ابراهیم بیك : ١٣٩
ابراهیم خان عمارلو : ١٥٤
ابراهیم (سلطان) ادهم : ٤٩
ابراهیم خان زند : ١٦٥
ابراهیم خان ذو القدر : ١٦٤
ابو محمّد ابراهیم بن عثمان بن نهیک : ٣٤
ابراهیم بن موسی الکاظم : ٣٨ ، ١٢ع ، ١٣ع
اتابك — انظر محمّد تقی خان
احتشام الوزاره : ٩٣ ، ٩٦
احمد الرّازی : ١٥٦
احمد (خواجه) فندرسکی : ١٦٤
احمد شمید : ٢٢
احمد طویل : ١٣٨
احمد خان قاجار علاء الدّوله : ١٦٥

احمد میرزا : ١٦٥

احمد (ابو الحسین) بن حسن ناصر الکبیر : ١٤٠

احمد (سلطان) خان بن سلطان حسن : ١٠٧ ، ١٤٩

احمد (استاد) بن حسین . ٤٧ ، ١٨ع ، ٢١ع

احمد (قطب الدّین) بن ملّا علی الاسترابادی : ٧٤ ، ٢٥ع

احمد بن عمر : ١٠٢

احمد بن محمّد السّکی : ١٣٧

احمد (ملك) بن سلطان محمّد بن ملك شاه سلجوقی : ١٣٨

احمد (ابو الحسین) بن محمّد القائم : ١٣٩

احمد (ابو العبّاس) بن نوح : ١٣٨

آذرولاش بن مهر : ١٣٣

ارجاسف (پادشاه مبارز الدّین) بن فخر الدّوله گرشاسف : ١٤٨

اردشیر بابکان : ١٣٣ ، ١٦٤ ، ١٦٦

اردشیر (حسام الدّوله) بن باحرب : ١٤٥

اردشیر (حسام الدّوله) بن حسن : ٢٦ ، ٣٩ ، ٥٢ ، ٥٣ ، ٨٤ ، ٩٠ ،
١٣١ ، ١٣٢ ، ١٣٥ ، ١٣٦ ، ١٤٨ ، ١٥٥ ، ١٥٩ ، ١٦٦

اردشیر (حسام الدّوله) بن کینخوار : ٣٥ ، ٥٣ ، ١٣٦

اردشیر (حسام الدّوله) بن نماور : ١٤٥ ، ١٥٤

اردشیر میرزا ملک آرا : ١٦٥

ارغش وهادان [فرهادون] : ١٤١

ارغون : ١٣٩ ، ١٦٤

ازرک : ٤٦

استر : ۷۲
استره : ۷۲
استن : ۲۶
اسحاق (ابو) بن المرزبان : ۱۴۷
اسحاق (امیر ابو) : ۱۴۷
اسد بن جندان : ۱۳۱
آسرب (ابو جعفر) : ۱۴۷
اسفار بن شیرویه : ۴۱ ، ۱۳۳ ، ۱۴۰
اسفندیار (ابن) [محمّد بن الحسن بن اسفندیار] : ۲ — ۴ ، ۱۴ ، ۱۵ ، ۲۹ ، ۳۳ ، ۳۴ ، ۳۸ — ۴۰ ، ۴۵ ، ۵۱ ، ۵۲ ، ۵۴ ، ۶۹ ، ۷۱ ، ۱۰۲ ، ۱۰۸ ، ۱۱۲ ، ۱۱۴ ، ۱۱۸ ، ۱۲۱ ، ۱۲۲ ، ۱۲۹ ، ۱۳۰ ، ۱۳۱ ، ۱۳۳ ، ۱۳۵ ، ۱۳۶ ، ۱۴۶ ، ۱۵۰ ، ۱۵۲ ، ۱۵۴ — ۱۶۰ ، ۱۶۶
اسکندر کبیر : ۸۶ ، ۱۳۲ ، ۱۳۳ ، ۱۵۳
اسکندر شیخی بن افراسیاب چلابی : ۳۱ ، ۱۳۹ ، ۱۴۲ ، ۱۵۶
اسکندر (جلال الدّوله) بن زیار : ۳۰ ، ۱۴۵ ، ۱۵۲
اسکندر (شرف المعالی) بن قابوس : ۱۴۱
اسکندر (جلال الدّین) بن کیومرث : ۱۴۴ ، ۱۴۶ ، ۱۵۴
اسکندر بن نماور : ۱۵۴
اسمعیل کدخداء ورزن : ۲۹
اسمعیل (استاد) نجّار آملی الرّازی : ۴۷
اسمعیل بن احمد سامانی : ۱۳۸
اسمعیل بن عبّاد : ۱۳۸

اسمعیل بن ابو القاسم بن حسن ناصر الکبیر : ۱۴۰
اسمعیل (شاه) اوّل صفوی : ۱۴۲ ، ۱۴۴ ، ۱۴۹
اشتاد : ۱۵۵
اشرف بن تاج الدّوله : ۱۴۶
اشرف (سیّد) بن کمال الدّین : ۱۵۹
اصطخری : ۹۰
اعتضاد الدّوله — انظر انو شروان خان
اعتماد الدّوله پسر اعتضاد الدّوله : ۱۶۵
اعتماد السّلطنه — انظر محمّد حسن خان
افراسیاب : ۱۱۱ ، ۱۵۵
افراسیاب (کیا) چلاوی : ۳۵ ، ۱۴۲
افریدون بن قارن : ۱۴۵
آقاخان (میرزا) نوری صدر اعظم : ۱۲ ، ۲۲
اکبر : ۷۳ ع
الله یار خان : ۱۶۴
آلندا بن قارن : ۱۳۴
الوند سلطان : ۱۳۹
الوند دیو : ۱۴۴
الیاس بن الیسع : ۱۳۸
امام قلی خان قاجار : ۱۶۵ ، ۴۴ ع ، ۴۵ ع
آمله : ۱۵ ، ۳۳ ، ۱۵۵
امیر(سیّد) کیا ملاطی : ۶۱ ع ، ۶۲ ع

امیر (سیّد) کیا بن هادی ملاطی : ١٤٩
امیر خان سردار — انظر نصرت الله میرزا
امیر اسعد : ١٦ ، ٢٠ ، ٢٣ ، ٢٤
امیر توپخانه — انظر حاجّی محمّد صادق خان
امیر مکرّم : ٣٦
انتظام الدّوله — انظر میرزا عبد الله خان
انو شروان : ١٤ ، ٨٠ ، ٨٢ ، ٨٧ ، ١٣٣ ، ١٥ع
انو شروان (شرف المعالی) بن قابوس : ١٤١
انو شروان خان اعتضاد الدّوله خان سالار : ١٦٥
انو شروان خان عین الدّوله : ١٦٥
اولیاء الله آملی : ٣٤
اویس بن کیومرث : ١٥٥
ایرج : ٥١ ، ١١١ ، ١٥٦

ب

بابر (معین الدّین ابو القاسم) : ٧٤ ، ٨٥ ، ١٦٤ ، ٢٥ع
بابک : ١٤
باحرب (امیر) : ١٤٧
باحرب (سیف الدّوله) بن زرّین کمر : ١٤٥
باحرب بن منوچهر : ١٤٧ ، ١٦٦
باذغاش : ١٤٨
با کالانجار بن ویهان : ١٤١
با کالانجار (امیر) بن جعفر : ١٤٨

بالا (اقا) : ٥٤ ع
باو : ١٣٣ — ١٣٥ ؛ ١٦٠
باو : ٥١
بايزيد (امير جلال الدّين) الجليلى الحسينى : ٧٥
بايسنغر : ١٦١
بدرخان افشار : ١٦٤
بديع الزّمان ميرزا : ٧١ ع ، ٧٢ ع
بديع الزّمان ميرزا صاحب اختيار بن محمّد قلى ميرزا : ١٠٣ ، ١٦٥
براهيم كيا بن حاجّى محمّد اشكورى : ١٤٩
بكر بن عبد العزيز بن ابى دالف العجلى : ١١١
بكر (ابو) شاسمانى : ١٦٢
بندار بن مونى : ١٣٧
بهاء الدّوله — انظر امير حسن
بهاء الدّين — انظر امير على
بهرام بن استاد محمّد نجّار ساروى : ٥٨ ، ٢٤ ع
بهرام (اسپهبد) بن حسام الدّوله شهريار : ٦٩، ١٣٥
بهمن بن بيستون : ١٤٦
بيرى بن گودرز بن بلاش : ١٦٤
بيستون بن اشرف : ١٤٦
بيستون بن جهانگير : ١٤٦
بيستون (شرف الدّوله) بن زرّين كمر : ١٤٥
بيستون (ظهير الدّوله) بن وسمكير : ١٤١

بیهقی : ١٤١ ، ١٦٠ ، ١٦١

پ

پادوسبان بن افریدون : ١٤٥
— بن خورزاد : ١٤٥
— بن گرد زاد : ١٤٧
— بن گیل : ٧ ، ١٤٥
پازواری (امیر) : ٤٦ ، ١٥٢
پری سلطان بنت سلطان محمّد : ٦٢ ع
پهلوان حسن : ١٦٤
پرویز (اسپهبد) : ١٤٧
پیر [پیرک] پادشاه بن لقمان : ٧٢ ، ١٦٤

ت

تاج الدّوله — انظر زیار — یزدجرد
تاج الدّوله بن اسکندر : ١٤٦
تاج الدّین — انظر توران شاه — شهریار
تاج الملوك — انظر مرداویج
تاجی دویر — انظر حسین بن سهل
تراب (ابو) بن سیّد رضی کیا : ٥٨ ع
تراب (شیخ ابو) : ٣٦
تقی الآملی : ٤٧ ، ٤٢٠
تکش (سلطان) بن ارسلان خوارزمشاه : ٥٣ ، ٨٤ ، ٩٠، ١٣١ ، ١٤٨
تنسر : ١

تور : ٥١
توران شاه (تاج الدّين) بن زردستان : ١٤٨
توران شاه (ابن تاج الدّين) : ١٤٨
توقداری داز : ٩٣
تیم بن سنان : ١٣٧
تیمور : ٣٣، ٣٥، ٥١، ٥٣، ٨٤، ٩٠، ١٣٢، ١٤٢، ١٤٤، ١٥٦، ١٦٢، ١٦٤

ث

الثّائر — انظر جعفر — هارون

ج

جریر بن یزید : ١٣٧
جستان بن نوشروان : ١٤١
جشنسف انظر گشنسب
جعفر (امام) : ١٦، ٥٥، ٢٢ ع، ٤١ ع
جعفر (ابو القاسم) بن حسن ناصر کبیر : ١٤٠
جعفر بن شهریار : ١٣٥
جعفر (الثّائر ابو الفضل) بن محمّد : ١٣٩، ١٤٠
جعفر (ابو) — انظر اسرب — حسن — محمّد
جعفر (ابو) باوند : ١٤٨
جعفر (شیخ ابو) الحنّاطی : ٣٩
جعفر قلی خان ایلخانی : ١٦٥

جلال (کیا) بن احمد بن جال : ١٤١
جلال الدّوله — انظر اسکندر — کیومرث
جلال الدّین — انظر اسکندر — بایزید — محمّد خوارزمشاه — محمود
جمشید خان : ١٦٤
جمشید بن قارن غوری : ٥٣ ، ١٣٩
جنتیمور : ١٣٩
جهانسوز میرزا امیر نویان : ١٦٥
جهانگیر بن عزیز : ١٤٦
» » کاوس : ١٤٦
» » کیومرث : ١٤٦
» » سلطان محمّد : ١٤٦
جهضم بن خباب : ١٣٧
جورماغون نوین : ١٣٩

چ

چنگیز : ٧٦
چونی : ٩٨

ح

حاجّی : ٨٣
حاجّی (شیخ) اقا : ١٣ ع
حافظ ابرو : ٩٠
حبیب الله خان سعد الدّوله : ٢٢ ، ٢٣ ، ١٠٦ ، ١٦٥

ابو الحجّاج — انظر مرداویج
حجّاز بن یوسف : ۱۳۱
حسام (کاکو) : ۱۵٤
حسام الدّوله — انظر اردشیر — تاش زر— ین کمر — شهریار
حسام الدّوله دیلمی : ٥٤
ابو الحسام مرزبان لارجان : ۱٤۷
حسان بن نوشروان : ۱٤۱
حسن (سیّد) : ۱٤٤
حسن بیکک : ۱٤۲
حسن (رکن الدّوله) بویه : ۱۳۸
حسن (مادر) بویه : ۲۷
حسن (امیر) بهاء الدّوله : ۱٤۸
حسن (سلطان) لاودی : ۱٥۸
حسن (ابو جعفر) بن احمد بن الحسن : ۱٤۰
حسن بن استاد بایزید : ٤۷، ۲۰ ع
حسن شیخ تیمور : ۱٦٤
حسن بن حسین : ۱۳۷
حسن (سیّد ابو القاسم) بن حمزه العلوی : ۳۹
حسن (شرف الملوک) [علاء الدّوله] بن رستم : ۲٦ ، ۱٤۷ ، ۱٤۸
حسن بن زید : ۱۱ ، ۱٤ ، ۳٤ ، ٥۲ ، ۱۰۸ ، ۱۳۱ ، ۱۳۹
حسن بن صبّاح : ۱٤۱
حسن بن علی بن ابی طالب : ۱۳ ، ۳۳ ، ۳۹ ، ٤۱ ع

حسن (داعی) بن علی — ناصر الکبیر : ۳۵ ، ۳۸ ، ۱۳۹ ، ۱۴۰
حسن بن علی الصالحی الجیلانی : ۵۹ع
حسن بن فیروزان : ۱۳۸ ، ۱۴۰
حسن بن قاسم — داعی الصغیر : ۲۷ ، ۳۴ ، ۳۹ ، ۱۳۹ ، ۱۵۶
حسن بن قحطبة : ۱۳۷
حسن (فخر الدّوله) بن کیخسرو : ۳۵ ، ۴۶ ، ۱۳۴ ، ۱۳۵ ، ۱۴۱ ، ۱۴۲
حسن (سلطان) بن سلطان محمّد : ۱۴۹
حسنی : ۶۳ع
حسین : ۱۵ع
حسین (استاد) : ۲۲ع
حسین (اقا) : ۲۴ع ، ۵۸
حسین (امام) : ۴۰ع ، ۴۱ع
حسین (بابا) : ۷۴ ، ۱۶۴ ، ۳۵ع
حسین (سیّد) : ۱۴۴
حسین خان بیگلر بیگی : ۱۶۴
حسین خان زیاد اغلو قاجار : ۱۶۴
حسین (سلطان) بیقرا : ۱۶۴
حسین (سلطان) میزا صفوی : ۱۳۹
حسین (شاه سلطان) صفوی : ۱۰ع ، ۳۷ ، ۱۴۴ ، ۱۶۰
حسین (سیّد) ناصر : ۱۶۶
ابن حسین خان فیروز جنگ : ۱۳۹
حسین بن استاد احمد نجّار ساروی : ۲۵ع ، ۶۵
حسین (استاد) بن احمد الرّازی : ۲۵ع ، ۵۹

حسين (استاد) بن على بن احمد المسافر اللاهجانى: ٦٤ ع
حسين (امير) كيا بن على بن لهراسب : ١٤٢
حسين (كاركيا سلطان) بن سلطان محمّد : ١٤٩
حسين بن موسى كاظم : ٢٢ ع ، ٥٥
حسين (مير) بن كاركيا يحيى كيا : ١٤٩
حسين قلى خان قاجار : ١٢١ ، ١٦٤ ، ١٦٦
حسين قلى خان : ١٦٥
ابو الحسين (سيّد) — انظر المؤيّد بالله
حشمت الدّوله — انظر عبد الله ميرزا
حمد الله مستوفى قزوينى : ٥٣ ، ٨٠ ، ٨٤ ، ٨٥ ، ٨٩—٩١ ، ١٥٣ ، ١٦٢ ، ١٦٦
حمزه (سلطان) بن سلطان هاشم : ١٤٩
حمزه (ابن الكاظم) بن يوسف السّهمى الجرجانى : ١٦١
ابنِ حوقل : ٢ ، ٣٣ ، ٣٥ ، ٨٤ ، ٨٥ ، ٨٩ ، ٩٠
حيدر سلطان قوى حصارلو : ١٣٩

خ

خازم بن خزيمه التّميمى : ١٣٦
خالد بن برمك : ٣٣ ، ١٣٦
خجسته (سيّد) بن فخر الدّين بابلكانى : ٤٧
ابو خزيمه : ١٣٦ ، ١٦٥
خسرو : ٣٣
خسرو خان : ٧٤ ، ١٦٤ ، ٢٩ ع

خسرو بن فیروز : ۱۳۰
خرشید (اسپهبد) گاو بره بن‌دازمهر : ۲ ، ۳۳ ، ۵۲ ، ۱۰۲ ، ۱۲۱ ، ۱۲۵ ، ۱۳٤ ، ۱۵۵ ، ۱۵۹ ، ۱٦٦
خرشید بن ابو انقاسم : ۱٤۷
خرشید (هژبر الدّین) بن کیکاوس : ۱٤۸
خرشید بن گیل : ۱۳٤
ابو الخضیب بن مرزوق السّعدی : ۱٤ ، ۵۲
خلیفه بن سعد بن هارون الجوهری : ۱۳۷
خلیل خان : ۱٦٤
خور (سیّد) کیا [سیّد حرم کیا ؟] : ۵۲ع ، ۵۷ع ، ۵۸ع
خورزاد بن پادوسبان : ۱٤۵
خیر النّساء بیگم : ۱٤۳

د

دابویه بن گیل : ۱۳۳ ، ۱۳٤ ، ۱٤۵
دارا بن رستم : ۱۳۵
دارا بن قابوس : ۱٤۱
دارا بن منوچهر : ۱٤۱
دارا (مجد الدّین) : ۱٤۸
دارای (کاکو) امیره : ۱۵٤
داز مهر بن زر مهر : ۵۲ ، ۱۳۳
داز مهر بن فرّخان بزرك : ۱۳٤
داعی — انظر حسن بن علی

داعی الی الحقّ — انظر رضا — هادی — محمّد بن زید
داعی الصّغیر — انظر حسن بن زید — حسن بن قاسم
داعی الکبیر — انظر حسن بن زید
داود (سیّد) کیا بن هادی : ١٤٩
دمشق : ١٣١
دولتشاه : ٤٩ ، ١٥١ ، ١٥٣ ، ١٦١ ، ١٦٢
دیو سفید : ١٥٤

ر

رافع بن هرثمه : ١٣٨
رامین : ١٦٤
رحیم خان گزیلی : ١٦٤
رستم زال : ٥١ ، ١١٠ ، ١٦٢ ، ٤٤ع
اقا رستم روزافزون : ١١٢ ، ١٤٣
رستم (مجد الدّوله) بویه : ١٣٥
رستم بورکله : ١٤٨
رستم کبودجامه : ١٤٧
رستم (امیر سابق الدّوله) : ١٤٨
رستم خان عمارلو : ١٥٤
رستم (نصیر الدّوله شمس الملوك شاه غازی) بن اردشیر : ٢٦،١٣٥،١٣٦
رستم بن دارا : ١٣٥
رستم بن سرخاب : ١٣٥
رستم بن شروین : ١٣٥ ، ١٤٧

رستم بن شهریار : ١٣٥
رستم (نصرت الدّین شاه غازی) بن علی : ٣٥، ١٣٥، ١٤٧، ١٤٨، ١٥٠، ١٦٦
رستم (شمس الملوك) بن قارن : ١٣٥
رستم (شرف الملوك) بن کیخسرو : ١٣٦
رضا (سیّد) مفیدی : ١٦١
رضا (کیا بزرك داعی الی الحقّ) بن هادی : ١٦٦
رضی (سیّد) کیا بن سیّد علی کیا : ٥٨ ع ، ١٤٩
رضی (سیّد) بن مهدی الحسنی الباشکجا ی : ١١ ع ، ١٢ ع
رضی الدّین الحسینی : ١٥٩ ، ١٩ ع
رضیّه : ٧٣
رفیع (حاجّی ملاّ) : ٦٦ ع
رکابزن (سیّد) کیا : ١١٢ ، ١٤٠ ، ١٤٨
رکن الدّوله — انظر حسن — ابو علی — کیخسرو
رکن الدّین : ١٤٧
رمجه هرویه : ١٥٥
روح بن حاتم بن قیصر بن محلّب : ١٣٦ ، ١٣٧
روح الله (سیّد) : ١٤٤
روزان صول : ٨٨
رینش بهارد : ١٦٤

ز

زاهد(شیخ) : ٣٩ ، ١٢ ع
زاهد (امیر شیخ) طارمی : ١٦٤

زبدر (سیّد) : ١٥٦
زردستان (سراج الدّین) بن فخر الدّوله گرشاسف : ١٤٨
زرمهر : ١٣٣
زرّین کمر (جسام الدّوله) بن جستان : ١٤٥
زرّین کمر (حسام الدّوله) بن فرامرز : ١٤٥
زکی خان : ١٦٦
زنگیشاه (حاجّی) ناظر: ٧٥ ع
زیار : ١٤١
زیار (تاج الدّوله) بن کیخسرو : ١٤٥
زید : ١١
زید (ابو القاسم) بن ابی طالب محسن المسدّد بالله : ١٤٠
زین العابدین بن اسمعیل : ٦٥ ، ٢٥ ع
زین العابدین (سیّد) بن کمال الدّین بن محمّد : ٥٥ ، ١٤٢
زین العابدین کاشانی : ٧٥ ع
زینل خان : ١٦٤

س

سابق الدّوله — انظر رستم
سارویه بن فرّخان بزرك : ٥١ ، ٥٢ ، ١٣٤
سالار مقتدر — انظر میر سعد الله خان فندرسکی
سالم فرغانه : ١١٩
سبکتگین : ١٣٨
سپهدار اعظم — انظر محمّد ولی خان تنکابنی

سپهسالار — انظر میرزا محمّد خان
سدید شقّی : ١٤٩
ابن سراپیون : ٩١
سراج الدّین — انظر زردستان
سرافراز سلطان : ٤٧٠
سرخاب بن شهریار : ١٣٥
سرخاب بن مهرمردان : ١٣٥
سردار افخم — انظر محمّد علی خان
ابو سعد — انظر منصور
سعد الدّوله — انظر حبیب الله خان تنکابنی — طوس
سعد الله (میر) خان فندرسکی سالار مقتدر : ٩٥
سعید بن دعلج : ١٣٧ ، ١٥٥
سعید بن سلمه : ١٣٧
سعید بن العاص : ١٣٦
سعید بن مسلم : ١٣٧
ابو سعید (سلطان) : ١٦٤
درویش سکندر بن عزّ الدّین : ٥٤ ، ٤٢٤
سکینه بنت موسی کاظم : ٤٧ ، ٥٥ ، ٤٢٢
سلام ترك : ١٣٨
سلم : ٥١
سلیمان : ١٥٧
سلیمان (خلیفه) : ٥١ ، ٧٢ ، ١٣٦!
سلیمان خان خانان : ١٦٥

سلیمان خان سرتیپ صاحب اختیار : ١٦٥
سلیمان (پیر) ابن حمزه دارابی : ٧٠ ع
سلیمان بن عبد الله : ١٣١
سلیمان بن عبد الملك : ١٣٧
سلیمان بن موسی : ١٣٧
سنجر : ١٤٨ ، ١٦٦
سندی بن شاهك : ١٥٩
سهراب بن باو : ١٢١ ، ١٣٥
سهراب بن رستم : ٥١ ، ١١٠
سهراب بن ابو القاسم : ١٤٧
سهل بن المرزبان : ٤٠ ، ١٤٧
سهم الدّوله — انظر یار محمّد خان
سوخرا بن آلندا : ١٣٤
سوید بن مقرّن : ١٣٦
سیف الدّوله — انظر باحرب — مظفر تبکچی — حاجّی سلطان محمّد میرزا
سیف الدّین — انظر فرامرز
سیف الملك — انظر وجیه الله میرزا
سیمجور (ابو علی) : ١٣٨

ش

شاپور ذو الاکتاف : ٨٤
شاپور بن شهریار : ١٣٥
شاری : ١٣٧

شاهرخ : ٤٧١
شاهرخ خان : ١٦٥
شاه غازی — انظر رستم — نماور
شاه غازی (فخر الدّوله) بن زیار : ١٤٥
شاهی (میر) بن عبد الکریم : ١٤٣
ابو شجاع — انظر فناخسروا
شرف : ٩٨
شرف خان : ١٣٩
شرف خان بن شمس الدّین بدلیسی — شرف الدّین بدلیسی
شرف الدّوله — انظر بیستون
شرف الدّین (سیّد) : ١٥٦
شرف المعالی — انظر اسکندر — انو شروان —
شرف الملوك — انظر حسن — رستم — علی
شروان (بی بی) : ٨٧
شروین بن رستم : ١٣٥
شروین بن سرخاب : ١٢١ ، ١٣٥
شفیع (میرزا) : ١٥٦
شمر : ٤٤١
شمس طبرسی : ٣٨
شمس الدّین (امیر) لاهجانی : ٤٥٩
شمس الدّین دیو : ١٤٤
شمس الدّین غوری بن جمشید : ١٣٩
شمس الدّین (سیّد) بن عبد العزیز بابلکانی : ٤٧ ، ٤٢٠

شمس الدّین (امیر) بن کمال الدّین : ۴۷ ، ۱۴۲ ، ۲۱ع ۲۲ع
شمس الدّین (مولانا) بن نصر الله المطهّر : ۱۵۹ ، ۱۹ع
شمس آل رسول الله — شمس آل محمّد : ۳۸
شمس المعالی — انظر قابوس
شمس الملوك — انظر رستم — محمّد
شمس علی (ملاّ) لمسکی : ۷۱ ، ۵۵ع
شهاب الدّین (استاد) بن نظام الدّین قزوینی : ۵۸ع
شهراکیم (فخر الدّوله) بن نماور : ۲۶ ، ۱۴۵
شهر نوش بن هزاراسف : ۲۶ ، ۱۴۵
شهریار بن پادوسبان : ۱۴۵ ، ۱۵۴
شهریار بن پادوسبان بن افریدون : ۱۴۵
شهریار بن جمشید : ۱۴۵
شهریار (تاج الدّین) بن خرشید : ۱۴۷
شهریار بن دارا : ۱۳۵
شهریار بن شروین : ۱۳۵ ، ۱۵۱ ، ۱۵۵
شهریار بن قارن بن شروین : ۱۳۵
شهریار (حسام الدّوله) بن قارن : ۵۳ ، ۱۳۵
شهریار (نصیر الدّوله) بن کیخسرو : ۱۴۵ ، ۱۵۴
شهریار (نصیر الدّوله) بن یزد جرد : ۱۳۶
شیبك خان : ۱۶۴
شیخ : ۶۹ ، ۵۴ع
شیخ الاسلام : ۱۵۶
شیرزاد بن ابو الحسام : ۱۴۷

شیرزاد بن ابو القاسم : ١٤٧
شیرین بنت رستم : ١٣٥

ص

صاحب — انظر اسمعیل بن عباد
صاحب اختیار — انظر بدیع الزّمان میرزا — سلیمان خان سرتیپ
صادق : ٣٧ ع
صادق (بابا) : ١٦٤
صدر الدّین شیخ الاسلام : ١٦ ع
صدر الدّین خان استاجلو : ١٦٤
شاه صفی : ٣١ ع
صول ترك : ٨٩

ض

ضحّاك : ٤٠

ط

ابو طالب (میر) رشتی : ٦٥ ع
ابو طالب — انظر هارون — وشمگیر — یحیی
طاهر (سیّد) : ١٠٨
طاهر بن عبد الله بن طاهر : ١٣٧
طاهر (سلطان) بن موسی کاظم : ١٨ ع
طغا تیمور : ١٦٤
طغرل : ١٤١

شاه طهماسپ اوّل : ۲۳ ، ۸۰ ، ۸۶ ، ۱۴۳ ، ۱۴۴ ، ۳۸ ع
شاه طهماسپ ثانی : ۱۶۱ ، ۱۶۴
طوس (سعد الدّوله) بن زیار : ۱۴۵
طوس نوذر : ۱۶۰

ظ

ظهیر الدّوله — انظر بیستون — محمّد تقی خان
ظهیر الدّین (میر) مرعشی : ۱۳ ، ۱۴ ، ۲۶ ، ۲۸ ، ۳۰ ، ۳۳ ، ۳۴ ، ۴۱ ، ۴۶ ، ۵۴ ، ۶۹ ، ۱۰۵ ، ۱۰۷ ، ۱۰۸ ، ۱۱۰ — ۱۱۷ ، ۱۱۹ — ۱۲۲ ، ۱۲۹ ، ۱۳۲ ، ۱۳۴ ، ۱۳۶ ، ۱۴۶ ، ۱۴۹ ، ۱۵۰ ، ۱۵۲ — ۱۵۵ ، ۱۵۷ — ۱۵۹ ، ۱۶۱ ، ۱۶۶
ظهیر الدّین بن علی بن قوام الدّین : ۲۷

ع

عادل شاه : ۶۳ ، ۱۶۵
عبّاس (شاه) اوّل صفوی : ۷ ، ۸ ، ۱۳ ، ۱۷ ، ۳۶ ، ۴۳ ، ۴۵ ، ۴۸ ، ۴۹ ، ۵۶ ، ۵۸ ، ۶۲ ، ۶۳ ، ۷۴ ، ۸۰ ، ۸۶ ، ۱۲۰ ، ۱۴۴ ، ۱۵۱ ، ۱۶۴ ، ۴ع ، ۲۵ع ، ۲۷ع
عبّاس (شاه) ثانی : ۷۵ ، ۳۷ع
عبّاس خان : ۷۵ ، ۴۲ع بیگلر بیگی ۱۶۵
عبّاس (شاهزاده) : ۲۳ع
عبّاس میرزا ملك آرا : ۱۶۵
عبّاس قلی اقا غلام باشی : ۲۳
ابو العبّاس (شیخ) قصّاب : ۳۹

ابو العبّاس (حسام الدّوله) طوسی : ۱۳۶ ، ۱۳۸
ابو العبّاس — انظر احمد — تاش — عبد الله
عبد الحمید مضروب : ۱۳۷
عبد الحیّ (سیّد) بن نصیر الدّین : ۱۰۵
عبد الرّحمن (سیّد) بن محمّد الادریسی : ۱۶۱
عبد الرّحمن — انظر ارغون
عبد الرّحیم بن محمّد : ۹ع
عبد الرّحیم بن امیر مرتضی : ۱۵۹
عبد العزیز سلطان بن عبید خان : ۱۶٤
عبد العزیز مهدی : ۱۱۸ ، ۱۹ ع
عبد الفتّاح فومنی : ۱۲۹
عبد الفتّاح نجّار لاهجی : ۵۷ ع
عبد الکریم (اقا) : ۳۶
عبد الکریم بن عبد الله بن عبد الکریم : ۱٤۳
عبد الکریم بن عبد الله خان : ۱٤۳
عبد الکریم بن محمّد : ۱٤۲ ، ۱۹ ع
عبد الکریم بن امیر مرتضی : ۱۵۹
عبد الله (امامزاده) : ٤۰ ع ، ٤۲ ع
عبد الله دروگر : ۱۲ ع
عبد الله (استاد حاجبی) : ۷۱ ، ۵٤
عبد الله میرزا حشمت الدّوله : ۱۶۵
عبد الله (میرزا) خان انتظام الدّوله : ۱۶۵
عبد الله بن آمر : ۸۹

عبد الله بن حازم : ٣٤ ، ١٣٧ ، ١٥٥

— بن الحسين بن سهل تاجي دوير : ١٤٧

— بن خرداد به : ١٣٧

— بن سيّد روح الله : ١٤٤

— بن سعيد الجريشي : ١٣٧

— بن عبد العزيز بن حمّاد : ١٣٧

— بن عبد الكريم : ١٤٢

— بن عمر : ١٣

— بن عمر بن العلاء : ١٥٥

— بن طاهر : ٥٢

— بن قحطبه : ١٣٧

— (ابو العبّاس) بن محمّد بن نوح بن اسد : ١٣٨

— (مير) خان بن مير سلطان محمود : ١٤٣

— بن مالك : ٣٤ ، ١٣٧

— بن ونداد اميد : ١٤٥

ابو عبد الله — انظر محمّد

ابو عبد الله : ٧٤

عبد المحيط (سيّد) بن مير توانى : ٥٩ ، ٢٤ع

عبد الملك (خليفه) : ١٣٧

عبد الملك بن قعقع : ٣٤ ، ٥٢ ، ١٣٧

عبد الواحد بن اسمعيل ابو المحاسن : ٣٨

عبد الوحيد : ٥٦ع

عبيد خان خوارزم : ١٦٤

عتّاب بن ورقا شیبانی : ۱۳۲

عثمان (خلیفه) : ۱۳۶

عثمان خان : ۲۵

عثمان بن نهیک : ۱۳۷

عزّ الدّوله — انظر قباد — هزاراسپ

عزّ الدّین — انظر گرشاسف

عزّ الدّین بنّا : ۵۰ ع

عزّ الدّین (سیّد) : ۱٤٤

عزیز (سیّد) بن بهاء الدّین آملی : ۳۹، ۱٤ ع

عزیز (سیّد) بن شمس الدّین بابلکانی : ٤۷، ۱۹ ع

عزیز (میر) خان بن میر عبد الله : ۱٤۳

عزیز بن کیومرث : ۱٤٦

عسکر (قاضی) : ۱۵ ع

عضد الدّوله — انظر فناخسرو — المؤیّد بالله

عضد الدّوله طوس — انظر سعد الدّوله طوس

علاء الدّوله — انظر احمد خان قاجار — حسن — علی

علاء الدّین بن درویش محمّد عبد الوفا : ۵۵، ۲۱ ع

علاء الدّین — انظر محمّد خوارزمشاه

علی (شیخ) خان زند : ۵۳

علی (کیا) اشکوری : ۱٤۹

علی (شاه) سلطان استاجلو : ۱٦٤

علی (حاجّی) رویانی : ۱۵۵

علی (حاجّی) شیروانی : ۷۰ ع

علی غزنوی : ۱٦ ، ۷ ع
علی (سیّد) مرعشی : ۳۸
علی (کربلای) : ٥۰
علی بُو القلندر : ۱٦٤
علی (پاشا) : ۱٤۸
علی بن احمد الجرجانی الادریسی : ۱٦۱
علی (علاء الدّوله) بن اردشیر : ۱۳٦
علی (استاد) بن استاد اسمعیل نجّار آملی : ۲۰ ع
علی (سیّد) کیا بن امیر : ۱٤۸ ، ۱٥٤ ، ٥۹ع ، ٦۱ع ، ٦۳ ع
علی (امیر) بهاء الدّین ابن امیر جلال الدّین بایزید : ۳۹ ع
علی شاه بن تکش : ۱۳۸
علیَ (شمس الدّین) بن جمشید قارن : ۱٦٤
علی (کارکیا) بن سلطان حمزه : ۱۳۹
علی (شرف الملوك) بن رستم : ۱۳٥
علی بن شمس الدّین : ۷۱ ، ٥٥ع
علی بن شمس الدّین بن یوسف لاهجی : ۱۳۲، ۱٥۳
علی (حاجّی) بن شهاب الدّین لاهجی : ٥۸ع
علی (علاء الدّوله) بن حسام الدّوله شهریار : ۱۳٥ ، ۱٤۷
علی ابن ابی طالب : ۱۱ ، ۲۲ ، ۹۹ ، ۱٥۳ ، ۳۰ع ، ۳۱ع ، ٤۱ ع
علی بن کامه : ۱۳۸ ، ۱٥٥ ، ۱٥٦
علی (سیّد) بن کمال الدّین مرعشی : ۱۳۲ ، ۱٤۲ ، ۱٥٦ ، ۱٥۹ ، ۱۸ع
علی (میرزا) بن سلطان محمّد : ۱٤۹
علی (میر) خان بن سلطان محمود بن عبد الکریم : ۱٤۳ ، ۱٤٤

علی بن موسی کاظم : ٤١ ع
علی بن موسی بن جعفر : ٣٨ ع
اقا علی اشرف مشائی : ٣٧
علی اصغر (میرزا) : ١٦٥
علی زین العابدین : ٤١ ع
علی محمّد خان مفاخر الملك : ٩٥
علی نقی : ٤١ ع
علی نماور بن زیار : ١٤٧
ابو علی — انظر سیمجور — محمّد بن احمد
ابو علی ابن احمد بن محمّد المظفّر : ١٣٨
ابو علی (استاد) جرجانی : ١٣٨
ابو علی (رکن الدّوله) بویه : ١٣٥ ، ١٦٦
علیار بیگک ایمیر : ١٦٤
عماد (سیّد) : ١٤٤
عماد الدّوله — انظر فرامرز
عماد الدّین — انظر محمود
عمادی : ١٥٢
عمر (خلیفه) : ١٣ ، ٩٩ ، ١٣٦
عمر بن العلاء : ١٤ ، ٣٣ ، ١٣٧ ، ١٥٥
عمید الملك — انظر کیومرث میرزا
عنصر المعالی — انظر کیکاوس
عوفی : ١٦٢
عین الملك — انظر انوشروان

غ

غازی محمّد خان : ٥٦ع

میر غضنفر : ١٤٤

غلام شاه گوکچه سلطان : ٧٥ ، ٧٦ ، ١٦٤ ، ٣٨ع

غیاث الاسلام : ٥٠ع

غیاث الدّین بن کمال الدّین : ١٥٩

غیاث الدّین — انظر محمّد

ف

فائق : ١٣٨

فتّاح (ملاّ) تنکابنی : ١٥٣

فتحعلی خان قاجار : ١٦١ ، ١٦٤

فتحعلی شاه قاجار : ٤٦ ، ٥٥ ، ١٠٣ ، ١٥٥ ، ١٦٥ ، ١٧ع ، ٣٤ع ، ٦٥ع ، ٦٨ع ، ٧٣ع

فخر الدّوله — انظر حسن — شاه غازی — شهرا کیم — گرشاسف — مسعود — نماور

فخر الدّوله بویه : ١٣٨

فخر الدّوله گلپا یگانی : ١٤٨

فخر الدّین (کیا) جلال : ٤٦ ، ١٤٢

فخر الدّین بن قوام الدّین مرعشی : ١١٢ ، ١١٥ ، ١٥٧ ، ١٥٨

فخر عماد الدّین بن امام زین العابدین : ٥٦

ابو الفداء : ٣٠ ، ٧٣

فرامرز (سیف الدّین عماد الدّوله) بن رستم : ١٣٥

فرج الله (میرزا) خان مستنصر السلطنه : ٦ع

فرّخان بزرك بن دابويه : ٣ ، ١٥ ، ٥١ ، ٨٨ ، ١١٤ ، ١٣١ ، ١٣٢ ، ١٣٤ ، ١٤٦ ، ١٥٤ ، ١٦٦
فردوسى : ٣ع
فرشواد : ١٤٦
فرهاد خان قرامانلو : ١٣٩ ، ١٦٤
فريدون : ٣٩ ، ٤٠ ، ٥٤ ، ٦٩ ، ١١١ ، ١١٥ ، ١٥٦ ، ١٥٨
فريدون خان چركس : ١٦٤
فضل بن المرزبان : ١٤٧
فضل بن يحيى : ١٣٧
فضل الله بن ظهير الدّين : ٢٧
فضل على خان : ٤٦ ، ١٦٥ ، ١٧ع
ابو الفضل بن محمّد : ١٤٥ ، ١٦٦
ابو فضل دابو : ١١٣
ابو فضل — انظر جعفر
فضّه (بى بى) خاتون بنت امير صاعد : ١٣٨
فلك المعالى — انظر منوچهر
فناخسرو (ابو شجاع) عضد الدّوله بويه : ١٣٨
ابن فورك : ٣٩
فيروز شاه : ١٥ ، ٣٣
فيروز ساسانى : ١٥٣
فيروز حاكم بيرون تميشه : ١٣٨
فيروز بن الليث : ١٤٧
فيروزان بن حسن بن فيروزان : ١٤٠

فیروزان بن نعمان : ۱٤۰

ق

قاآن : ۱٤۷
قابوس (شمس المعالی ابو الحسن) بن وشمگیر : ۸٤ ، ۸٦ ، ۸۷ ، ۱۳۵ ، ۱٤۱ ، ۱٤۵
قارن : ۱۲۵
قارن بن سوخرا : ۱۳٤ ، ۱۵۲
قارن بن شهریار . ۱۳۵
قارن (نجم الدّوله) بن حسام الدّوله شهریار : ۱۳۱ ، ۱۳۵
قارن تابریابی بن ابو القاسم : ۱٤۷
قارن بن گرشاسف : ۱٤۸
قاسم (شاهزاده) : ۵۳ع
قاسم خان هژبر خاقان : ٦۰
ابو القاسم (میر) خراسانی : ۱۳۹
ابو القاسم (میر) فندرسکی : ۸۲
ابو القاسم بن ابو المحاسن الرّویانی : ۳۸ ، ۳ع
ابو القاسم — انظر بابر — جعفر — حسن — زید — المؤیّد بالله
قای خان بن گوی خان بن اغوز خان بن قرا خان : ۱۰۱
القائم — انظر ابو الحسین احمد
قباد (عزّ الدّوله) بن شاه غازی : ۱٤۵
قباد بن فیروز بن یزدجرد : ۱۳۰ ، ۱۳۳
قثم بن العبّاس : ۱۳

قراتکین ترک : ۱۳۸
قجق : ۹۸
حاجّی قربان اقا : ۷٤ ، ۲٦ع ، ۳٤ع
قزوینی : ۸۹
قطب الدّین — انظر احمد
قطری بن فجأة المازنی : ۱۳۸
قلیج (ملاّ) خان : ۹٤
قلیج خان : ۱٦٤
قنسول روس : ۹٥
قوام الدّین المرعشی بن عبد الله بن صادق : ۳٦ ، ۳۷ ، ۱۳۱ ، ۱٤۲، ۱٥٦ ، ۱٥۹

ک

کا (امیر) بن ورداسف : ۱٤٦
کاظم : ۲۳ع
کاظم (امام زاده) : ٦۹
کاظم (استاد) بن علی نیشاپوری : ٥٥ع ، ۷۱
ابن کاظم [ابو کاظم] — انظر حمزه
کا کو — انظر اردشیر — حسام — دارا
کا کی بن نعمان : ۱٤۰
ابو کالانجار بن ویهان القوهی : ۱٤۱
کاوس بن اشرف : ۱٤٦
کاوس بن جهانگیر : ۱٤٦

کاوس بن کیومرث : ۱۴۴ ، ۱۴۶
کچل شاه وردی سلطان استاجلو : ۱۶۴
کریم خان زند : ۱۵ ، ۲۲ ، ۶۳ ، ۱۵۴ ، ۱۶۵ ، ۱۶۶
کلیپ : ۴۳
کمال الدّین بن شمس الدّین : ۱۴۳
کمال الدّین بن قوام الدّین : ۵۳ ، ۵۵ ، ۱۳۲ ، ۱۴۲ ، ۱۵۹
کمال الدّین بن محمّد : ۱۴۲
گنار بن فیروزان : ۱۴۰
کوچك علوی : ۲۹
کیخسرو : ۷۲ ، ۱۴۱ ، ۱۶۰
کیخسرو آملی : ۱۴۸
کیخسرو (شاه) بن شهراکیم : ۱۴۵
کیخسرو (رکن الدّوله شاه) بن یزد جرد : ۱۳۶
کیفرین شاه بن شمس الدّین : ۷۵ ، ۴۲ ع
کیکاوس (عنصر المعالی) بن اسکندر : ۱۴۱
کیکاوس بن فخر الدّوله گرشاسف : ۱۴۸
کیکاوس بن هزاراسف : ۲۶ ، ۳۵ ، ۱۴۵
کیمدور (سلطان) : ۱۰۹
کینخوار بن باخرب : ۱۴۷
کیوس بن قباد : ۱۳۳ ، ۱۶۰
کیو مرث میرزا عمید الملك : ۱۶۵
کیو مرث (حاجی) میرزا : ۱۶۵
کیو مرث بن بهمن : ۱۴۶

کیومرث (جلال الدّوله) بن بیستون : ۱۴ ، ۱۰۸ ، ۱۱۵ ، ۱۴۴ ، ۱۴۵
کیومرث بن کاوس : ۱۴۶

گ

گاوبره — انظر گیل
گرشاسف (عزّ الدّین) : ۱۴۸
گرشاسف (فخر الدّوله) : ۱۴۷
گرگین میلاد : ۷۱ ، ۸۸
گشنسف : ۱۳۳
گورگوز : ۱۳۹
گوکجه سلطان قاجار — انظر غلام شاه
گیل گاوبره : ۱ ، ۱۳۴
گیلانشاه بن کیکاوس : ۱۴۱

ل

لهراسب بن حسین بن اسکندر : ۱۴۲
لیثم دیلمی : ۱۱۱
لیلی بن نعمان : ۱۴۰

م

مازیار بن قارن : ۱۵ ، ۳۴ ، ۴۵ ، ۵۲ ، ۶۹ ، ۱۳۴
ماکان بن کاکی : ۱۴۰
مالك بن الحارث الاشتر النخعی : ۱۳ ، ۳۳ ، ۳۴
مأمون [عبد الله] : ۳۳ ، ۳۴ ، ۱۳۰ ، ۱۳۴ ، ۱۳۷ ، ۱۵۹
مبارز الدّین (پادشاه) — انظر ارجاسف

المطيع بالله : ١٣٥
مثنّى بن حجّاج :
مجد الدّوله — انظر رستم
مجد الدّين — انظر دارا
مجد الدّين (ملاّ) مكّى : ٥٥
اقا محسن : ٤٣ع
محسن بن كاظم : ٣٥ع
محمّد برادر امام رضا : ٧٠
محمّد خان حاكم استراباد : ١٦٤
محمّد خان دادو سواد كوه : ١٥ ، ٥٣ ، ٦٣ ، ٦٦ ، ١٦٥
محمّد خان قوانلو : ٤٦ ، ١٦٥
محمّد شاة قاجار : ٤٦ ، ١٧ع
محمّد كاتبى ترشيزى : ١٦١
محمّد (اقا) خان قاجار : ١٢ ، ١٣ ، ٢٢ ، ٥٣ ، ٥٤ ، ٥٦ ، ٥٨ ، ٦٣ ، ٦٨ ، ٧٦ ، ٧٨ ، ٨٠ ، ١٦١ ، ١٦٤ ، ١٦٦ ، ٢٣ع ، ٤٣ع
محمّد (حاجّى) خان : ٦٨ع ، ٦٩ع
محمّد (حاجّى) : ٧٥ ، ٣٩ع
محمّد (حاجّى سلطان) ميرزا سيف الدّوله : ١٦٥
محمّد (سلطان) خدا بنده صفوى : ١٤٣
محمّد (سلطان جلال الدّين) خوارزمشاه : ٣٥
محمّد (سلطان) لاهجانى : ١٠٥
محمّد (سيّد) : ١٠٨
محمّد (سيّد) كيا دبير صالحانى : ١٠٩

محمّد (علاء الدّين) خوارزمشاه : ٣٥ ، ٥٣ ، ٩٠ ، ١٤٧
محمّد (كربلاى) بنّا : ٤٦ع
محمّد (ميرزا) خان سپهسالار : ١٦٥
محمّد (نصرت الدين) : ١٤٧
محمّد (سيد) بن ابراهيم : ١٠٨
محمّد (ابو على) بن احمد الحسن : ٣٥ ، ١٤٠
محمّد (ابو جعفر) بن احمد النّاصر : ١٤٠
محمّد (شمس الملوك) بن اردشير : ١٣٦
محمّد بن الاشعث : ١٣٦
محمّد بن اوس : ١٠٨
محمّد بن جعفر الصّادق : ٨٩
محمّد (سلطان) بن جهانگير : ١٤٦
محمّد بن الحنفيّه بن على : ٣٩
محمّد بن خالد : ١٣٧
محمّد (اقا) روزافزون بن رستم : ١٤٣
محمّد (ابوعبدالله) بن زيد — داعى الى الحقّ : ٥٢ ، ٩٠ ، ١١١ ، ١٣٩
محمّد (امير) بن سلطان شاه لاودى : ١٥٨
محمّد (شمس الملوك) بن شهريار : ١٣٦
محمّد (شمس الملوك) بن كيخسرو : ١٤٥
محمّد بن صعلوك : ١٣٨
محمّد بن العزيز : ١٣٨
محمّد بن عبد الله بن طاهر : ١٣٧
محمّد (غياث الدّين) بن جلال الدّين عبد الوهاب : ١٤٢

محمّد (سلطان) ذو القدر بن علاء الدّوله : ٧٤ ، ١٦٤ ، ٢٧ ع

محمّد (استاد) بن استاد علی الرّازی : ٤٧ ، ١٩ع ، ٢٠ ع

محمّد (سیّد) بن علی کیا : ٦ ع ، ٦١ ع

محمّد بن علی الحسینی : ٧ ع

محمّد بن علی زین العابدین : ٤١ ع

محمّد بن فضل : ١٤٧

محمّد (شمس الملوک) بن کیخسرو : ١٤٥

محمّد (سلطان) بن سلطان مراد : ١٤٣

محمّد بن مرتضی : ١٤٢ ، ١٥٩ ، ١٩ع

محمّد (سلطان) بن ملک : ١٣٠

محمّد بن موسی : ٣٤

محمّد بن موسی بن حفص : ١٣٧

محمّد بن موسی بن عبد الرّحمن : ١٣٧

محمّد (کارکیا سلطان) بن ناصر : ٦٠ ع ، ٦٢ ع

محمّد بن هارون : ١٣٨

محمّد (ابو جعفر) بن وندرین باوند : ١٠٢ ، ١٤٨

محمّد (استاد) بن یادگار ساروی : ٥٥ ع ، ٧١

محمّد (کارکیا) کیا بن یحیی : ١٤٩

محمّد (میرزا) باقر : ٧٥ ، ٤٠ ع

محمّد تقی : ١٧ ع ، ٤١ ع

محمّد تقی (میرزا) : ٧ ، ١٣٩

محمّد تقی بن یوسف دماوندی : ١٩ ع ، ١١٨

محمّد تقی خان اتابک : ١٥ ، ٣٤ ع

محمّد تقی خان ظهیر الدّوله : ١٦٥
محمّد حسن خان اعتماد السّلطنه : ٤٣ ، ١١٦ ، ١٤٤
محمّد حسن خان جلایر : ٨٣
محمّد حسن خان قاجار : ٤٦ ، ٥٣ ، ٦٣ ، ٦٥ ، ٧٢ ، ٨٠ ، ١٦١ ، ١٦٤ ، ١٦٥
محمّد (میر) حسین : ٤٦ ، ١٧ ع
محمّد حسین خان قاجار : ٧٤ ، ١٦٤ ، ٢٦ ع ، ٣٤ ع
محمّد رحیم خان بجنوردی : ١٦٥
محمّد رضا میرزا : ٦٥ ع
محمّد رضا (حاجی) : ٢٦ ع
محمّد زمان بیگ : ١٦٤
محمّد زمان خان عزّ الدّینلو : ١٦٥
محمّد شفیع (میرزا) : ١٥٢
محمّد شفیع (میرزا) میرزای عالمیان : ١٣٩
محمّد شریف (استاد) سنگ تراش : ٣٨ ع
محمّد صادق (حاجی) خان شامبیاتلو امیر توپخانه : ١٦٥
محمّد طاهر (سلطان) بن موسی کاظم : ١٥٩
محمّد علی (حاجی) : ٧٥ ، ٤١ ع
محمّد علی خان سردار انجم : ١٦٥
محمّد علی شاه قاجار : ٩٥ ، ٩٦
محمّد علی میرزا ملک آرا : ٥٥ ، ٥٦
محمّد قلی بیگ : ٦٩ ، ٥٣ ع
محمّد کاظم : ١١٨ ، ١٩ ع

محمّد مهدی : ۱۸ع
محمّد نصیر خان : ۱٦٥
محمّد ولی خان قاجار : ۱٦٥
محمّد ولی خان سردار : ۱٦٥
محمّد ولی خان تنکابنی نصر السّلطنه : ۱٦ ، ۱۹، ۲۰ ، ۲۲ ، ۲۳ ، ۹٤، ۱۰٦ ، ۱٦٥
محمّد یاد گار (استاد) بن حاجّی مسافر تبریزی : ۷ع
محمّد یارخان بن عبد الله یارخان : ۱٦٤
محمّد یارخان بن علیار بیگ : ۱٦٤
محمود (عماد الدّین) : ۱۳۹
محمود (استاد) حجّار قزوینی : ٦۱ع
محمود (میرزا جلال الدّین سلطان) : ۱٦٤
محمود (استاد) بن شهاب الدّین دروگر : ۱۱ع
محمود (سلطان) بن سلطان مراد — میرزا خان : ۱٤۳ ، ۱٤٤
محمود بن قطب الدّین : ٦۱ع
محمود بن یحیی بن خالد بن برمک : ۱۳۷
مراد (میر) بن سلطان محمود : ۱٤۳
مراد (میر سلطان) بن شاهی : ۱٤۳
مراد (میر) بن میرزا خان : ۱٤۲
مرتضی (سیّد) بن علی بن شمس الدّین : ٦٤ع
مرتضی (میر) بن علی بن شمس الدّین : ٥۸ ، ۲٤ع
مرتضی بن علی بن کمال الدّین : ۱٤۲ ، ۱٥۹ ، ۱۹ع
مرتضی بن کمال الدّین : ۱٤۲

مرتضی قلی خان پرناک : ١٦٤
مرتضی قلی خان قاجار : ١٦٦
مرداویج بن بسو : ١٣٨ ، ١٤١
مرداویج (تاج الملوك) بن علی : ٢٦
مرداویج (ابو الحجّاج) بن زیار : ١٤١
مرزبان بن رستم : ١٣٥
مرضیّه : ٧٣
مزدك : ١٤
مستنصر السّلطنه — انظر میرزا فرج الله خان
مستوفی قزوینی — انظر حمد الله
مسعود (سلطان) سلجوق : ١٦٦
مسعود بن حسینجان شیرازی : ٤٢ ع
مسعود (فخر الدّوله) بن محمّد : ١٤٧
مسعود (امیر) بن سلطان محمود غزنوی : ١٤١ ، ١٦٦
مسعودی : ١٦٤
مسلم (ابو) : ٩٢
مسمغان : ١٣١ ، ١٦٦
مسمغان ولاش — انظر ولاش
مصطفی خان : ١٦٥
مصطفی خان میرپنج : ١٦٥
مصطفی قلی خان : ١٦٥
مصقله بن هبیره شیبانی : ٨٨ ، ١٣٦ ، ١٥٤
مظفّر (خواجه سیف الدّوله والدّین) بن خواجه فخر الدّوله والدّین احمد

تبکجی : ۷٤، ۷٦، ۲۷ع، ٤۸ع، ۵۰ع
مظفّر (سیّد) بن سیّد حسین مرتضائی : ۱٤٤
مظفّر الدّین شاه : ٦۰
معاویه : ۱۳٦
معتزّ : ۱۳۷
معتصم : ۱۳۷
معتمد : ۱۳۸
معتمد الدّوله : ٦۵ع
معین الدّین : ۱٤٤
مفاخر الملك — انظر علی محمّد خان
مفلح : ۱۳۷
مقاتل : ۱۳۷
مقدّسی : ۲۷، ۳۵، ۵۱، ۵۲، ٦۷، ۷۲، ۸۰، ۸٤، ۸۸ — ۹۲
مقری (حاجّی) ابن حاجّی علی جرجانی : ۷۵، ۳۷ع
مقیم خان : ۱٦۵
ملك آرا — انظر عبّاس میرزا — محمّد قلی میرزا
ملك (شاه) آقا : ۷۲ع
ملکشاه سلجوقی . ۸۹
ملك محمّد قزوینی : ٦۸ع
منجّم باشی : ٦۵ع
منصور (خلیفه) : ۱۳٦، ۱۵۵
منصور (شاه) بن شاه ملك اقا : ۷۲ع
منوچهر : ۲۹، ۳۰، ۵۱، ۱۱۱، ۱۵۵، ۱۵۹

منوچهر مرزبان لارجان : ۱۱۵ ، ۱۴۷ ، ۱۶۶
منوچهر (حاجّی) خان : ۱۶۴
منوچهر (فلک المعالی ابو منصور) بن قابوس : ۱۴۱ ، ۱۶۱
منوچهری : ۱۶۱
منینی : ۹۰
مهدی بیگ خلعت بری : ۲۲
مهدی علوی : ۱۶۶
امیر مهدی قارنوند : ۱۴۷
مهدی خلیفه بن مأمون : ۳۳ ، ۱۳۷ ، ۱۵۵
مهدی خان بن محمّد خان دادو : ۱۶۶
مهدی (ابن) مامطیری : ۴۵
مهر بن ولاش : ۱۳۳
مهراب خان : ۱۶۴
مهرمردان بن سهراب : ۱۳۵
مهلّب بن ابی صفرا : ۱۳۶
موسی (امیر) خان : ۱۶۵
موسی بن حفص : ۱۳۷
موسی بن عیسی بن عبد الله : ۱۳۷
موسی بن یحیی بن خالد : ۱۳۷
موسی کاظم (امام) : ۳۸ ، ۷۳ ، ۴۱ ع
مؤمن (امیر) : ۱۳۸
المؤیّد بالله (ابو الحسین) عضد الدّوله بن حسین : ۲۵ ، ۵۳ ، ۱۲۱ ،
۱۳۲ ، ۱۴۰

مؤيّد الدّوله بويه : ۱۳۸
میربزرك — انظر قوام الدّین
میرفندرسکی : ۸۲
میرسیّد (کارکیا) بن کارکیا محمّد کیا : ۱۴۹
میرزا خان — انظر سلطان محمود
میرزای عالمیان — انظر میرزا محمّد شفیع
میرك دیو : ۱۴۴
میزان : ۵۴ ع

ن

نادر : ۱۲ ، ۵۳ ، ۶۳ ، ۷۲ ، ۷۴ ، ۸۷ ، ۱۶۱ ، ۱۶۴ ، ۲۶ ع
ناسر بن احمد شمید : ۲۲
ناصر علوی : ۱۶۶
ناصر (کارکیا) کیا بن محمّد : ۱۴۹ ، ۶۰ ع ، ۶۲ ع
ناصر الدّین شاه قاجار : ۷ ، ۱۵ ، ۶۰ ، ۶۱ ، ۸۵ ، ۸۶ ، ۱۵۷ ، ۶۶ ع
ناصر الکبیر — انظر حسن بن علی
النّاطق بالحقّ — انظر یحیی
نامدر (حاجّی) : ۳۸
نجم الدّوله — انظر قارن
نریمن : ۱۶۲
نصر بن احمد سامانی : ۱۶۰
نصر بن حسن بن فیروزان : ۱۳۸ ، ۱۴۰
نصر (شاه ابو) بن اسمعیل : ۷۴ ، ۲۸ ع

نصر (ابو) شقّی : ۱٤۹
نصر الله (استاد) : ۷۱ ، ٥٥ ع
نصر السّلطنه — انظر محمّد ولی خان تنکابنی
نصرت الدّین کبود جامه : ۱٤۷ ، ۱٤۸
نصرت الدّین — انظر رستم
نصرت الله میرزا امیرخان سردار : ۱٦٥
نصیر الدّوله — انظر رستم — شهریار
نصیر الکتّاب : ۸۳ ، ۹٦
نظام : ۷۱
نظام الملک : ۳۸
نظر خان زند : ٥٤ ، ٦۳ ، ۱٦٥
نظر علی خان : ۷٥ ، ۳٥ ع
نماور (فخر الدّوله) بن بیستون : ۱٤٥
نماور (فخر الدّوله شاه غازی) بن شهراکیم : ۱٤٥
نماور (فخر الدّوله) بن نصیر الدّوله شهریار : ۱٤٥
نوسال : ۱۳۹
نوشروان — انظر انوشروان
نیارک (استاد) : ٦۹ ، ٥٤ ع

ه

هادی (کیا بزرک داعی الی الحقّ) : ۱٦٦
هادی (سیّد) کیا بن امیرکیا : ۱٤۹
هادی خان بن مهدی خان تنکابنی : ۲۲

هادی بن هانی : ١٣٧
هاروسندان بن تیدا : ١٤٤
هارون (سیّد) : ١٤٤
هارون الرّشید : ٣٤ ، ٣٩ ، ٥٢ ، ١٣٠ ، ١٣٧
هارون (ابو طالب) الثّائر بن محمّد : ١٤٠
هاشم (سیّد) : ١٤٤
هاشم (میرزا) : ١٣٩
هاشم (سلطان) بن سلطان محمّد : ١٤٩
هدایت خان : ٢٢ ، ١٥٤ ، ٦٩ع
هرمزد کامه بن یزدان گرد : ١٤٦
هزاراسف بن شهرنوش : ٢٦ ، ١٤٥
هزاراسف (عزّ الدّوله) بن نماور : ١٤٥
هزارفنّ : ١٤٠
هژبر الدّین — انظر خرشید
هژبر خاقان — انظر قاسم خان
هشام (قاضی) : ٣٨
هندو (امیر) کا : ١٦٤
هولاکو : ١٣٩

و

وجیه الله میرزا سیف الملک امیر خان سردار : ١٦٥
وشتاسپ (کیا) جلال : ١٣٢ ، ١٤٢
وشمگیر (ابو طالب) بن زیار : ١٤١

وکیل الدّوله انگلیس در استراباد : ۹۹
ولاش (مسمغان) : ۱۳۳ ، ۱۴۶
ولاش : ۱۳۳ ، ۱۶۰
ولاش بن دازمهر : ۱۳۳
ولی خان تنکابنی : ۲۲
ولی (امیر) بن شیخ علی هندو : ۷۲ ، ۱۶۴
وندا امید بن شهریار : ۱۱۹
وندا هرمزد بن آلندا : ۱۲۱ ، ۱۳۰ ، ۱۳۴
وندا هرمزد بن سوخرا : ۱۳۴
موبد ویس : ۱۶۴

ی

یادگار (استاد) دروگر : ۱۱ع ، ۱۲ع
یار محمّد خان سهم الدّوله بجنوردی : ۱۶۵
یاسر بن احمد شمید : ۲۲
یاقوت : ۳۰ ، ۴۱ ، ۹۰ ، ۹۲ ، ۱۲۹ ، ۱۴۱ ، ۱۵۰
یحیي کرابی : ۱۶۴
یحیي (النّاطق بالحقّ ابو طالب) بن حسین : ۱۴۰
یحیي بن زید : ۹۲
یحیي بن عمر بن یحیي بن حسین : ۱۱
یحیي (سیّد) بن قوام الدّین : ۱۵۹
یحیي (کارکیا) کیا بن کارکیا محمّد کیا : ۱۴۹
یحیي بن مخناق : ۱۳۷

يحيى بن موسى كاظم : ۱۲ ع ، ۲۲ ع ، ۳۷ ع ، ۵۵
يحيى (شاه) بن سيّد ناصر كيا : ۱۰۵ ، ۱۴۹
يحيى (سيّد) كيا بن سيّد هادى كيا : ۱۴۹
يحيى بن يحيى : ۱۳۷
يزدان : ۱۵۵
يزدجرد (تاج الدّوله) بن شهريار بن اردشير : ۳۵ ، ۱۳۶
يزيد : ۳۶ ع ، ۴۱ ع
يزيد بن مرثد : ۱۳۷
يزيد بن مهلّب : ۵۱ ، ۷۲ ، ۸۹ ، ۱۳۶
يعقوب بن ليث : ۱۳۷
يوسف بن شكرى دربندى : ۷۵ ، ۴۲ ع

فهرست الاماکن والقبائل

ا

ابّاران : ٤١
آب انبارکش : ١٥٣
ابخمه : ١٢٩
ابدال ده : ١١٠
ابر : ٧٩ ، ٨٣
ابراهیم کوتی : ١٢٥
آبرنگ : ٦ ، ١٠٧
آبسرفت : ١١٣
آب سفید : ٣١
آبسکون : ١ ، ٨٥ ، ٨٨ ، ٩٠ ، ٩١ ،
١٣٨ ، ١٦٢
آب شور : ٩١
آ بکسر : ١٢١
آب گرم : ١٦ ، ١٨ ، ١٩ ، ١٠٧
آب گرم بزرک : ١٩
آبلو : ١٠١ ، ١٠٣
آبلور : ١٢٥
آبمال : ١٢٠ ، ١٥٩
آبّندان : ١٦٢
آبّندان سر : ١١٩
آبّندانک : ١٠٩
آبّندانکش : ١١٩
آبّندان کوه : ١١٠ ، ١١٥
ابن نوه : ١١٩
ابهی : ١١٤
ابو الحسن آباد : ١١٣ ، ١١٨
ابو الحسن کلا : ١٩ ع
ابیورد : ١٥٣
اتابای : ٨١ ، ٩٣ ، ٩٥ ، ٩٨ ، ٩٩
اتجان : ٤٣
اترابن : ١٥٩
اترپ : ١٢
اترپ کیله : ٦٢
اترک : ٧٢ ، ٨٠ ، ٨٨ ، ٩١ ،
٩٧ — ١٠١ ، ٣ع
اترک چال : ٨٠ ، ١٢٧
اترکلا : ١١٥
آتش کده : ٢١ ، ٢٣ ، ٢٤
اتک : ٨٠ ، ٨٥ ، ٩٣ ، ٩٧ ، ٩٩ ،
١٠٠

اتکرم : ۱۲۶
اتو : ۱۱٦
اتی کلا : ۱۲۲
اتینی : ۱۲۲
اجبار کلا : ۱۱۳
اجغ : ۸۰
اجورد : ۱۲۳
اجو رسر : ۱۲۱
آجی بیشه : ۱٦
اچ رستاق : ۵۷ ، ۱۲۳
اچه رود : ۱۸
آح : ٤۰
احا : ۱۱٤
احا کلا : ۱۱۳ ، ۱۱۹
احمد آباد : ۱۱۳ ، ۱۱۵ ، ۱۲٤
احمد چال : ۱۱۷
احمد چاله پی : ٤٤ ، ۱۱۸
احمد سرا : ۱۰۵
احمد کلا :
احیو : ۱۱۵
آخر : ۹۲
اخواند محلّه : ۱۸ ، ۱۰۵ ، ۱۰٦
اخونزی : ۱۱٤
اخی پیدرّه : ۱۱۰
اخی ناپلار : ۱۱۰
ادرستاق : ۱۲۲
آذر بیجان : ۱
ارامنه : ۱ ، ۱۳
اران : ۱۲۱ ، ۱۲۹
ارتا : ۱٦۵
ارته : ۵۰ ، ۱۲۲
ارجمند : ٤۰
ارچی : ۱۱۸ ، ۱۱۹
اردار سیره : ۱۲۳
اردبیل : ۸
اردشیر : ۷۳
اردشیر آباد : ۱۲۹
اردشیر محلّه : ۱۲٤
آرد کلا : ۱۱۸
اردل : ۱۲۹
اردلان : ۱۲
ارده رود : ۲۵
ارز : ۱۲۹
ارزگ : ۱۲٤
ارزلو حاجیّ کلا : ۱۱۹
ارزم : ۱۲۲

ارسم : ۱۲۳
ارسنجان : ۱۲۱
ارفه ده : ۱۱۵
ارفه رودبار : ۱۱۵
آرم : ۱۱۵ ، ۱۲۱ ، ۱۲۳
ارم : ۱۱۳
ارم خواست : ۲
ارمك اله رودبار : ۱۱۸
ارمك كلا : ۱۱۳
ارمنج : ۱۵۱
ارمنستان : ۱۵۰
ارميج كلا : ۱۱۷
ارميج كلا مرى : ۱۱۷
ارنس : ۱۱۵
آرنگه : ۲
ارود : ۱۰۷
اروس قلعه : ۱۶۰
ارى : ۱۱۷
اريم : ۱۱۵
ارينه دشت : ۱۱۳
اريه : ۱۵۳
آز : ۱۲۱
آزاد سفيد كوه : ۱۲٤
آزاد كلا : ۱۱۸
آزاد گله : ۵۸ ، ۱۲۰ ، ۲۳ ع
آزادگون : ۱۱۸
آزاد مان : ۱۱۲
آزاد محلّه : ۱۲۵
ازباران . ۱۱۲
ازدار سيره : ۱۲٤
ازدارك : ۱۲۱
ازدرّه : ۱۶۵
ازر بند : ۱۱۹
ازرت : ۱۲۳
ازرود : ٦ ، ۲٤ ، ۱۰٦ ، ۱۵۱
ازرود : ۱۱۵
ازن رود : ۱۱۵
ازن كوه : ۱۵۷
ازنوا : ٤۸
ازو : ۱۱٤
اساران : ۱۱٦
اساروپى : ۱۲۱
اسپاهى كلا : ۱۱۲
اسپ چر : ۱۲٦
اسپ چين : ٦ ، ۲۵ ، ۱۰۵ ، ۱۵۱ ، ۱۵٤

اسپرنجان : ۱۲۸
اسپ سمده : ۱۰۹
اسپنت : ۱۱۳
اسپنج : ۱۱۳
اسپنجاری : ۱۲۶
اسپهبد : ۳ ، ۵۱ ، ۵۲
اسپهبدان : ۳ ، ۵۲
اسپهبدیّه : ۱۳۵
اسپه روز — اسپه رود : ۶ ، ۲۶ ، ۱۵٤
اسپو : ۱۱۷
اسپوردشت : ۱۱۲
اسپو ریزی : ۱۲۲
اسپوکلا : ٤٤ ، ۱۱۸ ، ۱۲۰
اسپو محلّه : ۱۲۵
اسپ ونیزه : ۵۹ ، ۶۵ ، ۱۲۶ ، ۱۶۶
اسپیار بن : ٤٤ ، ۱۱۳
اسپی انجیل : ۶۱
اسپی آو : ۱۵۷
اسپی چشمه : ۱۱۶
اسپید جوی : ۱۵٤
اسپید دارستان : ۱۳۰
اسپی دز : ۸۶
اسپی روز — اسپی ریز : ۱۵٤
اسپی کلا : ۱۱۱
اسپی کلاجی : ۱۱۹
اسپی کوه : ۱۲۵
اسپیگر کلا : ۱۱۹
اسپیه بنه : ۱۵۳
اسپیه چن : ۱۵۳
اسپی واشی : ۱۲۲
استارا : ۳ع
استارم — استالم : ۵۷ ، ۱۲۳
استانک رود : ۱۰۹
استانه سرای : ۳۳
استا جنان : ۱۲۳
استرآباد — بلده : ۲ ، ۷ ، ۸ ، ۱۵ ، ۶۳ ، ۶۶ — ۸۱ ، ۸۵ — ۸۸ ، ۹۰ ، ۹۳ — ۹۷ ، ۹۹ — ۱۰۳ ، ۱۵۱ ، ۱۵۷ ، ۱۶۱ ، ۱۶۲ ، ۱۶۳ ، ۳ع ، ۵ع ، ۷ع ، ٤۷ ، ۲۵ع — ۵۲ع
استرآباد — ولایت : ۱ ، ۳ ، ۵۶ ، ۶۶ ، ۶۷ — ۸۵ ، ۱۰۵ ، ۱۲۵ — ۱۳۲ ، ۱۳۸ ، ۱٤۷ ، ۱۵۰ ، ۱۵۲ ، ۱۶۱ ، ۱۶٤ ،

۲۷ ع ، ۳۰ ع ، ۳۳ ع
استرآباد — خلیج : ۵ ، ۶۲ ، ۶۴ ،
۶۷ ، ۱۶۲
استرآباد رستاق : ۷۸ ، ۸۱ ، ۹۷ ،
۱۰۵ ، ۱۲۷ ، ۱۲۸
استرك : ۷۲
استره کوه : ۱۲۶
است میر محمّد : ۱۲۲
استندار : ۳ ، ۲۶ ، ۱٤٦ ، ۱۵۲
استنداریّه : ۳ ، ۲٦
استوج : ۱۰۷
استو روای کفشگر : ۱۲۳
استو روای گیل : ۱۲۳
استون آباد : ۷۹ ، ۱۲۵
استوناوند : ۱٤۰
استیله سر : ۱۲٤
استی محلّه : ۱۲۳
اسحاق — اسحاق صو : ۹۱ ، ۱٦۱
اسد آباد : ۱۲۲
اسرامیل : ۱٦۵
اسرم : ۵۹ ، ۱۱۹ ، ۱٦۵
اسری کلا : ۱۱۹
اسطلخ بجار : ۱۰٦
اسطلخ سر : ۲۳ ، ۱۰٦ ، ۱۲۱ ،
۱۲۳
اسفراءین : ۷۹ ، ۸۰
اسفرنجان : ۱۲۹
اسفندان : ۱۲۰
اسفندیار : ۱٦۵
اسفندیار محلّه : ۱۱۷ ، ۱۲۰
اسفندین : ۱۳ ، ۱۵۹
اسفنکلا : ۱۰۸
اسفی ورد : ۵٦ ، ۱۲۱
اسک : ٤۰ ، ۱۱٤
اسکار کلا : ۱۱۲
اسکم : ۵۹
اسکند آباد : ۵۸
اسکندر کلا : ۱۲۰
اسکنه ده : ۱۱۳ ، ۱۱۹
اسکنه کوه : ۱۰٦
اسکو محلّه : ۱۱۳
اسکی : ۳٦
اسل : ۱۱٦
اسل محلّه : ۱۰۷
اسمعیل کلا : ۱۲۰
اسمعیل محلّه : ۱۲۳

اسملی : ١٨ ، ٥٩

آسمیان : ١٢٨

اسه : ١١٥

اسولات : ١٠٧

آسیاب پیش : ١٢٢

آسیاب سر : ١٠٥ ، ١٠٦ ، ١٢٢

اسیر کلا : ١١٩

اسی ویشه : ١١٤

اشاغی باشی : ٨٦

اشتاد — اشتاد رستاق : ١٥٥

اشتاس : ١٢٦

اشتر : ٤١

اشرف : ٣ ، ٨ ، ١٠ ، ١٥ ، ٣٢ ،
٥٧ ، ٥٨ ، ٦٠ — ٦٥ ، ٦٧ ،
٦٨ ، ١٠٣ ، ١٠٥ ، ١٢٥ ،
١٦٠ ، ١٦١

اشرف محلّه : ١٢١

اشغانیان : ١٦٤

اشك : ٨٠ ، ١٦١

اشکر بن : ١٠٧

اشکرز : ٤٤

اشکور : ١٨ ، ٢٠ ، ٢١ ، ١٠٥ ،
١٤٠ ، ١٥٣

اشوراده : ٦٠ ، ٦١ ، ٦٧

اشیلادشت : ١٢٩

اصرم — انظر اسرم

اصغر آباد : ٦ ، ١٠٦

اصفهان : ٣١ ، ٤٣

اصفهان کلا : ١٢٧

اغوز بن : ٤٨

اغوز بن اسپو : ١٢٣

اغوز دار بن : ١٠٧

اغوز دار کلا : ١٠٧

اغوز دار کوتی : ١٠٦

اغوز درّه : ١٢٣

اغوز کلا : ١٠٦

اغوز گله : ١٢٤

افچه : ٣١

افرا : ١١٧

افرا باغ : ١٢٢

افرا بن : ١٥٩

افرا پل : ١٢١

افرا تخت : ١١٣

افرا چال : ١١٣ ، ١٢٤

افرا سرا : ١١٣

افرا سیاب کلا : ١١٠ ، ١١٧

افراکش : ۱۲۱
افرا کوتی : ۵۰ ، ۱۲۲
افراهمام : ۱۰٤
فراوه : ۹۲
افطلت : ۱۲۳
افغان : ۱۱ ، ۱۲ ، ٦۱ ، ٦۲
افنه سر : ۱۱٤
آق امام : ۱٦۳
اقا زمان : ۱۲۳
اقا سیّد نیکی : ۱۱۱
اقا سیّد قاسم : ۱۰۷
اقا محمّد : ۱۱۹
اقا محمّد آباد : ۱۲۸
اقا مشهد : ۱۲۱
اقا ملک : ٤٦
اقا ملک دلاور : ۱۱۷
آق اولر : ۸
اقری کل : ۹۱
اقزه کلام : ۸۵
آق قلعه : ۸۵ ، ۸٦ ، ۹۱ ، ۱٦۵
آق ناور : ۹۳
اقیره جار — اگیره جار : ۹۱ ، ۹۳
اکارجه : ۱۱۳
اکبدار : ۱۰۸
اکبر آباد : ۱۰٦
اکرتیج کلا : ۱۱۷
آکند : ۱۲۰ ، ۱۵۹
آکنه : ۱۰۵
اکوله سر : ۱۰٦
اگره : ۱۲۳ ، ۱۲۷
اگره سر : ۱۵۳
الارد : ۲ ، ۱۵۰ ، ۱۵۷
الارز بوم : ۱۲۳
الارز شوراب : ۱۲۳
الازد : ۱۵۰
الاشت : ٤۲ ، ۱۱٦
الامل : ۲۷ ، ۱۰۸
الامه سر : ۱۱۳
البرز : ۳ — ۷ ، ۲۱ ، ۷۸ ، ۷۹ ، ۱۵۸ ، ۱٦۱
البه کلی : ۹۱ ، ۹۳
البره : ۱۰۷
آلتپه : ٦٤ ، ۱۲۵
التین تخماق : ۹۹
الدرّه : ۱۰۹
الرب : ۱۱۳

الرم : ٤١
الرو ولرو : ٤١
الزم : ١١٤
الشا : ١١٨
الف کلا : ١٠٨
الکا محلّه : ١١٠
الکان : ١١٧
الله کرک : ٩٣
آب الله قلی : ٨٢
الم توت زار : ١١٣
آلمدر محلّه : ٤٤
المده : ١١٣ ، ١٥١
الم رود : ٦ ، ٣١
المشیر : ١٢١
المکانلی : ٩١
الموت : ٢٠ ، ٢٣ ، ١٦٦
المیر : ١٠٨
الند : ١٠٨
النگ : ١٢٥
اله چال کارد گر : ١١٧
اله رودبار : ١١٩
اله سر : ١٢٢
الوا : ١١٠
الوار : ٧٠ ، ١٢٥
آلوستان : ١٢٨
آلوکلا : ١٠٦ ، ١٢٧
آلوکنده : ١٢٠
الوندکیا : ٦٩ ، ٧٠ ، ١٦١
الیاس محلّه : ١٢٣
الیاس تپّه : ٩٧
الیانی : ١٣٠
الیس : ١١٤
الیشرود : ٣ ، ٦ ، ٢٦ ، ١٥٥
امام تقی تپّه : ٦١
امام رود : ٢٧ ، ١٠٨ ، ١٥٤
امام زاده ابراهیم : ٣٣ ، ٣٦ ، ٣٨ ، ٥٥ ، ١٢ ع
— ابو جواب : ٤٥ ، ٤٦ ، ١٩ ع
— ابن امام موسی : ١١٥
— ابو المعصوم : ١٥٨
— اسحق : ٧٣ ، ٣٩ ع
— اسندج : ٥٠
— اقا سیّد حسن : ٦٥
— اقا سیّد معصوم : ٣٢
— امام دادرس : ١٥٩
— بلند امام : ٥٨ ، ٦٥ ، ٢٥ ع

امام زاده بی بی آسیه خاتون : ۱۵۸
— بی بی حور : ۷۳
— بی بی سبز : ۷۳
— بی بی نور : ۷۳
— پنج تن : ۷۱
— پنجهٔ عبّاس علی : ۷۳
— پیر سلیمان : ۷۰ ع
— چهار امام : ۶۱
— چهار پادشاه : ۵۶ ع
— چهار شنبه : ۷۳ ، ۷۵
— حسن : ۱۱۶
— خواهر امام : ۶۶ ع
— داود : ۲۷
— دختر امام : ۶۵
— درویش عزیز الله : ۴۴
— دوشنبه : ۷۳
— دو قبران : ۱۲۸
— رکاب امیر : ۱۵۸
— رو بند برو : ۷۳
— روشناباد : ۷۰
— زین العابدین : ۵۱ ، ۵۵ ،
۲۱ ع
— سعید سر : ۵۵

امام زاده سفید : ۱۱۶
— سلطان محمّد طاهر : ۵۰ ، ۱۸ ع
— سه تن : ۳۸ ، ۱۴ ع
— شاه زاده حسین : ۵۵
— شاهزاده سلطان محمّد
رضا : ۵۵
— شاهزاده قاسم : ۷۳
— شاه غازی : ۵۵
— شزدان : ۵۹
— شهدا : ۱۵۸
— عبّاس : ۵۸ ، ۲۳ ع
— عبد الله : ۴۸ ، ۵۵ ، ۶۴ ،
۷۳ ، ۷۵ ، ۱۵۸ ، ۴۱ ع
— عیسی خندق : ۵۰
— فیلده رودبار : ۷۱ ع
— قاسم : ۵۵ ، ۱۵۸ ، ۵۳ ع
— قدمگاه خضر : ۷۳
— قوام الدّین : ۳۳ ، ۳۱ ، ۳۷
— محسن : ۷۳ ، ۳۵ ع
— محمّد : ۱۱۸
— محمود : ۱۵۸
— مراد بخش : ۷۳ ، ۷۵ ،
۳۸ ع

امام زاده معصوم: ۳۶، ۱۵۸، ۱۶۱

— ملاّ مجد الدّین: ۵۱، ۵۵

— میرسه روزه: ۵۵

— نکا: ۵۸، ۵۹، ۱۶۰، ۲۴ع

— نه تن: ۷۳

— نه گوران: ۱۶۱

— نوامام: ۱۱۸

— نور: ۷۳، ۷۵

— هاشم: ۴۰

— هفت تن: ۱۵۸

— یحیی: ۱۵۸، ۲۲ع

امجله پی: ۴۴

آمد خیل: ۱۲۶

امراب: ۱۱۴

امرانلو: ۱۳، ۶۵

امره: ۱۱۰

امروباو: ۸۰

امرو بلو: ۸۰

امری: ۱۲۱

امزی ده: ۱۰۹

آمل: ۲، ۳، ۷، ۸، ۱۴، ۱۵، ۲۱، ۲۷، ۳۰، ۳۲ — ۴۱، ۴۳، ۴۴، ۴۷، ۵۳، ۵۶، ۸۹، ۱۰۵، ۱۱۱ — ۱۱۵، ۱۱۸، ۱۱۹، ۱۲۹ — ۱۳۲، ۱۳۸ — ۱۴۰، ۱۴۲، ۱۴۴، ۱۴۸، ۱۵۰، ۱۵۱، ۱۵۳ — ۱۶۰، ۱۶۵، ۱۶۶

آملی: ۳۶

امّ مهانکک: ۴۱

امیچ کلا: ۲۵، ۱۰۶

امیدوارکوه: ۲

امیرآباد: ۶۱، ۸۵، ۱۰۶، ۱۰۹، ۱۲۷

امیرده: ۱۱۷، ۱۲۷

امیررود: ۶، ۲۸

امیرکا: ۱۳۳، ۱۴۶، ۱۵۲

امیره کوه: ۲

امیره منکاس: ۱۱۰، ۱۱۱

امیری: ۴۰، ۱۱۴

امین آباد: ۱۰۶

امین اباد نیم مردان: ۱۶۲

انّاده: ۱۱۰

انارین: ۱۱۴

انارجار: ۱۱۰

انار ستان : ۱۲۹
انارم : ۱۱۵
انارما : ۱۲۳
انار مرز : ٤۸ ، ٤۹
انار مرزچل : ٦۱
انارور : ٦ ، ۲۹ ، ۱۰۹
انّاور : ٤۲
انتشار آباد : ۱۰٦
انجدان : ۳ ، ۱۱۵
انجی : ۱۱٤
انجیر : ۱۳۰
انجیره بن : ۱۹
انجیلاب : ۱۲۵
انجیلستان : ۱۲۲
انجیلو خیل : ۱۲۸
انچه پل : ۱۱۳
انچلی : ۹۱ ، ۹۳، ۹٤، ۹۹ ، ۱۰۰
اندرات : ۱۲۳
اندراچم : ۱۲۳
اندرود : ۱۲ ، ۱۳ ، ٤۹ ، ۱۱۹
اندرون تمیشه : ۳ ، ۱۵
اندرون تنگه : ۵۷
اندشیر آباد : ۱۲۷
اندع آباد : ۱۲۷
انده کلا : ۱۱۸
انده ور : ۱۱۹
اندین : ۱۲۳
انزان : ٦۱ ، ٦٤ ، ٦٦—٦۸ ، ۷۰ ، ۷۸ ، ۱۰۳ ، ۱۰۵ ، ۱۲۵
انزان پشت آب : ۵۷
انزان رستاق : ۷۸
انزان کوه : ۵۷ ، ۱۲۳
انزلی : ۵
انساران : ۱۱٦
انصاری محلّه : ۱۱۳
انکتار ودی : ۱۱۰
انکسی : ۱۱۳
انگاس : ۳۰ ، ۱۰۸
انگرود : ۱۱۱
انگشتر : ۱۱۳
انگل : ۱۰۸
انگه پام : ۱۲٤
انگه مار : ۱۱٤
انگوران : ۱۰۸
انند : ٤۳ ، ۱۱٦
انوش تنگه : ۱۲۷

انوشه داذن : ۱۲۹
آهار : ۱ ، ۲۷
اهل البیوتات : ۱٦٥
اهلم : ۳۲ ، ۱۱۲ ، ۱٥٥ ، ۱٥۸
اهلم رستاق : ٤۰ ، ۱۱۲
اهلم رود : ٦ ، ۳۱ ، ۳۲
اهلمه : ٦ ، ٤۷
آهنگر : ٦٦ ، ۷۰ ، ۱۱٦
آهنگر کلا : ۱۰۸ ، ۱۱۲ ، ۱۱۳ ، ۱۱۷ ، ۱۲۰ — ۱۲۳
آهنگر محلّه : ۱۲٤ ، ۱۲۷
آهن محلّه : ۱۱۲
آهودشت : ۱۱۰
آهو سرا : ۱۲۷
اواجن : ۱۲۹
اوارت : ۱۲٥
اوت : ۱۱٦
اوجابیت : ۱۰۸
اوجا نالار : ۱۱۷
اوجابن : ۷۱ ، ۸۰ ، ۱۱۷ ، ۱۲٦
اوجاتوک : ۱۲۷
سادات اوجاق : ۱۱۳
اوجاق سر : ۱۱۷
اوجا کلا : ۱۱۲ ، ۱۲۰
اوجی آباد : ۱۱۳
اوچکاده : ۱۱۱
آودرّه : ۱۰۳
اودروه رود : ۸۲
آودز : ۱۲۹
اودیه : ۱۲۹
اورار آباد : ۱٦٥
اوران : ۱۲٥
اورتشت : ۱۱۳
اورسوسی : ۱۱۱
اورشت : ۱۲۳
اورنگ : ٦ ، ۱٥٤
اورنگ کیله : ۲۷
اوز : ۱۱۱
اوزبک : ۱٥ ، ۸۰
اوز رود : ۳۲ ، ۱۱۱
اوز کلا : ۱۱۱
اوزینه : ۱۲۷
اوسرزین : ۱٦٥
آوسیا : ٦
آوسیارود : ۲۰ ، ۱٥۱ ، ۱٥۳
اوشان : ۲۷

اوشیان رود : ۱۸
اوشیب : ۱۱۸
اوصانلو : ۱۱ ، ۱۲ ، ۱۹
اوطاق سرا : ۱۰۹
اوطاق سرا چال : ۱۱٤
اوفر : ۱۳۲
اوگز : ۹۸
اولان مهان : ۱٤٦ ، ۱۵۲
اولند : ۱۲٤
اولنگ درّه : ۱۲۸
اولیت : ۱۲٤
اومار : ۱۱۹
آوه : ۱۱۹
اوهر : ۵۱
اویجان : ۵۱
اویجدان : ۱۰۷
اویر : ۱۰۸
اویل : ۱۰۹
ایتا : ۱۱۱
ایترجلو : ۱۲۹
ایجر : ۱۵۳
ایرا : ۱۱٤
ایرت بن : ۱۱٦
ایرائی : ۳٦
ایرن آباد : ۱۲۰
ایزد : ۱۰۸
ایساس : ۱۲۲
آیك سر : ۱۳۲
ایگدر : ۹۸ ، ۱۰۱
ایل : ۱۱۰
ایلال : ۱۲۲ ، ۱٤۸
ایلان گرگان : ۱۲۸
ایلت : ۱۰۸
ایلغارتپّه : ۸۱
ایلغی : ۹۸
ایفی : ۱۰۵
ایمانآباد : ۱۱۸
ایمیر : ۸۲ ، ۹۸
این : ۱۰۸
ایوت : ۱۰۵
ایول : ۱۲٤
ایوه : ۱۱۱ ، ۱۲۱

ب

بابا بیگ کمانگر : ۱۱۷
باب الطّاق : ۹۰

باب الیهود : ۹۰

باب رودبار : ۱۰۶

بابل : ۶، ۴۴ — ۴۶، ۴۸، ۱۳۰، ۱۴۸

بابل پشت : ۱۱۶

بابلکان — خاصهٔ بابلکانی : ۱۱۸

سدات بابلکانی : ۱۶۰

بابل کنار : ۱۲۹

بابلور : ۱۲۰

بابوده : ۲۷، ۱۰۷

بابی ها : ۱۴

باج تپّه : ۸۵

بادله : ۵۸، ۱۲۳، ۱۶۳

بادله کوه : ۱۲۳

بادکوبه : ۱۰۴

بارفروش : ۳، ۷، ۸، ۱۰، ۱۳،
۱۹، ۳۳، ۴۲ — ۴۸، ۵۰،
۵۳، ۵۴، ۱۰۵، ۱۱۷ —
۱۱۹، ۱۴۲، ۱۵۰، ۱۵۱،
۱۵۷، ۱۵۸، ۱۴ع، ۱۸ع

بارفروش ده : ۴۵

بارکلا : ۱۲۴

بارکوتی : ۱۱۳

باریگک آب : ۱۲۶

باریکک آب سر : ۱۲۱

باریکک محلّه : ۱۱۲

بازار سر : ۱۰۷، ۱۱۰

بازارگاه : ۱۱۹

بازار محلّه : ۱۰۵، ۱۱۶

بازیار : ۱۱۸

بازیار کلا : ۱۱۳

بازیگر کلا : ۱۰۹

باشیر : ۱۲۹

باش یوزخه : ۹۱، ۹۴، ۱۰۰

باعو : ۴۴

باغبان کلا : ۱۱۰

باغبان محلّه : ۱۲۳

باغ چوپان : ۱۱۴

باغ شاه : ۴۵، ۵۵

باغشت : ۱۱۹

باغ گلبن : ۱۲۷

باغو : ۶۷ — ۶۹، ۱۲۵

باف چال : ۱۰۹

باقر آباد : ۱۲۵

باقر تنگه : ۴۸، ۱۱۶

باقلی آبندان : ۶۰

باکر محلّه : ۱۲۵

بلا برکلا : ۱۰۳
بالا بلوگ : ۴۸ ، ۱۱۷
بالا بند : ۱۹ ، ۲۵ ، ۱۲۴
بالا تجن : ۴۸ ، ۱۱۷
بالا جاده : ۷۰ ، ۱۲۵ ، ۱۲۶
بالا خانه سر : ۱۱۹
بالا را : ۱۶۵
بالا رستاق : ۵۷ ، ۱۲۳
بالاعین : ۱۲۹
بالا کلا : ۱۲۲ ، ۱۲۴
بالا کاوان : ۱۱۷
بالا لارجان : ۱۱۴
بالا لم : ۱۸
بالا محلّه : ۱۰۶
بالان : ۱۰۷
بالمان : ۱۳۱
بالو : ۱۰۹
بالو محلّه : ۱۲۰ ، ۱۲۱
بامر کلا : ۱۱۳
بامسر : ۱۵۷
باهین : ۱۵۷
بانصران : ۶۹
بانصر کلا : ۴۶ ، ۱۱۲ ، ۱۱۶
بانصری مشهد : ۱۵۹
بانعمان : ۱۲۵
بانوده : ۱۱۳
باو آویجان : ۵۱
باوج محلّه : ۱۰۵
آل باوند ۳۵ ، ۵۲ ، ۵۴ ، ۱۳۳ — ۱۳۶ ، ۱۴۶ ، ۱۴۸ ، ۱۵۲ ، ۱۵۹
بای : ۸۲
بایجان : ۴۰ ، ۱۱۴
بای کلا : ۱۲۰
آب باینل : ۱۰۰
بایه کلا : ۱۵۵
بجت : ۱۲۵
بجه کلا : ۱۱۳
بجلو : ۱۲۱
بجنورد : ۹۹ ، ۱۰۰ ، ۱۵۱ ، ۱۶۱ ، ۱۶۵
بچه چاله سر : ۱۲۱
بچه گرماب : ۱۹
بحر الارم : ۴۵
بختیار کوتی : ۱۱۳
آب بخشان : ۸۱
سادات بداب سری : ۱۲۵

بدراق : ٩٨
بدليس : ١٣٥
بديع خيل : ١٠٨
برار : ١٠٧
برارده : ١٢٠
براز : ١٢٩
بربر : ١٣ ، ٣٦ ، ٧٨
بُربُر : ١٢٧
بربری خيل : ١١٩
برد : ٥٧ ، ١٢٣ ، ١٦٣
بردم : ١٢٤
بردون : ١١٠
برج زردی : ٤٨
برج علی نقی : ٤٨
برج گوهر باران : ٤٨
برجنده : ١١٣
برج نكا : ٤٨
برزندی : ٦٥
برزو : ٦٤
برسمين : ١١٩
برسه : ١٠٧
برسو — انظر برزو
برشه بر : ٢٤ ، ١٠٦
برشی : ١٩ ، ١٠٥
برف آب پی : ١١٤
برفتان : ٨١ ، ١٢٨
بركار : ٥٧ ، ١٢٣
بركام : ١٦٢
بركان : ١٥٥
بركلا : ٦٥ ، ٧٩ ، ١٠٣
بركوه : ٥٩
برگير كلا — بارگير كلا : ١٢٤
برلور : ١٣٠
برمار ودبار : ١٢٣
برنا : ١٢٣
برناچی : ١١٠
برنجان : ١٢٩
برنجبين : ١٢٩
برنج يكی : ١٢٨
بروحه سر : ١٢٢
بروم : ١٢٤
بريا : ١١٥
بريجان : ١٢٢
بريشرود : ٦ ، ١٥١
برين : ١٢٩
بزرودپی : ١١٧

بزکوه : ١٥٧

بزمینا آباد : ١٢٠

بزمینان : ١١٣

بزنام : ١٢٤

بزوار : ١٥١

بژم : ١٥٧

بژم عبّاس کوتی : ١١٣

بژم موسی : ١٣١

بستان : ٤١

بستک : ٤١ ، ١١٤ ، ١١٥

بستم : ١٠٩

بسطام : ١ ، ٥٩ ، ٧٨ — ٨١ ، ٨٣،
٨٤ ، ٨٨

بسل کوه : ١٠٥

بسو : ٦٤

بسی سر : ١٢٨

بشل : ١٢٢

بصرا : ١١٨

بطاهر کلا : ١١٠

بکرآباد : ٨٩

بکنده : ١٣٠

بکّه : ٩٨

بلارک : ١٢٢

بلانجرک : ١٢٩

بلجه کان : ١٠٩

بلخ : ٣٣

بلخاس : ١٢٤

بلده — اشرف : ٦٤ ، ١٢٥

— آمل : ٤٠

— بارفروش : ٢١ ، ٢٤ ، ١٠٥،
١٥٣

— ساری : ٥٦ ، ١٢٠

— فرح آباد : ٤٩ ، ١١٩

— کجور : ٣٠ ، ١٠٨

— مشهد سر : ٤٦ ، ١١٦

— نور : ٣٢ ، ١١٠ ، ١١٥ ،
١٥٧

— هزارجریب دودانگه : ١٢٢

بلس : ١٠٧

بلسه بنه : ١٦

بلف کلا : ١١٩

بلم بران : ٥٩

بلند اجا : ٥٨

بلند امام : ٦٥

بلند سفاله : ٧٩ ، ١٦٣

بلوچ — بلوچی : ١١ ، ١٢ ، ٧٦ ، ٧٨

بلويج : ١١٠
بليسه : ١٧
بمتو : ١١٩
بنافت : ٥٧
بنجاكل : ٦ ، ٣١
بندارخيل : ١٢١
بندار كلا — بنداره كلا : ١١٨ ، ١٣٠
بند امير : ٩٣ ، ٩٤
بندايمير : ٨٢
بندبن : ١٠٤
بندپى : ٢٨ ، ٣٠ ، ٤٢ ، ٤٨ ، ١٠٩ ، ١١٠ ، ١١٧ ، ١١٨ ، ١٥٠
بند خوى : ١١٨
بندر : ١٠٩
بندر گز : ٥٨ ، ٦٦ ، ٦٨ ، ٧٢ ، ٧٩ ، ٩٨ ، ١٠٣ ، ١٠٤ ، ١٢٥
بند قرفه : ١١٤
بند نرد : ١٢٦
بنده فروش : ١٢٢
بنفشه : ١٠٧
بنفشه تپّه : ١٢٥
بنفشه گون : ١٠٩
بنفه : ١١٢
بنكشى : ١٣ ، ٢٦
بن كلا — بن كلاته : ١١٦ ، ١٢٦
بنگر كلا : ١١٧
بنو ناجيّه : ١٥٧
بنى اسكندر : ١٤٤ ، ١٤٦
بنى كاوس : ١٤٤ ، ١٤٦
بنى كريمى : ٧٦
بنى هاشم : ١١٠
بهار سرا : ٢٨
بهارك : ١٢٦
بهرامان : ١٥٢
بهرام خان : ١٢٦
بهرام ده : ١٦٥
بهرام على كيله : ٦١ ، ٦٧
بهرام كلاده : ١٢٩
بهرستاق : ٤٠ ، ١١٤
بهستان : ١٢٠
بهلكه : ٨٧ ، ٩٨ ، ١٠١
بهمن آباد : ١١٤
بهمنان : ١١٦
بهمن شيو : ١٦٦
بهنمير : ٤٨ ، ١١٦

بو الکلام : ١١٤
بوانه : ١٢٧
بوته ده : ١١١
بوته گران : ١١٣
بودوسرا : ١٢٦
بورا : ١١٧
بوراه‌سر : ١٠٥
بوران : ٣٥
بوران کلا : ١١٣
بوردتان : ١٠٧
بوره خیل : ١٢١
بوره سر : ١٠٨
بورود : ١٠٨
بوسته مین : ١٢٦
بوعلی : ٦٦
بون : ١٠٩
بون ده : ١١٢
آل بویه : ٤١ ، ٧٢ ، ٨٠ ، ١٣٣ ، ١٣٨
بیابان شلیب : ١٣٢
بی بالان : ١٠٦
بی بی شروان : ٨٧
بیجا : ١١٨
بیج کلا : ١٢١
بیجنو : ١٠٨
بیجوری : ١٢٩
بیجی کلا : ١١٨
بیخبن : ١٢٥
بیدار : ١١٣
بیدر : ١٢٤
بیرام الم : ٩٩
بیرام شالی : ٩٨
بیرون بژم : ٢٧ ، ١٠٧
بیرون تمیشه : ٣ ، ١٥ ، ٦٩ ، ١٣١ ، ١٣٨ ، ١٤٧
کیای بیستون : ١٥٨
بیشه : ٤٨ ، ١١٨
بیشه بند : ١٢٣
بیشه بند معینی : ١٢٣
بیشه سر : ٤٨ ، ٥٦ ، ١١٦ ، ١٢٠
بیشه کلا : ١١٣ ، ١٢٢
بیکلا : ١١٧
بیگلری : ٨٢
بیم درّه : ١١٥ ، ١١٦
بین : ١٥٥
بینتاسی : ١٠٩

بینمد : ١١٢
بینه سونك : ١٢٢
بیه پیش : ٧ ، ١٤٩ ع

پ

پاتخت : ١٠٨
پاجی : ١٢٢
پادشاه قلیجه : ٤٩ ع
پادشاه میر کلا : ١١٩
جوب پادنگ رود : ٦ ، ٢٠
آل پادوسبان : ١٣٣ ، ١٤٤ ، ١٤٥
جبل پادوسبان : ٢
پارادیمه : ١١٢
پارچ : ١٢٣
پارسا : ١٢٣
پارسیان : ١٢٩ ، ١٦٢
پارسیان قانچی : ٧٩ ، ١٢٩
پارم : ١٢٥
پارود : ٤٤
پازوار : ٤٦ ، ١١٧
پازور : ١٣١
پاس : ٧٠
پاسگاه میر مرحوم : ١٣١
پاسند : ٦٥ ، ١٢٥ ، ١٦١
پاسنگ : ١٠٩
پاشا کلا : ١٠٩ ، ١١٢ ، ١١٣ ، ١٢١ ، ١٢٢
پاقلعه : ١٢٨
پالوجده : ١٠٩
پاوند : ١٢٥
پای تو : ١٢٣
پای دشت : ٢٦ ، ٣٣ ، ١٦٤
پای ده : ١٠٩
پائزبن : ١٢٦
پائزسر : ١٢٦
پایزه کوه : ٢
پای کلا : ١٠٨
پاین بند : ٢٥
پاین ده : ١٢٢
پاین رودپی : ١١٧
پاین سرا : ١١٠
پاین کلا : ١٢٢
پاین کوه : ١١٤
پاین لارجان ٤٠ ، ١١٤
پاین مازو : ١٥٣
پته : ١٠٦

پراه : ١٢٤
پرچوا : ١٢٤
پرچور : ١٠٦
پرچین ده : ١١٢
پرچینك : ١٢٠
پردسر : ١٠٦
پردمه : ١١٥
پردمه کلا : ١١٣
پرده کلا : ١٢٢
پرس : ١٦٢
پرسپ : ١٦٢
پرستاق : ١٣١
پرکنار : ١٢٢
پرمز : ١٠٧
پره سنگك : ١١٤
پره کوه : ١٢٣
پرور : ١٢٢
پروین : ١٢٠
پریجا کلا : ١٢٠
پریجان : ١١٦
پریچه : ١٦٥
پری کلا : ١١٩
پریم : ١٥٠
پریمك : ١٢٥
پسا کلا : ١١٦
پسپرس : ١٠٩
پس دا کوه : ٢٥
پسرك : ١٢٩ ، ١٦٢
پسکلایه : ١٠٧
پسند رود : ٦ ، ٢٤ ، ٢٥
پسنده : ١٠٦
پسنگیکا : ١١٥
پشت جوب : ١٠٦
پشت رودبار : ١٢٣
پشت کوه : ٥٧
پشت گردو کوه : ١٢٦
پشته : ١١٤
پشتهٔ ازرك دون : ٤٦
پشتو : ١٢٦
پشرت : ١٢٤
پشین کلا : ١٢٦
پکی باغ : ٢٥
پل بستل : ٤٣
پل خرده : ١٢٧
پل دختر : ٤٣
پل دوازده پاله : ٣٣ ، ٣٦ ، ٤٤

پل سفید : ٤٢ ، ٤٣
پل گردن : ١٢١
پل لیشام : ١١١
پل محمّد حسن خان : ٣٣ ، ٤٤
پل نکا : ٥٩ ، ١٦٠ ، ١٦٦
پلت کلا : ٦ ، ٢٤ ، ١٠٦
پلت کلا دنباله : ٦
پلت کوه : ١٠٨
پلر : ١٠٩
پلرم : ١٢٨
پلم کوتی : ١١٤
پلند : ١١٦
طایفهٔ پلنگ : ١٢٥ ، ١٢٨ ، ١٣١
پلنگ آباد : ١٠٦
پلنگان : ٥٨ ، ٦٠ ، ٦١
پلنگان اسطلخ . ٦١
پلنگ دروازه : ١١١
پلنگ رود : ٦ ، ١٩ ، ٢٦ ، ١٥١
پلنگ کلا : ١٠٦
پله سرا : ١٠٦
پلهم کوتی : ٦٤
پلور : ٢ ، ٥٨ ، ١١٤
پلور : ٤١ ، ٤٢ ، ١٥٧
پلور محلّه : ١٢٤
پلورود : ١٧ ، ١٨
پلوریّه : ١١٠
پلیم دشت : ١٥٣
پنبه چولی : ١٣ ، ١٢٠
پنبه زرکوتی : ١٢٠
پنجاب : ٤٠ ، ١١٤ ، ١٥٧
پنج امام : ٧٤ ، ٢٩ع ، ٥٥ع
پنجاه هزار : ٦٩ ، ١٢٥ ، ١٣١ ، ١٦٠ ، ١٦٥
پنج تن : ٣٩
پنج رستاق : ٣٠
پنجك رستاق : ٣٠ ، ١٠٩
پنج هزار : ٦٢ ، ٦٤ ، ١٢٥
پهپشت : ١٢٣
پهدر رود : ٦ ، ٢٠
پهمه ور : ١٢٢
پهن آب : ١٢١
پهن کلا : ١٢٠ ، ١٢١
پوده : ١٠٦
پورندان : ٢١
پوستکلا : ١١٧
پولادکلا : ١٢١

پولاد محلّه : ١٢٦
پیازك : ٤١
پیازمرکر : ٤٢
پیازه چال : ١٠٨
پیترود : ٤٨ ، ٤٩
پیته نو : ١٢٣
پیج ده : ١١١
پیچا کلا : ١٢٢
پیچاك محلّه : ٧٩ ، ١٢٧ ، ١٢٨
پیچه بن : ١٠٧
پیچه کلا : ١٢٠
پیچه لو : ١٠٨
پیرجه : ٥٧ ، ١٢٤
پیرده : ١٠٨
پیر کلا : ١٢٥
پیرگردوکوه : ١٣١
پیرنعیم : ١١٦
پیش الوار : ١٠٨
پیش آهنگ : ١٢٧
پیش دا کوه : ٢٥ ، ١٠٢
پیش کوه : ١٥٣
پیشمبر : ٨ ، ١٠٨
پیل : ١١١
بیلکك : ١١٤
پیله دار بن : ١٠٧
پیمت : ٣١ ، ١٠٩
پینه ارم : ١١٦

ت

تابر : ١٢٨
تابکون : ١٢٦
تات : ٦٣ ، ٧٠
تاتار : ٨٢
تاج الدّوله : ١١٨
تاج الدّین محلّه : ١٢٠
تاجر خیل : ١٢٥
تاجیکك : ٧٨
تاجی کلا : ١٢٠
تاچکی : ١٠٩
تارسم : ١٢٣
تاریکك محلّه : ٢٠ ، ١٠٧
تاری محلّه : ١١٦
تازه آباد ٩٩ ، ١٠٥ ، ١٠٦ ، ١٠٩ ، ١٢٦
تازه آباد کلکك : ٦٠
تاش : ٥٧ ، ٦٤ ، ٦٥ ، ٧٩ ، ٨٠ ،

٨١، ١٢٦، ١٣١
تاکر. ١١١
تالار: ٦، ٤٢، ٤٣، ٤٨، ٤٩،
٥٠، ٥٦
تالارپشت: ١١٩
تالارپی: ٤٦، ١١٧
تب کلا: ١٠٨
تبکی: ١٥٢
تبونه: ١٥٩
تپر: ١٣٢
تپّه سرو: ١٢٧
تپّه مورندین: ١٢٢
تته رستاق: ٣٢، ١١١
تجر: ٧٩
تجری اسپ شورپی: ١١٨
تجن ـ تجین: ٦، ٤٨ — ٥٠،
٥٦ — ٥٨، ١٢٢، ١٥٩
تجن جار: ١١٣
تجن جارلارجان: ١١٣
تجن رود: ١٢١
تجن گوکه: ١٦، ٧٦ع
تجنك: ١١٢، ١١٩، ١٢٠
تخت بند: ١١٤

تخت خسرو: ١٢٨
— دیکا: ١٢٨
— رستم: ٥٩، ١٢٨
— سلیمان: ١٥٣، ١٦١
— عمر: ١٢٨
— میل: ١٢٧
تخشی محلّه: ١٢٦
ترازده: ١٢٢
تراکمه. ١٥، ٤٥، ٥٣، ٦٠، ٦٢،
٦٣، ٦٦، ٦٧، ٧٠، ٧٢، ٧٨ —
٨٣، ٨٥، ٨٦، ٩٣ — ١٠١،
١٠٣، ١٢٧، ١٦١، ١٦٣ — ١٦٥
تراگل: ١١٩
تربت حیدری: ١٥٥
ترخان: ١٥٢
ترخانی: ١٥٢
تردوینی: ١٦٦
ترس: ١١٩
ترسه: ١٢٩
ترسو: ٣٢، ١٠٨
ترسیاب: ١١٢
ترسی کلا: ١١٧، ١٢٢
ترك — اتراك: ١٢، ٧٠، ٧٦، ٨١

۸۳ ، ۹۰ ، ۱۳۲
ترك : ۱۲۴
ترك اسطلخ : ۶۱
ترکام : ۱۲۴
ترکما : ۱۲۶
ترك چال : ۱۲۷
ترك دشت : ۱۲۴
ترك ده : ۱۰۹
ترکران : ۱۱۴
ترکود : ۶ ، ۱۸ ، ۱۰۶
ترکستان : ۷۴ ، ۲۶ع
ترك کلا : ۱۱۳
ترك محلّه : ۴۴ ، ۱۱۹ ، ۱۲۴
ترك میدان : ۱۲۷
تره زر : ۱۱۱
ترنگ تپّه : ۱۲۷
ترنگ سر : ۱۵۳
تره : ۱۲۹ ، ۱۶۲
تره ومج : ۱۵۷
تروجن : ۶۲ ، ۱۲۵
تریچه : ۱۳۱ ، ۱۳۲ ، ۱۶۵
تزکلا : ۱۵۵
تسکا : ۱۰۹
تسکابن : ۱۱۴
تسی کلا : ۱۱۳
تفنگا : ۴۷ ، ۱۱۳ ، ۱۵۷
تقرتپّه : ۱۲۷
تقی آباد : ۱۲۳ ، ۱۲۷ ، ۱۲۹
تکله : ۱۰۷
تکمجان : ۲۱
تکیهٔ ابو محلّه : ۱۵۸
— ارباب : ۶۴
— آستانه : ۱۵۸
— اسکیها : ۳۶
— اعتماد دیوان : ۱۵۸
— اقا : ۶۵
— اقا سیّد ربیع : ۱۵۸
— انبارنو : ۱۵۹
— آهنگر کلا : ۱۵۸
— اوجابن : ۱۵۸
— باب باقر : ۱۵۸
— بازار محلّه : ۶۴
— باشی : ۶۴
— بیج ناجی : ۱۵۸
— بیرام تر : ۱۵۹
— بیسر تکیه : ۷۳ ، ۱۵۸ ، ۱۵۹

تکیهٔ پنا کلا : ۱۵۸
— چهار تکیه : ۱۵۹
— چهار شنبه پیش : ۱۵۸
— حاجی آباد : ۱۵۹
— حصیر فروشان : ۱۵۸
— دبّاغان : ۷۵ ، ۴۰ ع
— درب شهدا : ۱۵۸
— درویش خیل : ۱۵۸
— راضیهٔ کلا : ۱۵۸
— رودگر محلّه : ۱۵۸
— زرگرها : ۱۵۸
— سبزمیدان : ۱۵۸
— سر حمّام : ۱۵۸
— سر دروازهٔ استرآباد : ۱۵۹
— سیّد جلال : ۱۵۸
— شاه زنگی : ۱۵۸
— شاه غازی بن : ۱۵۹
— شپش کوشان : ۱۵۹
— شکرآباد : ۱۵۹
— شمشیر گر محلّه : ۱۵۸
— طوق دار بن : ۱۵۸
— عبّاس خانی : ۱۵۹
— قتل گاه : ٦٤
تکیهٔ قرا کلا : ۱۵۸
— قصّاب کلا : ۱۵۸
— قوپچی : ٦۵
— گرجی : ٦٤
— گلشن : ۱۵۸
— لیلاک محلّه : ۱۵۸
— محلّه اصفهانی : ۱۵۹
— مراد بیک : ۱۵۸
— محمّد تقی خان : ۱۵۹
— ملاّ اقا بابا : ۱۵۹
— میرزا هادی : ۱۵۸
— میر مشهد : ۱۵۹
— ناصر خان : ٦٤
— نخیب کلا : ۱۵۸
— نعل بندان : ۱۵۹ ، ۳٦ع
— نفطی محله : ۱۵۸
— نو : ۱۵۹
— نو علم : ۱۵۸
تگلی قراصو : ۹۳
تلاجیم : ۱۲۲
تلارك : ۱۲۱
تلارم : ۱۲۳
تلبن — تولبین : ۷۹ ، ۱۲۹

تلم : ۱۰۶
تلما درّه : ۱۲۳
تلمه : ۱۶۳
تلمیار : ۱۲۸
تلنگ سرا : ۱۲۹
تله : ۱۱۵
تلو کلا : ۱۲۵ ، ۱۲۷
تلو کلاته : ۱۲٤ ، ۱۲۸
تلو کوتی : ۱۵۵
تلیان : ۱۰۶
تلیباغ : ۱۲۲
تلیکران : ۱۱۹
تلی کلا : ۱۲۲
تلیکه سر : ۳۲ ، ۱۱۲
تلیم : ۱۱۶
تلینو : ٦۵ ، ۱۱٤
تماجان : ٦٤ع
تمار : ۱۵۰
تمام : ۱۲۲
تمتمه کلا : ۱۱۹
تمر تاش خیل : ۱۲۶
تمسک : ۱۱۳
تمشان سر : ۱۱۲
تمشك تنگ : ۵۹
تمسکی دشت : ۱۳۲
تمل : ۱۰۵
تمنجاده : ۱۱۳
تمنگا — فرضهٔ تمنگا : ۱۱۳
تمنگا ده : ۱۱۳
تموش کلا : ۱۰۶
تمیجان : ۸
تمیجانه : ۲۰ ، ۱۰۷
تمیشه : ۳ ، ٦۷ ، ٦۹ ، ۸۸ ، ۱۰۲ ، ۱۳۳ ، ۱٤٦ ، ۱۵۰ ، ۱۵۵ ، ۱۵۷ ، ۱٦۵
تمیشه بانصران : ۱٦۱
تمیشه کوتی بانصران : ۱٦۱
تنبلا : ۱۲۲
تنپرست : ۱٦٦
تندرلی : ۹۳
تنشون : ۱۵۵
تنکا : ۱۵۳
تنکابن : ۳ ، ۱۲ — ۱۵ ، ۱۸ ، ۱۹ ، ۲۱ — ۲٤ ، ۲۷ ، ۳۰ ، ۱۰۵ — ۱۰۷ ، ۱۱۱ ، ۱۳۱ ، ۱۳۳ ، ۱۳۹ ، ۱٤۰ ، ۱٤۸ — ۱۵۰ ، ۱۵۳ ، ۱۵٤ ، ۱۵٦

تنگاو : ٤٢
تنگ درّه : ١٠٦
تنگران : ١٠٠
تنگراه : ١٦١
تنگ سرا : ١١٨
تنگ شمشیربر : ٥٩ ، ١٢٦
تنگ شوراب : ٥٩ ، ١٦٣
تنگ لودیان : ٦٥
تنگ واشی : ١٥٨
تنگهٔ چهل در : ٤٣
تنگهٔ مقیمی : ٦١
تهجان : ١٠٧
تنورکش : ١٥٣
تهارم : ١٢٠
آب تهرم : ٦ ، ٢٠
تهنه در : ١١٨
توابع : ٢١ ، ٢٤ ، ١٠٦ ، ١٠٧
توار : ٢٧ ، ١٠٨
توبن : ١٠٦
توجانب کلا : ١١١
توجی : ١٣١ ، ١٣٢ ، ١٤٢ ، ١٥٧
تودراو : ٥٦
تودی : ١٠٧

توران : ٣، ١٥، ٦٩، ٧٤، ١٢٨ ، ٢٦ع
توران چر : ١٣٢
تورودبار : ٥٩
توری : ٧٧
توسستان : ١٠٦
توسکابن : ٦١
توسکا چشمه : ١٢٤
توسکا رود : ٦٠
توسه : ١٢٣
توسه کلا : ١٠٧
توسه کلام : ١٠٧
توشکون : ٢٣ ، ١٠٧
توشن : ١٢٦ ، ١٢٧
توگل باغ : ١٧٦
تولت : ١٢٣
تولنده : ١١٢
توله سرابی نمد : ١١٣
تولی دشت : ١٥٣
توملج : ١٢٤
توی درّه : ١٠٨
تیاف : ١١٢
تیامه جان : ٦٤ع
تیران کلا : ١١٠

تیرتاش : ٦٥
تیرخانی : ۱۱۹
تیرکار : ٥۷ ، ۱۲٤
تیرکار کلا : ۱۲۱
تیرکلا : ۱۱۹
تیرم : ۲۰
تیرونشی کلا : ۱۱۹
تیس : ۱۳۰
تیغه زمین : ۱۲۹
تیل پرداب سر : ۲٤
تیل پرد سر: ٦، ۲٤، ۱۰۷، ۱۵۱، ۱۵٤
تیل رود سر: ٦ ، ۲٦ ، ۱۰٦، ۱۵۱
تیلك : ۱۲۲
تیل کنار : ۱۰٦
تیله بن : ۱۲۲
تیله وا : ۸۳ ، ۱٦۲
تیلوره سر : ۲٦
تیموری : ۱۳۳ ، ۱۳۹
تیموی لنگ : ۱۲۳
تینه : ۱۱۵

ث

ثورکلاته : ۱۲۷

ج

جابران : ۱٦۵
جاچرم : ۳ ، ۷ ، ۱۵، ۷۸ ، ۷۹
جاجرود : ٤۰ ، ۱۵۵
جاجگلی : ۱۲٦
جارچیان : ۱۲٤
جاری : ۱۱۸
جاشم : ۱۲۲
جاشم تنگسر : ۱۲۲
چال : ۱۵۳
جالدرّه : ۱۵۳
جامخانه : ۱۲۰
جامنو : ۱۲۲ ، ۱۳۱ ، ۱۳۲
جامه بازار : ۱۱۷
جانباز : ۱۵۸
جانگدار محلّه : ۱۱۲
سادات جبرائلی : ۱٤٤
جربست : ۱۳۰
جرجان : ۳۷ع
جرکان : ۱٦۲
جرکلباد . ۱۵، ۵۸ ، ٦۵ — ٦۸ ، ۷۸
جرین : ۱۲۷

جرین برین : ١٦٦
جرینده : ١٠٨
جزما : ١٠٧
جزین : ١١٢
جزیه سلامی خیل : ١٢١
جش : ١١٦
جشن : ١١٦
جص : ١٦٢
جعفرآباد : ٨٥ ، ١٢٦ ، ١٢٧
جعفر بای : ٧٠ ، ٩٣ ، ٩٦ ، ٩٨ ، ٩٩
جعفر کلا : ١١٣ ، ١٢٢
جفا کنده : ٦٦ — ٦٨ ، ١٢٥
کیای جلال : ٤٦ ، ٥٣ ، ١٣٣ ، ١٤١ ، ١٤٢
جلال ازرك : ٤٦ ، ٤٨ ، ١١٨
جلاین : ١٣٠
جلودار محلّه : ١١٨
جلیل کل : ١١١
جلین : ١٢٧
جلین برین : ٧٩
جماجان — جماجو : ٩٠
جمال الدّین کلا : ١٢٤
جمشید آباد : ٢٦ ، ١٠٦
جند : ١٣٠
جنده رودبار : ١٥٣
جنده کلی : ١٢٥
جنف کلا : ١١٩
جنگار : ١١٣
جنگدین : ٦٤
جنگل ده : ١٢٨
جنه : ١٦٠
جنید : ١١٧
جنی کلا : ١١٢
جهان آباد : ١٢٧
جهانبیگلو : ١٣ ، ١٥٩
جهانشاه : ٦٦
جهان نما : ٧٨ ، ٧٩ ، ١٠١ ، ١٠٣ ، ١٢٦ ، ١٦٣
جهنّم درّه : ١٣٠
جهینه : ٨٤ ، ١٣١
جوانگان : ١٦٢
جوب پشت : ١١٩
جوبار : ١٣ ، ٤٨
جوبر : ١٢٠
جوچار : ١١٥

جور بند : ١٩ ، ٢٥ ، ١٠٥
جور پشته : ١٣٠
جوردستان : ١٦٢
جورده : ١٨ ، ١٩
جور شحرد سعید آباد : ١٠٨ ، ١٦٥
جوركلا : ١١٠
جوزا كلا : ١١٣
جوزچال : ١٢٨
جوزستان : ١٣٠
جوغان : ١٦٢
جوكی : ٧٧
جولی خان : ١٢٦
جوی مهروان : ١٦٦
جوین : ٨٠
جیجال طوخانی : ١١٧
جیحون : ١٥٣
جیر بند : ٢٥ ، ١٠٥
جیسا : ١٠٦
جیل : ٦٠ع ، ٦٣ع

چ

چابك سر : ١٨
چات : ١٠١
چاتلی : ٩٩
چار : ١٠٩
چارتابن : ١٢١
چارمان : ١٦٠
چاروا : ٩٣ ، ٩٧ — ٩٩
آب چاروا : ١٠١
چاخانی : ١٥٣
چاخونی : ١٥٣
چاشم : ١٣١
چاكل : ٢١
چال : ١١١
چال باش : ١٦١
چال خانه : ١٢٦
چالش محلّه : ١٢٥
چالك : ٢٨ ، ١٠٩
چالكی : ١٢٥
چاله پل : ٦٢ ، ١٢٢
چاله زمین : ١٢٢
چاله سرا : ١٢٦
چاله كوه : ١٠٧
چالو : ٥٧ ، ١٢٣ ، ١٢٤
چالود : ١٢٢
چالوس : ٦ ، ٢١ ، ٢٧ ، ٣٠ ، ١٠٨ ،

١١١ ، ١٥٠ ، ١٥١ ، ١٥٤ ،
١٥٥
چالوسه رستاق : ٢٧
چاه سر : ١٢١ ، ١٥٤
چاه ويجن : ٢
چايجان : ١٨
چپی : ١٢٠
چپك رود : ٦ ، ١٣ ، ٤٢ ، ٤٨ ،
٤٩ ، ١٢٠ ، ١٦٥
چتم : ١٠٩
چرات : ٤٢ ، ١١٦
چراهر : ١٢٢
چرز : ١٠٦
چرسون : ١١٦
چرکت : ١٢٣
چرين ده : ١١٢
چشته هارون : ١١٥
چشمه : ١١٦
— آب : ٢٨
— بن : ١٢٣
— سر : ٦٠
— سفيد : ١٥٧
— شاه : ١١٥
چسمه على : ١٦٣
— كيله : ٦ ، ٢٠ ، ٢٤ ، ١٥١
چقّر : ١٢٥
آب چقّر بيگدلی : ١٠٠
چقلّی : ٨٢ ، ٩١
چکاده : ١٠٦
چکدلی : ٩٣
چکشلر : ٩٣ ، ٩٩
چکور : ١٢٨ ، ١٦٢
چگنی : ٧٧
چل : ١١١
چلاب : ١١٢
چلابی — كيای چلاو : ٣٥ ، ٤٠ ،
١٣٠ ، ١٣٤ ، ١٤١ ، ١٤٢
چلاو : ١٣٣ ، ١٣٤
چلچا : ٨٣
چلچليان : ٦٥ ، ٧٩ ، ١٣٠
چلکرود : ٦ ، ٣٠ ، ١٠٥ ، ١٥١
چلکی : ١٥٣
چلندر : ٢١ ، ٢٩ ، ٣٠ ، ١٠٩ ،
١٥٤ ، ١٥٥
چلوسر : ١٠٥
چلی : ١٢٨

چلین : ۱۲۹
طایفهٔ چلیندان : ۱۵۳
چمازان : ۱۱۹
چمازده : ۱۱۶ ، ۱۱۸ ، ۱۲٤
چمازدون کلا : ۱۱۸
چمازك : ۱۲۰
چماز کلا : ۱۱۳ ، ۱۱۹
چماز کوتی : ۱۲۰
چمان : ۱۲۰
چمستان : ۱۱۰
چمن دارا : ۱۲٦
چمن ساور : ۵۷ ، ۱۰۲
چمن قشلاق : ۱۲۹
چمنو : ۱۲۲ ، ۱٦۵
چمنی : ۱۲۹
چمه بن : ۱۱۲
چمور : ۹۳ ، ۹۷ ، ۹۹
چمور کوه : ۱۰۸
چنار بن : ۱۰۵ ، ۱۱۸ ، ۱۲۳ ، ۱۵٤
چنار بینی : ۱۲٤ ، ۱۲٦
چناشك : ۷۹ ، ۸۳ ، ۸٤ ، ۱۲۹ ، ۱۳۱ ، ۱٤۸ ، ۱٦۲
چندرسیت خیل : ۱۲٦
چندر محلّه : ۱۱۳
چندلا : ۱۱٦
چنس : ۱۰۷
چنگ میان : ۱۱۳
چنگور : ۱۱۹
چنیجان : ۱۷
چهار : ۱۱۹
چهار افرا : ۱۱۳
چهار امام : ٦۱ ، ٦۷ ، ۱٦۰
— باغ : ۵۷ ، ۷۹ ، ۱۲٦ ، ۱٦۳ ، ۵۰ع
— چنار : ۱۲۷
— خانه سر : ۱۷
— دانگه : ۵۱ ، ۵٦ ، ۵۷ ، ۱۲۳ ، ۱۲٤
— ده : ۵۸ ، ۵۹ ، ۷۰ ، ۷۹ ، ۱۰۲ ، ۱۲۵ ، ۱۲۷ ، ۱٦۳
— ده رودبار : ۱۲۲
— سو ۱۵٤
چهارمان : ۱٦۰
چه جاه : ۱۲۸
چهل برّه : ٤۱
چهل جای : ۱٦۲

چہل چشمہ : ۱۱۵
چہل گیسو : ۱۲۷ ، ۱۶۲
چو پلانی : ۱۲۷
چور رود : ۶
چورسر : ۱۹ ، ۲۰ ، ۱۰۵
چورن : ۱۰۹
چوری : ۱۱۳
چوسر محلّہ : ۱۱۳
چوکلا : ۱۲۰
چولی : ۱۲۲
چوماسان : ۱۵۵
چونی : ۹۳
چیرستان : ۱۲۶
چین پرچ : ۱۲۳
چینہ پل : ۱۲۴
چینو : ۱۲۸

ح

حاجیّ آباد : ۶۵، ۷۵ ، ۱۰۶، ۱۱۳، ۱۲۶ ، ۱۲۸ ، ۴۰ ع
حاجیّ باغ : ۶۶
حاجیّ بکندہ : ۱۶
حاجیّ دیلا : ۱۱۵
حاجیّ سعید کا نگر : ۱۱۷
حاجیّ عبد العظیم کا نگرہ : ۱۱۷
حاجیّ کلا : ۴۸ ، ۱۱۲ ، ۱۱۳، ۱۱۷ ، ۱۱۸ ، ۱۲۱
حاجیّ کلا کاردگر : ۱۱۸
حاجیّ لر : ۷۶ ، ۷۸ ، ۸۳ ، ۸۴ ، ۱۰۰ ، ۱۶۲
آب حاجیّ لر : ۱۰۰
حاجیّ محلّہ : ۲۴، ۱۲۵، ۱۵۱، ۱۵۴
حاجیّ یادار : ۱۲۷
حازمہ دز : ۱۳۰
حازمہ سر : ۱۳۰
حازمہ کوی : ۳۴
حبشہ بر : ۲۱ ، ۲۳ ، ۲۴ ، ۱۰۶
حبشی : ۷۰
حبیب آباد : ۲۸ ، ۱۰۶ ، ۱۰۹
حجاز : ۱۱
حچہ رود : ۶ ، ۲۷ ، ۱۵۱
حدّاد : ۱۱۰
حرمون : ۱۱۵
حرنداب : ۱۳۰
حسن آباد : ۲۴، ۲۸، ۱۰۶، ۱۰۹، ۱۲۲
نہر حسن آباد : ۶ ، ۳۱

حسن کلا : ۲۳
حسن کلایه : ۱۰۶
حسن کیف : ۱۰۸ ، ۱۵۵
حسنی : ۱۳۹ ، ۱۴۰
حسین آباد : ۷۱ ، ۱۰۹ ، ۱۲۲ ، ۱۲۵ ، ۱۲۹ ، ۱۵۳ ، ۵۵ ع
حسین آباد ملك : ۱۲۷
حسینی : ۷۰ ، ۱۳۹ ، ۱۴۰
حشواه : ۱۱۱
حلال حور محلّه : ۱۱۷
حلب : ۲۲
حلرم : ۱۲۳
حلمی : ۱۲۴
حلوای کلا : ۱۱۷
حمّام اشرف سلطان : ۳۶
— اقا عبّاسی : ۳۶
— رفیع خان یاور : ۳۶
— یوسف خان : ۳۶
حمزه کلا : ۴۶
حمید آباد : ۴۹ ، ۱۵۹
حنا : ۱۲۴
حوات : ۱۶۳
حورحاباد : ۱۶۲
حوض کوتی : ۲۱ ، ۲۹ ، ۱۰۹
حیدرآباد : ۸۰ ، ۱۰۵ ، ۱۲۵
حیدر خیل : ۱۲۶
حیدر کلا : ۴۸ ، ۱۱۸ ، ۱۱۹
حیدر محلّه : ۱۲۷
حیدریّه : ۱۱۰

خ

خاتون بارگاه : ۴۱
خاجکه سر : ۶ ، ۲۶ ، ۱۰۶
خاچك — خواج — خواجك : ۲۸ ، ۱۰۸
خارجی : ۱۳۱
خارکلا : ۱۲۸
خارمیان : ۱۲۰
خاره گت : ۱۲۳
خاریك : ۱۲۰
خاصه کلا : ۱۱۳
خاف : ۱۱۴
خاکستر دله : ۱۲۶
خالده سرای : ۳۳
خان ببین : ۸۲ ، ۱۲۸
خان دوز : ۱۲۸ ، ۱۶۳

خان دوشر : ١٢٩
خان عبّاسی : ١٢١
خانقاه : ٤٢ ، ١١٥
خانقاه پی : ٤٢ ، ١١٥
خان قلّی محلّه : ١٢٢
خانه بن : ١٥٣
خانه سری : ١٢٦
خانه کیان : ١٥٣
خانیان : ١٠٧
خجند : ١٥٣
خجیر کلا : ١١١
خداداد : ١١٠
خر : ١٦٢
خراب : ١٠٨
خراب ده : ١١٩ ، ١٦٣
خرابه سر : ١٠٥
خرابه شهر : ١٥ ، ٦٧ ، ٦٩ ، ٧٠ ، ١٢٥ ، ١٦١ ، ٥٣ع
خرابه مشهد : ١٢٥
خراسان : ٢ ، ٣٨ ، ٨٤ ، ٨٨ ، ٩٤ ، ١٣٧ ، ١٥٠ ، ١٥١ ، ١٦٤
خراطه کلایه : ٣٥
خرچنگ : ١٢٢
خرده مرد : ١١٩
خرسگلو : ١٢٧
خرسنگ : ١١٥
خرشید : ٥٩ ، ١١٨ ، ١٢٥
خرشید کلا : ٦٥ ، ٦٧ ، ١٢٥ ، ١٦١
خرطیر : ٩٢
خرقان : ١
خرکام : ١٢٤
خرک رود : ٦ ، ٢٦ ، ١٥١
خرکوران : ٦٢
خرکون : ١١٤
خرلاش : ١٥٢
خرما : ٦١
خرّم آباد : ١٦ ، ١٩ — ٢١ ، ٢٣ ، ٣٤ ، ١٠٧ ، ١٢٢ ، ١٢٩ ، ١٦٥
خرما رود : ٨٢ ، ٨٣ ، ٩١ ، ٩٢ ، ١٦٢ ، ١٦٣
خرمالو : ١٢٨ ، ١٦٤
خرمنده چال : ١١٦
خرمه زر : ١٣٠
خرنه : ١١٤
خرو : ١٢٨
خروس آباد : ١٢٦

خريد : ١٢٢

خريه : ١١٠

بحر جزر : ١ ، ٣ — ٦ ، ١٢ ، ١٣ ، ١٧ ، ٢١ ، ٢٤ ، ٢٦ ، ٢٨ ، ٣٠ ، ٣٢ ، ٤١ ، ٤٢ ، ٤٨ ، ٥٦ ، ٥٩ ، ٦٢ ، ٦٤ ، ٦٧ ، ٦٨ ، ٧٠ ، ٧٨ ، ٨٦ ، ٩٠ ، ٩١ ، ٩٣ ، ٩٧ ، ١٥٨ ، ١٦٠ ، ١٦٢

خسرو آباد : ١١١ ، ١٢٧

خسين كلا : ١١٩

خشاميان : ٢٦ ، ١٠٦

خشتستان : ١٢٤

خشتسر : ١١٢

خشكدرّه : ١٠٧

خشكبر : ١٠٦

خشكرو : ١١٩

خشكرود : ١٨ ، ٤١ ، ١٥٧

خشكرودبى : ١١٧

خشكسرى : ١٢٢

خشكسل : ١٥٣

خشكفل : ٦٩

خشكلات : ٦ ، ١٨ ، ٢٩

خشه چال : ١٥٣

خشواش : ١١٤

خضر : ١١٤

خطيب كلا : ١١٠ ، ١١٦

خطير : ١١١

خطير خيل : ٥٧

خطير كلا : ١١٧

خلابر : ٢٢

خلخالى محلّه : ١٠٥

خلرت : ١٢٤

خلعت برى : ٢١ ، ٢٢

خلعت پوشان : ٧١

خلك : ١٩

خلفا : ٨٠ ، ١٣٣ ، ١٣٦ — ١٣٨

خليج : ١١٣

خليل خيل : ١٦١

خليل كلا : ١١٦

خليل محلّه : ١٢٥

خمام رود : ١٦

خمير كنده : ١٢٠

خناز : ١١٦

خنر محلّه : ١٢٢

خنگک : ١٣١

خواج — خواجك : ٢٨
خوجه : ١٠٠
خواجه خضر : ٧١
خواجه كلا : ١١٦ ، ١٢٣
خواجه نفس : ٨٥ ، ٨٦ ، ٩١ ، ٩٣ ، ٩٤ ، ١٠٠
خواچك : ١٠٩
خوار : ٧
خوار زم : ٣٥ ، ٨٦ ، ٩٣ ، ١٤٧ ، ١٤٨ ، ١٦٢ ، ١٦٤
خوار زم شاهان : ١٣٣ ، ١٣٨
خواسته رود : ٤٩ ع
خوبان رزگاه : ١٠٧
خورت : ١٢٤
خور داوند : ١٤٦
خورد رو : ٤٩
خورده ايموقلى : ١٢٩
خوردون كلا : ١١٢ ، ١١٣
خورسفلى : ١٣٠
خورمه كلا : ١١٧
خوره : ٥٩
خوره تاوه رود : ١١٠
خوشاب : ١٢١
خوش امد : ١٢٦
خوش انگور : ٥٧
خوش رودبار : ١٢٤
خوشل : ١٠٩
خوش ييلاق : ٨٢ ، ١٢٨
خوليندر : ١٢٨
خوناچاه : ١٦
خيابان شاه عباس : ١ ، ٧ ، ٨ ، ١٧ ، ٤٣ ، ٤٩ ، ٥٠ ، ٥٨ ، ٦٢ ، ٦٤ ، ٦٩ ، ٧٠ ، ٧٩ ، ١٠٤ ، ١٢٠
خير آباد : ١١٨
خيرات : ٧٩ ، ١٢٧
خيرود : ٦ ، ٢٨ ، ١١٠ ، ١٥١
خيرود كنار : ٢٨ ، ٣٠ ، ١٠٩ ، ١٣١
خيره سر : ١٠٩
خيشان : ٧٠

د

دابو : ٤٠ ، ١١٢ ، ١١٣ ، ١١٦ ، ١٥٥
دابوان : ١٣٣ ، ١٣٤ ، ١٤٦ ، ١٥٢
دابقه ده : ١١٣
قصرداد قان : ١٠٢

دارا : ١٦٢
آب دارا : ١٦٠
داراب کلا : ٥٩، ١٢٠، ١٦٠
دارا رود : ١٦٠
دار الحکومهٔ استر آباد : ٤٣ع
دار الملك : ٧١
دار المومنین : ٧١
داران : ١٦٦
دارجار : ١١٠
دارجان : ١٠٧
دار رود : ١٦٠
دار کلا : ٢١، ٨٢، ١٠٧، ١٢٦، ١٢٨
دار کنار : ١١٠
دار کندان : ١١٠
دارموش کلا : ١٠٨
دارنا : ١١٢
داره سرا : ١٠٥
داز : ٩٣، ٩٨
داغ داغان اسطلح : ٦١
دا کوه : ٢٥، ١٠٧
دالستان : ١٢١
داماد کلا : ١٢٢
دامسر : ١٢٠
دامغان : ١، ٢٦، ٥٦، ١٣٠، ١٦٣
دانکوه : ١٢٨
دانیال : ٨، ١٠٦
داود کلا : ١١٨، ١٢٢
داود محلّه : ١٢٣
دای کلا : ١١٧
دبّاغ : ١٢٤
دبّاغ کل : ١٢٧
دج : ٢٢
دراران : ١١٣
درارکش : ١٠٧
درازده : ١١٠
دراز زمین : ١٠٨
دراز کلا : ١١٩
دراز گیسو : ٧٦
درازه بال کیله : ٦
دراسته : ١١٠
دران ده : ١١٣
در بند کولا : ١٢١
در بند شینوه : ١٦٦
در بیب : ١٢٢
در بیب شهاب الدّین : ١٢٤
درجور : ١٥٥

درخی : ١١٧
دردین : ١١٩
درزی : ٧٠
درزی ده : ١٠٧
درزی کلا : ١٠٩، ١١٧، ١٢٠، ١٢٤
درزی کلای اخوند : ١١٨
درزی کلای حاجّی نصیرا : ١١٨
درزی محلّه : ١١٩
درزین کلا : ١١٣، ١١٨
درکا : ٥٧، ١٢٣
درکاپی : ١١٣
درکا دشت : ١١٩
درکاس : ١١٤
درکاسر : ١٢١
درکلا رود : ١٦٦
درگاه : ٢١
درلبش : ٣٩
درم : ١٢٣
درمانترك : ١٢٤
درمه کلا : ١١٣
درّه پشتان : ١٢٠
درّه قدمگاه : ١٢٩
درّه گز : ١٢
درّه ملك سلیمان : ١٢٨
درّه و یه : ١٢٨
دروار : ١٢١، ١٢٢
دروازهٔ استرآباد : ٥٤
— بارفروش : ٣٦، ٥٤، ٥٥، ١٥٩
— بسطام : ٧٢، ٧٣، ٥٠ ع
— تلیکسر : ٣٦
— چهل دختران : ٥٤، ٧٢
— چهل در : ٥٤
— دریا : ٣٣
— دنکوان : ٧٣
— سبز مشهّد : ٧٢
— صید : ٥٢
— طهران : ٣٦
— فرح آباد : ٥٤
— فوجرد : ٧٢، ٧٣، ٨٥، ٩٤
— کوهستان : ٣٣، ٥٢
— گرگان : ٣٣، ٥٢، ٧٣
— گیلان : ٣٣، ٥٢
— لارجان : ٣٦
— مازندران : ٧٠، ٧٢، ٧٣
— ملاّ مجد الدّین : ٥٤

دروازهٔ نور : ٣٦
دروپی : ١٢٢
دروك : ١٢٣
درون کلا : ١١٨
درویش علم بازی : ١٢١
درویش محلّه : ١١٩
درویشه خاك : ٤٤ ، ١١٨
دریا پسته : ١٧ ، ١٠٦
دریاسر : ١٧ ، ١١٣ ، ١٥٣
دریسانك : ٢١
دریك : ١٢٠
درین : ١٢٠
دزا : ١٢١
دزآباد : ١١٧
دزادون : ١٢١
دزان : ١١٥
دزبن : ١٧
دزتنکا : ١٥٣
دزدارا : ١٦٠
دزدك : ١٠٩ ، ١٥١
دزدکه رود : ٦ ، ٢٨
دزدکه روی سر : ١٠٩
دزگاه : ١٢٧
دزگران : ١٠٧
دزمنوچهر : ٢٩
دزنی کنده : ٤٩ ، ١١٩
دسته : ١١٧
دشت : ٢٧ ، ١٠٧ ، ١٦١
دشت رباط : ١٥١
دشت سر : ٤٠ ، ١١٣ ، ١١٩
دشت کلا : ١٢٥
دشت میان : ١٢٢
دشت ناظر : ١٠٩
دشلی : ٨٤
دعوی سرا : ١٠٦
دلاباد : ١٦٢
دلارز : ١٢٥
دلاّك : ٧٠
دلم : ١٥٤
دلما : ٩١
دلوکلا : ١١٧ ، ١١٨
دلی چای : ٤١
دلیر : ٢٧ ، ١٠٨
دلیرگان : ١١١
دماوند : ٧ ، ٤١ ، ١٣٣ ، ١٥٠ ،
١٦٣

دمرو : ٢٨

دنجه کلا : ١٢٢

دنکلان : ٧٠ ، ١٢٥

دنکی : ١٢٢

دنگپایه : ١١٣

دنگسرك : ١٢٠

دنگله ده : ١٢٢

ده جولی : ١٢٩

ده چر : ١٠٧

ده درّه : ١٠٣

ده دو : ١٢٤

دهستان : ٣ ، ٨٥ ، ٨٨ ، ٩٢ ، ١٣٨ ، ١٥٠

ده سرا : ١١٢

ده فلول : ١١٥

دهك : ٤٦

ده گری : ١٠٩

ده ملاّ : ١١٩

ده میان : ١١٥

دهنهٔ تنگران : ١٠٠

دهنهٔ فارسیان وفیرنك : ١٠٠

آب دهنهٔ کتول : ٨١

دهنهٔ گرگان : ١٠٠ ، ١٦١

دهون : ١١٨

دوآب : ٤١ ، ٤٢ ، ٤٣ ، ١١٦ ، ١٦٥ ، ١٦٦

دوآبِ بالا : ٤٢ ، ١١٥

دوآب برزندی : ٦٥

دوتیره : ١١٣

دوجز : ١٢٩

دوجمان : ٦ ، ٢٧ ، ١٠٨

دوجی : ٨١ ، ٩٣ ، ٩٨

دوخر : ١٢٩

دودان : ١٣١

دودانگه : ٥١ ، ٥٦ ، ٥٧ ، ١٢٢ ، ١٢٤ ، ١٢٧

دودرجن : ١٢٩

دود محلّه : ١١٣

دوران : ١٥٣

دورانه سر : ١١٢ ، ١٢٥

دوراه اسطله : ١١٦

دورود محلّه : ١٢٥

دوروك : ١٢٩

دوز : ١١٠

دوزین : ١٠٠

دوست کوه : ١٧ ، ١٨

دوسگر : ١٠٨
دوغ الوم : ٩١
دوقبران : ١٢٧
دوك : ١٢١
قلعه دوك : ١١٢
دوكل : ١٢٤
دوكه بن : ١٢٦
دوگور : ١٥٣
دولادار : ١٥٤
دولار : ١٣٠
دولت آباد : ٥٣ ، ١٢١ ، ١٢٢ ، ١٢٧
دوله رودبار : ١١٧
دولّو : ٧٦
دومركلا : ١٢٢
دون : ١١٠ ، ١١٢
دونا : ١٠٨
دونج كلا : ١١٢
دونسر : ١١٧
دونك : ١٢٠
دونگا : ١١٣
دونگسى : ١٠٩
دوهزار : ١٩ ، ٢١ ، ٢٣ ، ١٠٧ ، ١١٢ ، ١٥٣
دويلات : ١١١
دياجم : ١٢٤
دياريان : ١٠٣
دى درّه : ١٢٦
ديدوان : ١٠٣
ديزان : ١٠٨
ديفرى : ١١٢
ديلارستاق — ديله رستاق : ٤٠ ، ١١٥
ديلم : ١ ، ١١ ، ٢٧ ، ٨٢ ، ١٣٢ ، ١٤٠ ، ١٥٠ ، ١٥٣ ، ١٦٦ ، ٦٠ع ، ٦٣ع ، ٧٣ع
ديلمان : ١٦ ، ٢٥ ، ١١٤ ، ١٢٩ ، ١٣٩ ، ١٤٠ ، ١٤٨ ، ١٦٦
ديلم رودبار : ١٢٤
ديلمستان : ١١٢
ديلى : ٧٧
ديم تپّه : ٤٩
ديم توران : ١٢٠
ديمرون : ١٠٥
ديمه : ١١٢
ديمو : ١٠٧
دينارجارى : ١

دینار کفشین : ٥١
دینار کوتی — دینار گوشی : ١٢١
دیناره جاری — دینار جای : ٣ ، ٨٠
دینان : ١١٤
دینه چال : ٤٨
دینه سر : ١٢٤
دیو : ١٣٣ ، ١٤٤
دیوا : ١١٧ ، ١٢٣
دیو بند کلا : ١١٩
کوه دیوتنگه : ٥٦
دیوچال : ١١٧ ، ١٢٠
دیودشت : ١١٩
دیودلا : ١١٨
قلعه دیو سفید : ٤٣
دیوسیاه : ٤١
دیوشل : ١٧
دیو کلا : ١١٢ ، ١٢٠ ، ١٢١
دیو کوتی : ١٢٠
دیولیلم : ١١٦

ذ

ذاغ رود : ٤٢
ذاغ مرز : ١٢ ، ٢٢ ، ٤٨ ، ٥٨ ، ٦٠ ، ٦١ ، ١٦٠
ذکیر کلا : ١٢٤

ر

رابر : ١٥٣
رادکان : ٥٩ ، ٦٤—٦٦ ، ٧٩ ، ٩٣ ، ١٠١—١٠٣ ، ١٢٦ ، ١٤٨
رازی : ١٢٠
راست آب پی : ٤٢ ، ١١٥
راست آب کوچک : ٤٢
راست پی : ٤٢ ، ٤٣
راست کوی : ٣٤ ، ٣٥
راش : ١٥٣
رامیان : ٧٩ ، ٨٢ ، ٨٥ ، ١٢٨ ، ١٦١
ران : ٦٥ ، ١٢٥
رانکوه : ٢ ، ٨ ، ١٧ ، ١٠٦ ، ١٥٠ ، ١٦٥ ، ٦٢ع ، ٦٤ع
رانوس : ١٠٩
رانوس رستاق : ٣٠ ، ١٠٩
راه پشته : ١٥١ ، ١٥٤
راه دارخانه : ١٢١

رباط : ٦٤ ، ١٢٥
الرباط : ٩٢
رباط ابن طاهر : ٩٢
— ابو العبّاس : ٩٢
— تاش : ٦٥
— تجر : ٧٩
رباط حفض : ٨٠ ، ١٥٧
— سفید : ٩٦ ، ١٢٦
— عشق : ٨ ، ١٥١
— قرابل : ٨ ، ١٥١
— قزلق : ٧٩ ، ١٦٣
— گزینی : ٩٢
— مقسی : ١٠٣
رباطو : ١٢٨
رباط وزاره : ٨٠
ربیع کلاته : ١٢٧
رجبلی : ٨٢
رجه : ١١٥
رجو : ١٠٧
رچه کلا : ١١٣
رح کلا : ١١٤
ردا کلا :
رزان : ١١١ ، ١٠٧
رزپت : ١٠٥
رزدکه : ١١٣
رزکی بسته : ١١٣
رزه کنار : ١١٨
رزی : ١٢٨
رستم حاجّی علی : ١١٧
رستمدار : ١—٣ ، ١٤ ، ٢٢ ، ٢٦ ، ٢٨ ، ٣٠ ، ١٠٨ ، ١١١ ، ١١٢ ، ١٣٠ ، ١٣٢ ، ١٣٩ ، ١٤٢ ، ١٤٤ ، ١٤٥ ، ١٥٠ ، ١٥٢ ، ١٥٥
رستمدار کلا : ١٢٢
رستم رود : ٦ ، ٣١ ، ١١١ ، ١٥٥
رستم زمان کفشگر : ١١٧
رستم کلا : ٦٢ ، ١٢٥
رستم کلای سادات : ١٢٧
رستم کلای عبّاس بیگ : ١٢٧
رسگت : ١٢٤
رسو : ٥٩
رسول : ١٢٦
رسول آباد : ١٢٦
رسوم رودبار : ١٢٢
رسیا : ١١٦

رشت : ٨، ١٦، ٢٢، ٢٣، ٩٩، ٣ع، ٦٥ع—٦٧ع، ٦٩ع، ٨٠ع

رشت آباد : ١٦

رشتی : ٧٠

رشین : ١٦٢

رضا کلا : ١١٧، ١١٨

رضا محلّه : ١٠٥

سادات رضی الدّینی : ١٤٤

رضی محلّه : ١٨، ١٠٦

رضیّه کلا : ١١٩

رعیت خیل : ١٢٥

رفیع آباد : ١٠٥

رکاب دار کلا : ١٢١

رکاپشته : ١٠٦

رکاج کلا : ١١٨

رکاوند : ١٢٥، ١٦١

رکن : ١١٨

رکن دشت : ١٢١

رکن کلا : ١٢١

رمدان — خاصهٔ رمدانی : ٥٧

رمدان خیل : ١٢٥

رمك : ٦، ١٩، ١٠٦، ١٥١

رمنت : ١١٨

رنگریز : ١١٨

ره کلا : ١١٩

روا : ١٦٥

رواپرنده : ١١٣

روارکلا : ١١٩

روار محلّه : ١٠٦

جبل روبنج : ٢

روجینه : ١٠٧

رودبار : ٢١، ١٢٣، ١٢٤، ١٢٩، ١٣٠، ١٦٥، ٦٤ع

رودبار اعلی : ١٢٣

رودبار الموت : ١٩

— پیچ : ١٣١

— دشت : ١١٣

— سفلی : ٣٢، ١١١

— علیا : ٣٢، ١١١

رودبارك : ١٠٨، ١١٠، ١٢٢

رودبار کش : ١١٣

رود بارکنار : ١٠٥

رودبارکی : ١٠٦

رودباری : ٢٢

رودپشت : ٤٦، ١٠٦، ١٠٧، ١١٣، ١١٧، ١١٨، ١٢١

رودپشت پایینی : ١٢١
رودپی : ٤٩ ، ١٢٠
رودخانه : ١٠٦
رودسر : ٨ ، ١٦ ، ١٧ ، ١٦٦ ، ٦٤ ع
رودعه : ٦ ، ١٩
رودکش : ١١٣
رودگر : ٦٦
آل روزافزون : ١٣٣ ، ١٤٣
روزکی : ٢٣
روزکیاده : ١٢٤
روس : ١٦٣
روسها : ٥٢ ، ٦٧ ، ١٦٠ ، ١٦١
روسیه : ١٠ ، ٩٨ ، ١٠٠ ، ٣ ع
روشن آب : ١٢٢
روشن آباد : ٦٧ ، ٧٠ ، ٧١ ، ١١٩ ،
١٢٦ ، ٥٤ ع
روشناخره : ٩٠
روشنائی محلّه : ١٢٨
روشندون : ٤٨ ، ١١٦
روشن کلا : ١٢٧
روعد — روغد : ٨٤ ، ١٥٠
روك : ١٦٢
روکتم : ١٢٤
رونج کلا : ١١٠
روهین : ١٣١ ، ١٤٨
رویان : ١٤ ، ٣٠ ، ١٠٨ ، ١١٠ ،
١١١ ، ١٣٣ ، ١٤٤ ، ١٤٧ ،
١٤٨ ، ١٥٠ ، ١٥٤
روین — روئین : ١٣١ ، ١٦٢
ری : ١ ، ٢ ، ٤١ ، ٨٩ ، ١٣١ ،
١٣٢ ، ١٥٢ — ١٥٤ ، ١٥٧
ریتو : ١٢٦
ریزاو : ١٢٦
ریزسرده : ١٢٤
ریزوشم : ١٢٣
ریک : ٨
ریکنده : ١٢٠
ریگ چشمه : ١٢٨
رینه : ٤٠ ، ١١٤
رینهٔی : ٣٦

ز

زابلستان : ٥١
زارم رود : ٥٨ ، ١٢٤
زارم رودی : ٧٠
زاغ ده : ١١٤

زاغ رود — انظر ذاغ رود
زاغ سرا : ۱۵۶
زاغ مرز — انظر ذاغ مرز
زاهد : ۷۰
زاهد کلا : ۱۱۸
زاهد محلّه : ۱۲۲
زایگان : ۱۳۲
زاینده رود : ۱۶۰
زبج : ۱۶۲
زبله : ۱۶۳
زرا محلّه : ۱۶۶
زرداب : ۱۱۳
زرد سر : ۱۵۳
زرد کمر : ۱۱۱
زرد کیله : ٦
زردل : ۱۱۵
زرده بان : ۱۱۵
زرده کوه : ۱۵۷
زردوا : ۸۳ ، ۱٦٤
زردوان : ۱٦۳
زردی : ۱٦۰
زردی چال : ۱۲۱
زرزمین : ۱۱۵

زرشک چال : ۱۰۳ ، ۱۲٦
زرشك خونی : ۱۰۳!
زرشوران : ۱۱۷
زرکیا : ۱۱۰
زرگر : ۱۱۷
زرگران : ۱۲۷
زرگرباغ : ۱۲۰
زرمش کوه : ۱۲۸
آل زرمهر : ۱۳۳ ، ۱٤٦
زرمی خواست : ۱۳۱
زرو : ۱۵۳
زروجان : ۱۲۱
زرّین آباد : ۱۲۳
— بالا : ۱۲۱
زرّین ده : ۱۲۲
زرّین کلا : ٤۹ ، ۱۰۹ ، ۱۲۰
زرّین کلاته : ۱۲۹
زرّین گل : ۸۱ ، ۸۲ ، ۱۲۸
زغال چال — ذغال چال : ۵۸ ، ۱۲۰
زاکوار : ۱۲٦
زکین محلّه : ۱۰٦
زلان کوتی چل : ٦۱
زلم : ۱۵۳

زله بان : ۱۲۷
زمین جوب : ۶ ، ۲۰
زمین کین : ۲۳ ، ۱۰۷
زن بینی : ۱۲٤
زند : ۵۳ ، ٦۲
زندان چال : ۱۲۹
زندانه کوی : ۳۹
زندرستاق : ۳۰ ، ۱۰۹
زنکیان : ۱۱٦
زنگت : ۱۲۳
زنگی : ۷۰
— شاه محلّه : ۱۰۵
— کلا : ۱۱۳
— کلاته : ۱۳۲
— محلّه : ۷۱ ، ۷۸ ، ۱۲٦
زوات : ۱۰۸
زوار : ۲۱ ، ۲۵ ، ۱۰٦
زوارده : ۱۱۷
زوار کیله : ۱۵۰ ، ۱۵٤
زوار محلّه : ۱۲۲
زوین : ۱٦۲
زیادی : ۲۱
زیادلو : ۷٦
آل زیار : ۷۲ ، ۸۰ ، ۱٤۰
زیار : ٤۲ ، ۱۱٤ ، ۱۳۳
زیارت : ۷ ، ۹ ، ۸۱ ، ۱۲۷ ، ۱۲۸ ، ۱٦۳
زیارت بر : ۱۰٦
زیارت خواسته رود : ۷٦ ، ۱۲۸
زیارت خاسه رود : ۱۲۷
زیارت سیّد محمّد کیاد بیرصالحانی : ۱۰۸
زیارت کلا : ۱۲٤
زیارت میروزان : ۱۳۱
زیت — زید : ۱۳ ، ۱۲۰
زیراب : ٤۲ ، ٤۳ ، ۱۱٦
زیرانی : ۷۷
زیر بند سهل پل : ۱۲۳
زیر مارکوه : ۱۹ ، ۱۰٦
زیروان : ٦۲ ، ۱۲۵ ، ۱٦۵
زیکش : ٤۹
زیله : ۱۲۸
زیمشاه : ۱۲۹
زینوان : ۱۳۲
زینوند : ٦۱

س

سابق محلّه : ۱۲٤

سادات : ۱، ۱۱، ٦٦ ، ۷۰ ، ۷۱،
۷٦ ، ۸۲
سادات محلّه : ۲۱ ، ۱۰٦ ، ۱۰۷ ،
۱۱۷
سارستان : ۱۵۰
سارلده : ۱۱۱
سارم : ۱۰٦
ساره : ۱۱۸
سارو : ٦٤ ، ۱۲۵ ، ۱٦۱
سار وتی : ۱۵۲
ساروج محلّه : ۱۱۰
سارو چشمه : ۱۲۷
ساروغاپی : ۱۱۵
ساروکلا : ۱۲۰
سارو یه : ۵۲
ساری : ۱—۳، ۷، ۸، ۱۰—۱۳،
۳۳ — ۳٦ ، ٤۲ ، ٤۵ ، ٤۸ ،
۵۰—۵۸ ، ٦۳ ، ٦۵ ، ۱۰۲ ،
۱۰۵ ، ۱۲۰—۱۲۲ ، ۱۲۹ —
۱۳۲ ، ۱٤۲ ، ۱٤٦ ، ۱۵۰ ،
۱۵۱ ، ۱۵۷ — ۱۵۹ ، ۱۹۲ ،
۱٦۵ ، ۱٦٦
ساری رودپی : ۵٦ ، ۱۲۱
ساری صو : ۹۱
ساریه : ۲
ساس : ۱۰۹
آل ساسان : ۱۵۰ ، ٤ ع
ساسی کلام : ٤٦، ٤۸، ۱۱۹
ساق محلّه : ۱۲۳
سالا : ۱۲۹
سالده : ۱۱۱
سالارود کلا : ۱۱۷
سالوس — سالوش : ۲۷
سالو محلّه : ۱۸
سالیان : ۵ ، ۱٦۵
سالیان تپّه : ۸۱ ، ۸٦
آل سامان : ۱۳۳ ، ۱۳۸
سامته : ۱٦۵
سامرّا : ۵۲
ساور : ۵٦ ، ۵۷ ، ۷۹ ، ۱۲۷
ساور علیا : ۱۲۷
ساور کلا : ۱۲۸
سایر : ۱۲۹
سبز مشهد : ۷۵
سبز میدان : ۱۷ ، ۲۳ ، ۳۲ ، ۳۸ ،
۳۹ ، ۱۰۷

سبکک رود : ۱۱۶
سپانلو : ۷۶
سته ده : ۱۱۹
سجه محلّه : ۱۱۰
سختسر : ۵ ، ۶ ، ۱۶ ، ۱۸ ، ۱۹ ، ۲۱ ، ۲٦ ، ۱۰۶ ، ۱۵۱ ، ۱۵۳
سدّ انو شروان : ۱۵
سدّ پی : ۱۲۲
سدّ سکندر : ۱۵۳
سدن : ۱۲۶
سدن رستاق : ۶۷— ۷۰، ۷۸، ۹۷، ۱۰۵، ۱۲۵ ، ۱۲٦
سراب : ۱۳۲
سراب گرم : ۱۰۶
سراج محلّه : ۶۵ ، ۶۷ ، ۱۲٤
سراج کلا : ۱۱۸ ، ۱۲۰
سرادار کلا : ۱۱۹
سراست : ۱۱۰
سربدال — سربدار : ۱۶۲
سربرد : ۱۰۶
سرتخته : ۱۲۸
سرتکوسرا : ۱۰۶
سرتنگک : ۱۶۳ ، ۱۶٦
سرتوکک : ۶۱ ، ۱۶۰
سرتیزی : ۱۵۲
سرتیکه : ۵۷ ، ۱۲٤
سرجه سرا : ۱۵۳
سرحانوند : ۱٤٦ ، ۱۵۲
سرحدّ : ۲۱ ، ۱۰٦
سرحك : ٤۱
سرخان : ۱۱۸
سرخان کلا : ۱۲۷
سرخان محلّه : ۸۱
سرخانی : ۳ ، ٦ ، ۱۸ ، ۲۱ ، ۳ ع
سرخ چاده : ۱۲۷
سرخ چشمه : ۱۲۸
سرخ دشت : ۱٦۱
سرخ ده : ۱۲۳
سرخ دیم : ٦۱ ، ۱٦۰
سرخ رباط : ٤۲ ، ٤۳ ، ۱۱۵
سرخرود : ٦ ، ٤۱ ، ٤۷ ، ۱۱۳
سرخکک : ٤۱ ، ۱۱۵ ، ۱۵۷
سرخ کلا ۵۰ ، ۱۱۸
سرخ کمر : ۱۳۲ ، ۱۵۷
سرخ گیریه : ۵۱ ، ۵۷
سرخ محلّه : ۸۱ ، ۸۲

سرخه چال : ۱۱۵
سرخه ده : ۱۲۲
سرخه کلا : ۱۱۳ ، ۱۱۶ ، ۱۲۱
سرخوای : ۱۶
سرداب رجه : ۱۵٤
سرداب رود : ٦ ، ۲۷ ، ۱۵۱ ، ۱۵٤
سرداب سر : ۱۵۳
سردابه : ۱۰۷
سردار : ۳۱
سردای محلّه : ۱۱۳
سردروازه : ۷۹ ، ۱۲٦
سردشت : ۱۱۵
سرده : ۱۰۸
سردورقادی : ۱۱۸
سرس : ۱۱۹
سرطاق : ٦۸ ، ۱۲۵
سرقلعه : ۱۰۳
سرکا : ۱۰۸
سرکام : ۱۲٤
سرکت : ۱۲۲
سرکلا : ۱۱٦ ، ۱۲٦ ، ۱٦۱
سرکیله : ۱۵۵
سرگل چاک : ۱۵۳
سرگنجه کیله : ٦۷
سرانـگا : ۱۰٦
سرما خورده : ۱۲۷
سر محلّه : ٦۷—٦۹ ، ۱۱٤ ، ۱۲۵
سرمرد : ۱۲۳
سرنگک : ۱۲۹
سرنه : ۱۳۲
سرنو : ۱۳۲
سرهلاله : ۵۹
سرهنگک کوتی : ۱۱۳
سروك : ۱۲۲
سروکن حاجّی کفشگر : ۱۲۳
سروکلا : ۱۲۰
سرومه میان : ۱۱۸
سروی : ۱۱۰
سروی ده : ۱۰۹
سروینه باغ : ۱۲۱
سری : ۱۱۱
سریانی : ۱۲۷
سریجان : ۱۱۳
سرین : ۱۱٦
سطل کیا : ۲۸
سعادت آباد : ۱۰۹

سعامك : ١١٤
سعد آباد : ١٠١ ، ١٠٣ ، ١٢٦ ، ١٢٨
سعد الدّين كلا : ١١٤
سعد ده : ١٠٩
سعيد آباد : ٣٠ ، ١٥٠ ، ١٥٥
سعيد محلّه : ١٢٢
سعيده : ١٢٤
سعيدوها : ١٤٦ ، ١٥٢
السّعيدى : ١٦٥
سفيدآب : ٤١ ، ١١٥ ، ١٥٧
سفيد تميشه : ١٨ ، ١٩ ، ١٥١
سفيد چاه : ٦٩
سفيدار دشت : ١١١
سفيد رود : ١ ، ١٦
سفيد طور : ١١٧
سفيد كوه : ١٢٣
سكرچى : ١١٤
سلاخ : ٩٨
آل سلجوق : ١٣٣
سلده : ٦ ، ٢١ ، ٣٠—٣٢ ، ١١٠ ، ١٥٥
سلستى كوه — سلسله كوه : ١٣٢
سلش : ١١٦ ، ١٣١ ، ١٣٢
سلطان آباد : ١٢٧
سلطان آباد لمسرى : ٦٤ ع
سلطان دوين : ٨٥ ، ٩١
سلطان على كيا سلطان : ٢٨ ، ١٠٩
سلطان كلا : ٦ ، ٢٤
سلف : ١٠٧
سلمبر : ١٠٧
سلم رود : ٦ ، ١٩ ، ١٥١
سلم رود سر : ١٠٦
سله مال : ١٥٣
سلوكلا : ١٢١
سلى : ١٢٢
سليا كوتى : ١١٠
سليم آباد : ١٠٨
سليم بهرام : ١٢١
سليم شيخ : ١٢١
سليمان آباد : ٢١ ، ١٠٥ ، ١٦٢
سليمان داراب : ٧٠ ع
سليمان كلا : ١١٧
سليمان محلّه : ١٢٠ ، ١٢٣
سلينه : ١٦٢
سما : ١٠٨ ، ١٠٩
سمارو : ١٢٧

سمام : ۱۵۰ ، ٦۰ ع — ٦٤ ع
سمام کوه : ۱۸
سمبر : ۹۱
سمسکنده : ۵۸ ، ۱۲۰
سملقان : ۱٦۱ ، ۱٦۲
سمنان : ۲٤ ، ۲٦ ، ٤۳ ، ۵٦ ، ۱۳۱ ، ۱۳۲
سمندك : ۱۲۰
سمنگان : ۱۰۸
سمه چول : ۱۲۳
سمور : ۱۰۹
سنتی : ۱۲۲
سنّر : ۱۰۷
سنعه خیل : ۱۲۲
سنگ : ۱۲۳
سنگ امام : ۱۲٦
سنگا محلّه : ۱۲٤
سنگ بن : ۱۲٦
سنگ بست : ۱۱۳
سنگ تاب : ۱۱۰
سنگ تپّه : ۱٦۰
سنگ تجن : ۱۰۹
سنگ تراشان : ۱۲۱
سنگتو : ۱۲۱
سنگ چال : ۱۲۳
سنگ چال دادملا : ۱۱۷
سنگ چالك : ۱۲۲ ، ۱۲۷
سنگ خواست : ۸۰ ، ۱۵۱
سنگ ده : ۱۲۳
سنگ دوین : ۱۲۷ ، ۱۲۸
سنگر : ۹۷ ، ۱۲۹ ، ۱۵۱
سنگر احمد علی خان : ۱۲۷
سنگر تپّه : ۹۹
سنگر حاجّی لر : ۷۸ ، ۸۳ ، ۱۲۹
سنگر سوات : ۸۷
سنگر کبود جامه : ۸۲ ، ۱۲۹
سنگرمال : ۱۰۷
سنگر نیم مردان : ۹۹
سنگروج : ۱۲۵
سنگسر : ۵٦ ، ۱۳۱
سنگسرا : ٦ ، ۲٤ ، ۱۰۷ ، ۱۰۹
سنگسرك : ۱۱۵
سنگ سوراخ : ۷۹
سنگ کلان : ۱۲٦
سنگ نشات : ۱۱٦
سنگ نو : ۱۰۹

سنگه بن : ۱۹
سنگه پوش : ۱۱۹
سنگین ده : ۱۱۱
سنّو : ۴۲
سنّی : ۱۴ ، ۷۳ ، ۷۹
سه پشته چل : ۶۱
سه پل : ٤٤
سه دله : ۵۲
سه رو : ۱۲۹
سه روز بالا : ۱۲۱
سه گنبد : ۵۱ ، ۱۵۹
سه لر : ۱۱۰
سهمار : ۱۵۰
سهمین کلا : ۱۱۷
سه هزار : ۲۱ ، ۲۳ ، ۱۰۷ ، ۱۵۳
سه هیر : ۱۲۹
سوات : ۴۲
سواد رودبار : ۱۱۶
سواد کوه : ۲ ، ۳ ، ۷ ، ۱۵ ، ۳۳ ، ٤۲ ، ٤۳ ، ۵۳ ، ۵٦ ، ٦۳ ، ۱۰۵ ، ۱۱۵ ، ۱۱٦ ، ۱۱۹ ، ۱۲۱ ، ۱۳۱ ، ۱۳۲ ، ۱٤۳ ، ۱٤٤ ، ۱۵۷ ، ۱٦۵
سواسیه : ۹۱
سوامره : ۱۲٤
سو پرده : ۱۰۵
سوتک : ٤۱ ، ۱۰۷
سوتکلا : ۱۱۷
سوته : ٤۹ ، ۱۱۸ ، ۱۵۹
سوته اغوز : ۱۲٤
سوته خیل : ۱۲۵
سوته ده : ۱۲۵
سوته سر : ۱۱٦ ، ۱۲۷
سوته کلا : ۳۲ ، ۱۱۳ ، ۱۲۳
سوته نداف : ۱۲۳
سوجوال : ۹۹
سوحلما : ۱۲٤
سوخته سرا : ۱۲۸
سوخته کلا : ۱۱۷
سوخرانیان : ۱۳۳ ، ۱۳٤
سوراخ مازو : ۱۱۲
سورتج : ۵۷
سورتجی : ٦٦
سورك : ۵۹ ، ۱۱۳ ، ۱۱۹ ، ۱۲۰ ، ۱۲۳
سورکا : ۱۲۰

سوره بن : ١١٩
سوری : ١٦٣
سوریم : ١٢٠
سوزدیم : ٦٤
سولك : ١٠٧
سوه : ١١٠
سوواشی : ١٥٧
سیارکلا : ١١٢
سیاه آب : ٧٠
سیاه انارباغ : ١٢٢
سیاه بالا : ٨٥
سیاه بلوی تمار : ١٢٣
سیاه بند : ١٠٧ ، ١٥٧
سیاه بیشه : ١١١
سیاه پره : ١٢٣
سیاه پلس : ٤١
سیاه پله سرا : ١٥٣
سیاه تلو : ١٢٧
سیاه جو : ٦٧
سیاه چال : ٤١
سیاه چنار : ١٢٢
سیاه خان پی : ٧٩
سیاه خانی : ١٢٥ ، ١٦٣
سیاه درگا : ١١٩
سیاه درّه : ٧٠
سیاه دشت : ١٢٢
سیاه ده : ١١٧
سیاه رستاق : ٢١ ، ١٠٦
سیاه رو : ١٠٩
سیاه رود : ٦ ، ١٦ ، ٢٦ ، ٣١ ، ٤٢ ، ٤٨—٥٠ ، ١٢٢ ، ١٥٨
سیاه رودبار : ٦ ، ٤٧
سیاه رودپی : ١٣٢
سیاه سنگر : ١١٠
سیاه کتو : ١١٤
سیاه کمر بند : ١١٥
سیاه کل : ١٥٣
سیاه کلا : ١١١
سیاه کلا محلّه : ١١٩
سیاه کله رود : ١٨ ، ١٥٣
سیاه کوه : ١٢٤٠ ، ١٥٣
سیاه گاو : ١٥٣
سیاه گده : ١٥٣
سیاه گله : ١٥٣
سیاه لم : ١٨
سیاه لن : ١٥٣

سیاه مرکوه : ٥٩ ، ١٢٨
سیاه مشتد : ٢٥
سیاه واشه : ١١٥
سیاه ورز : ٢١ ، ٢٤ ، ١٠٧
سیاه وش کلا : ٥٩ ، ١٢٢ ، ١٢٥
سیب چال : ٨٤ ، ١٢٩
سیب باغ : ١١٩
سیبده : ١٠٨
سیبن : ١٠٦
سیپی : ١١٦
سیتك : ١٠٩
سیچکانی : ١٠٦
سیّد آباد : ١٠٧ ، ١٢١ ، ١٢٤
سیّد خیل محلّه : ١٢٤
سیّد عزیز گشتسب : ١١٨
سیّد کاشی : ١١٨
سیّد کلا : ١٧ ، ١١٧ ، ١٢٤ ، ١٢٨
سیّدک محلّه : ١٢٣
سیّد گور : ١٢٤
سیّد محلّه : ٦ ، ١٧ ، ١٩ ، ٤٩ ، ٥٠
١٠٦ ، ١١٤ ، ١١٧ ، ١٢٠ ، ١٥١
سید میران : ١٢٦
سیر : ١٠٧ ، ١٢٢
سیرجاران : ١١٣
سیرجاری : ١٢٤
سی رستاق : ٦٩
سیرگاه : ١٠٧
سیره کلا : ١١١
سیستان : ٩٤ ، ١٠٦
سیستانی : ٧٠
سی سنگان : ٣ ، ٢٦ ، ٣٠
سیف زرگر : ١١٠
سیگا رود : ١٥١
سیگره رود : ١٥٣
سینا : ١٢٩
سیه رود : ١٠٥
سی هزار : ١٠٧
سیه سر : ١٠٥
سیور : ١٢٤
سیومک : ١٢٩
سیووجه : ١١٥

ش

شاد کوه : ١٣٢
شارک : ٤٢
شارمام — شارمان : ١٦٠

شاسب پر : ۱۱٤

شاسمان : ۹۰ ، ۱٦۲

شاطر گنبد : ۵۸

شاطر لنگه : ۱٦۰

شالا : ۱۲۳

شال تپّه : ٦۲

شالکه : ۱۰٦

شال محلّه : ۱۰٦

شالی کلا : ۱۱۱

شام : ۱۱ ، ۱۱۵

شامبیاتی : ۷٦

شانتاش : ۲٤

شانه تراش : ۲٤ ، ۱۰٦ ، ۱۱۷

شاه آباد : ۱٦۱

شاهان دشت : ۱۱٤

شاه پسند : ۱۰٤

شاه کوه : ۱۲٦

شاه حسین حیدر دریا آبادی : ۲۳

شاه در کوه : ۵۷

شاه دز : ۳۰

شاه ده : ۷۰ ، ۱۲٦

شاه رود : ۵۸ ، ٦٤ ، ٦۵ ، ۷۸ — ۸۱ ، ۱۳۰ ، ۱٦۳

شاه زاد : ۱۲۱

شاه زید : ۱۱۳

شاه سفید کوه : ۱۵۳

شاه سوار : ۲۰ ، ۲۳ ، ۲٤ ، ۱۰۷

شاه کلا : ۱۱۳

شاه کلای گلیج : ۱۱۳

شاه کلا محلّه : ۱۱۸

شاه کوتی : ۱۱۹

شاه کوه : ۳ ، ۵۷ ، ۵۹ ، ۷۸ ، ۷۹ ، ۸۱ ، ۱۳۰ ، ۱٦۳

شاه کوه بالا : ۷۹ ، ۱۲٦

شاه کوه پائین : ٦۵ ، ۱۲٦

شاه کوه گـکشان : ۸۱

شاه کوه وسارو : ۷۸ ، ۸۰ ، ۱۰۵ ، ۱۲٦ ، ۱۲۷

شاه کیله : ٦٤ ، ٦۷ ، ۱۲۵ ، ۱٦۱

شاه مازی بن : ۱۱۱

شاه محلّه : ۱۱۳ ، ۱۲۱

شاه مراد کیله : ٦ ، ۲۸

شاه مراد محلّه : ۱۰٦

شاه مرز : ۱۵ ، ۸۵ ، ۹٤

شاه میرزاد : ۱۲۲

شاه نجّار : ۱۰۹

شاهی کلا : ١١٣
شاور : ٥٩ ، ٧٨
شب خس کج : ١٠٩
شب خس کوتی : ١٠٧
شب کلا : ١١٩ ، ١٢٤
شجی : ١٥٣
شرامه کوتی : ١١٣
شران : ١٢٩
شرز : ١٥٠
شرّز : ١٣٢
شرزك : ١١٩
شرف : ٩٣
شرف آباد : ١٢١
شرفتی : ١١٢
شرف دارکلا : ١٢١
شرف ده : ١١١
شرم کلا : ١١٤
شروین کوه : ٢ ، ٤٢ ، ١٢٩ ، ١٥٠
شری : ١٠٧
شریعت آباد : ١٠٩
ششتا : ١٠٥
شش رودبار : ١١٦
شصت کلا : ٧٠ ، ٧١ ، ١٠١ ، ١٦١
شعبودشت : ١٣٢
شغال تپّه : ٦٢ ، ٨٥
شفته کلا : ١١٩
شفیع آباد : ١٢٨
شکری کلا : ١٠٩
شگرکوه : ١٠٨
شل : ١٢٣
شلاب : ١٣٢
شلر : ١٢٣
شلسکوه : ١٣٢
شلفین : ٢ ، ٤٢
شلمان : ١٧
شلوزانی : ٧٧
شلیار : ٦ ، ٤٧
شلیر کنده : ١٢١
شلیمك : ١٢٢
شمس آباد : ١٢٧
شمشیر بر : ١٢٦
شمشیرزن : ١١٨
شمع جاران : ٦ ، ١٠٩
شمع جارود : ٢٨
شمله دون : ١٢١
شمن : ١٣٢

شمهار : ١٥٠
شموشك : ١٢٦
شمی کلا : ١١٩
شنگلده : ١١٤ ، ١٦٣
شهاب : ٦٦
شهاب الدّين كلا : ١١٧ ، ١١٨
شه دله : ٥٢
شهر آباد : ١٦٢
شهر اشوب : ١٢٦
شهر بت : ٧٩ ، ١٢٨
شهر بند : ١١١
شهر تجری : ١١٨
شهردشت : ١٢٣
شهر دوين : ١٢٩ ، ١٣٢
شهر خواست : ٤٩ ، ١٢٠
شهر ستان : ٣٠ ، ٨٩ ، ١٠٧
شهر ستان تپّه : ١٢٧
شهر ستانك : ٢٧
شهر ستانه مرز : ٣٣
شهرك : ١٦٢
شهر كجور : ٣٠
شهر كلا : ١١٠ ، ١١١
شهرك نو : ١٦٢
شهر نو : ٩١ ، ١٦٢
شهر يار : ١٢ ، ١٥٢
شهر يار درّه : ١٢٣
شهر يار كنده : ١٢٠
شهر يار كوه : ٢ ، ١٣٠ ، ١٣٤ ، ١٣٨
شهزاد كلا : ١٢٥
شهمار : ١٥٠
شهميرزاد : ٤٢ ، ٤٣ ، ٥٦
شهنا كلا : ١١٣
شهنه كلا : ١١٢
شو پسند : ١٠٤
شوراب : ١٢١ ، ١٢٤
شوراب سر : ١٩ ، ٦٢ ، ١٠٦ ، ١٢٥ ، ١٥١
شورج : ٢٢
شورستان : ١١٢
شورچشمه : ١٢٧
شورك : ١١٩
شوركلا : ١١٧ ، ١٢٧
شوركله :
شوركوه : ١١٦
شورماست : ١١٥

شوریان : ۱۲۶
شوش : ۹۰
شوکت آباد : ۱۲۸
شِوندشتی : ۳۶
شوندی : ۱۱۶
شویلاشت : ۱۲٤
شیام : ۱۲۳
شیب ابندان : ۱۲۰
شیت : ۱۲٤
شیخ : ۱۱۷
شیخ الاسلامی : ۱۰۶
شیخانبر : ۱۷ ، ۱۱ ع
شیخ ذکیا : ۱۱۸
شیخ رود : ۶ ، ۳۱
شیخ صیقل : ۱۱۰
شیخ طبرسی : ۱٤
شیخ قلی کلا : ۱۱۱
شیخ کدیر : ۱۱۹
شیخ محلّه : ۱۱۰ ، ۱۱۶ ، ۱۲۵
شیخ موسی : ۱۱۹
شیدان : ۱۲۹
شیرآباد : ۸۲ ، ۱۱٤ ، ۱۲۸
شیراز : ۱۲ ، ۲۲ ، ۳۱ ، ۵۳ ، ۶۳
کیای شیرایه : ۱۱۲
شیرایه کلاته : ۱۱۲
شیربتی : ۶۶
شیرجان : ۱۵۳
شیرج خیل : ۱۰۷
شیرج محلّه : ۱۰۷
شیرخان لیو : ۶۰
شیرخواست : ۱۳
شیردار بن : ۶۹
شیردار کلا : ۱۱۹
شیرداری : ۱۲۵
شیردرّه : ۱۱۶
شیرسوار کلا : ۱۱۷
شیرش : ٤۲
شیرکتا : ۱۲۲
شیرکرز : ۲۰ ، ۱۰۷
شیرکلا : ۱۰۶ ، ۱۱٤ ، ۱۱۶ ، ۱۲٤
شیرگاه : ٤۲ ، ٤۳ ، ۵۶ ، ۱۱۹ ، ۱۲۱
شیرمحلّه : ۱۸
شیرنگ : ۷۶ ، ۱۲۷
سادات شیرنگی : ۷۶ ، ۱۲۷
شیره رود : ۶ ، ۱۷

شیره زکک : ١١٩
شیره زیل وند : ١٤٦
شیره‌سل : ١١٥
شیروان محلّه : ١٠٧
شیروج کلاته : ١١٧
شیرود : ٦ ، ٢٠ ، ٤٤ ، ٤٧ ، ١٠٥ ، ١١٢ ، ١٣٢ ، ١٥١ ، ١٥٣
شیزه : ١٥٣
شیعه : ١٤ ، ٣٤ ، ٧٣ ، ٧٩ ، ٨٩ ، ٩٠
شیطان محلّه : ٦٢
شیل درّه : ١٢٣ ، ١٢٤
شیمرود : ١٦ ، ١١١
شیه رود : ١٠٥

ص

صادقانلی : ١٦٤
صادقلی : ٨٢
صاری صو : ٩١
صالح آباد : ١١٠
صالحان : ١٠٨ ، ١٥٤
صاحبی ویشکلا : ١٢٠
صحرای شاه حسین : ٦٠
صحرای گاو پیچان : ٧١
صدر آباد : ١٢٦
صرین کلا : ٦ ، ٢١ ، ٢٩ ، ٣١
صفارود : ٦ ، ١٨
صفّاری : ١٣٣ ، ١٣٧
صفوح : ١٣١
صفوی : ١٤ ، ٤٩ ، ٦٢ ، ٧١ ، ٨٠ ، ٨٨ ، ١٣٣ ، ١٣٩ ، ١٤٢ ، ١٦٤
صفی آباد : ٦٢
صفی محلّه : ١١٦
صلاح الدّین کلا : ٦ ، ٢٩ ، ١٠٩
صلاح الدّین محلّه : ١٢٠
صلبی : ٧٠
صلحدار کلا : ١١٧
صنعم : ١١٧
صندوقه : ١٠١ ، ١٦٣
صورت : ١١٧
صوفی محلّه : ١٠٥
صول : ٨٨ ، ١٤٦
صیقل اقابابا بیگک : ١١٠
صیقل دوست علی : ١١٠

ض

ضیارود : ۱۱٤

ط

طابران : ۱٦٥
طالبو : ۱۲۷
طالش : ۱۲ ، ۲۲ ، ٦۳
طالش محلّه : ۱۰٦
طالقان : ۲ ، ۲۰ ، ۲۱ ، ۲۳ ، ۱۰۸ ، ۱۱۱ ، ۱٤۲ ، ۱٥٤
طالقانی : ۲۲
طالو : ۱۲۸
آل طاهر : ۳٤ ، ٥۲ ، ۱۳۳ ، ۱۳۷
طاهر ده : ۱۲۰
طبرسا : ۱۲۷
طبرستان : ۱—۳ ، ۱۳ ، ۱٤ ، ۲۹ ، ۳۰ ، ۳۳ — ۳٥ ، ٤۰ ، ٥۱ ، ٥۲ ، ۸۸ ، ۸۹ ، ۱۰۲ ، ۱۲۱ ، ۱۲۹ — ۱۳۱ ، ۱۳۳ ، ۱۳٤ ، ۱۳۸ ، ۱٤۰ — ۱٤۲ ، ۱٤۷ ، ۱٤۸ ، ۱٥۰ ، ۱٥۲ ، ۱٥۳ ، ۱٥٥ ، ۱٥۷ ، ۱٦۲
طبقه ده : ۱۲۰
طبقه کلا : ۱۲۳
طرقچی محلّه : ۱۱۸
طغان : ۱۱۸
طلابخت : ۱۲۸
طلاین : ۱۰٦
طلوت : ۱۱۹
طلور : ٦٦ ، ۱۲٦
طهران : ۷ ، ۱۲ ، ۲۱ ، ۲۳ ، ۲۷ ، ۳۰ ، ۳۱ ، ٤۰ ، ۷۹ ، ۹٥ ، ۹٦ ، ۱۱٥ ، ۱٦٤
طوا : ۱۲۷
طوس : ۱۳ع
طوسان : ۱٦۰
طوسکلا : ٥۹
طولندرّه بی : ۱۱۷
طوله کلا : ۱۱٤
طیبار : ۱۱۲
طیزنه رود : ۱٤٦
طیفوری : ۹۱

ظ

ظهیر آباد : ۱۲۷

ع

عابدین خطیر : ١٢٣

عایشه بر : ١٥٣

عایشه کرگیلی دژ : ١٢١

عباسا : ١١٠

عبّاس آباد : ٦ ، ٢١ ، ٢٥ ، ٢٦ ، ٦٤ ، ١٠٥ ، ١٠٨ ، ١١٥ ، ١٦١

عبّاس خطیری : ١٢٦

عبّاس علی کش : ٤٩

عباس کلا : ١٠٧ ، ١١٠

عبد الله آباد : ١٠٦ ، ١١٠

عبد الله محلّه : ١٢٣

عبد اللّهی : ١٢٣

عبد الملکی : ١١ ، ١٢ ، ٢٢ ، ٦٠

عبد الملکی کیله : ٦ ، ٦٠

عبد المناف : ١١٠

عبّهٔ بند : ٩٤

عبّهٔ خلی خان : ١٠٠ ، ١٢٩

عثمان سرا : ١٠٦

عثمان کوه : ١٥٧

عدول ده : ١١١

عراق : ١٠ ، ١١ ، ٤٢ ، ٥٦ ، ١٥٧

عرب : ١٣ ، ٢٧ ، ٧٠ ، ٨٨ ، ١٥٥ ، ١٦٥

عرب خیل : ١٠٨ ، ١١١ ، ١١٦

عروسی کلا : ١٢٨

عزّ الدّین لو : ٧٦

عزّت : ١٠٩

عز خورده : ١١٠

عزده : ٦ ، ٣١ ، ٣٢ ، ١١٠

عزیزک : ٤٨ ، ١٢١

عزیز کلا : ١١٩

عشرت آباد : ١٠٦

عطایان : ١١٣

عقیلی : ٧٠ ، ٧٦

علازمین : ١٢٨

علامن : ١٢٧ ، ١٢٨

علمدار پی : ١٢٤

علمدار ده : ١٢٤

علم ده : ١٠٩

علم کلا : ١٠٩

علم کوه : ١٢٤

علو فن : ١٢٦

علویان : ١١ ، ٧٧ ، ١٣٣ ، ١٣٩

علوی کلا : ۳۰ ، ۱۰۸ ، ۱۰۹ ،
۱۱۳ ، ۱۱۹
علوی محلّه : ۳۱
علی آباد : ۶ ، ۷ ، ۸ ، ۲۷ ، ۲۹ ،
۳۹ ، ۴۳ ، ۵۰ ، ۵۶ ، ۶۳ ،
۷۹ ، ۸۱ ، ۱۰۵ ، ۱۰۷ ، ۱۰۹ ،
۱۲۰ ، ۱۲۲ ، ۱۲۷ ، ۱۲۸ ،
۱۵۰ ، ۱۵۶ ، ۱۶۳
علی آباد بزرک : ۶ ، ۲۸ ، ۱۰۹
علی آباد میر : ۲۸
علی آباد اصغرخانی : ۲۸ ، ۱۰۹
علی آباد کیله — دنباله : ۲۸
علی اللّهی : ۱۴ ، ۱۰۶
علی جنگل : ۱۱۳
علی دراز : ۱۰۷
علی زمین : ۱۱۷
علی کلاوه : ۳۹
علی کنده : ۵۹ ، ۱۲۰
علیه کلا : ۱۱۶
علی وک — علی واک : ۵۰ ، ۱۲۰
عمارت سر : ۶۲
عمارت موسی خان : ۸۵
عمر آباد : ۱۵۵
عمر کلاته : ۱۵۵
عموغلی محلّه : ۱۰۵
عوامّة کوی : ۳۸
عیب چین : ۱۲۴
عیسی خندق : ۱۲۱
عیسی رود : ۶
عیشه بن : ۱۰۸
عین الهمّ : ۱۵۸

غ

غریب : ۷۰
غریب آباد : ۱۲۸
غریب محلّه : ۱۲۵
غزّ : ۹۰
غلام : ۷۰
غلامه راه : ۱۳۰
غلامی : ۵۷ ، ۱۲۳
غلبیر بند : ۷۷
غیاث کلا : ۱۱۳

ف

جبل فادوسبان : ۲
فارس : ۲۷

فارسیان : ۸۳
فارسیان فیرنگک : ۱۲۹
فارسیان وقانچی : ۸۳
فتح فضلب : ۱٦٥
فتوکک : ۱۰٦
فتیده : ۱۷
فخر عماد الدّین : ۷۸ ، ۸۱ ، ۱۲۷
فرا : ۱۱٦
فرّاش : ۱۱۳
فراوه : ۹۲
فرج آباد : ۱۰۸
فرح آباد : ۳ ، ۷ ، ۱۳ ، ٤۳ ، ٤٥ ،
٤۷ — ٤۹ ، ٥٥ ، ٦۱ ، ٦۳ ،
۱۰٥ ، ۱۱۹ ، ۱۲۰ ، ۱٥۹
فرّخان فیروزکوه : ۲
فرسپ : ۲ ، ۱٥۷
فرسی کلا : ۱۱۱
فرشوادگر : ۱ ، ۱٥۰
فرغانه : ۱٥۳
فرغول : ۹۲
فرم : ۱۱۸
فرّن آباد : ۱۱۰
فره : ۱۱٥
فره زن : ۱۰۸
فریکنار : ٦ ، ۷ ، ٤۷ ، ۱۱۲
فریم : ۲ ، ٥۷ ، ۱۳٥ ، ۱٥۰ ، ۱٦٥
فریمان : ۱۲۸
فریمون : ۱۱۲
فشکوه : ۱۰۸
فقیه : ۲۲
فقیه آباد : ۲٤ ، ۱۰٦ ، ۱۰۸
فقیه محلّه : ۱۰٥
فلاّح : ٥۰
فلاس : ۱۱٤
فلرد : ۱۱٥
فلزی کلا : ۱۰۹
فلـکک ده : ۱۰۷
قلعه فلول : ۱۱٥
فلیمرز : ٦ ، ۳۱ ، ۱۰۹
فندرسکک : ۷۸ ، ۷۹ ، ۸۱ ، ۸۲ ،
۹۷ ، ۱۰٥ ، ۱۲۸ ، ۱٦۳
فندری نماور : ۱۱۷
فنگک چال : ۱۱۷
فوتم : ٥۰ ، ۱۲۰ ، ۱۳۱
فوجرد : ۸٥ ، ۱۲۷
فوزه کلا : ۱۲٦

فوكلا : ١١٧
فولاد كلا : ١١١
فولاد محلّه : ٥٨ ، ١٢٢ ، ١٣٠ ، ١٣١ ، ١٦٣
فومش كنار : ١١٧
فيتسك : ١٢٢
فيتسك آهنگر : ١٢٢
فيرنگ : ٨٣ ، ١٢٩
فيروز آباد : ١٠٨ ، ١١٤
فيروزجاه : ١٤٣
فيروزچاه : ١١٧
فيروز خسرو : ١١٤
فيروز كلا : ٣٠ ، ٣١ ، ١٠٩ ، ١١٣
فيروز كند : ٥٠ ، ١٦٢
فيروز كنده : ١٥ ، ١٢٠
فيروز كوه : ١ ، ٢ ، ٧ ، ٣٣ ، ٤٢ ، ٥٦ ، ١٠٩ ، ١١٦ ، ١٣٠ ، ١٣١ ، ١٥٨
آب فيروزكوهى : ٥٠ع
فيرويز : ١٣٠
فيص آباد : ١٢٧
فيكارود : ٦ ، ٢٠
فيكسره : ١١٥
فيلده رودبار : ٧١ع
فيل زمين : ٤١
فيول : ١١١

ق

قاجار : ١ ، ١٢ ، ٦٦ ، ٧٠ ، ٧٦ ، ٨٠ ، ٨٦ ، ١٦٤ ، ١٥ع
قاجار : ١١٣
آب قاجار : ٨١
قاجار خيل : ٤٩ ، ١٢٠
قادار آباد : ١٢٨
قادر كلا گر : ١١٨
قادى كلا : ١١٣ ، ١٢٠ ، ١٢٤
قادى كلايه : ١٣١
قادى كياب : ٦٢ ، ١٦٥
قادى محلّه : ١١٧ ، ١٢٤
قارلق : ١٢٧
آل قارن — انظر قارنوند
جبل قارن : ٢ ، ١٢١ ، ١٣٣ ، ١٥٠
قارن آباد : ١٢٥
قارن آباد دشت : ١١٩
قارنوند : ١٣٣ ، ١٣٤ ، ١٤٦ ، ١٥٠ ، ١٥٢ ، ١٦٥

قاری آب : ۸۱ ، ۹۳
قاری قلعه : ۱۶۳
قاری کلا : ۱۱۸
قاسم آباد : ۱۸ ، ۱۲۶ ، ۱۵۳
قاضی محلّه : ۱۰۷
قالی باف : ۱۱۰
قانچی : ۸۳ ، ۱۲۹ ، ۱۶۲
قانیخمز : ۸۲ ، ۹۸
قای : ۱۰۱
قبران : ۱۲۶
قبر خاتون : ۵۸
قبر سفید : ۷۹
قپچاق : ۱۵۲
قتارمه : ۱۲٤
قجق : ۸۲
آب قجق : ۹۱
قدمگاه : ٤۲
قدمگاه خضر : ۳۹ ، ۷۱
قرا آغاج : ۱۲۷
قرا باغ : ۷۸
قرا تپّه : ۱۲ ، ٦۱ ، ٦۲ ، ٦۷ ، ۱۲۵ ، ۱٦۳
قرا جنگل : ٦٦
قرادوین : ٦۳ ، ٦۵ ، ٦۸
قراخیل : ۱۱۸
قراسانلو : ۷٦
قراسنگر : ۹۹
قراصوه : ۱۵ ، ٦۷ ، ۷۰ ، ۷۷ ، ۸۰ ، ۸۱ ، ۸۵ ، ۸٦ ، ۹۱ ، ۹٤ ، ۹۹
قراطغان : ۱٦ ، ٦٤ ، ۸۲ ، ۱۲۵ ، ۱٦۱ ، ۱٦۵
قرا کل : ۱۲۷
قرا کلا : ۱۱۲
قرا کلاته : ۳۵
قرا محلّه : ۱۱۲
قراول چای : ۹۱
قراوای تپه : ۸۷
قرسلی : ۹۱
قرن آباد : ۱۲۷
قرنجمین : ۱۲۸
قرنگوم : ۱۱٤
قرنگی امام : ۸۵ ، ۹۳ ، ۹٦ ، ۱٦۳
قریب محلّه : ۱۲۲ ، ۱۲۳
قریه منصور : ۲
قز قلعه : ۱۲۷
قزل اروت : ۹۲

قزل الان : ١٤ ، ٧٨ ، ٨٠ ،
٨٥—٨٧
قزل امام : ١٦٣
قزل رباط : ٩٢
قزلق : ٧٩ ، ٨١ ، ٩٦ ، ١٢٦ ، ١٦٣
قزلّی : ٦٢
قزوین : ٢١ ، ٣٠ ، ٣٥ ، ١٤٣ ،
١٥٢ ، ٦٨ ع
قشلاق : ١٢٩
قصّاب بوستانی : ١١٧
قصّاب محلّه : ١٧
قصّاب میان ده : ١١٧
قصران : ١٥٠ ، ١٥٥
قصر تور : ٥١
قطری کلاده : ١٣١
قفقاز : ٦٣
قلزم کلا : ١١٧
قلعه : ١٠٦ ، ١١٦ ، ١٢٦ ، ١٦٣
قلعهٔ اولاد : ٤٣
— اولاد دیو سفید : ٤٣
— ایلگلدی خان : ٩٣
— بن : ١١٤
— پایان : ١٢٥ ، ١٦١
قلعه پرز : ٢٤
— پشته : ١٠٧
— پلنگان : ١٦٠
— پوران : ١٢٨
— تنبت برزین : ٨٤
— حسن : ١٢٧
— حسین آباد : ١٢٥
— خندان : ٧١ ، ١٠٧
— دارا : ١٣٠ ، ١٦٠
— درگاه : ١١٤
— دیو سفید : ٤٣
— روسیان : ١٦٠
— زردی : ٦
— زینوند : ١٢٥
— سر : ١٠٩ ، ١٢٢ ، ١٦٣
— سرا : ١٢٩
— سیاه بالا : ١٢٧
— علی نقی بیگ : ٦
— کافة : ١٠٠ ، ١٢٩
— کجین — کچین : ٨٤
— کش : ٤٦ ، ١١٠ ، ١١٨
— کهرود : ١١٥
— گردن : ١٥٥ ، ١٦٣

قلعه ماران : ۱۲۸ ، ۱۶۲
— محمود : ۸۰ ، ۹٤ ، ۱۲٦
— مرز : ۱۱۲
— مور : ۲۹
— ناصر آباد : ۱۲۵
— همایون : ۸٤
— ولیج : ۱۰۹
قلندر عیش : ۱۲٦
قلندر محلّه : ۱۲٦
قلی آباد : ۱۰٦ ، ۱۲۷
قلی تپّه : ۱۲۹
قلی داغ : ۹۱
قلیلا : ۱۲۸
قمی کلا : ۱۱۹
قنات بازید : ۷۵ ، ٤۰ع
قهسبه : ۱۳۰
قوانلو — قوانلی : ۷٦ ، ۸۲
قورق : ۳۱ ، ۱۲۱
قوشچی : ۱۱۸
قوش کبری : ۹۱ ، ۹۳ ، ۱۲۸
قولی تیمور : ۱۵۲
قومس : ۱
قوی اوصلّو — قوی حضارلو : ۱۲ ، ۲۲ ، ۱۰۷

ك

کابولج : ۱۰۹
کارچه کلا : ۱۱۳
کاردگر : ۱۱۰
— الیشرود : ۱۱۰
— خطیر : ۱۱۷
— کلا : ۱۱۲ ، ۱۱۷
— محلّه : ۲۳ ، ۱۰٦
— نماور : ۱۱۸
کار کنده : ۵٦ ، ٦۸ ، ٦۹ ، ۱۲۱ ، ۱۲۵
کارو : ۱۱۵
کاری : ٤٤
کازر : ۱۱۳
کاسمنده : ۱۱۳
کاسه گر محلّه : ۱۰۹
کاشغر : ۱٤۲
کاشی دار : ۸٤ ، ۱۲۹
کاشی کلا : ۱۱۷
کاظم آباد : ۱۰۵ ، ۱۱٦

کاظم بیگی : ٤٤ ، ٤٦ ، ۱۱۹
کاظم رود : ٦ ، ۲۵ ، ۱٥۱
کاظم کلا : ٦۷ ، ۱۰٦ ، ۱۱۹
کاغذلی : ۸۲
کافردوین : ۱۲۷
کافی بافی : ۱۲۳
کاکران : ۱۱٦
کاکو — کاکوان : ۱٥۳ ، ۱٥٤
آل کاکی : ۱۳۳ ، ۱٤۰
کالپوش : ۱۲
کالیج : ۳۰ ، ۱۰۹
کام : ۱۱۱
کام کلا : ۱۱۳
کاوان آهنگر : ۱۱۷ ، ۱۱۸
کاودان : ۱۳۰
کاوردان : ۱۳۰
کای : ۹۱
کبریا کلا : ۱۱۹
کبوتردون : ۱۱۳
کبوترگاده : ۱۱۳
کبود جامه : ۷٦ ، ۷۸ ، ۸۳ ، ۸٤ ، ۱۰۰ ، ۱۳۳ ، ۱٤٦ ، ۱٤۷ ، ۱٥۰ ، ۱٥۲ ، ۱٦۲
کبود چاله : ۱۲٦
کبود چشمه : ۱۲۸
کبود کلا : ۱۱۲
کبود کلایه : ۱۰۷
آب کبود وال : ۸۱
الکبیره : ۲۷ ، ۱٥٤
کپر : ۱۰۸
کپوربرون : ٦۷
کپورچال : ٥۰ ، ۱۱۷
کپی : ۱۱٤
کت چشمه : ۱۲٥ ، ۱۲٦
کت رم : ۱۲٤
کت کلا : ۱۰٦
کتله گردن : ۱۱۰
کتم بسته : ٤۱
کت محلّه : ۱۲٥
کته پشت : ۱۱۳
کته خواست کوتی : ۱۱۳
کته رودبار : ۱۲۳
کته سرکلا : ۱۰۸
کته کش : ۱۲٤
کتول : ۷٦ ، ۷۸ ، ۷۹ ، ۸۱ ، ۸۳ ، ۸٦ ، ۹٥ ، ۹۷ ، ۱۰٥ ، ۱۲۸

کتول : ۱۱۰
کتیا : ۱۱۰
کج : ۱۶۲
کجه : ۲۷ ، ۱۵٤
کجو : ۱۵ ، ۱۵٤ ، ۱٦٥
کجور : ۳ ، ۲۱ ، ۲۲ ، ۲٤ ، ۲۷
۳۰، ۳۱، ۱۰۵، ۱۰۸—۱۱۱ ،
۱۳۲ ، ۱٤٤ ، ۱۵۳
کجویه : ۱۵٤
کجید : ۱۱٦
کچ : ۱۱۹
کچپ : ۱۱۲
کچپ محلّه : ۱۲۵
کچکن : ۱۰۷
کچل‌ده : ۱۱۱
کچه : ۱۵٤
کچه رستاق : ۳۰ ، ۱۰۹
کچه رود : ٦ ، ۳۱ ، ۱۰۹
کچه رودبار : ۱۱۲
کچه‌رودسر — کچه روی‌سر : ۱۰۹
کچه قراشور : ۱۰۰
کچه گاه : ۱۱۱
کچو : ۱۵٤
کچین انظر کجین
کدمینو : ۱۲۵
کدیر : ۱٤ ، ۱۵٤
کراب : ۱۲۳
کرات : ۲۰ ، ۱۲٤ ، ۱٦۳
کرات کتی — کرات کوتی : ۱۰۵
کراچی : ۱۳
کراجو : ۲۳
کرامك : ۱۲۰
کربلا : ۳٦ع ، ۳۷ع ، ٤۱ع
کربلای علی کشت : ۵۰۰
کرت کلا: ۱۱۰
کرت کن : ۹۳
کرجی : ۱٤٦
کرجیان : ۱۰۵ ، ۱۰۷ ، ۱٤۹ ،
۱۵۳ ، ۱۵٤ ، ۱٦٦
کرجی کوه : ۱۰۵
کرچا : ۱۲٤
کرچک : ۳۲ ، ۱۱۲
کرد : ۱۱ ، ۱۲ ، ۸۲ ، ۱۰۰ ، ۱۵۹
کرد : ٦٦
کرد آباد : ۱۱۱ ، ۱۱٦ ، ۱۲۸ ،
۱۵۷

کرد امیر : ١٢٤

کردان : ٢٣

کرد بروکلا : ١١٧

کرد پی : ١١٩

کرد خیل : ١٢٢

کرد دشت محلّه : ١٢٣

کرد رودبار : ١١٧

کرد شاه رودبار : ١١٠

کرد کلا : ١٣ ، ٤٨ ، ٤٩ ، ١٠٥ ، ١١٧ ، ١١٩ ، ١٢٠

کرد محلّه : ٦٦ـــ٧٠ ، ٩٩ـــ١٠٤ ، ١٢٣ ، ١٢٥ ، ١٦٢

کرد ملاّ یعقوب : ١١٠

کردی چال : ١٠٨

کردیل کلا : ١١١

کرز مانسر : ١٠٧

کرسم : ١٢٤

کرسی : ١١١

کرسی کلا : ١١٤

کرف : ١١٥

کرک : ١٠٨

کرک : ٨١

کرکام : ١٢٢

کرکت محلّه : ١٠٦

کرک چشپان : ١١١

کرک رود : ٦ ، ٢٨

کرکره چال : ١٠٧

کرک رود سر : ١٠٩

کرکسا : ١٢٦

کرکم : ١٣٠

کرکه پای دشت : ١١٤

کرکو : ١٥٤

کرکو رود ـ کرکو روسر : ١٥١

کرگا نرود : ٨

کرگو گردن : ١٥٥

کرلو : ٧٦

کرمتر ـــ کرمتو : ١٢٨

کرمزد : ٤٢ ، ١١٦

کرّمی : ٧٦ ، ٧٧

کره کنار : ١١٧

کره کوه : ٢٤ ، ١٠٦

کروا : ١٢٠

کروکلا : ١١٨

کریم آباد : ٦ ، ٢٠ ، ٨٥ ، ١٠٥ ، ١٠٨ ، ١٢٧ ، ١٥١

کریم کلا : ١١٨

کزونك : ٤۱
کست : ۱۲۲
کسلیان : ٤۲ ، ٤۳ ، ۱۱٦ ، ۱۵۷
کسوب : ۱۲٤
کش : ۱٦۲
کشا جا کك : ٦٤ ع
کشایه : ۲۱
کشتلی : ۱۱۷ ، ۱۱۹
کشتلی عزیز علمدار : ۱۱۸
کشته : ۱۲۷
کشفل : ۱۳۰
کشکا : ۱۱۷
کشکوه : ۱۰۵
کشنا باد : ۱۱۹
کشه : ۱٦۳
کشیر : ٦٦ ، ۷۰
کفار الکا : ۱۱٤
کفا کاری : ۱۱۰
کفترخان : ٦۱ ، ۹۷
کفترکار : ۱۲۵
کفتر کلی : ۵۷
کفشگر کلا : ۱۱۷ ، ۱۲۰
کفشگیری : ٦۷ ، ۷۰ ، ۷۱ ، ۱۲۵
کل : ۱۱۱
کلا : ۱۱٦ ، ۱۲۰ ، ۱۲۱ ، ۱۲۳
کلاپی درّه : ۱۲۳
کلاته : ٦۵ ، ۷۹ ، ۱۲٦
کلاته اسپی : ۱۰۷
کلاته خیج : ۸۰ ، ۸۳
کلاجان : ۱۲۵
کلاده : ۱۱۲
کلادوش : ۱۱٤
کلار : ۲۷ ، ۱۰۹ ، ۱٤٦ ، ۱۵٤ ، ۱٦۵
کلارآباد : ۱۰٦ ، ۱۵۱
کلاردشت : ۱۲ ، ۲۷ ، ۱۰۸
کلارستاق : ۳ ، ۸ ، ۱۵ ، ۲۱ ، ۲۲ ، ۲٦ ، ۲۷ ، ۳۰ ، ۳۱ ، ۱۰۵ ، ۱۰۷ ، ۱۰۸ ، ۱۵٤ ، ۱۵۵
کلارسی : ۱۱۸
کلارم : ۱۲۳
کلارودبار : ۱۲٤
کلارودپی — کلاروپی : ۱۱۷ ، ۱۱۹ ، ۱۵۰
کلاره چه : ۱۲٤

کلاره کلا : ۱۱۹
کلاریجان : ۴۲ ، ۱۱۶
کلازل : ۱۵۷
کلاسنگیان : ۱۲۵
کلافت : ۱۲۴
کلاك : ۱۰۷ ، ۱۱۱ ، ۱۱۳ ، ۱۲۰ ، ۱۲۵ ، ۱۶۱
کلا کرد : ٦٦
کلا کیله : ٦٧
کلا گر کلا : ۱۱۹
کلا گر محلّه : ٤٤ ، ۱۲۳
کلا محلّه : ۱۱۳
کلامه سر : ۱۰۵
کلامو : ۱۲۵
کلان : ۱۱۳
کلانتریّه : ۲۲ ، ۱۵۳
کلاندون : ۱۱٦
کلایه : ٦٤ ع
کلایه بن : ۱۰۵
کلب : ۱۰٦
کلباد : ۳ ، ۱۵ ، ۵۸ ، ٦۵ ، ٦۳ ، ۱۲۵
کلبست : ٤٦ ، ۱۱۷
کلبستان : ۱۲۰
کلباد : ۱۱۲
کلپاشا : ۱۱٤
کلتله سر : ۱۵۳
کلچوب : ۱۱۹
کلدرّه : ۱۷
کلفرا : ٦۸
کلم : ۱۳۰
کلما : ۱۲۰
کلمازی بن : ۱۰٦
کلمر : ۱۲۰
کلمه : ۱۰۸
کلیشکیجا : ۱۲٦
کلنگرود : ۱۰۹
کلنگسر : ۱۱۲
کلنو : ۱۰۸
کله چاه : ۱۵۳
کله سرا : ۱۰٦
کله می : ۱۱۹
کلهودشت : ۱۱۳ ، ۱۱۷
کلورا : ۱۲۳
کاود : ۱۱۰
کاوده : ۱۱۲

کاورد : ۱۲۱
کاورودپی : ۳۰ ، ۱۰۹
کاوز : ۱۲۳
کاوسا : ۱۱۲
کاوکن : ۱۲۸
کاوکای : ۱۲٦
کلی : ۱۱۷ ، ۱۲۲
کلیای خطیر : ۱۲۳
کلیپ : ۱۵۷
کلیت : ۱۲
کلیت : ٦۲ ، ۱۲۵
کلیج : ۱۲۱
کلیج کلا : ۱۱٦ ، ۱۲۲
کلیدبر : ۱٦
کلیدر : ۱۲۲
کلیرد : ۱۲۱
کلی رو — کلی رود : ٦ ، ۳۱
کلیس — در بند کلیس : ۱۵۷
کلیشم : ۱۰۷
کلیک : ۱۱۰
کلیکا : ۱۱۸
کلیکان : ۱۱۳
کلیم خواجه : ۱۲۲
کل ییلاق : ۱۲۸
کماسی : ۱۲۷
کمالان : ۱۲۸
کمال خان : ۱۲۷
کمال غریب : ۱۲۷
کمال کلا : ۱۱۱ ، ۱۱۳
کمال کلاته : ۱۱۲
کما نگر کلا : ۱۱۲ ، ۱۱۸
کم چاك : ۱۰۸
کمر : ۱۱۰
کمر بن : ۱۰۸ ، ۱۲۳
کمر بند : ۱۱٤
کمردشت : ۱۵۷
کمر رود : ۳۲ ، ٤۲ ، ۱۱۰
کمر کلا : ۱۲٤
کمرو — کمرود : ٤۳ ، ۱۱۵ ، ۱۱٦
کمشیان : ۱۲۰
کمنان : ۱۳۰
کمند : ۱۱٦
کمندین : ٤۲ ، ۱۱٦
کمنزدشت : ۱۳۲
کمیمنان : ۱۵۰
کنارسر : ۲٤ ، ۱۰۱ ، ۱۰٦

کناره : ۶۲ ، ۶۶ ، ۷۹ ، ۱۲۷
کنداب : ۱۰۳ ، ۱۲۶
کند آباد : ۱۱۲
کندر : ۱۳۰
کندسان : ۱۵٤
کندلو : ۱۱٤
کندلوس : ۱۰۹
کنده خر : ۱۲۹
کنده سر : ۱۰٦
کنده کلا : ۱۱۹
کندوان : ۱۰۸
کنّز کلا : ۱۰۹
کنس : ۲٦ ، ۲۹
کنسانه بند : ۱۱۰
کنسه پا : ۱۱٤
کنسه رود : ٦ ، ۳۱ ، ۱۵۵
کنسه مرز : ۱۱٤
کنسی : ۱۱٤
کنگرج محلّه : ۱۱۲
کنگل آب رجه : ۱۱۱
کنگل چاه : ۱۵۳
کنگله چال : ۱۱۰
کنیم : ۱۲٤
کهر رود : ۱۱۵
کهرود : ٤۰ ، ٤۲
کهلیرد : ۱۱۳
کهنه دشت : ۱۱۸
کهنه دون : ۱۱۳
کهنه ده : ۱۲۲
کهنه کلباد : ۱۲۵
کهنه کوه : ۱۲۵
کهنه گون : ۱۲۵
کهو : ٤۱
کهیر : ۱۰۹
کو بیج کلا : ۱۱۳
کوپ : ۳۲ ، ۱۱۰
کو پاسرا : ۱۱۷
آب کو پان : ۷۰
کوت : ۱۲٤
کوتره : ۱۰٦
کوتل : ۱۰۸
کوتل جهان نما : ۷۰ ، ۹۳
— دوکٔ : ۷۹
— قلعه سر : ۱۰۳
— کش : ٤٤
— ویجمنو : ۷۹

کوتی ابراهیم کاردگر : ۱۳۰
کوتی سر : ۱۲۲
کوتی سردشت : ۱۲۲
کوچانی محلّه : ۱۱۹
کوچسفهان : ۱٦
کوچک : ۸۲ ، ۹۸
کوچه بوسی : ٦ ، ۲۵
کوچه گازران : ۳۳
کوده : ۲۰
کورجو : ۲۳
کورزیل : ۱۰٦
کورشید : ۱۰۸
کورشید رستاق : ۲۹ ، ۳۰ ، ۱۰۸ ، ۱۱۰
کوره سر : ۱۵۳
کوری : ۱۱۰
کوریا : ۱۱٦
کوزا : ۱۲۱
کوزک : ۱۱٤
کوسان : ٦۲ ، ۱۲۵ ، ۱٦۰ ، ۱٦۵
کوسرکنده : ۱۲۰
کوسکوه : ۱۰٦
کوش : ۳۰ ، ۱۰۹
کوشک جاوه لی : ۱۵٦
کوشک دشت : ۱۵٦
کوشکسرا : ۱۲۰
کوشک‌ـک : ۱۰۹ ، ۱۱۱
کوشک نداف : ۱۲۳
کوشه زر : ۱۱۳
کوفه : ۱۱
کوکباغ : ۱۲۰
کوکده : ۱۱۳
کوکلایه : ۲۰ ، ۱۰۵
کوکوورسر : ۱۰۳
کولا : ۱٤۸ ، ۱٦۵
کولاپی : ٤۲
کولانج : ۱۵۲
کولاویج : ۱۳۰ ، ۱٤۸
کولدین : ۱۲٦
کولسان : ۱۱٦
کولـکسرا : ۱۰۹
کولنگه : ۱۰۳
کوله درّه : ۱۳۰
کومیان : ۱۲۸
کونچی ملاّ : ۹۱ ، ۹۳
کوه اصطبل : ۱۱۵

کوه بژم : ۵۶ ، ۵۷
کوه بینار : ۱۳۰
کوه پر : ۳۰ ، ۱۰۹
کوه تیرپرو : ۵۷
کوهسار : ۵۷ ، ۷۸ ، ۸۲—۸٤ ، ۱۰۵ ، ۱۲۳ ، ۱۲۹ ، ۱٦۲
کوهستان : ۲۷ ، ۱۰۷ ، ۱۰۸
— اندرون تنکه : ۱۲۳
— دو بژم : ۱٦۵
— گرنام : ۱۲۳
کوه سرد : ۱۵۷
کوه عبد اللهی : ۵۷
کوه قد مگاه : ۱۱٦
کوه قروق : ۳۱
کوه نیلی : ۱٦۲
کوهی خیل : ٤۹
کوهیر محلّه : ۱۱۷
کویتر : ۱۰۷
کویج : ۱۳۰
کویر : ۱۵٤
کیا : ۷۰
کیاده : ۱۲۲
کیاسر : ۱۲۳
کیا کلا : ۵٦ ، ۱۰۸ ، ۱۰۹ ، ۱۱۱ ، ۱۱۷ ، ۱۲۱
کیا کلاته : ۱۵۵
کیان : ۱۱۵
کیت : ۱۲۲
کیج : ۸۰
کیخا : ۱۱۹
کید : ۱۰۵
کیسلیان : ۱۵۷
کیسنا : ۱۲٤
کیسه : ۵۲
کیش کلا : ۱۱۱
کیکلایه : ۱۷ ، ۱۸
کیکه بن : ۱۱۰
کیکو : ۱۰۹
کیلاپی : ۱۱۲
کیلارجان : ۱۳۰
کیلنکور : ۱۱٤
کینج : ۱۰۹
کینخواریّه : ۱۳٦
کیه وز : ۱۰۷
کیوان بژم : ۱۳۰
کیوان کوه : ۵۷

کیوسر : ٥٧ ، ١٢٤
کیوسیّه : ١٣٥

گ

گارپام : ١٢٣
گازرگاه : ١٥٦
گازه محلّه : ١١٩
گالش بر : ٣٢
گالش پل : ١١٢
گالش کلا : ١١٣ ، ١١٧
گالش محلّه : ١٠٥
گامیش بنه : ١١٢
گاوائی محلّه : ١٢٧
گاوبر : ١٠٧
آل گاوبره : ١٣٤
گاوپا : ١٢٦
گاورد : ١٢٢
گاوزن — انظر گوزن
گاوزن محلّه : ١١٧
گاوزنه کلاته : ١١٠
گاوسالار : ١٢٣
گاوسنگ : ١٢٦
گاوکل : ١٥٣
گاوکوه : ١٢٦
گاولنگر : ١١٩
گبر : ٣٧
گتاب : ١١٨
گتابسرا : ١١٠
گته پشت : ١٠٩
گته رودبار : ١٢٣
گته کش : ١٢٣
گچه سر : ٢٧
گچیان : ١٠١
گدوک : ٤٢ ، ٤٣ ، ١٥٧
گدوک شاه : ٤٢
گراکوه : ١٠٥
گرامجان : ١٠٨
گران : ٢٨ ، ٣٠ ، ١٠٩
گرائی محلّه : ١٢٧
گرپ : ٩١ ، ٩٣
گرجی : ١ ، ١٣ ، ٦٣
گرجی کلا : ١٢١
گرجی محلّه : ٦٢ ، ١٢٥
گرجیه سرا : ١٠٦
گرداب : ١٠٥
گردآسیاب : ١١٥

گرد زمین : ۱۳۰
گردشی : ۱۲۱
گردو : ٦
گردکوه : ۲۰
گردگو : ۱۵۳
گردن بری : ۱۱۹
گرشسب : ۷۰
گرلسپه سر : ۱۵۳
گرفنگ : ۱۲۹
گرکلا : ۱۰۷
گرگان : ۱، ۳، ۷، ۱۵، ۵۳، ۷۱، ۷۲، ۷۷—۹٤، ۹٦—۱۰۰، ۱۲۹، ۱۳۱، ۱۳۲، ۱۳۷، ۱۳۸، ۱٤۱، ۱٤۸، ۱۵۰، ۱۵۱، ۱۵۷، ۱٦۱—۱٦۳، ۱٦۵
گرگ پا : ۱۲٦
گرگ تاج : ۱۲٤
گرگرود : ۱۰۵
گرگو : ۱۵٤
گرماب دشت : ۱۲٦
گرماب رود— گرمابه رود : ۱۱۳، ۱٤۷
گرماب سر : ۱۱٤
گرمابه سرا : ۱۲۷
گرماوك : ۱۰۷
گرمدشت : ۷۹، ۱۲۸
گرمرود : ۱۰٦، ۱۲۱
گرمرود پی : ٤۰، ۱۱۳
گرمستان : ۱۲۱
گرمسر محلّه : ۱۱۳
گرمش کلا : ۱۱۸
گرمیج کلا : ۱۱۸
گرمی کلا : ۱۱۷
گرنا : ۱۱٤
گرنام : ۱۲۳
گره : ۲۱
گرّوس : ۱۲
گریلی : ۱۱، ۱۲، ۷۰، ۷٦، ۷۸، ۸۲، ۸۳، ۱٦۰
گز : ٦۷—٦۹، ۷۸، ۷۹، ۱۰۳، ۱۰٤، ۱۲۵
گزانک : ۱۱٤
گزاف رود : ۱۸، ۱۰٦
گزدرّه : ۱۰٦
گزنه : ۱۱٤
گزنه سرا : ۱۱۰، ۱۲٦

گسکری محله : ۱۸
گشاده : ٦۱
آل گشنسف : ۱۳۳
گکچه : ۸٦
گل افشان : ۱۲۰ ، ۱۲۱
گل باغ : ۱۲۷
گل باغچه : ۱۱٦
گل بن : ۱۲۷
گلبا نگاه : ۱۱۱
گلپا یگان : ۱۳۱ ، ۱۳۳ ، ۱٤۸ ، ۱٦۲
گلپشته : ۱۰۷
گلتپّه : ۸۵ ، ۱۲۷
گلجاری : ۱۲۳
گلچشمه : ۱۲۸
آب گلچشمه : ۸۲
گل چینی : ۱۲۱
گل خانه : ٤۱
گل خانه سر : ۱۰۷
گل دست : ۱۵۳
گلردك : ٤۱ ، ۱۱۵
گلزای : ۱۲
گلزرود : ۱۰۷
گلستان : ۷۹ ، ۸۳ ، ۱۰۷ ، ۱۲۹
گل سرا : ۱۲۹
گل سفید : ۱۷
گل گل : ۱۲۲
گلمندرو : ۱۱۰
گله بوسی : ٦ ، ۲۵
گله چال : ۱۲۸
گله کوه : ۱۰۵
گله گچ : ٤۱
گلو : ۱۲۵ ، ۱۲٦
گلور : ٦ ، ۲٦ ، ۱۰٦ ، ۱۵۱
گلوکن : ۱۲٦
گلوگا : ۱۳ ، ۵۸ ، ٦٤ ، ٦۵ ، ٦۸ ، ۱۱۷ ، ۱۲۵
گلیا : ٤۰ ، ۱۱۹
گلیج : ۲۲ ، ۱۰٦ ، ۱٤٦
گلیجان : ۱٦ ، ۲۰—۲۲ ، ۱۰۵ ، ۱٤۹
گلیجان رستاق : ۵٦ ، ۱۱۰
گلین خونی : ۱۱۰
گمدسی : ۱۵۷
گمش تپّه : ۸٦ ، ۹۱ ، ۹۳ ، ۹٤ ، ۹۹ ، ۱۰۰

گمیش کلا : ۱۱۹
گنبد چهار در : ۱۵۹
گنبد چهارراه : ۳۹
گنبد سلم وطور : ۵۱ ، ۵٤
گنبد سه‌تن : ۳۸
گنبد شمس طبرسی : ۳۸
گنبد قابوس: ۸۳ ، ۸۵ ، ۸۷، ۹۱،
۹۳ ، ۹٦ ، ۹۹ ، ۱٦۲
گنبد محمّد آملی : ۳۹
گنبد ناصر الحقّ : ۳۸
گنجرود : ٦ ، ۲۵
گنج کلا : ۱۱۷
گنج گرداب : ۱۲۲
گنجو روز : ٤٦ ، ۱۱۸
گنجینه : ۱۳۰
گنداب : ٦۵
گنداب رود : ٦ ، ۲۸ ، ۱۵۵
گندک محلّه : ۱۲٤
گندل تپّه : ۱۰۱
گندلک : ۱۲٤
گندیاب : ۱۱۰
گنگر : ۱۰۸
گنو : ۱۲۸
گوا : ۱۲۳
گوا زونو : ۱۲۱
گواسل : ٦۱
گودر : ۱۳ ، ٦۳
گود ناظر : ۱۳۰
گوراب جور : ۱٦
گوراب گسکر : ۸
گوران تالار : ۱۱۹
گور داعی : ۹۰
گور سرخ : ۸۹
گورشبرد — گورشجرد — گورشیر —
گور شیرد : ۱۰۸
گورك : ۱۱۳
گورك سفید : ۹۹
گورمجان : ۱۵٤
گورزلدین‌خیل — گورزین‌العابدین
خیل : ۱۱۵
گوزن : ۷۵ ، ۱۲۷ ، ٤۰ ع
گوسری : ٦ ، ۲۰
گوشواره : ۱۳۳ ، ۱٤۸
گوشواره کوه : ۱۳۰
گوکلان : ۱۳ ، ۸۲ ، ۸٦ ، ۸۷ ،
۹۳ ، ۹٤ ، ۹٦ ، ۹۷ ، ۱۰۰ ،

١٠١ ، ١٦٢

گوكله شور : ٦١

گوكه : ١٦

گوكوه : ١٢٦

گوليج — انظر گليج

گونى محلّه : ١٢٧

گوهرباران : ٦ ، ١٦٠

گوهرده : ١٢٢

گوئى گله : ١٠٦

گيا بندان : ١٥٧

گيسا : ١٠٥

گيشه دمرده : ١٦

گيل : ١٥٠

گيلاآباد : ١٢٠

گيلاس : ١١٤

گيلاموش : ١٦

گيلان : ١ ، ٣ ، ٨ ، ٩ ، ١٥ ، ١٦ ،
١٨—٢٢ ، ٢٦ ، ٩٠ ، ١٠٦ ،
١١٠ ، ١٣٣ ، ١٣٩ — ١٤١ ،
١٤٤ ، ١٥٠ ، ١٥٢ — ١٥٤ ،
٣ع ، ٧ع ، ٦٠ع ، ٦٨ع

گيلاناآباد : ١٦٥

گيلان ده : ١١١

گيلانه جوى : ٥٢

گيل چاله سر : ١٢٠

گيل خواران : ٤٩ ، ١٢٠ ، ١٢٢

گيلك : ١١ ، ٣٠ ، ٦١

گيلكجان : ١٨

گيلكش محلّه : ١٢٣

گيل كلا : ١٠٩ ، ١١٢ ، ١١٨

گيل نشين : ١٢٠

گيله دون : ١٢٠

گيله كلا : ١٠٨ ، ١٢١

گيله محلّه : ١٠٦

گيله رود : ٤٩

گيلور : ١١٦

گيليان : ١٥٧

گيودرّه : ١٦

لابيج : ٣١

لات : ١٠٦ ، ١٠٧

لات كنار : ١٠٥

لات محلّه : ١٠٦

لار : ٣١ ، ٣٣ ، ٤٠—٤٢ ، ١١٥ ،
١٥٧

لارجان : ۲ ، ۳ ، ۱۵ ، ۳۲ ، ۳۳ ،
۴۰ ، ۴۲ ، ۱۰۵ ، ۱۱۴ ، ۱۱۵ ،
۱۴۰ ، ۱۴۷ ، ۱۵۰ ، ۱۵۵ ،
۱۵۷ ، ۱۶۶
لارجان : ۱۳۳ ، ۱۴۶ ، ۱۵۲ ، ۱۶۶
لارقصران : ۳ ، ۳۴
لارک : ۱۲۴
لارکوه : ۴۱
لارما : ۱۲۱ ، ۱۲۴
لاری کلا : ۱۱۷
لاریم : ۶ ، ۱۳ ، ۴۲ ، ۴۸ ، ۴۹ ،
۱۲۱ ، ۱۵۸
لاری محلّه : ۱۱۷
لاغرزمین : ۱۱۸
لاشک : ۱۰۹
لاشکنار : ۳۱ ، ۱۰۹
لاک آبندان : ۱۱۹
لاک تاش : ۱۲۴
لاک تراش : ۱۲۴
لاک تراشان : ۱۲ ، ۱۲۰ ، ۱۵۳
لاک دشت : ۱۲۰
لالا : ۱۲۲
لالاباد : ۴۶ ، ۴۸ ، ۱۱۸
لاله رود : ۱۶
لا لیم : ۵۸
لامیلنگ : ۱۲۵
لاهجان : ۸ ، ۱۶۶ ، ۱۷ ، ۱۰۷ ،
۱۴۸ ، ۱۶۰ ، ۷ع ، ۵۶ع —
۶۰ع ، ۷۳ع ، ۷۴ع
لاهو : ۱۰۸
لاویج : ۱۱۰
لاویجی : ۱۱۰
لای : ۱۲۴
لای پسند : ۱۲۴
لپاوک : ۱۰۸
لپه رودبار : ۱۵۳
لپه سر : ۳۰ ، ۱۰۵
لپوت : ۱۵۸
لترا : ۱۳۰
لتنگان : ۶ ، ۲۸ ، ۱۰۹
لته بند : ۱۱۵
لته پشت : ۱۱۵
لته کوه : ۱۳۵
لج : ۱۰۵
لدر : ۱۱۹
لُر : ۶۶

قلعه لرز : ١٣٠
لرزنه : ١١٦
لرستان : ١٢
لرگان : ١٠٩
لرگه سری : ١١١ ، ١١٤
لرگم : ١٠٨
لره : ٧٩ ، ١٦٣
لره سر : ١٠٥
لره کوه : ١٢٦
لزر : ١٥٣
لزربن : ١٠٦
لزرجان : ١٨٠
لزور : ٤٠ ، ١٠٩ ، ١٣٠
لزورك : ١١٤
لزیر : ١٠٩
لسغی : ٦٣
لسن : ١١٤
لشتو : ١٠٥
لشکرك : ٢٤ ، ١٠٧ ، ١١٥
لش کنار : ١٠٩
لشاوار : ١١٤
لشه ازور : ١٣١
لعلزن کیا کلا : ١١٨
لعلکیاده : ١١٢
لفوت : ١٥٨
لفور : ٤٨ ، ١١٨ ، ١٣٣ ، ١٤٧ ، ١٥٢ ، ١٥٧ ، ١٦٥
لفورك : ١١٨
لکك : ١١ ، ١٢ ، ٢٢
لکتر : ١٠٩ ، ١٥٥
لکری : ١٥٣
لکه موزی : ٣٢
لله باغ : ١٢٨
لله پرچین : ٣٤
لله دوین : ٨٠ ، ١٢٥
لله مرزچل : ٦١
لله فن : ١٢٥ ، ١٢٦
لله گندو : ٨١
لله ونگه : ٦١
للوك : ١١٨
لمتر : ١٠٦
لمراسك : ٦٥ ، ١٢٥ ، ١٥٧
لمرد : ١٢٣
لمسك : ٧١ ، ١٢٥ ، ١٢٦ ، ٥٥ع
لمسکلا : ١١٩
لمسوکلا : ١٢٤

لموک : ۱۲۱
لنجرود : ٦٤ع
لند : ۱۳۰
لند اسپو : ۱۲۳
لندر : ۱۳۰
لندرود بار : ۱۲۳
لندک : ۱۳۳، ۱٤۷، ۱٦۳
لنده کوه : ۱۲٦
لنکج : ۱۱٤
لنکران : ٦۳
لنکورخان : ۱۳۰
لنگا : ۲۱، ۲٥، ۱۰٥، ۱۰٦
لنگرود : ٥، ۱٦، ۱۷، ٦٤ع
لنگور : ۱۱۰، ۱۰۹
لهاش : ۱۱۲، ۱۱٥
لهیر : ۱۱٥
لوبا : ۱۱۲
لوبیور : ۱۱٦
لوتیا : ۱۲۸
لوجنده : ۱۲۳
لودیان : ٥۹
لورا : ۱۱۰
لوران : ۱۱۳
لوسان : ٤۱
لوسر : ۱۰۳
لوسکنده : ۱۲٥
لوشگان : ۲۱
لوشلوئی : ۱۱٤
لوط : ۱۱٤
لوات : ۱۲۲
لولده : ۱۰٦
لولیان : ٥۹
لولی محلّه : ۱۰۷
لومن دون : ۱٦۰
لولک : ۱۱٦
لوندر : ۱۱٤، ۱۳۱
لیارستان : ۱۷
لیاسی : ۲۱
لیتکوه : ٤۰، ۱۱۳
لیچم : ۱۳۰
لیرود : ۱۲۸
لیسه گو : ۱۲٦
لیکانی : ۱۲۹
لیکش : ۱۱۰
لیلاسر : ۱۲٦
لیلان : ۱٥۳

لیلم دشت : ۱۱۸
لیله کوه : ۱۷
لیلی کلا : ۱۲۱
لیماك : ۱۰۵
لیرز : ۲۰
لیموجو : ۱۸
لیمونجو : ۱۰۶
لیمونده : ۱۲٤
لیند : ۱۱٦
لیوار : ٦۹
لیوان : ٦٦ ، ٦۷ ، ۱۲۵
لیوجان : ۱۱٤

ماته : ۳۳
ماچك پشت : ۱۲۱
ماخواران : ۱۱٤
مادو رستاق : ۱۲٤
ماران : ۲۳ ، ۱۰۷
ماران کلا — ماران کلاته : ۱۲۷ ، ۱۲۸
ماران کوه : ۸۳ ، ۱۰٦ ، ۱۲۸

مارکوتی : ۱۱۳
مارگیرده : ۱۰۹
مارم : ۱۲٤
ماز : ۱۵
مازندران : ۱—۱۵ وغیره
مازندرانی : ۱۱ ، ۱۲ ، ۳۰ ، ٦٦ ، ۷۰ ، ۱۵۲ ، ۱٦۰
مازوارم : ۱۲۸
مازوبن : ۱۰٦ ، ۱۰۷
مازوکش : ۱۲۸
مازولنگه : ۱۰۵
مازی بن : ۱۲٦
مازی کلام : ۱۰۵
مازی گاه : ٦ ، ۲۸
مازیه چال : ۱۰٦
مازیه سر : ۱۰٦
ماس : ۱۵۷
ماسال : ۱۰۷
ماسور آباد : ۱٦۲
ماشخ : ۱۱٦
ماشو کلا : ۱۱۷ ، ۱۲۳
مافروزجك : ۱۲۱
ماقلاصان : ۱٦۲

ماكران : ۱۲۰
ماكركلا : ۱۱۸
مالكه دشت : ۳٤
مالكي : ١٤ ، ٣٤
ماليه كلا : ۱۱۰
ماطير : ٤٥ ، ۱۳۳ ، ۱٤۷ ، ۱٦٥
املاك ماونى : ۱۳۰
ماندر : ۱۱٥
مانهير : ۳ ، ۲٦ ، ۲۹
مانى زرگر : ۱۱۷
ماه : ۱۲۰
ماهانه سر : ۱۱٤ ، ۱٤۲
ماه فيروز محلّه : ۱۲۰
ماهيه سر : ۱۱٤
ماهيه‌سر دز : ۱۱٤
ماوجكوه : ۱٥۸
ماوراء النّهر : ۱٥۹
ماياك : ۷۰
مايان : ۱۲۸
مايستان : ۱۰٦
مباركك آباد : ۷۸ ، ۸۰ ، ۸٥ ، ۸٦ ،
۹۳
متجى : ۱۲٤
متكازين : ۱۲۳
منه كلا : ۱۱٦
متوريج : ۱۱۳
متى كلا : ٤٤ ، ۱۱۹ ، ۱۲۰
مجاور محلّه : ۱۲۰
مجل : ۱۰۸
مجلس ملّى : ۹٥
مجيد آباد : ۲۷ ، ۱۰۹
مچورى : ۱۳۰
مثلّث الثلاثه : ۲۲
محلّهٔ آب دنگك سر : ۳٦
— ابو محلّه : ۱٥۷
— اسپت تكيه : ۱٥۷
— اسپى كلا : ۳٦
— آستانه : ۱٥۷
— استرآبادى محلّه : ۱٥۷
— آسياب سر : ۳٦
— اصفهانى محلّه : ٥٤
— افغان : ٥٤
— آقارود : ۱٥۷
— امامزاده عبد الله : ٥٤
— امامزاده يحيى : ٥٤
— آمليها : ۳٦

محلّهٔ آهنگر محلّه : ۱۵٦ ، ۱۵۷
— اوجابن : ۱۵۸
— اوردشت : ۱۵٦
— اوصانلو : ٥٤
— باب باقر ناظر : ۱۵۷
— باجلو : ۱۵٦
— بادحیل : ٦۸
— بازار محلّه : ٦٤
— باغبان محلّه : ۱۵٦ ، ۱۵۷
— باغ شاه : ٦٤ ، ۷۳
— باغ شاه کهنه : ٥٤
— بای خیل : ٦۸
— بخشی محلّه : ۱۵۷
— بربری خیل : ۳٦
— بربری محلّه : ۳٦
— بلوچ : ۷۳
— بلوچی خیل : ٥٤
— بنگشی خیل : ۳٦
— بهار آباد : ٥٤
— بیا کلا : ۱۵۷
— بیچ ناجی : ۱۵۷
— بید آباد : ۱۵۷
— بیرامتر : ٥٤ ، ٥٥

محلّهٔ بیسر تکیه : ۱۵۷
— پای چنار : ٥٤
— پای سرو : ۷۳
— پائین بازار : ۳٦
— پل بیور : ۳٦
— پنا کلا : ۱۵۷
— پنجشنبه بازار : ۱۵۸
— تجن جار : ۱۵٦
— ترک محلّه : ۱۵۸
— تکیه ار باب : ۱۵۸
— تکیه خان : ۷۳
— تکیه دوشنبی : ۷۳
— تکیه عبّاس علی : ۷۳
— تمیشکانه خیل : ٦۸
— چاله باغ : ٥٤
— چاه سر : ۳٦
— چشمه سر : ٦٤
— چمندیان : ۷۳
— چنار بن : ۱۵٦
— چهار تکیه : ٥٤
— چهار شنبه : ۱۵۷
— چهار شنبه پیش : ۱۵۸
— چوباق محلّه : ۱۵۷

محلّهٔ حاجیّ جعفر : ١١٨
— حصیر فروشان : ١٥٧
— حمزه کلا : ١٥٧
— خش واش : ١٥٦
— خیابان حرم : ١٥٧
— دباغان : ٧٣ ، ٤٠ع
— دبّاغ خانه پیش : ١٥٧
— درب شهدا : ١٥٧
— درب نو : ٧٣
— درزی کوتی : ١٥٧
— درزی محلّه : ١٥٦
— در مسجد : ٥٤
— درویش تاج الدّین : ١٥٧
— درویش خیل : ١٥٧
— درویش محلّه : ٣٦
— دوچناران : ٧٣
— دیو محاله : ١٥٧
— راضیهّ کلا : ١٥٨
— رودگر محلّه : ٣٦ ، ١٥٦ ، ١٥٧
— زرگر محلّه : ١٥٨
— سبزمشهد : ٧٣ ، ٣٧ع
— سبزمیدان : ٣٦ ، ٥٤ ، ١٥٨
— سرپیر : ٧٣
محلّهٔ سرچشمه : ٧٣
— سر حمّام اقا حسن : ١٥٨
— سوخته تکیه : ٧٣
— سیّد جلال : ١٥٨
— سیّد زین العابدین : ١٥٨
— شاه : ٦٨
— شاه پسند : ٦٨
— شاهزاده حسین : ٥٤
— شاه زنگی : ١٥٨
— شاه غازی بن : ٥٤
— شاه کلا : ١٥٨
— شپش کشان : ٥٤
— شعر باف محلّه : ١٥٨
— شکرآباد : ٥٤
— شمشیرگر محلّه : ١٥٨
— شوندشتی — شاهان دشتی :
٣٦
— شیرکش : ٧٣
— شیشه گر : ٥٤
— عرب خیل : ١٥٧
— عطّار محلّه : ١٥٧
— طالش محاله : ٦٤
— طوق دار بن : ١٥٨

محلّهٔ فرّاش محلّه : ٦٤
— قادريّه محلّه : ١٥٨
— قاضى كوتى : ١٥٨
— قرا كلا : ١٥٨
— قصّاب كلا : ١٥٨
— قليجلى محلّه : ٥٤
— كاردى محلّه : ١٥٦
— كاسه گر محلّه : ١٥٧، ١٥٨
— كردخيل : ٦٨
— كلاج مشهد : ١٥٧
— كهنه مشهد : ١٥٦
— كوره سر : ١٥٧
— كوه صهرا : ٦٨
— كوى خيل : ٦٨
— گالش خيل : ١٥٦
— گالش محلّه : ٦٤
— گاو بندان : ٧٣
— گرجى محلّه : ٣٦، ٦٤
— گريلى محلّه : ٦٤
— گلشن : ١٥٧
— گورك : ١٥٦
— ليلك محلّه : ١٥٧
— مراد بيك : ١٥٧

محلّهٔ مسجد جامع : ١٥٧
— مشائها : ١٥٦
— ملاّ مجد الدّين : ٥٤
— ميان دسته : ١٥٧
— ميان قطع : ١٥٧
— ميچگاه محلّه : ١٥٧
— ميخچه گران : ٧٣
— ميدان : ٧٣
— ميرزا كوچك : ١٥٧
— ميرسه روزه : ٥٤
— مير كريمى : ٧٣
— مير مشهد : ٥٤
— نخيب كلا : ١٥٧
— نعلبندان : ٥٤، ٧٢، ٣٦ ع
— نفطى محلّه : ١٥٧
— نقّارچيان : ٧٣
— نقّاش محلّه : ٦٤
— نيا كى : ٣٦
— هارون محلّه : ٣٦
— هاشمى : ٣٦
— هتكا كلا : ١٥٧
— هزار بن : ١٥٧
— هيمه دوزان : ٧٣

محلّهٔ یهودی محلّه : ١٥٨
محمّد آباد : ٧٨ ، ٩٢ ، ١٠٨ ، ١٢٤ ، ١٢٧ ، ١٢٨ ، ١٣١ ، ١٦٢
محمّد حسین آباد : ٦ ، ٢٥ ، ١٠٥ ، ١٥١
محمّد کیله : ١٦٠
محمود آباد : ٢١ ، ٣٢ ، ٤١ ، ٤٥ ، ٤٧ ، ١١٢ ، ١١٤ ، ١٢٧
مدانلو : ١٣
مدرس : ١١٣
مدرسه : ١٠٧
مدرسهٔ ارباب : ٦٤
— احمد ملاّ صفر علی : ١٦٠
— افا محسن : ٧٣ ، ٤٣ع
— امامیّه : ١٥٩
— حاجّی ابراهیم : ١٥٧
— حاجی سیّد حسن مولانا : ١٥٧
— حاجّی محمّد تقی خان : ٧٣
— حاجّی محمّد صالح : ٧٣
— حاجّی ملاّ رضا : ٧٣
— حاجّی مصطفی خان : ١٥٩
— دار الشّفاء : ٧٣
مدرسهٔ دروازه نو : ٧٣
— روحیه : ١٥٨
— زین الشّرف : ٣٩
— سادات : ٧٣
— سپهسالار : ٧٣
— سلیمان خان : ١٥٩
— سیّد امام خطیب : ١٥٦
— صدر : ١٥٧
— علامه : ١٥٧
— عمادیّه : ٧٣
— قادریّه : ١٥٧
— قهّاریّه : ١٥٧
— کاظم بیگی : ١٥٧
— گلشن : ٦٤
— مادر شاهزاده : ١٥٩
— محمّد تقی خان : ٧٥ ، ٣٤ع
— مسجد جامع : ١٥٩
— میرزا زکی : ١٥٧
— نوّابیّه : ١٥٩
مدو : ١٣٠
مراتع : ١٢٠
مراد چال : ١٠٧
مراد چشمه : ١٢٨

مراوه تپّه : ۹۹
سادات مرتضائی : ۱۳۳ ، ۱٤٤
مرج : ۱۱۱
مردمان کلا : ۱۱۸
مرد مؤمن : ۷٦
مردو : ۱۱۰
مردین کلا : ۱۱۱
مرزان آباد : ۱۰۷ ، ۱۲۷
مرزان ده : ۱۰۸ ، ۱۱۱
مرزان کند : ۱۰۵
مرزان کیله : ۱٥٤
مرزبال : ۱۱۸
مرزبان : ۱٤٦ ، ۱٥۲
مرزبان آباد : ۱۳۰ ، ۱٦۰
مرزبان کلاته : ۱۲۸
مرزکنار : ۱۱۸
مرزناک : ۱۱۹ ، ۱۲۹
مرزن گور : ۱۱۲
مرزه بند : ۱۱٤
مرزود : ۱۲۰
مرزون آباد : ۱۱۸
مرزون کلا : ۱۱۳
مرس : ۱۰۸
مرسده : ۱۰۸
مرسنگک : ۱۲۸
مرشتاوند : ۱٥۳
سادات مرعشی : ۲۷ ، ۳٦ ، ۱۱٤،
۱۳۳ ، ۱٤۲ ، ۱٤۳
مرغانه پرد : ۱٦
مرکوره : ۱۲۱
مرگاو : ۱۲۲
مرمت : ۱۲۰
مرند کشل : ۱۲۳
مرو : ۱٥۳
مروردی : ٦ ، ۲۸ ، ۱۰۹
مریار : ۱٥۷
مریج محلّه : ۱۱۲
مریجان : ۱۱٤
مرید چر : ۱۱٤
مری کنده : ۱۱۸
مریم آباد : ۱۲۷
مزدران : ۳
مرزر : ۸۲ ، ۱٥۱
مزر : ٦ ، ۲۰ ، ۲۳
مزردشت : ۱۰۷
مزرعه : ۱۲۸

مزرعهٔ سیّد اسد : ٤٩ ع
مزرک : ۱۳۰
مزرک : ۱۰۷
مزرلات : ۲۰ ، ۲٤
مزنگ : ٦٦ ، ٦۷
مزید : ۱۱۱
مسجد آخوند : ٦٤
— ارباب : ٦٤
— استانه : ۱٥۸
— استرآبادی محلّه : ۱٥۸
— افا شیخ حسین اندلیت : ۱٥۸
— افا عبّاسی : ۳٦
— اقا عبد الکریم : ۳٦
— اقا میر مومن : ۷۳
— اکبریّه : ۷۳ ع ، ۷٥ ع
— امام حسن : ۳۹ ، ۷۳
— امامیّه : ۱٥۹
— اوجا بن : ۱٥۸
— ایرائها : ۳٦
— بازار : ۷٤ ، ۲۹ ع
— باشی : ٦٤
— باغ پلنگ : ۱۳
— باغ شاه : ۷۳
مسجد بنگشیها : ۷۳
— بیسر : ۷۳
— پای سرو : ۷۳
— پناه بیگی : ۷۳
— پناه کلا : ۱٥۸
— ثقة الاسلام : ۱٥۸
— جامعٔ استرآباد : ٦۷ ، ۷۳ ، ۷٤ ، ۲٥ ع ، ۲٦ ع ، ۲۹ ع ، ۳٤ ع
— جامعٔ اشرف : ٦٤ ، ۱٦۰
— — آمل : ۱٤ ، ۳۳—۳۷ ، ۱٦۰
— جامعٔ بارفروش : ٤٥ ، ٤٦ ، ۱٥۸ ، ۱۷ ع
— جامعٔ رانکوه : ٦۲ ع
— — رشت : ٦٥ ع
— — ساری : ٥۲ ، ٥٤ ، ۱٥۹
— جامعٔ لاهجان : ۱٦۰ ، ۷ ع
— چال : ٦۲ ، ۱٥۸ ، ۱٥۹
— حاجی اقا محمّدی : ۷۳
— حاجی تبریزی : ۷٤ ، ۲۹ ع
— حاجی جعفر : ۱٥۸

مسجد حاجّی حسین : ١٥٨
— حاجّی سیّد حسین مولانا :
١٥٨
— حاجّی علی : ٧٣
— حاجّی فرج : ٦٥
— حاجّی محمّد حسن معمار : ٧٣
— حاجّی محمّد خان : ٦٨
— حاجّی محمّد رضا : ٧٣
— حاجّی محمود اقا : ٧٣
— حاجّی مصطفی خان : ١٥٩
— حاجّی میرزا هدایت : ١٥٨
— حصیر فروشان : ١٥٨
— دار الشّفاء : ٦٤
— دبّاغان : ٧٣ ، ٤٠ع
— در مسجد : ١٥٩
— دروازهٔ فوجرد : ٧٣
— دوچناران : ٧٣
— دیلمیها : ٧٣
— زرگر محلّه : ١٥٨
— رضا خان : ١٥٩
— روحیّه : ٣٦ ، ١٥٨
— ساغری سازان : ٧٠ع
— سالار : ٣٩

مسجد سراب دنگک : ٦٤
— سرچشمه : ٧٣
— سرپیر : ٧٣
— سلیمان خان : ١٥٩
— سفید : ٧٣ ، ٧٤ ، ٢٩ع
— سقّا : ١٥٨
— سیف الاسلام : ١٥٨
— شاهزاده قاسم : ٧٣
— شاه غازی : ١٥٩
— شیخ عبد الرّصول : ١٥٨
— شیرکش : ٧٣
— طشته زنان : ٣٣
— علامه : ١٥٨
— علی خان : ٧٣
— قاجارها : ٧٣ ، ٤٤ع
— قادریّه : ١٥٨
— قادی : ٧٣
— قرا کلا : ١٥٨
— قصّاب کلا : ١٥٨
— قهّاریّه : ١٥٨
— کاسه گران : ٧٣
— کاظم بیگی : ٤٥ ، ١٥٨ ،
١٤ع

مسجد کوچک : ۷۳

— گرجی : ٦٤

— گرجی محلّه : ۳٦

— گرزین : ۹۰

— گلشن : ٦٤ ، ٦٥ ، ۷۳ ، ۱٥٦ ، ۱٥۷

— محمّد باقر خان : ۷۳

— مشهدی محمّد خراسانی : ۱٥۸

— مصلّی : ۷۳ ، ۷٤ ، ۲۹ ع

— مقبره : ۷۳

— ملاّ حسین علی : ۱٥۸

— ملاّ عبّاس : ٦٥

— ملاّ علی : ۷۳

— ملاّ مجید : ۱٥۸

— ملاّ میرزا حسین : ۷۳

— میخچه گران : ۷۳

— میرزا محمّدعلی : ۳٦

— میرزا مهدی اشرفی : ۱٦۰

— میر کریمی : ۷۳

— ناصر خان : ٦٤

— نخیب کلا : ۱٥۸

— نعلبندان : ۷۳

— نعل بیگی : ۷۳

مسجد نقار چیان : ۷۳

— هاشمی : ۳٦

مسدان : ٤۸

مسله زرّین کول : ۱٦٥

مسکان : ۱۳۰

مسکوپا : ۱۲٤

مسگر : ۷۰

مسگران : ۱۲۷

مسگر محلّه : ۱۲۷

مسلم : ۱٤

مسی محلّه : ۱۱۹

مشان کیله : ٦ ، ۲۸

مشانی : ۱۲٥

مشبو کلا : ۱۲۳

مشتک قطب الدّین : ۱۲۸

مشتگان : ۱۱۳

مشخی کلا : ۱۲۲

مشک آباد : ۱۳ ، ٥٦ ، ۱۲۱

مشکان : ۱۳۰

مشکزار : ۱۰۳

مشکلا : ۱۰٥

مشکین دشت : ۱۱۱

مشل آباد : ۲٥

مشلک : ۶ ، ۲۸ ، ۱۵۱
مشهد : ۱۶۴
مشهد سبز : ۱۱۸
مشهد سر : ۳ ، ۵ ، ۷ ، ۱۰ ، ۴۰ ، ۴۵ ، ۴۶ ، ۴۹ ، ۹۸ ، ۱۰۵ ، ۱۱۶ ، ۱۱۷ ، ۱۱۹ ، ۱۵۰ ، ۱۵۶
مشهد گنجو روز : ۱۳ ، ۴۸ ، ۱۱۸
مشهد مصریان : ۷۲ ، ۱۰۱
مشهد میر بزرگ : ۳۶ ، ۳۷
مشهدی سرا : ۱۰۵
مشو : ۱۲۸
مصر : ۱۱۵
مصقل آباد : ۱۶۲
مصف : ۱۲۵
مصلّی : ۳۴ ، ۳۹ ، ۷۴ ، ۷۵ ، ۲۹ ع
مصیّب محلّه : ۱۲۳
مظفّر : ۱۱۷
مظفّر کلا : ۱۱۸
معاف : ۱۰۶
معصوم آباد : ۳۲ ، ۱۲۴ ، ۱۲۷ ، ۱۲۸
معلّم : ۷۰
معلّم کلا : ۱۱۲ ، ۱۲۰
مغان ده : ۱۱۱
مغول : ۱ ، ۳۰ ، ۳۵ ، ۵۳ ، ۶۹ ، ۸۰ ، ۸۸ ، ۹۰ ، ۱۰۱ ، ۱۳۳ ، ۱۳۵ ، ۱۳۹ ، ۱۴۷ ، ۱۵۰ ، ۱۵۲ ، ۱۶۲
مفید آباد : ۱۲۶
سادات مفیدی : ۷۶
مقری کلا : ۱۱۶ ، ۱۱۷
مقسی : ۱۰۱ ، ۱۰۲
مقسی سرپیچ : ۱۲۶
مقصود لو : ۷۶ ، ۷۸
مقیم : ۱۶۰
مکا : ۱۰۸
مکارود : ۱۰۸
ملاّ : ۱۰۹
ملاّ امیره : ۱۷
ملاّ حاجیّ محلّه : ۱۰۵
ملاحده : ۳ ، ۲۶ ، ۳۹ ، ۱۱۰ ، ۱۳۰ ، ۱۴۸ ، ۱۶۶ ، ۶۰ ع
ملاحم : ۱۱۶
ملاّ خان : ۶۶
ملاّ خیل : ۱۲۴
ملاّده : ۱۲۴

ملارد : ۱۱٤ انظر ملرد
ملارم : ۱۱۲
ملاّ صادق : ٦۰
ملاط : ۱ ، ۳ ، ۸ ، ۱۷ ، ۲٦
ملاّ علی : ۷۹
ملاّ قلیج خان : ۹۱
ملاّ کلا : ٤۷ ، ۱۰۹ ، ۱۱۲ ، ۱۱۳ ، ۱۱۷
ملاّ کیله : ٦ ، ٦۷ ، ۷۰ ، ۹۹
ملاّ محمّد : ۱۱۹
ملخ آباد : ۱۵۷
ملرد : ۱۱۵ انظر ملارد
ملفه : ۱۱۹
ملک : ۱۲۱
ملک آباد : ۱۱٤ ، ۱۲۰
ملکلار : ۲ ، ۲۸ ، ۲۹ ، ۱۰۹
چشمهٔ ملك جوب : ۱۸
ملکشاه محلّه : ۱۱۹
ملك کلا : ۱۱۷ ، ۱۱۹
ملك محلّه : ۱۲۳
ملك خیل : ۱۱۹
ملّه : ۱۳۰
ملهار : ۱۱٤
مله متّکا : ۱۱۵
ملو : ۱۲۳
ملوا : ۱۲٤
ملومه رنگ : ٦٦
ملیت : ٤٤
ملی گله . ۱۲۰
ملیه درّه : ۱۱۵
منارهشور — گلدستهٔ میدان شور : ۷٤ ، ۷۵ ، ۲۹ع ، ۳۰ع ، ۳۷ع
منجر : ۱۰۹
منحل : ۱۲۱
منحله : ۱۰٦
مندور : ۱۱۱
منزل درّه : ۱۲۳
منزه رود : ۱۵۳
منزولک : ۱۲٦
منشلک : ۱۰٦
منصور کنده : ۱۱۸
منکول : ۱۳۰
منکی چال : ٤۲
منگل : ۱۱٤
منوچهر کلا : ۱۰۹
منوچهری : ٦٦ ، ۷۰

منوّل : ١٠٩
مهتر کلا : ١٢٥ ، ٦
مهدی آباد : ١٢٩
مهدیان : ٧٠
مهدی خیل : ١١٣
مهدی سرا : ١١١
مهدی کلا : ١١٩
مهربان : ١٦٦
مهرجمین : ١٦٢
مهروان : ١٦٥
مهرون کلا : ١٢٢
مهری : ٥٠
مهستیّه : ١٣٠
مهکتان : ١١٤
مهلستان : ١١٨
مواضع : ٥٧ ، ١٢٤
موجه کوه : ١١٨
مور : ٢٩
موردستان : ١٥٠
مورستاق : ١٥٠
موریدار : ١٢٠
موز : ٣ ، ٢٩
موزاندرون : ٣
موزکک چل : ٦١
موزورج : ٤٤ ، ١١٨
موسی آباد : ٨٠ ، ١٠٩
موسی کلا : ١٢١
موغان : ٧ ، ٨ ، ٢٥
مولود خانه : ١٦١
مومه دەرده : ٦ ، ٢٥
مؤمن آباد : ١٢٧
مون : ١١٤
میارکلا : ١١٥
میامه : ٧٩ ، ٨٣ ، ١٦٤
میان آباد : ٨١ ، ١٢٧
میان بژم : ١٠٧
میان بند : ٢٥ ، ٣٢ ، ١٠٦ ، ١١٠
میان پشته : ١٧
میان چاه : ١٢٠
میان دشت : ١١٦
میان دج محلّه : ١٠٥
میان درّه : ٧٠ ، ١٢٤ ، ١٢٦
میان دورود : ١٢ ، ٤٩ ، ٦٢ ، ٦٤ ، ١٢٠ ، ١٢٦ ، ١٣٣ ، ١٤٦ ، ١٦٦

میان‌ده : ۱۳ ، ٦۹ ، ۱۰۵ ، ۱۰۷ ، ۱۱۰ ، ۱۱۲ ، ۱۳۰ ، ۱۵۷
میان سرا : ۱۰۷
میان سی : ۱۲٤
میان شهر : ۱۰۹
میانک : ۱۰۹
میان کلا : ٦۲ ، ۱۲۵
میان کله : ٤۸ ، ۵۸ ، ٦۰ ، ٦۱ ، ٦۷ ، ۱۳۱ ، ۱٦۰ ، ۱٦۱
میان کوه : ۱۰۷ ، ۱۵۳
میان کی : ۱۰۸
میان لدک : ۱۰۷
میان محلّه : ۲۳ ، ۲٤ ، ۱۰۷
میان یورت : ۱۲٦
میج : ۱۰۵
میجران : ۱۱۳
میچکر : ۱۰۷
میخساز : ۱۰۹
میدان تاپان : ۱۵۹
میدان رودبار باقلی پزان : ۱۵٦
میدان سر : ۱۱۹ : ۱۲٤
میدان شور — میدان شور آجوری : ۷٤—۷٦ ، ۲۹ ع
میدانک : ۱۲۳
میران : ۱۵۲
میران آباد : ۱۱٤
میراناده : ۱۱٤
میرانه رود : ۱۲۵
میربازار : ۱۱۷
میربان : ۱٦٦
میررود : ٦ ، ٤۲ ، ٤۷ ، ٤۸
میرزاده : ۱۲۲
میرزاد محلّه : ۱۱۷
میرشب : ۱۱۸
میرشریف : ۱۰۳
میرشمس الدّین : ۱۰۷
میرعلم ده : ۱۱۲
میرکلا : ۱۱۸
سادات میرکمال الدّینی : ۷٦
میرک محلّه : ۱۰٦
سادات میرمجیدی : ۷٦
میرمحلّه : ۸۱ ، ۱۲۷ ، ۱۲۸
میره : ۱۱۱
میرود : ۱۵٤
میروزان : ۱۳۱
میروند آباد . ۱۳۱

میسّر : ١٣١
میشه : ١٦٢
میشه کلایه : ٦ ، ١٩
میغان : ٨١
میکا محلّه : ١٢٣
می کلا : ١١٩
میکه : ١١٨
میل : ١٣٠
میلاآباد : ٨٠
میل رادکان : ١٠٢
میله : ١١٢ ، ١٢٠ ، ١٣٠ ، ١٣١ ، ١٥٧ ، ١٦٥
میمجی خیل : ١١٦
مینس کلا : ١١٨
مینگک : ١٠٩ ، ١١١
میوت گشن : ٨٧

ن

ناتر : ١٠٨
ناتل : ٢٧ ، ١١٠—١١٢ ، ١٥٠ ، ١٥٤ ، ١٦٥
ناتل رستاق : ٣٢ ، ١١٠ ، ١١١
ناتل کنار : ٣٢ ، ١١٠ ، ١١٢
ناردین : ٧٨ ، ٧٩ ، ٨٣ ، ٨٤
نارنج باغ : ٥٨ ، ٥٩ ، ٦٢ ، ١٢٧
نارنج بن : ٦ ، ١٨ ، ١٠٦ ، ١٠٩
نارنج بندان : ١٠٦
نارنجه کوتی : ٥١
ناریوران : ١١٧
ناسرود : ١٦٢
ناصرآباد : ١١٨
ناصرکلا : ١١٨
ناصروند :
نامشی : ١١٦
نامن : ١٢٦
نامنه : ١٢٥ ، ١٣١ ، ١٥٧
ناموس ده : ١١٢
نانوا کلا : ١١١
ناوسر : ١٣١
نائج : ١١٠
نجّار : ٧٠
نجّارده : ١٠٩
نجّارکلا : ٦٧ ، ١٠٨ ، ١١٧ ، ١٢١
نجو : ١٠٩
نچی کوه : ١٥٣
نخجیرکلایه : ١٧

نخ کلا : ۱۱٦
ندف خیل : ۱۲۲
ندکک : ۱۰۵
نرّاب : ۱۲۹
نردن کلا : ۱۱٤
نردی محلّه : ۱۰۵
نرس : ۱۰۷
نرسا : ۱۲۷
نرصو : ۱۲۸ ، ۱٦۲
نرگس جار : ۱۱٦
نرگس چال : ۱۱۷ ، ۱۲۸
نرگس کوتی : ۱۲۲
نرنه : ۱۰۵
نریمن صو : ۱٦۲
نزوار : ۱٦۳
نساء : ۱٦٤
نسل : ۱۱۰
نسن : ۱۱۱
نسیه رود : ۱۸
نسیه کلا : ۲۰
نسیه محلّه : ۲۰ ، ۱۰۵
نشال : ۱۱۷
نشتا : ۲۱ ، ۲٤ ، ۲۵ ، ۱۰٦
نشتارود : ٦ ، ۲٤ ، ۱۰٦
نشدا کوه :
نشکجان : ۱۰٦
نشل : ٤۰
نشو : ۱۰۹
نشون کلا : ۱۱۹
نصرآباد : ۲۳ ، ۱۰٦ ، ۱۰۹ ، ۱۲۷
نصرت آباد : ۱۲۸
نصرت سنگک : ۱۳۱
نصف جان : ۱۱۱
نصیر کلا : ٦
نصیر محلّه : ۱۱۹
نظر : ٦٦
نظر آباد : ۱۰۷
نعل : ۱۰۹
نعلبندان : ۱۲۲
نعل کلا : ٤٦
نعمت آباد : ۱۱۱
نفطو : ۱۲۸
نفط چال : ۱۱۸ ، ۱٦۰
نفطه چاک : ۱۵۳
نفطه کوتی : ۱۳۱
نقارچی محلّه : ۱۱۹ ، ۱۲۲

نقد یورت : ١٢٦
نقره بجار : ٦٤ ع
نقله بان : ١١٥
نقله سر : ١١٥
نقی آباد : ١٢٨
نقیب دشت : ١١٨
نقیب کلا : ١١٧
نکا : ٦ ، ٢٠ — ٥٦ ، ٦٢ ، ٧٨ ، ١٠٢ ، ١٢٠ ، ١٢٥ ، ١٦٠ ، ١٦٦ ، ٢٤ ع
نکران : ١٢٤
نگارستان : ١١٢
نلقشر : ١٧
نمار : ١١٠
نمارستاق : ٣٢ ، ١١٠
نمتلو : ٧٩ ، ١٢٨
نمک آب رود — نمکاوه رود : ٣ ، ٦ ، ٢١ ، ٢٦ ، ٢٧ ، ٣١ ، ١٠٧ ، ١٠٨ ، ١١٠ ، ١٥١
نمک جاه : ١١٥
نمه لو : ١١٢
نمیوند : ١٤٦
ننّل : ١١٥
نهابد ساری : ٨٨
نهابد صول : ٨٨
نهرمان : ٥٧
نوا : ٤٠ ، ١١٤
نوارتله : ١٥٣
نوائی کلا : ١١٨
نوج : ١١١
نوچمن : ١٢٦
نودرّه : ١٨
نودشت : ١٢٢
نوده : ١٦ ، ١٨ ، ٧٨ ، ٧٩ ، ٨٢ ، ٩١ ، ١٠٩ ، ١١١ ، ١٢٢ ، ١٢٤ ، ١٢٨ ، ١٦٣ ، ١٦٤
نودهٔ اسمعیل خان : ٨٣ ، ١٢٨
نودهٔ حاجّی شریف : ٨٣
نودهک : ١٠٨ ، ١١٧ ، ١١٨ ، ١٢٠ ، ١٢١ ، ١٢٥ ، ١٥٤ ، ١٦٠
نوده کلا : ١٢٢
نودهٔ میر سعد الله خان : ١٢٨
نودهٔ نظام الدّین : ١٢٧
نودیجه : ١٢٦
نودی کلا : ١١٩
نوذر آباد : ١٢ ، ٤٨ ، ١٣١

نور : ۳ ، ۱۲ ، ۲۱ ، ۲۲ ، ۲۷ ،
۳۰ — ۳۲ ، ٤۲ ، ۱۰٥ ،
۱۱۰ — ۱۱۲ ، ۱۲۹ ، ۱۳۰ ،
۱٤٤ ، ۱٥٥ ، ۱٥۷
نورامک کلا : ۱۱۰
نورود : ۱٦
نورودبار : ٦ ، ۲۹ ، ۱٥۱
نورود سر : ٦ ، ۲۷ ، ۱۰۸ ، ۱٥۱
نوروز آباد : ۱۳۱
نوری : ۳٦
نوری بن : ۱۲٤
نوسر : ۱۱٤
نوشا : ۱٥۳
نوشروان : ۱۱۷
نوشروان بوستانی : ۱۱۷
نوکلا : ۱۱۳ ، ۱۱۷ ، ۱۲۸
نوکنده : ٥٦ ، ٥۸ ، ٦٦ — ٦۸ ، ۷۹ ،
۱۰٤ ، ۱۲٥
نوکنده داروب : ۱۲٤
نوکنده‌کا : ۱۲۱
نوکوه : ۸۱
نومرو : ۱۲۸
نومل : ۷۹ ، ۱۲۲ ، ۱۲۷
نوهیا : ۱۱۱
نی : ۱۱۱ ، ۱۱٥
نیاردرّه : ۱٥۳
نیاسه : ٦ ، ۲۰ ، ۱۰٥
نیافت : ٥۷ ، ۱۲۲
نیاک : ۱۱٤
نیاکی : ۳٦
نیالا : ۱۲٤
نیتل : ۱۰۸
نیج : ۱۱۰
نیج کوه : ۳۲ ، ۱۰۹ ، ۱۱۰
نیرس : ۱۰۹
نیرگان : ۱۲۷ ، ۱۲۸
نیرنگ : ۱۰۹
نیرود : ۲۹ ، ۱٥۱ ، ۱٥٤
نیرودبار : ۱۲٦
نیرین : ۱۱٥
نیزه وران : ۱۱۱
نیس الوار : ۱۰۸
نیسه رود : ۱٥۱
نیشاپور : ۲
نیشاپوریّه : ۱٦٥
نیشاور : ۱۳۱

نیکنام ده : ۱۱۱

نیله کوه : ۱۲۸

نیلی : ۱۶۳

نیم : ۱۲٤

نیمچائی : ۱۲۵

نیم مردان : ۸۵ ، ۹۱ ، ۱۶۲

نیمه ور : ۱۰۹

ه

آب هارون : ٤٤

هارون کلا : ۱۱۳

هارون محلّه : ٤٤

هاسیت آباد : ۱۲۰

هاشم آباد : ۱۲۵

هاشم رود : ٦ ، ۳۱

هاشمی : ۳٦

هبراثان : ۹۲

هبزتن : ۹۲

هبنه : ۱۵۳

هتکاپشت : ۱۱۸

هجبی : ۱۱۱

هجیر کلا : ۱۱۹

هجران : ۱۱۵

هرات : ۲۲ ، ۷۹

هرات بر : ۱۰۵

هرجان : ۱۰۸ ، ۱۳۰

هرده رود : ٤۲

هرده کلا : ۱۰۸

هردورود : ۱۱۰

هرس : ۱۰۷

هرسه مال : ۱۱۹ ، ۱۳۰

هرسی : ۱۰۷

هرط : ۱۱۱

هرله : ۱۲٤

هرمزد کوه : ۲

هرمینا : ۱۲۲

هره بی : ۱۱۲

هره سنگ : ٤۱

هرهر : ۹۷

هرهز : ٦ ، ۳۱—۳۳ ، ۳۵ ، ۳٦ ، ٤۰—٤۲ ، ٤٤ ، ٤۷ ، ۱۳۰ ، ۱۵٦ ، ۱۵۷ ، ۱٦٦

هرهزبی : ۱۱۳

هزارتیره : ۱۰۹

هزار جریب : ۲ ، ۳ ، ٦ ، ۱۵ ، ۲٤ ، ٤۲ ، ۵۱ ، ۵۳ ، ۵٦ — ۵۸ ،

٦٤ ، ٦٨ ، ٧٠، ١٠٣، ١٠٥،
١١٥ ، ١٢٢ — ١٢٥ ، ١٣١ ،
١٣٣ ، ١٤٤
هزراچم : ١٠٨
هزارخال : ١٠٨ ، ١١٠
هزاره : ٧٨
هشتادتن : ١٥٥
هشتاديل : ٨٠ ، ١١٢
هشتيكه : ٦٧ ، ١٢٥
هفت تن : ٤٣
هفت تنان : ١١٤
هفت چشمه : ٧٩ ، ١٢٦
هفت لب : ١٢٣
هفته چال : ١١٤
هكا : ١٠٨
هلاوان : ١٦٥
هلبه : ١١٤
هلسن كش : ١١٤
هله كش : ١١٤
هله كلا : ١٠٦
هلو پشته : ١١٠
هلوچال : ١٢٣
هلودرّه : ١٠٧
هلوسان : ١٠٩
هلوه سر : ١١٣
هلو ير : ١٢٣
هلي چال : ١١٤
هلميرود : ٧
هلي كلا : ٦ ، ٢٤ ، ٤٩
هلي كنده : ١١٩
هلي پشت : ١١٩
هندوستان : ٧٤ ، ٧٧، ١١٥، ١٦٠،
٢٦ ع
هندومرز : ١٠٩
هندوكلا : ٤٤ ، ١١٣
هنسان : ١٥٧
هنگو : ١٠٦
هني : ١١٣
هود كان : ١١٢
هوسم : ١
هولا : ١٢٠ ، ١٢٢
هولار : ١٢١
هيان : ١٥٣ : ١٦٢
هيرت : ١٠٩
هيكو : ١٢٢
هيمه جان : ١٢٣

هی هی کیان : ۱۱۹

هیولا : ۵۸

و

واتاشان : ۱۱۱ ، ۱۱۲

واجی : ۱۰۸

واچک : ۶ ، ۲۰ ، ۱۰۵

وارفو : ۱۳۲

وارمی : ۱۲٤

وازک : ۱۰۹

وازه کوه : ۱۳۲

وازوار : ۱۰۹ ، ۱۲۲

وازی : ۱۱۰

واسکس : ۱۲۰

واکتان : ۱۱٤

والارود — ولاروز : ۱۱٦

وال قوش کبری : ۸۱

والمان : ۸٤ : ۱۲۹

وامنان : ۸۳ ، ۸٤ ، ۱۰۰ ، ۱۲۹

وانکس : ۱۱۳

وانه : ۱۱٤

واهه : ۱۰۸

واودرّه : ۱۲۳

واوسر : ۱۲۲

وباد : ۱۳۲

ورپام : ۱۲٤

ورت : ۱۲۲

ورچشمه . ۱۲۹

ورد داوند : ٤۱ ، ۱٤۰

وردگر : ۱۵۷

وردیمه : ۵۷ ، ۱۲٤

ورزن : ۲۹ ، ۱۱۱ ، ۱۵۵ ، ۱٦۳

ورزنه : ۱۱۷

ورسک : ۱۱۵

ورسن : ۱۲٦

ورسوکلا : ۱۲۱

ورکا : ٤۰ ، ۱۱۵

ورکارده : ۱۱۳

ورکه : ٤۰

ورکی : ۱۲۱

ورگه خوسه : ٦٤

ورمزآباد : ۱۲۲

ورمه زار : ۱۲٤

ورناباد : ۱۵٤

ورند : ۱۲۱

ورندان : ۱۲۰

وری : ۵۷ ، ۱۲٤
وریان : ۱۳۲
وری کنده : ۱۱۸
وزدول : ۱٦۲
وزرا : ٤۷
وزرا محلّه : ۱۱۳
وزملا : ۱۲۳
وزمه : ۱۲٦
وزوار : ٦٦ ، ۱۲٤
وزیه مال : ۱۰۹
وستون : ۱۲۲
وسسکر : ۱٦۲
وسطی کلا : ۱۱۳ ، ۱۲۰
وسم : ۱۲۳
وسوا : ۱۲٤
وسیه کش : ۱۱٦
وشکن : ۱۰۹
وطن : ۱۲۸
وطنا : ۸۳ ، ۱۲۵
وکسر : ۱۱٦
ولار : ۱۲٦
ولارود — ولاره رود — والاروز : ۱۱٦
ولاسان : ۱٤٦
ولاسره : ۱۲٤
ولاش آباد : ۱۲۷
ولاشان : ۱۵۲
ولاشت : ۱۲۲
ولاشکی : ۱۲٦
ولاشگرد : ۱٦۵
ولاشیت : ۱۱۱
ولبن — انظر وله بن
ولتور : ۱۲۰
ولد : ۱۰۸
ولسپ : ۱۰۹
ولفرا : ٦۷ — ٦۹ ، ۱۲۵
ولم : ۱۲۵
ولم رود : ۲۳
ولمه : ۱۱۰ ، ۱۱۱
ولنه : ۱٦۳
وله : ۱۱٦
وله بن : ۱۳۲
وله جوی : ۱۳۲
وله مازو : ۱۲۵
وله موزی : ٦۵
ولو : ۱۲۵

ولوپی : ٤٢ ، ١١٦

ولوکش : ١١٦

ولول : ١٠٨

ولوند : ١١٩

ولویه : ٥٧ ، ١٢٤

ولی آباد : ٢٤، ٢٧، ١٠٧، ١٠٨، ١٥١

ولی مرز : ١٠٧

ولیجه : ٥٩

ولیسه ده : ١١٣

ولیك : ١١٤

ولیك آباد : ١٢٧

ولیکان : ١٣٢

ولیکك بن : ١٢٣

ولیکك چال : ١٢٣

ولیکك دون : ١١٨

ولیگان : ١٠٩ ، ١١٠

ولین آباد — ولینوا : ٥٩

وماد : ١٣٢

ونداد امید کوه : ٢ ، ١٥٦

ونداد هرمزد کوه : ٢ ، ١٥٠

ونداهزه کوه : ٢ ، ١٢٩

ونده چال : ١١٥

ونشت : ١٢٣

ونه : ٤٠ ، ١٢٣ ، ١٥٧

ونه بن : ١٥٥

ونوش — ونوشده، ونوشه ده : ٢٩، ٣١، ١٠٩، ١٢٩

وهی : ١١٣

ویره گردن : ١٠٦

ویسر : ١٠٩

ویلیر : ١١٤

ویلیرد :

ویمه : ٢ ، ١٢٣

ویناآباد : ١٣٢

وینه بن : ١٢٥

ویوا : ١٢٣

ی

یاجینی : ١٢٦

یارم تپّه : ٩١

یازر رود : ٩٢

یازین : ١٠٥

یاس تپّه : ٩٧ ، ١٠٠

یاسل : ١١١

یامیمین کلا : ١١٣

یامیمین کلا شایخ : ١١٣

یاسمین کلا و رزی : ۱۱۳
یاغ دشت : ۱۰۷
یاغی الم : ۹۹
یاغی کلا : ۱۱۸
یاغی گورک : ۱۶۰
یالو : ۳۱ ، ۷۰ ، ۱۱۱ ، ۱۲۶ ، ۱۵۷
یالو رود : ۳۲ ، ۱۱۱
یانسر : ۴۱ ، ۵۱ ، ۵۶ ، ۵۷ ، ۷۹ ، ۱۵۷
یاسر برگیر : ۱۲۳
یتیم کش : ۱۵۳
یج : ۱۰۷
یخدم : ۱۲۴
یخکش : ۵۱ ، ۵۷ ، ۶۴ ، ۱۲۵
یزدان آباد : ۱۵۵ ، ۱۶۵
یزدری : ۸۲
یزدی : ۷۰
یساقی : ۷۴ ، ۱۲۶ ، ۲۷ ع
یسرم : ۱۲۲
یعقوب پیغمبر : ۸۵
یعقوب لنگه : ۶۰ ، ۱۶۰
یکتوت : ۶۰
یکلک حاجی : ۹۴
یکه مازور : ۸۵ ، ۹۴
یکورلیو : ۶۰
یلاپان : ۱۱۱
یلده چشمه : ۱۰۰
یلما : ۱۲۳
یلّی چشمه : ۹۱ ، ۱۰۰
یهشتم : ۱۱۰
یهودی : ۱ ، ۱۳ ، ۴۵
یهودیّه : ۱۲۵
یموت : ۶۸ ، ۹۳ — ۱۰۱ ، ۱۶۳
یورت اقارضا : ۱۲۶
— چناره : ۱۲۷
— خان احمد خان : ۱۱۵
— خانلرخان : ۴۱ ، ۱۱۵
— سه درّه : ۴۱ ، ۱۱۵
— شارک : ۱۲۶
— شاه : ۱۱۵
یوسف آباد : ۱۱۲
یوش : ۱۱۱
یوقاری باش : ۸۶
یونانیان : ۱۱ ، ۱۵۰